What Is College Reading?

Across the Disciplines Books

Series Editor, Michael A. Pemberton

The Across the Disciplines Books series is closely tied to published themed issues of the online, open-access, peer-reviewed journal *Across the Disciplines*. In keeping with the editorial mission of *Across the Disciplines*, books in the series are devoted to language, learning, academic writing, and writing pedagogy in all their intellectual, political, social, and technological complexity.

The WAC Clearinghouse, Colorado State University Open Press, and University Press of Colorado are collaborating so that these books will be widely available through free digital distribution and low-cost print editions. The publishers and the series editors are committed to the principle that knowledge should freely circulate. We see the opportunities that new technologies have for further democratizing knowledge. And we see that to share the power of writing is to share the means for all to articulate their needs, interest, and learning into the great experiment of literacy.

Other Books in This Series

What Is College Reading?

Edited by Alice S. Horning, Deborah-Lee Gollnitz, and Cynthia R. Haller

The WAC Clearinghouse
wac.colostate.edu
Fort Collins, Colorado

University Press of Colorado
upcolorado.com
Louisville, Colorado

The WAC Clearinghouse, Fort Collins, Colorado 80523

University Press of Colorado, Louisville, Colorado 80027

ISBN: 978-1-64215-000-1 (PDF) | 978-1-64215-001-8 (ePub) | 978-1-60732-860-5 (pbk.)

Printed in the United States of America

Library of Congress Cataloging-in-Publication Data

Names: Horning, Alice S., editor. | Gollnitz, Deborah-Lee, 1955– editor. |
  Haller, Cynthia R., 1957– editor.
Title: What is college reading? / edited by Alice S. Horning, Deborah-Lee
  Gollnitz, and Cynthia R. Haller.
Description: Fort Collins, Colorado : WAC Clearinghouse, [2017] | Series:
  Across the disciplines books | Includes bibliographical references.
Identifiers: LCCN 2017059420| ISBN 9781607328605 (pbk. : acid-free paper) |
  ISBN 9781642150018 (epub) | ISBN 9781642150001 (PDF)
Subjects: LCSH: Reading (Higher education)—United States.
Classification: LCC LB2395.3 .W42 2017 | DDC 418/.40711—dc23
LC record available at https://lccn.loc.gov/2017059420

Copyeditor: Brandy Bippes
Book Design: Mike Palmquist
Series Design: Tara Reeser
Cover Art and Design: Malcolm Childers
Series Editor: Michael A. Pemberton

This book is printed on acid-free paper.

The WAC Clearinghouse supports teachers of writing across the disciplines. Hosted by Colorado State University, and supported by the Colorado State Univeristy Open Press, it brings together scholarly journals and book series as well as resources for teachers who use writing in their courses. This book is available in digital formats for free download at wac.colostate.edu.

Founded in 1965, the University Press of Colorado is a nonprofit cooperative publishing enterprise supported, in part, by Adams State University, Colorado State University, Fort Lewis College, Metropolitan State University of Denver, Regis University, University of Colorado, University of Northern Colorado, Utah State University, and Western State Colorado University. For more information, visit upcolorado.com. The Press partners with the Clearinghouse to make its books available in print.

Contents

What Is College Reading?

Introduction

Alice S. Horning

OAKLAND UNIVERSITY

In 2013, after I (Alice) had published two pieces in *Across the Disciplines*, Michael Pemberton invited me to serve as guest editor for an issue of the journal focused on reading and writing across the curriculum. The result was the special issue of the journal that appeared in December of that year. It included eight articles exploring reading issues in a variety of disciplines. Subsequently, Michael asked me to edit this book, a task I readily agreed to take on with the help of two colleagues I respect: Cynthia Haller of York College/City University of New York and Deborah Gollnitz, a curriculum coordinator for a public school district in Michigan. It includes an expanded and/or updated version of some of the articles from the special issue and some additional new material. Following the publication of the two volumes of *What Is College Writing?* edited by Patrick Sullivan and Howard Tinberg, I came up with the title *What Is College Reading?* thinking that it would be a good companion volume. What I did not know at the time was that Sullivan and Tinberg had a similar idea. Their volume, *Deep Reading: Teaching Reading in the Writing Classroom*, which they co-edited with Sheridan Blau, was published this year by NCTE. They kindly agreed to provide the Afterword to this collection.

Despite these happy collaborative developments, my general sense about the status of reading at the college level is that we have taken two steps forward and one step back. A brief review of recent research makes clear the sources of my sense about the inconsistent nature of our progress. The steps forward are comprised of two kinds of increased attention for reading: first, a focus on "informational text" in the Common Core State Standards to better prepare high school students for college work. A second step forward lies in more attention devoted to work on reading in first-year writing to help students develop the skills they will need in both the reading and writing aspects of academic critical literacy for their work in college and beyond. This increased attention arises from two recent books about reading and first-year writing: Ellen Carillo's *Securing a Place for Reading in Composition* and Daniel Keller's *Chasing Literacy*. Both report helpful research findings on reading. These developments are significant positive steps toward addressing students' reading problems and toward improving their abilities. The step back is that studies continue to show that students lack the critical reading skills needed in college and beyond (Stanford History Education Group, 2016).

As a forward step, the Common Core State Standards for English Language Arts (hereafter CCSS) are designed to place the responsibility of developing strong reading and writing skills on all K-12 educators. The standards include performance and demonstration of these skills in Social Studies, Science and Technology courses. Educators in K-12 environments across the US are being asked by the CCSS to do more than just raise awareness of the need for literacy skills students should develop before graduating from high school. Their work requires shifting the paradigm about who is responsible for literacy development, because it shifts responsibility to all teachers in all disciplines. That is, this work is now the responsibility not only of English teachers who push students to think deeply about literature and other texts, even those that students do not find engaging, but also of all teachers of all subject areas and courses, even if they feel unprepared to teach literacy.

However, this expectation from the CCSS is not easily realized because not all K-12 teachers feel that they are prepared to teach reading and writing. Even high school English teachers will readily admit that they are not reading teachers. Their training is in teaching the themes of literature, approaches to effective writing, and overall communication skills. With a new responsibility to meet the Standards presented in Common Core, teachers are now asked to develop readers who can comprehend multiple texts on one topic and synthesize that information into new ideas that might be expressed in writing, oral presentations or in some digital format. Comprehension and synthesis are intended to lead to problem-solving and creativity. This demand places students and teachers in new territory, with new challenges that require new methods of instruction and increased interdisciplinary collaboration. So, much work remains, but there is good reason to think K-12 teachers are rising to this challenge. While there is much discussion of the assessment of the Common Core and related issues, the new requirements concerning students' reading and understanding of informational text is definitely a positive first step forward.

In the best of all worlds, the reading and writing capabilities developed in K-12 should seamlessly transition into those fostered in first-year writing courses. Fortunately, a recent revival of interest in connecting reading and writing pedagogy in first-year composition courses may help to facilitate this smooth transition, offering a second step forward. While discussions of reading pedagogy have always, to some extent, been a part of composition studies, there has been a relative dearth of attention to the topic since the early 1990s. The strong scholarly and pedagogical interest in reading seen in the 1980s and early 1990s, Carillo (2015) suggests, dwindled within the discipline in part because it became complicated by debates on the relationship between composition and the literature curriculum within English studies. However, she argues that common threads from the 1980s and 90s research, as well as newer, though less plentiful, scholarship on reading and learning transfer, can lay a good foundation for new ways of reconnecting reading and writing pedagogy in first-year composition courses. These are an important second step forward in helping students be better readers. Past work in reading scholarship outlines a variety of pedagogical approaches to draw on. Helmers' *Intertexts:*

Reading Pedagogy in the College Writing Classroom (2003) collects a number of ideas from contributors who have deliberately sought to enhance student reading in their writing classes. Hermeneutic and reader-response theory, which situate meaning-making not in the writer or reader but in their interaction, remind us to foreground students' interpretive practices and encourage them to be more self-aware as readers. Salvatori's "difficulty paper" assignment asks students to identify difficult places in readings as opportunities to delve more deeply into meaning-making (Salvatori & Donahue, 2005). Carillo's (2015, pp. 132–135) problem-based passage paper assignment explicitly asks students to make connections between selected portions of a text and its overall meaning, which helps them enact the hermeneutic circle.

In addition to works on reading that target college faculty, student-directed resources are available to guide students toward better college reading. Bartholomae, Petrosky, and Waite's textbook *Ways of Reading* (2014) pays special attention to helping students read well for college. In Wendy Bishop's *The Subject is Reading* (2000), both student and faculty contributors offer advice about college reading, based on their own experiences. Padgett (1997) presents creative techniques with which students can approach texts.

No matter which ideas are adopted for reading pedagogy in college classrooms, it is clear that, for successful college reading, students need to become self-aware and reflexive regarding their own processes. In her chapter on mindful reading, Carillo (2015) argues that students need to be taught a variety of reading practices, but also be taught to reflect on those practices so they can engage them appropriately as needed in diverse contexts. As Carillo points out, instructors of first-year composition must also attend to the reading/writing needs that students will encounter throughout their academic programs. Drawing upon the scholarship of learning transfer, Carillo suggests that compositionists deliberately foster "mindful" reading, foregrounding students' ability to think metacognitively about their own reading and to adjust their reading approaches as needed within different contexts.

Getting students to read mindfully is not easy, but it can be facilitated by making the invisible processes of meaning-making more visible to students, so they can "see" and reflect on those processes. In his Read Like a Writer (RLA) approach, Bunn (2011) advocates that students think deliberately about the choices writers have made as they read texts, thinking about which of those choices might be useful for their own writing. Double-entry journals (Berthoff, 1981) encourage students to become conscious of and differentiate between the processes they use to comprehend a text's meaning and the processes they use to respond to that meaning. Salvatori's (Salvatori & Donahue, 2005) triple-entry variation of this reading journal practice further helps students become more aware of their reading. These authors ask students to first respond to the text, then comment on the moves they made as readers, and finally, assess the particular meaning of the text their recursive reading produced. These types of activities and assignments, which ask students to bring a multiplicity of cognitive processes to bear on their reading and to reflect on those processes, can help student readers move toward the three awarenesses engaged in by Horning's (2012) expert readers: metacontextual, metalinguistic, and metatextual. In addition, assignments should be designed so that students use a variety of cognitive skills (analysis, synthesis, application, and evaluation) to interpret texts.

Certainly, asking students to engage in "mindful" reading in first-year composition can enhance their approaches to reading in other academic and nonacademic contexts. However, just as K-12 reading instruction must permeate the entire K-12 school curriculum to be effective, so, too should reading instruction be part of every course in the college curriculum to reinforce and develop students' abilities in both reading and writing. While the research discussed here moves in these directions, much of this attention is within English Language Arts and Rhetoric and Composition, where we could politely be described as "preaching to the choir." English teachers, writing instructors and others in the literacy profession don't need much of a sales pitch to get on board with reading, though some do resist as they feel they have more than enough to do in teaching writing alone. As I argued in my Introduction to my guest-edited issue of *Across the Disciplines*, however, reading needs attention across the disciplines, in every course, every term. The challenge is that academic reading is difficult and sometimes unappealing, and it is competing against the speed and superficial reading common in students' reading of many types of text, both print and online.

To explore the need for more consistent attention to reading instruction across the curriculum, we have assembled this volume to define and address the nature of college reading and ways to work on it with students across the curriculum. All of the pieces provide a definition of college reading from the authors' perspective from their individual contexts, offering strategies and approaches that can be used in a wide range of courses. Before the chapters begin, we want to provide some key background discussion to set a broader context for the work presented here. We will begin by providing, first, a basic and collaboratively developed definition of *college* reading created from contributions of all the authors. Then, we review research indicating just how difficult such reading is for our students. We will also make clear why we think the book will be useful to our likely audiences, and which chapters in the book might best support the goals and address the needs of those various audiences.

Defining "College Reading"

A phrase like "college reading" is not one easily found in the dictionary. In lieu of looking to the dictionary, we called on our assembled group of authors to give us their individual definitions of college reading. Some of them came from the texts of the chapters presented here, but some of them came in response to our specific request for each author's personal definition. With an eye toward creating a shared definition that would capture the common elements among these writers, we asked all the authors to submit their personal definitions separately from their texts, either quoting from their chapters or writing a separate statement, drawing on their individual experience as well as their work with students. When all the definitions were fed to a word cloud tool, which functions by looking at word frequencies in a text, a few key concepts show up quite clearly in our collective thinking about the definition. The purpose of this exercise was to find a definition that captures commonalities.

The words that appear prominently in the word cloud are these: reading, readers, college-level, complex, process, actively, critically, academic, meaning, recursive, understanding, definition, texts and connections. With a bit of syntactic super glue, here's the resulting definition:

> College-level academic reading can be defined as a complex,
> recursive process in which readers actively and critically under-
> stand and create meaning through connections to texts.

There are five key terms in the collaborative definition that frame the contributions to this collection: complexity, recursion, active, critical, and connection. These elements reveal how college reading differs from the reading students may do in other contexts and clarify why the approaches presented here are relevant to every discipline. Because college reading is complex, it needs to be taught in every discipline and every course. Because it is a recursive activity, students need to be reminded that they need to work on reading as they work on subject learning and mastery. Because it is an active process, reading assignments need to be set up so that students must do the reading and engage with the material in some overt way. Because reading should always be critical, students must learn the elements of critical evaluation of everything they read (authority, accuracy, currency, relevancy, appropriateness, bias) and be able to apply them online and on paper. And finally, because of the need for connection, faculty must help students read in context, not only within their courses, but also within their disciplines, to make connections to materials and ideas beyond the classroom. The chapters presented here offer an array of strategies for achieving these goals so that students develop their "college reading" abilities for every course in college and beyond. Faculty and administrators across the disciplines can all contribute to this work in every course, every term.

College Students and Reading—the Don't, Won't, Can't Problem

It's not your imagination and it's not your fault: students' ability to read extended nonfiction prose has been declining for quite some time. The trend is not improving overall. The evidence is quite clear from a large number of sources, both quantitative and qualitative: students generally don't read much extended nonfiction prose of the kind used in college courses (textbooks, research reports, journal articles and the like) and they won't unless teachers assign reading in a specific and intentional way and make what students do count in their grades. Assigning reading in this way is necessary because the evidence suggests that students really can't read in the ways most faculty intend. There are a number of reasons to be concerned about students' reading abilities: reading has an impact on their success in college as well as on their success beyond college in their personal and professional lives, and as members of a democratic society. Moreover, reading is necessary to success in every course across the disciplines, so everyone needs to pay attention to it. For all these reasons, it is important to understand what studies reveal about where students are before we can address the situation; the evidence of students' difficulties with reading comes from both quantitative and qualitative sources.

Quantitative Studies

Quantitative studies provide one kind of evidence for students' reading abilities, or lack of them. One major quantitative study was released by the ACT organization in 2006. ACT tracked 563,000 students in three cohorts, looking at performance on the Reading section of the ACT and students' success in college. The Reading section of the ACT is a multiple-choice timed test in which students read four passages on different topics, one or more of which might be drawn from a literary work. At least one of the passages is on a Social Studies topic and one on a Science topic; these are factored into students' scores in those areas. There are 40 questions all together, ten on each passage. ACT claims it is testing for factors essential to critical reading, summarized in the mnemonic RSVP: relationships, richness, structure, style, vocabulary and purpose (ACT, 2006, p. 17). These factors are certainly key elements in critical reading, though of course not a comprehensive list.

In the 2006 report, ACT defined success using these criteria: a score of 21 or better on the Reading portion of the test, a 2.0 GPA in the first year, and returning for a second year of college. Given that definition, 51% of students were "successful." The trend shows a decline in the number of students who meet this definition: in 2015, 46% hit the slightly higher cut-off score of 22 nationally (ACT, 2015, p. 4), among those members of a graduating class of 1,924,436 students. More than half of the students you see Monday morning, then, don't hit this minimal criterion for "success."

It is possible to argue that there are plenty of things wrong with the ACT Reading test. It uses short passages; it's a timed test; it does not look at students' prior knowledge of the topics or their interest or motivation. On the other hand, a very large number of students have taken the test, and the passages and questions do tap some key aspects of "college reading." Moreover, other studies, as discussed below, show that students do really have a hard time with reading; it seems reasonable to think their reading problems are a factor in college attainment when the US Department of Education reports that half of the students who start some kind of post-secondary education never finish a degree (2015). While the fact that drop-out rates and "success" rates according to ACT are similar does not mean they are necessarily connected or related in any way, it seems reasonable to think that students' reading difficulties play some role in college success or the lack of it. It's important to note and keep in mind that these are students in every field, likely to choose from the full array of majors offered by colleges and universities. Reading is everyone's problem.

The ACT can be criticized for other reasons besides the fact that it is a multiple-choice test on short passages. While a very large number of students take the ACT, they are, on the whole, self-selected because the exam is taken by students hoping to go to college. However, a similar picture of students' reading performance arises from a more truly representative quantitative measure of students' ability at the point of high school graduation, the National Assessment of Educational Progress (NAEP). NAEP is run by the federal government; it is an instrument that draws a truly representative national sample of K-12 students, tracking performance in reading, mathematics and other areas at several grade levels. Thirty-seven percent of twelfth-grade students performed at or above the *Proficient* level in 2015 in reading; the sample was 18,700 students from across the country (National, 2015). Performance was lower for African-American and Latino students and also lower for males than for females. In the classroom, this result means that more than half of your students do not read as well as they should, both for success in college and for full participation in our society.

Students' reading difficulties are not just a US problem either. Another quantitative measure is the Programme for International Student Assessment (PISA), which is administered to 15-year-olds in 72 first-world countries. It is run by the Organization for Economic Cooperation and Development (OECD). The 2015 results are based on the administration of the 2-hour test to about half a million students worldwide. Parts of the test are multiple choice, computer adaptive, and machine scored, and parts call for open-ended answers scored by people. The results show that US students are just average in this group on reading; "about 20% of all students in OECD countries, on average, do not attain the baseline level of proficiency in reading. This proportion has remained stable since 2009" (OECD, 2016).

It is worth taking a moment to look at the PISA outcome a bit more closely, given the size and international character of the students being tested. The definition offered by PISA that is the basis of the 2015 test is very close to our generically-derived definition: "Reading literacy is understanding, using, reflecting on and engaging with written texts, in order to achieve one's goals, to develop one's knowledge and potential, and to participate in society" (PISA 2015, p. 9). Comprehension and engagement are key elements here. Because reading was not the focal area in the

2015 exam, full results have not been reported; however, the 2012 results provide more information and overall there is little change according to the 2015 results (OECD, 2016). According to those 2012 results, only 25% of students score at the top levels, achieving scores above 625 on a 1000 point scale (PISA 2015, p. 43). Moreover, as noted, 75% of students are not at that top level of proficiency, as measured by PISA. So, it's not just American students who aren't as good in reading as they need to be; students in other countries also have difficulty with reading.

As noted, all the quantitative studies have a number of flaws, even if the sample of students taking a particular instrument is a fair and representative one or a very large one. Such studies do not examine students' ability to read longer texts to follow a full argument, for example. They also do not examine students' ability to find, read, evaluate and use materials they find on the Internet, whether conventional articles or multimedia materials of various kinds. To get a better and closer look at these kinds of abilities, qualitative research and other kinds of studies are needed. The results of these more detailed studies confirm students' reading difficulties based on an assortment of instruments, measures and analyses.

Qualitative Studies

Highly respected reading researcher David Jolliffe and his graduate student (at the time) Alison Harl (2008) did do a qualitative study in which they paid 21 first-year composition students at the University of Arkansas at Fayetteville (a research-intensive public university) to complete course reading and assignments and to keep records of their reading and responses. The writing was in response to specific prompts from Jolliffe and Harl, requiring the students to analyze, synthesize, evaluate and make use of the material they read. This study shows clearly that students have difficulty with this kind of higher-level work with assigned reading material (2008, pp. 611–613). They point to the need for all college faculty (not just English or writing instructors) to work on reading of the kind needed for college and beyond (pp. 613–615); this work should include both traditional texts and those found or accessed online that encourage students to engage more fully with the material. This study points to the need for connections to texts and to active, critical reading as specified in our generic definition.

A different kind of qualitative study was conducted by a school and public library librarian. Frances Harris published a book with a fine title: *I Found It on the Internet*, which has appeared in a second edition, published by the American Library Association (2011). Harris is a librarian who has worked as a school librarian, now on the faculty at the University of Illinois at Urbana-Champaign. She draws on her years of experience in both roles to discuss the present landscape of the Internet for all sorts of uses by teens and young adults. Her review suggests that librarians need to understand the overall situation of all aspects of the Internet; students in high school and college draw on all of it in various ways. It is essential that students be taught not only to search and find, but also to evaluate and to consider the ethics of sources as well as source use. Harris notes that schools have three main strategies for helping students use the Internet effectively and appropriately: regulatory, technological and pedagogical approaches can all be called upon to help students find and use material efficiently and effectively for their own purposes, whatever they might be (pp. 122–123). While this work is not a study of reading *per se*, it does show that libraries and librarians have an essential role to play in helping students read, understand and use whatever they find online. It also points to a role for librarians and other faculty in helping students develop the critical reading abilities our generic definition suggests are part of "college reading."

Additional qualitative data comes from focused work with students' reading and research derived from the highly-regarded Citation Project, begun in 2011 (http:// site.citationproject.net). This study, led by Sandra Jamieson and Rebecca Moore Howard (2012), has examined a sample of almost 2000 references in 174 first-year students' research papers drawn from 16 schools and colleges in the US. The findings reveal the following outcomes: only 6% use real summary; 46% cite from the first page of a source; 70% of citations come from the first 2 pages of the source material, and the majority of sources are cited only once. As Jamieson (2013) points out in her analysis of the data and its relationship to students' reading, it is clear students are reading their source materials in a minimal way, relying heavily on quotation rather than full understanding of an article that might support their own ideas. The Citation Project researchers claim that theirs is a representative sample of college-level writing from across the country and across the disciplines because the vast majority of colleges and universities require first-year writing in some form. They worked with statisticians to insure they had an appropriate sample of papers to represent college writing. The Citation Project results suggest that faculty need to help students develop skills in recursive processing of a text to understand and follow complex arguments, elements of college reading on which they need help.

Students' writing from sources studied in the Citation Project—and their inability to read, understand and use those sources appropriately—is not the only data revealing the reading problem. Faculty might want to think that when students go online, they read more effectively, but research does not support this idea. One large-scale study, for example, directly examines students' information literacy skills. Project SAILS (Standardized Assessment of Information Literacy Skills) was designed by faculty and librarians at Kent State University, drawing on the work of the Association of College and Research Libraries, the part of the American Library Association for faculty librarians. SAILS is an untimed test of students' ability to find, evaluate, understand and make appropriate use of materials found online. Findings from recent administrations of the SAILS instrument show that only half of students have the skills needed to read online materials effectively (https://www.projectsails.org). A study of student performance on SAILS was led by scholars under the auspices of the Association of Research Libraries, a nonprofit organization of major research libraries in North America. A sample of more than 61,000 students from 76 institutions shows that while performance in their ability to evaluate, document and use online source materials effectively (the tasks in the SAILS instrument) does improve as students move through their undergraduate and graduate careers, and while the ability to find relevant material also improves, most students score around 50% (Radcliff, Oakleaf & Van Hoeck, 2014, p. 802).

The SAILS results point again to the need for more focus on critical reading of the kind expected at the college level.

Other reasonably current qualitative studies provide the same kinds of findings, showing students' difficulties in reading. These difficulties appear not only when students are reading traditional printed paper texts, but also with any kind of digital material. A careful study done by Alison Head at the University of Washington shows the problem clearly (2013). Head's work is part of Project Information Literacy, a large, on-going national study based at the University of Washington's School of Information (http://projectinfolit.org/about). This report has both quantitative and qualitative parts. First, Head and her colleagues examined library resources in high schools and colleges. They conducted interviews with a sample of 35 first-year students at six different colleges and universities and also did an online survey of almost 2000 high school and college students. So the interview data rely on self-reports, but draw on a sample of college students; these students reported having difficulty reading and understanding the material they were able to find. Their search abilities were limited as they found the use of academic library databases and other resources a challenge as well. In both the self-report data and the survey data, students report difficulty with both comprehension and evaluation of texts.

In a more current study of recent graduates from the same body of research at the University of Washington, half of the respondents reported difficulties with extracting needed information (i.e. reading and understanding material found through search), evaluating credibility, and using the information effectively for their own purposes. Again, this study relies on self-reported data, but the findings are drawn from a large sample with results reported anonymously (Head, 2015, p. 10). This study had 1,651 participants who graduated from college 2007–2012; they were from ten colleges and universities across the country representing an array of types of institutions in different parts of the US. So the students themselves perceive problems in reading and evaluating materials and making effective use of them.

All of these reports give some additional perspective on the problems students have with reading extended nonfiction prose in the ways faculty expect. Finally, two other recent qualitative studies point indirectly to students' reading problems: Keller (2014) and Carillo (2015) both make the case for more attention to reading in writing classes and beyond at the college level. Using case studies with nine high school students, and following four of them to college, Keller reports on their reading activities online and off. He proposes that faculty need to pay more attention to reading trends in the online environment to discourage what he calls "digital literacies tourism" (2014, p. 160), i.e. superficial reading. Carillo did a different kind of study under the auspices of the Conference on College Composition and Communication, a part of the National Council of Teachers of English, the major professional organization for English teachers including composition instructors. Reporting on a national survey of college writing faculty, Carillo argues for what she calls "mindful reading" (2015, p. 117f.), the kind of thoughtful, thoroughly engaged reading students do not do now according to all the studies cited previously. Keller's findings are particularly useful because of his focus on online reading as well as reading traditional texts, while Carillo's work reveals how instructors see what is happening with students' reading in the classroom. All of these qualitative studies and all the quantitative research discussed here show the problems students have with college reading as we have defined it in this book, a complex, recursive, active, critical process of connecting to texts.. This collection offers an array of new strategies and approaches to expand this discussion along with assorted ideas for addressing students' problems.

Overview of the Chapters

Literacy instruction is the work of all teachers, K-12 and beyond. It does not and should not end in elementary or secondary school. The goal of this collection is to provide replicable strategies to help educators think about how and when students learn the skill of reading, synthesizing information, and drawing inferences across multiple texts. This type of reading is stressed in the Common Core State Standards and teachers of secondary students are finding challenges in leading readers to mastery of these standards. It is not only the act of helping students read that creates challenge. The need for data to show progress and to determine the next phases of reading instruction has added another layer of complexity to the work of teaching literacy. Composition instructors and scholars should also find this collection of interest as well as faculty and administrators across the disciplines. The presented definitions of college reading can be helpful as high school faculty work to prepare students for the real work of learning in college, and as faculty in college work with students once they get there. And it must continue to include literature but now must also include extended nonfiction prose. This body of work should be of interest and practical use to those who are facing the need to offer more for students as they exit their high school career and begin the journey of post-secondary education. While the chapters not only address those elements in the generic definition, they fall into two broad categories that we have used to organize them. First, there are six chapters that describe work in cross-institutional settings of various kinds. In the second part, the seven chapters take up assorted disciplinary settings for work on reading.

To begin, Anson presents work connecting writing with rhetorical analysis to improve reading comprehension. Anson shows that connecting writing and reading leads to improved teaching and learning when assignments call for students to engage actively with texts. Gogan's chapter presents a fresh way of understanding college reading. Drawing from research on threshold concepts, he reports on interviews with eight students who had deep, transformative experiences with reading. Gogan writes:

> When practiced as a dynamic mode of reception, reading transforms the agency of the reader, allowing the passive receptor to become an active co-creator of meaning. When practiced as a relational arrangement, reading transforms the identity of the reader and of the text, as it stitches together texts, contexts, selves, and others in novel configurations. And when practiced as a recursive journey, reading transforms the approach or orientation of the reader to the text, affording the reader the opportunity to chart his or her course inside of the text. (p. 53)

These experiences, it should be clear, occur with a variety of different kinds of reading across disciplines, illustrating the recursive and complex nature of active reading.

Hollander, Shamgochian, Dawson, and Bouchard offer suggestions for scaffolding the reading task to help students understand content in a manner that deepens comprehension. To achieve this goal, their work suggests the importance of changing the reading "climate" on campus across disciplines to facilitate students' abilities to connect to texts. Using a different kind of cross-campus project, Maloy and her colleagues explore the ways that the use of a common book can be adapted on any campus to build students' reading abilities. This approach builds a sense of community on a campus, contributing as well to students' sense of themselves as *college* students. When Maloy et al. write that "What makes Queensborough's Common Read uncommon is that it is a yearlong collaborative experience for faculty participants and a curricular immersive experience for student participants. It provides much-needed community for our faculty and students . . . ," the program focuses attention on this sense of connection through reading.

Townsend's study of high-profile football players' reading reveals that it is important to challenge stereotypes about how different student populations engage in reading. Her research with college athletes shows that they are much more fully involved with reading and learning than either their ACT scores or the common negative stereotypes might suggest. The complexity of student athletes' reading practices and their active use of reading to learn offer surprising insights into this group of students. Young and Potter also offer this kind of wider view of reading from a P–16 perspective, drawing on the Common Core State Standards; they argue that the contemporary focus on testing distracts from students' need for critical reading skills essential to college and careers. As Young and Potter say: "Although not at the complete exclusion of approaches that are more direct, we argue that whole language and constructivist approaches offer a level of contextualization and engagement that best prepares students for the work they will do in the college environment" (p. 124). For high school teachers, particularly those working with grade 11 and 12 students, this chapter may be most pertinent. Young and Potter describe the current emphasis on data-driven decisions about teaching strategies and highlight the danger of losing authentic means of measuring student progress because of a political climate that requires specific types of reading assessment.

The second set of chapters pay closer attention to specific disciplinary settings in which reading can and should play a key role. As in the cross-disciplinary chapters of the first part, these chapters address the nature of "college reading" and ways to help students with its complex, recursive quality—the importance of active engagement that leads to critical connection with texts in various subject areas.

Leading off the second section, Nantz and Abbott, coming from outside the English Language Arts arena, describe an interdisciplinary team-taught honors course that challenged students to read texts across historical and economic perspectives on the concept of "empire." They focus on the development of both skill in and motivation for reading. Even though Nantz and Abbott experienced mixed results in their attempt to provide students with the tools they need for deep reading, they were working on critical reading within their respective disciplines, suggesting how this goal might be achieved. Davies provides another disciplinary perspective. Her chapter presents ways that biology and other science professors can model assignments on a sequential series to encourage students' recursive reading. Davies explicitly advocates modeling as a strategy. Moreover, she forthrightly states that "Conversations about student writing issues and/or students' lack of content knowledge at an institutional level need to be reframed and focused on students' reading practices" (p. 179). These chapters show that faculty in disciplines other than English can achieve their own teaching goals when they work on students' active critical reading.

Along with disciplinary variety, faculty in both high school and college settings deal with groups of students with particular needs in addition to their disciplinary learning. Freedman described a collaborative project where principles of ELL language learning were used to promote better reading in East Asian Studies courses. This chapter's focus on preparing TAs to work with students who are learning the language as well as disciplinary content is particularly valuable. Developing reading ability is, after all, part of learning a language. Similarly, Huffman describes her curricular transformation of a developmental reading class, a unique focus in this collection, to enable better comprehension, critical thinking, and pass rates. Course assessment results suggest that students using the rhetorical analysis and writing model may be more engaged and motivated in the course, and the reading they learn to do may make them more engaged writers; however, the approach may not help students better identify main ideas, key points, or bias, which points to the need to define what comprehension means explicitly. Readers of these chapters will find ideas for adding rigor and student engagement in any curricular area.

A different student group with particular needs is discussed by Melis, who is writing from a tribal community college. Composition instructors can learn from Melis' advocacy for a culturally responsive approach to college reading, one that both recognizes differences in student populations and also takes into account students' experiences with high school reading instruction. Melis addresses the importance of culturally responsive teaching, a more prevalent challenge than many educators recognize. It is a challenge that both secondary teachers and college professors face; the authors published in this text have aptly presented practices and research that can directly inform classroom practice in ways that acknowledge the complexity of reading for all kinds of students.

Odom suggests three ways disciplinary faculty can further support their students' reading: considering the types of assignments they give, explaining their goals when assigning reading, and providing guidance as students read challenging texts and/or texts in unfamiliar genres. A key idea in her chapter as well as in the book as a whole is, as she says: "Determining what does bring meaning to our students' textual experiences is a crucial first step in developing pedagogies that make successful reading, writing, and learning connections for students" (p. 256). Connecting to texts is a key aspect of college reading. Similarly, Sturtz, Hucks, and Tirabassi explore an initiative that links first-year writing with disciplinary studies at Keene State College, where education professors have joined forces with composition professors for a two-semester sequence on reading, writing and professional development for beginning students in their program. According to Sturtz et al., "[t]he structures of full-year linked courses, learning communities, and clustered learning programs connecting two or more courses that typically involve the same faculty and students offer researchers interested in transfer further opportunities to study how a whole cohort of first-year students apply, transform, integrate and reconstruct their learning about reading and writing processes across contexts . . ." (p. 288). These ways of creating connections to texts and among the students are essential to students' developing the elements of college reading.

College reading, however, is an issue that affects faculty in all disciplines, wherever students are expected to engage in academic reading and writing. Much of this book, therefore, moves beyond reading pedagogy in college composition courses (discussed in the Afterword and addressed by many chapters in *Deep Reading:*

Teaching Reading in the Writing Classroom) to consider how such pedagogy can be successfully implemented across disciplines and within discipline-specific courses. It should be clear that we have assembled these chapters to provide an array of options for instructors across these various settings. College reading must be part of the work of every member of the faculty. Using the variety of tools, strategies and approaches offered here, building on and collaborating with colleagues in first-year writing and in the library, faculty can help students become faster, more effective readers, writers and critical thinkers in every course, every term.

References

ACT. (2006, March 1). Reading between the lines: What the ACT reading test reveals about college readiness. Retrieved from http://www.act.org/path/policy'reports/reading.html.

ACT. (2015). The condition of college and career readiness—Michigan. Retrieved from http://www.act.org/newsroom/data/2015/states/pdf/Michigan.pdf.

Bartholomae, D., Petrosky, A. & Waite, S. (2014). *Ways of reading: An anthology for writers.* (10th ed.). New York: Macmillan.

Berthoff, A. (1981). *The making of meaning: Metaphors, models, and maxims for writing teachers.* Portsmouth, NH: Boynton/Cook.

Bishop, W. (2000). *The subject is reading: Essays by teachers and students.* Portsmouth, NH: Heinemann.

Bunn, M. (2011). How to read like a writer. In C. Lowe & P. Zemliansky (Eds.), *Writing spaces: Readings on writing, Vol. 2* (pp. 71–86). Andersen, SC: Parlor Press. Retrieved from https://wac.colostate.edu/books/writingspaces2/.

Carillo, E. C. (2015). *Securing a place for reading in composition: The importance of teaching for transfer.* Logan: Utah State University Press.

Harris, F. J. (2011). *I found it on the Internet: Coming of age online.* (2nd ed.). Chicago: American Library Association.

Head, A. J. (2013). *Learning the ropes: How freshmen conduct course research once they enter college.* Project Information Literacy Passage Studies research report. Seattle: University of Washington. Retrieved from http://projectinfolit.org/pdfs/PIL_2013_Freshmen Study_FullReport.pdf.

Head, A. J. (2015). *Project Information Literacy's research summary: Lifelong learning study phase two: Trends from the online survey.* Seattle: University of Washington School of Information.

Helmers, M. (2003). *Intertexts: Reading pedagogy in writing classrooms.* New York: Routledge.

Horning, A. S. (2012). Reading, writing and digitizing: Understanding literacy in the electronic age. Newcastle-upon-Tyne: Cambridge Scholars Press.

Horning, A. S. & Kraemer, E.W. (Eds.). (2013). *Reconnecting reading and writing.* Anderson, SC: Parlor Press and The WAC Clearinghouse. Retrieved from https://wac.colostate.edu/books/reconnecting/.

Jamieson, S. (2013). Reading and engaging sources: What students' use of sources reveals about advanced reading skills. *Across the Disciplines*, Special issue on Reading and Writing Across the Curriculum. Retrieved from https://wac.colostate.edu/atd/reading/jamieson.cfm.

Jamieson, S. & Howard, R. M. (2012). The citation project. Retrieved from http://site.citationproject.net/.

Jolliffe, D. J. & Harl, A. (2008). Texts of our institutional lives: Studying the reading transition: from high school to college: What are our students reading and why? *College English, 70*(6), 599–617.

Keller, D. (2014). *Chasing literacy: Reading and writing in an age of acceleration.* Logan: Utah State University Press.

Lombardo, S. (2016). Evaluating sources. Handout available at Kresge Library, Oakland University.

National Assessment of Educational Progress. (2015). Are the nation's twelfth-graders making progress in mathematics and reading? Retrieved from http://www.nationsreportcard.gov/reading_math_g12_2015/#reading.

Organisation for Economic Cooperation and Development. (2016). PISA 2015 results in focus. Retrieved from https://www.oecd.org/pisa/pisa-2015-results-in-focus.pdf.

Padgett, R. (1997). *Creative reading: What it is, how to do it, and why.* Urbana, IL: National Council of Teachers of English.

PISA 2015 draft reading literacy framework. (2015). Retrieved from http://www.oecd.org/pisa/pisaproducts/Draft%20PISA%202015%20Reading%20Framework%20.pdf.

Radcliff, C., Oakleaf, M. & Van Hoeck, M. (2014). So what? The results and impact of a decade of IMLS-funded information literacy assessments. In S. Durso, S. Hiller, M. Kyrilliou & A. Pappalardo (Eds.), *Proceedings of the 2014 Library Assessment Conference* (pp. 801–805). Washington, DC: Association of Research Libraries. Retrieved from http://libraryassessment.org/bm~doc/proceedings-lac-2014.pdf.

Salvatori, M.R. & Donahue, P. A. (2005). *The elements (and pleasures) of difficulty.* New York: Pearson.

Stanford History Education Group. (2016). *Evaluating information: The cornerstone of civic online reasoning.* Stanford, CA. Retrieved from https://sheg.stanford.edu/upload/V3LessonPlans/Executive%20Summary%2011.21.16.pdf.

Sullivan, P. & Tinberg, H. (Eds.). (2006). *What is "College-Level" writing?* Urbana, IL: National Council of Teachers of English. Retrieved from https://wac.colostate.edu/books/collegelevel/.

Sullivan, P., Tinberg, H. & Blau, S. (2017). *Deep reading: Teaching reading in the writing classroom.* Urbana, IL: NCTE.

United States Department of Education. (2015, July 27). Fact sheet: Focusing higher education on student success. Retrieved from http://www.ed.gov/news/press-releases/fact-sheet-focusing-higher-education-student-success.

Part 1. Cross-Institutional Approaches to Theory and Practice in College Reading

Writing to Read, Revisited

Chris M. Anson

NORTH CAROLINA STATE UNIVERSITY

A recent meta-analysis (Graham & Hebert, 2010) shows that certain writing practices and instruction help students improve their reading skills and comprehension. This chapter first summarizes the positive results of this meta-analysis, but then questions its pedagogical recommendations, which, while clearly helpful in fostering students' literacy development, lack attention to four important instructional dimensions: students' motivation and engagement; the cognitive complexity of the task and its relationship to the reading content; the teacher's incentive to be creative; and the social and collaborative nature of the classroom. The chapter explores ways that teachers in all disciplines can engage students in deeper and more intellectually meaningful reading through imaginative, carefully designed low-stakes writing-to-read assignments in a variety of genres. These methods are illustrated with examples from several disciplines and courses such as history, invertebrate zoology, biology, medical ethics, and geography. The examples show how writing-to-read assignments such as those advocated in Graham and Hebert's report—which do not guarantee careful reading, do not lead to engagement, and can easily be plagiarized—can be turned into low-stakes, low-burden, genre-flexible assignments that students find highly engaging and that teachers can use to stimulate livelier and more productive discussions and other forms of classroom interaction.

The situation is familiar. A teacher has assigned students some reading material for homework—an article, a chapter, a story, a webtext. When they show up in class, they're supposed to be prepared to discuss the reading or apply it during an activity the teacher has set up. Valiantly, the teacher struggles to draw out the students' reading knowledge—get them to make observations and connections, explain what they learned, or interpret something interesting or significant. But nothing happens. The students sit mutely, hoping the awkward silence will pass quickly and that, as usual, the teacher will end up telling them all the things they were supposed to figure out and discuss on their own. After all, it's so much easier for them than struggling to make sense of a text that they just skimmed quickly before class, or didn't even glance at.

All of us feel anguish over the prospect that our students don't read, can't read, won't read, or read superficially, passing indifferent eyes across lines of text that engage us but bore and alienate them. When I ask teachers during faculty workshops to list their gravest concerns about their students' learning processes and behaviors, reading comes up early and often—the suspicion that many of their students don't read assigned material, or that if they do read it, they don't read it critically, thoughtfully, or fully, from start to finish. Although we know that students are exposed to large amounts of text each day online, recent studies suggest that they often avoid academic reading (see Nantz & Abbott, this volume). On the 2014 National Survey of Student Engagement, which is administered to tens of thousands of students at hundreds of colleges and universities each year, 18% of first-year students and 20% of seniors self-reported attending classes often or very often "without completing readings or assignments," those numbers rising to 74% and 75% respectively when including "occasionally" (NSSE, 2014). In high school, the problem may be worse. Even when students are reading deliberately—as when they are collecting material for a research paper—their practices betray superficial reading: in one study of 1,911 student citations, almost three-fourths were from the first two pages of the source text (Jamieson, 2013). Students' tendency to quote sentences in isolation instead of summarizing or referring to broader pieces of text leaves us wondering whether they are truly understanding what they read (Howard, Serviss & Rodrigue, 2010, p. 187).

In 2010, the Carnegie Corporation's Advancing Literacy Program issued a report, *Writing to Read: Evidence for How Writing Can Improve Reading* (Graham & Hebert, 2010; see also 2011). This report is of special interest to those working in literacy studies because, over the past three decades, research on the relationship of writing and reading in higher education has ebbed. As the field of writing studies gained momentum, especially in the mid-1980's, reading saw consistent emphasis in edited collections such as Fulwiler and Young's *Language Connections: Reading and Writing Across the Curriculum* (1982), Newkirk's *Only Connect: Uniting Reading and Writing* (1986), and Peterson's *Convergences: Transactions in Writing and Reading* (1986) as well as in the scholarship of writing specialists such as Marilyn Sternglass (e.g., 1988), Elizabeth Flynn (e.g., Flynn & Schweickart, 1986), Ann Berhoff (e.g., 1978), David Bartholomae (e.g., Bartholomae & Petrosky, 1986), and (controversially) E.D. Hirsch, Jr. (e.g., 1987). At composition conferences throughout this period, it was not uncommon to encounter many sessions focusing on uniting writing research with scholarship on reading, including schema theory (Anson, Bommarito & Deuser, 1983), reader-response theory (Brandt, 1990), and transactional approaches to reading (Kucer, 1985). As Carillo (2015) puts it, this was the "moment wherein attention to reading flourished in composition" (p. 2).

Despite the obvious connections between reading and writing, the focus wasn't sustained. Fleeting revivals of interest occurred thereafter, but so little serious post-millennial research on reading has appeared in writing studies that scholars such as Alice Horning have been calling for a revitalization of inquiry into the relationship, especially because technology has put a new face on certain aspects of academic reading. New work (e.g., Carillo, 2015; Helmers, 2003; Horning, 2010;

Horning & Kraemer, 2013; Salvatori & Donahue, 2012; and this volume) is finally picking up where an earlier generation of scholarship left off. As Bazerman, Reiff, and Bawarshi (2013) argue, "As teachers of writing we cannot keep reading out of the picture. . . . The need to connect reading and writing is greater than ever as students negotiate new information technologies and a multi-mediated world" (pp. xi–xii). In the context of such calls, the Graham and Hebert (2010) report is welcome news, helping educators and policy-makers to know more about how writing can enhance what students do as readers and how they can become more proficient readers. But the picture is not entirely rosy. In contrast to the positive conclusions of the report's analysis, its pedagogical recommendations are dull and uninspired. We can do much better.

This chapter will first briefly review the findings of *Writing to Read*. Then, honoring the principle that practitioners, not researchers, are the best equipped to implement the findings of well-supported research, it will suggest ways that teachers in every conceivable discipline can engage students in deeper and more intellectually meaningful reading through brief, imaginative, focused writing assignments in a variety of genres. Creating those assignments, however, requires an analysis of the intellectual processes they are asking for—their "structure of activity"—as well as a strong dose of creativity and an interest in student engagement. Several examples of writing prompts from different college-level disciplines will demonstrate these principles.

Writing to Read: A Meta-Analysis

Writing to Read is the first meta-analysis to examine the relationship between various writing practices' effects on students' reading performance. The authors gathered 104 experimental and quasi-experimental studies conducted at a variety of grade levels.[1]

Research was thoroughly vetted, and studies that did not meet rigorous empirical criteria were rejected. The authors then looked at the effect sizes of all the studies relating to the specific relationship at hand. A full explanation of the study's careful methodology and statistical analysis appears in both the report and article (Graham and Hebert, 2010; 2011) and will not be repeated here.

While experimental research has its limitations as a method for understanding highly complex processes of learning, meta-analyses can be especially useful

---

1   The studies in *Writing to Read* focused entirely on K-12 educational contexts, in part because of the (problematic) social and academic assumption that students come to college already prepared as readers, which has generally limited both instruction and research in this area (see Bazerman, Reiff, and Bawarshi, 2013, p. xi). However, the findings are as relevant to the college setting as they are to primary and secondary education.

heuristically and sometimes politically, to the extent that they magnify the results of many individual experimental studies. For example, a meta-analysis of the effects of class size in higher education showed that when the delivery mode is to lecture to students and test them objectively, class size makes little difference; a class of 50 will behave the same way as a class of 100. But when it comes to other important attitudinal, motivational, and cognitive goals, class size makes a significant difference (Pascarella & Terenzini, 1991), with smaller class sizes proportionally enhancing specific learning outcomes. A study like this easily cuts through arguments based on the politics of school funding by asking what characteristics of learning and delivery systems we find most important to invest in. Similarly, in one of the most important meta-analyses of instructional methodologies for writing, Hillocks (1986) showed that none of the included studies provides any support for teaching grammar as a means of improving composition skills. If schools insist upon teaching the identification of parts of speech, the parsing or diagramming of sentences, or other concepts of traditional grammar (as many still do), they cannot defend it as a means of improving the quality of writing (p. 138).

Not only did direct grammar instruction fail to improve overall writing ability, but there was some evidence that students wrote worse at the end of such instruction than when they started. This study, which has not been refuted, continues to help progressive educators to forestall the reintroduction of mindless grammar drills in the name of developing students' broader literacy interests and abilities. In this sense, *Writing to Read* may be useful in support of programs that provide faculty development, incentives, and rewards for the integration of writing as a tool for reading in all subject areas—and especially for its increased attention at the college level. Overall, the analysis found that:

- "students' comprehension of science, social studies, and language arts texts is improved when they write about what they read,"
- "students' reading skills and comprehension are improved by learning the skills and processes that go into creating text," and
- "students' reading comprehension is improved by having them increase how often they produce their own texts" (p. 5).

The authors conclude that writing about reading "should enhance comprehension because it provides students with a tool for visibly and permanently recording, connecting, analyzing, personalizing, and manipulating key ideas in text" (p. 13).

In many ways, the recommendations in the report push against a dominant model of reading and writing in which students read first and then, through writing, are tested on their understanding and interpretations of the text. Writing is used not as "input," not as a way to come to terms with and construct the text's meaning, but as "output," as a measure or reflection of their (finished) reading. For this reason, the writing tends to be higher-stakes—an essay exam or a formal paper, for example—and is judged for its adherence to the conventions of those genres, which limits the nature and scope of the assignments teachers will create (see Figure 1).

Figure 1. A Conventional *Model of Reading and Writing in Academic Contexts*

Writing to Read, on the other hand, supports a reciprocal model of reading and writing that sees them as intertwined (Figure 2). Students may try to summarize a text and realize that they haven't fully grasped its details or significance, which propels them back into its words in the quest for fuller understanding—rethinking, reconsidering, and creating new meaning. Or they may write questions about the text and answer them as they read, further solidifying their understanding of the details. Used for such purposes, the writing is often brief, with less risk, designed not to measure the outcome of reading but to provide a means to think more fully about it.

Figure 2. A Reciprocal *Model of Writing and Reading*

The idea of writing informally about reading is not new (having been advocated for decades in writing studies). However, when we look across the entire landscape of higher education, in all content areas, it is rare to find the systematic integration of writing-to-read in coursework. Reading is typically seen as independent of (and usually done prior to) tests, formal papers, or classwork, which may take the form of lecture or discussion or even hands-on activity in labs and clinical settings.

In the context of a focus on the potential benefit of writing to students' comprehension of sophisticated content material across the curriculum, Graham and Hebert's first conclusion is especially important: that students' comprehension of texts improves when they write about them. By "writing," the authors mean the following activities, based on the studies they examined (2010, p. 5):

- Responding to a text in writing (writing personal reactions, analyzing and interpreting the text)
- Writing summaries of a text
- Writing notes about a text
- Answering questions about a text in writing

There is little question that these strategies, when well taught and implemented, can only enhance students' reading comprehension and also contribute to their development as writers (although it could be argued that the strategies move only slightly away from a "reading-to-write" model). But they also ignore some crucial aspects of teaching and learning, and although they may be supported across dozens of experimental studies, they go only so far in responding to the complex learning situations that most teachers orchestrate. In particular, the strategies fail to consider four dimensions of learning that, if accommodated, could significantly enhance the strategies' success:

- students' motivation and engagement (see Kuh, 2003);
- the cognitive complexity of the task and its relationship to the content;
- the teacher's incentive to be creative, i.e. to engage the pedagogical imagination; and
- the potential of the written text to contribute to collaborative learning and enhance the social dynamic of the class (which is of increasing importance and availability with digital access and tools for collaboration and dialogue).

These dimensions of teaching and learning have been recently given voice in the *Framework for Success in Postsecondary Writing* (2011), a report issued jointly by the Council of Writing Program Administrators, the National Council of Teachers of English, and the National Writing Project. Among those features defining preparation for postsecondary education are eight "habits of mind" that include curiosity, openness, engagement, and creativity (p. 1), all of which could be more effectively fostered than through writing summaries of texts or taking notes on them.

To further explore these dimensions in the context of Graham and Hebert's recommendations, consider a teacher of introductory biology who wants her students to read assigned textbook material more deeply and carefully. After each chapter assignment, she requires students to write a *summary* of the material. First, such an assignment fails the test of motivation and engagement: it's exceedingly boring and routinized, relying on a typical "canonical" academic task, and responded to without imagination. Second, it requires no creative pedagogical energy from the teacher, who almost mindlessly includes the requirement after each reading and is therefore unlikely to look forward to seeing students' responses or be surprised by them. Third, it requires a relatively low level of cognitive complexity (searching for macrostructures in the text and organizing them into a brief synthesis), with no surrounding context or complex connections to the meaning of the text itself.[2]

---

2   Evidence of this relatively shallow level of cognitive sophistication comes from the increasing capabilities of computers to create accurate summaries of longer texts or data (see Levy, 2012), in contrast to the absolute inability of computers to "read"—that is, understand, interpret, and discover meaning in natural-language texts (Anson, 2006).

Finally, it offers little potential to position readings in some richer social and inter-active space and open them up to deeper interpretive possibilities, igniting class-room interaction (beyond an equally dull activity in which, for example, students compare their summaries for accuracy). This is not to say that summary fails to engage students with the texts they are reading (see, for example, Marzano, Gaddy & Dean, 2000, Chapter 3); instead, it's to suggest that we can move far beyond simple summary in the design and implementation of writing-to-read assignments.

Beyond Meta: Creating Meaningful Writing-to-Read Assignments

To instantiate the model in Figure 2, it's necessary to place writing-to-read assign-ments along a continuum of formality and risk. Figure 3 shows such a continuum. Writing on the far left represents the most informal, lowest-stakes genres, which are familiar to most teachers of writing: journal entries, learning logs, dialogic blogs etc. Most of the recommendations of *Write to Read* fall on this end of the contin-uum, such as note-taking and personal reactions. Typically, the writing produced in response to such assignments may look acceptably associative, unorganized, and a-grammatical because it is almost always written in one draft without revision. Al-though some writing toward this end of the continuum may motivate and engage students (such as personal responses in which they relate the material to their own lives) or create interpersonal connections in the class (such as through blogs and forums), it generally fails to meet the four standards described above. Teachers need only assign an ongoing dialogue forum once, and students can end up finding it tedious or disengaging, or may write unthinkingly, with their minds on what some educators call "autopilot":

> I thought the reading for today was OK. It was pretty interest-ing. I had a hard time finishing it at first but then I got through it. I didn't think it was too complicated. The author made some good points.

As we move along the continuum toward the middle, assignments are still produced in one sitting and continue to be understood as involving little risk, dif-ferentiating them from formal assignments that should always require significant support and multiple drafts based on readers' responses. Here, however, students are provided with more constraints linked to the reading material—a context, a specified audience, a problem to solve.

Crafting these genres of assignments begins with the articulation of clear learn-ing goals relating to course material, a process generally known as "backward de-sign" (Wiggins & McTiege, 1998). These goals determine the scope and nature of the assignment. For example, a teacher who wants students to learn about a historical figure through some research, including his or her career, family and influential friends, contributions to society or science, what sort of time period he or she lived in, and so on, might ask students to use the online educational platform "Fakebook," which allows students to emulate a Facebook page that the historical figure might have set up at the time. The student then populates the page with "friends," interactive posts that are distillations of research on the figure, videos and still photos, and other material (see http://www.classtools.net/FB/home-page).

Low stakes/informal		High stakes/formal
Journals	Provided-data papers	Term Papers
Reading logs	Translation papers	Reports
Reflections	Invented dialogues	Formal essays
Minute papers	Mini-cases	Documented papers
Blogs	Problem analyses	Literature reviews
Notes	Wiki contributions	Proposals

Figure 3. A Formality-Based Writing Continuum

Because it would be very difficult to circumvent the need to gather information about the historical figure in order to build the Fakebook page, the teacher would almost surely realize his or her learning goal. In this sense, the assignment is "constructively aligned" (Biggs, 1996), meaning that it demonstrates symmetry between what it wants students to learn and what specific *activities* it sets up to guarantee that learning. In addition, the assignment engages the writer because the platform emulates familiar social media that usually motivate self-sponsored writing, provides a space that can be built up over time from the student's investigations, can sometimes be funny (as when important events are rendered in colloquial language or when the figure's "friends" post messages to the page), is both visually and textually appealing, and engages the imagination of viewers and opens up the possibility for highly successful student interaction and collaboration.

In the context of this volume, the general learning goal under consideration is that students will, through brief writing assignments, *read* their assigned material more fully, thoughtfully, and interpretively, in keeping with most definitions of college-level reading.[3] In addition to considering the value of constructive

---

3   From a cross-curricular perspective, college reading must be understood as much more complex than common definitions often allow. It is the process of actively constructing meaning from text, including multimedia manifestations of text, in the context of specific genres, domains of knowledge, and specialized uses of language. It involves a transaction between authorial intention, features of text, and the reader's instantiation of schemas and other forms of existing knowledge. These and other complex factors, well demonstrated in studies of eye movements during read-

alignment in shaping such writing assignments, two crucial questions must also be asked:

- What *specific* underlying intellectual activities does the assignment require that compel fuller, more thoughtful, more interpretive reading? (We might call this the "structure of activity" beneath the assignment: the various processes that surround, inform, and are informed by their reading.)
- Is it difficult or impossible to circumvent those activities?

Consider, for example, a writing-to-read assignment intended to compel students to read the first act or so of *King Lear*.

> After reading through Act 1, Sc. 3 of *King Lear*, write a brief (half-page) summary of what has happened so far in the play.

This brief writing assignment realizes the Graham and Hebert recommendations effectively: students must read the play carefully enough to explain what's going on in writing. But the structure of activity beneath the assignment is limited to pulling out the most salient pieces of the plot. While there is no question that the assignment requires effort and knowledge of the play's particulars, it could be much more engaging and dynamic. In addition, such assignments can be easily circumvented with a quick online search, the results of which can be paraphrased or even copied verbatim. Here is one of hundreds of online *Lear* summaries, from SparkNotes:

> Lear, the aging king of Britain, decides to step down from the throne and divide his kingdom evenly among his three daughters. First, however, he puts his daughters through a test, asking each to tell him how much she loves him. Goneril and Regan, Lear's older daughters, give their father flattering answers. But Cordelia, Lear's youngest and favorite daughter, remains silent, saying that she has no words to describe how much she loves her father. Lear flies into a rage and disowns Cordelia. The king of France, who has courted Cordelia, says that he still wants to marry her even without her land, and she accompanies him to France without her father's blessing.

With some imagination, an interest in student engagement, and an understanding of what makes for richer, more nuanced and meaningful writing-to-read assignments, a teacher might create the following alternative:

---

ing (see Anson and Schwegler, 2012), make college reading an experience whose difficulty varies constantly across contexts and requires considerable developmental and experiential support in all classroom instruction.

> After reading through Act 1, Sc. 3 of *King Lear*, imagine that
> there is one piece of modern technology in the world of the
> play: on online chat system. Create an online dialogue between
> Cordelia and Lear, drawing on what has happened so far in the
> play. Shakespearean language optional.

Beneath this small shift in the assignment is a more complex structure of intellectual activity. First, the student must know not just "what's happened," but what Cordelia and Lear might be feeling, what is revealed in their interaction, what Cordelia might be thinking about her sisters and their husbands. The assignment more successfully meets 1) the criterion of motivation and engagement (partly through the chat genre and the chance to enter the virtual Lear world); 2) the criterion of greater cognitive complexity (in addition to knowing the play, the writer must use various rhetorical strategies, write in the imagined or constructed voices of Cordelia and Lear, and even try out some Elizabethan English); 3) the criterion of teacher creativity (in a somewhat more imaginative assignment whose results might be more interesting to read than a batch of summaries); and 4) the criterion of potential social interactivity (students can read their dialogues aloud in small groups or to the class or post them to a website). Yet at the same time, these quickly written responses are understood to be *informal,* used to come to terms with the play rather than to be tested on it. The assignment doesn't require a thesis, support for assertions, and a logical structure; it requires an attempt to convey a developing understanding of the play in the form of an online chat between characters. The result is a more dynamic response, in contrast to the static summary, which gives a sense of completion and rigidity. The potential for interactivity around students' online chats is obvious.

It is this feature of write-to-learn assignments—their informality and low stakes—that also allows them to be created in any imaginable genre, regardless of the disciplinary goals or orientation of a course (see Anson, 2011, for a discussion of one such genre, dialogues). In business courses, for example, students are sometimes assigned to write extended obituaries of companies that have failed, providing the details of their demise. Few business students will find themselves routinely asked to write obituaries on the job, but unlike learning the professional genre of a financial report, a business memo, or a public relations document, the goal is not to "learn to write" more effectively but to "write to learn" more powerfully. Every conceivable genre is at the disposal of the teacher's imagination. The *King Lear* assignment could also take the form of a series of exchanged letters (sent by carrier pigeon) or a chain of voicemail messages. Or students could create a digital news forum reporting on Lear's denouncement of Cordelia with subsequent forum posts from any of the characters, who contribute their perspectives.

It is important to realize that lowering the stakes of the assignment—by reducing its "worth" in a grading system, by limiting the timeframe for composing it, and by downplaying the features of formal, stylized, carefully revised and edited academic prose—doesn't also weaken the intellectual effort students must put in to respond to it. Rather, effort and time are more easily linked to engagement than the formality or scope of a task; students can be largely unengaged in a substantial research paper. At the same time, *design* is crucial. From a teacher's perspective, lower-stakes writing-to-read assignments in no way diminish the pedagogical effort needed to think through how the assignment challenges students to read, reflect on, and respond to a reading. Part of that effort involves considering the *structure of activity* beneath the assignment and what, exactly, it does to promote more careful, thoughtful reading.

The Structure of Activity: Unpacking Writing-to-Read Assignments

In creating low-stakes writing-to-read assignments, analyzing the structure of activity beneath their design requires attention to all the processes students need to go through in order to complete the assignment. Consider the following writing-to-read assignment in a medical ethics course. Students must read an article reporting on the results of a major survey study that asked women and their non-gestating partners what they would prefer for the disposition of their unused frozen embryos following successful *in vitro* fertilization (Lyerly & Faden, 2007):

> In a paragraph or two, summarize the Lyerly and Faden article.

Compare this writing-to-read assignment with its revised version, which takes the form of what is sometimes called a low-stakes "voices" or "join the conversation" assignment:

> While reading and reviewing the Lyerly and Faden article,
> you find yourself in the company of several people who have
> read this study and are talking about it. The conversation is
> wide-ranging and, as is typical in discussions about complicated
> ethical issues, gets a little tense. At one point, Paul, who has been
> quietly listening, blurts out this response:
>
> "This study is bogus! The authors totally twist their results to
> support an anti-embryo-protection stance. The fact that 42%
> of patients can't be located after five years to say what they want
> to do with their embryos indicates that they want them cryo-
> genically preserved forever, that is, never destroyed. The authors
> report that a significant percentage (82%) of those who said

they *didn't* want their embryos donated to other couples wanted
to save them for themselves or keep them forever frozen. The
authors never talk about these results! Nor do they talk about the
fact that more "partners" felt it was OK to donate the embryos
than the infertile women who produced the eggs from which the
embryos were created. Totally biased!"

In a paragraph or two, respond back to Paul as if you're part of
the conversation. Is he right about the bias? How do you know?

Compared to the first version of the assignment, this one has required a little
investment of time and creativity from the instructor: a context, a made-up statement from a fictitious person, an assertion that may or may not accurately characterize the study, and the inclusion of both accurate and inaccurate statistics from
the original article (42%, 82%). From the student's perspective, the assignment
involves a structure of activity that includes the following processes:

- read the article;
- consider the fictitious but realistic interpretation of the article;
- re-read the article, checking for the sources of the "voice's" positions,
  opinions, and support (this requires reconsidering the methodology as
  well as the way the results are rendered);
- decide how to respond to the voice, agreeing or disagreeing with various
  points and correcting misinterpretations if necessary;
- render the response in a conversational genre in keeping with the case.

In addition to the way these processes "guarantee" the goal of deeper reading,
it's hard to imagine how students could circumvent their engagement with them.
A student could simply agree with Paul in a short statement, but would know that
doing so represents a significant risk, since the agreement needs to be corroborated
by a closer reading of the article. (In this course, the professor has found that "join
the conversation" assignments yield more careful reading of assigned material than
any other strategy she has used.)

Playing with fictitious personae and contexts can lead to especially creative and
engaging low-stakes assignments. In a course in the Geography of the Southwest
at the University of New Mexico, for example, Dr. Maria Lane has designed a
number of imaginative writing-to-read assignments that tap into students' creative
potential while also ensuring that they learn the relevant material.[4] Compare her
original version:

Describe how the Diné and the Spanish settlers in the Southwest
used the same land for agricultural purposes.

---

4   This assignment and the student's response are used with permission.

with the revised version:

> Imagine you are one of the sheep living in a Diné-controlled
> flock sometime around the year 1900. In about 700 words,
> provide a description of what your life is like *and* how it com-
> pares to the lives of some of your sheep ancestors who came to
> the Southwest in Spanish-controlled herds. Since you are writing
> for an audience of humans who have never experienced life as a
> sheep, be as explicit as possible about your relationship with the
> landscape and with the Diné community (or the Spanish colo-
> nial community, in the case of your ancestors).

The structure of activity behind the sheep case involves at least the following:

- critically read the required materials about land use;
- re-read, focusing on the content relating specifically to land use;
- compare information about land use between cultures;
- hypothesize differences in the use of land;
- render an account of land use through the experiences of sheep herds living in the different periods among the different cultures;
- create a narrative that has contemporaneous information with information from the sheep's past;
- add any creative elements desired.

As seen in the following excerpt from one student response, this low-stakes assignment not only realizes Maria's goal of ensuring that students read and learn the material about land use, but also highly engages students in the process, giving them practice—without risk—with language play, which accomplishes another goal indirectly, of improving students' writing abilities.

> Hey! Hey, you! Shoo! Shoo! You're standing on a premium patch
> of blue grama! Since all you're using it for is standing on, would
> you mind moving aside to some bare patch of ground so I can
> eat? Sorry to be so rude, but good grass is hard to come by these
> days. Frequently we sheep are forced to nibble forbs and woody
> species; yuck! Those can be hard to digest, with all that extra
> lignin and whatnot. Plus nothing's more embarrassing than
> getting a twig caught between your teeth. Once in a while we do
> get a tasty alfalfa treat, but those treats are becoming few and far
> between these days.
>
> Sometimes I wish I lived in the olden days when life was much
> better for us sheep. When I was just a wee lamb my great-

great-grandram used to tell us stories of the way things used to be. Flocks were smaller and the eatens were good. They got to continuously roam the land. Rotating from valley, to Piflon-Junipers, to upland meadows and everything in between gave the sheep of yore tasty vittles year-round. Constantly on the move with the Diné, they were. That's the life! Now we are restricted to the reservation and that means we don't move around as much. (etc.)

Like this assignment, mini-cases require imagination and an investment of time to create, but doing so places students into an imagined context where the material they are reading can take on new rhetorical and situational complexity and interest. Compare this assignment in an introductory (general-education) biology course:

After reading Chapter 3, describe the process of plant growth.

with this revised version:

The following experimental conclusion was published by Jan Baptista van Helmont in 1648 (translated):

I took an earthenware vessel, placed it in 200 pounds of soil dried in an oven, soaked this with rainwater, and planted in it a willow branch weighing 5 pounds. At the end of five years, the tree grown from it weighed 169 pounds and about 3 ounces. Now, the earthenware vessel was always moistened (when necessary) only with rainwater or distilled water, and it was large enough and embedded in the ground, and, lest dust flying be mixed with the soil, an iron plate coated with tin and pierced by many holes covered the rim of the vessel. I did not compute the weight of the fallen leaves of the four autumns. Finally, I dried the soil in the vessel again, and the same 200 pounds were found, less about 2 ounces. Therefore 169 pounds of wood, bark, and root had arisen from water only.

With the assistance of time travel and your newly acquired knowledge from the readings in BIO 106, please help M. van Helmont understand the source of the "169 pounds of wood, bark, and root." You must incorporate the following words from the readings in your answer: *carbon dioxide, oxygen, water, glucose, photosynthesis, sunlight, chloroplasts*, and *pigments*.

Here the structure of activity involves at least the following:

- read the chapter;

- read and consider the van Helmont experiment, including its method and controls;
- re-read the chapter in order to compare van Helmont's conclusion with the contemporary account of the processes of plant growth;
- study and understand the role of each of the listed terms in those processes;
- optionally invent a way to time travel;
- greet Mr. van Helmont and create a rhetorically appropriate exchange, or monologue, explaining what is really behind his experiment, being careful not to act too haughty or condescending in light of van Helmont's significant contributions to science;
- Optionally embellish with further imaginary features, including attention to language.

Like this assignment, a "provided-data" paper also relies on the provision of some information either pulled from or parallel to (and supplementing) the material in assigned readings. Compare the following assignment from a course in invertebrate zoology taught by Professor Gerald Summers at the University of Missouri:

> Describe the relationship between coral and zooxanthellae.

with its revised version:

> Arrange the propositions below in a logical order, connect the individual statements with appropriate transitions, and arrive at a conclusion that is supported by your argument. Using all of the points supplied below, write a brief response concerning "The relationship between coral and zooxanthellae."
>
> - Coral reefs are formed by scleractinian corals that typically occur in shallow (<60m) water.
> - Hermatypic corals contain photosynthetic algae (zooxanthellae) in special membrane-bound cavities inside the cells of the gastrodermis.
> - Reef corals are limited to clear water because suspended material interferes with the transmission of light.
> - Over two-thirds of the metabolic requirements of corals are provided by zooxanthellae.
> (Etc.; see http:// http://cwp.missouri.edu/teaching/syllabi /index.php)

Here the structure of activity includes at least the following, as compared with the original version:

- examine a random assortment of statements;
- interpret and judge the validity of each proposition (in a more complex version of the assignment, irrelevant statements are scattered throughout and must be rejected);
- create causal or other links between statements;
- arrange the statements into a hypothetical line of reasoning;
- test the line of reasoning; reconsider rejected statements;
- render analysis into expanded, persuasive prose.

As these examples demonstrate, low-stakes writing-to-read assignments can be created in hundreds of common but engaging genres and draw on the imaginations of both teachers and students, yet still require sophisticated, challenging thinking based on reading and re-reading of even difficult texts. Interestingly, anecdotal information suggests that students become more inspired and engaged in such assignments than in the usual conventional assignments that require little thought from the teacher giving them and yield the same predictable material from students.

Conclusions: Insisting on the Conditions of Innovation

Creating innovative low-stakes writing-to-read assignments pushes against several prevailing educational conditions. First is the tyranny of imposed assessments of student learning. When outcomes are narrowly defined (such as the "ability to accurately summarize reading material chosen at an appropriate developmental level"), teachers begin behaving pedagogically in ways that most directly match the expected assessments. In the K-12 context, this imposition of external assessment strips away pedagogical imagination and systematically denies teachers the opportunity to bring their creativity and instructional talents to the design of their own curriculums (see Pedulla, et al., 2003). College teachers may experience somewhat more freedom, but the same impulses exist, exacerbated by a reward system that does not fully encourage innovation in teaching. Assigning reading by itself, and then later testing for an understanding of it, with no attention to how students work through and interpret the text and then integrate it into their current knowledge and understanding, relies on a trial-and-error model that is less about teaching than sorting and ranking. Assigning reading accompanied by conventional, unimaginative tasks such as summarizing or note-taking represents a small step forward, but still does not fully align the goals of a course or curriculum with the methods that best reach those goals (see Biggs and Tang, 2011). Without sufficient incentives (and time), many research-oriented faculty won't put in the effort to engage students in ways that guarantee they will read assigned material with the kind of care and insight that are otherwise simply expected.

A second barrier to the innovation suggested here is constructed from dominant beliefs that teaching and learning should be dry and academic, unadorned by context, humor, and imagination. Thankfully, new approaches from the gaming community have pushed against these beliefs with tangible results (Gee, 2007). Greater attention is now also being paid to the complex role of reading across the curriculum (see Odom, this volume), and the relationship between engagement and both learning and completion (Kuh, 2003). But teachers often need "permission" to unleash their pedagogical imagination and begin thinking of ways to energize their instruction and engage their students. This impetus does not give in to a notion of students as "clients" or a watering-down of standards; rather, it *raises* the bar by enriching and making more complex what are otherwise static and unidimensional assignments.

A number of implications for writing-across-the-curriculum (WAC) and writing-in-the-disciplines (WID) programs arise from the potential of writing to enhance reading. Among the most important, WAC and WID leaders must represent their programs not only in their conventional (and publicly presumed) role, as serving the interests of "improving students' writing abilities," but also in the role of helping faculty to understand the interrelated nature of language and to move campus communities beyond the notion that students should "know how to read" when they come to college and that no attention should therefore be paid to the processes and results of their reading. Significant new faculty-development work is needed in this area, especially in helping all stakeholders, including students, to move beyond a focus on college reading as "remediation."

As the examples and processes in this chapter suggest, insisting on full, careful, critical reading of assigned material can re-energize courses across the curriculum and lead to much higher levels of academic achievement among students. Doing so will require that we encourage teachers' creativity, have faith in their ability to achieve agreed-upon educational outcomes in a variety of ways, and trust them to know when they are or are not achieving those and to redesign and restructure their teaching accordingly.

References

Anson, C. M. (2006). Can't touch this: Reflections on the servitude of computers as readers. In P. F. Ericsson & R. Haswell (Eds.), *Machine scoring of student essays: Truth and consequences* (pp. 38–556). Logan: Utah State University Press.

Anson, C. M. (2011). My dinner with Calais. *Pedagogy, 11*(3), 578–590.

Anson, C. M., Bommarito, E. & Deuser, J. (1983). From schemes to themes: Implications of schema theory for teaching writing. *Journal of Teaching Writing, 2*, 193–212.

Anson, C. M. & Schwegler, R. A. (2012). Tracking the mind's eye: A new technology for researching 21st century writing and reading processes. *College Composition and Communication, 64*(1), 151–171.

Bartholomae, D. & Petrosky, A. (1986). *Facts, artifacts, and counterfacts: Theory and method for a reading and writing course.* Upper Montclair, NJ: Heinemann.

Bazerman, C., Reiff, M. J. & Bawarshi, A. (2013). Series editors' preface. In A. S. Horning & E. W. Kraemer (Eds.), *Reconnecting reading and writing* (pp. xi–xiii). Anderson, SC: Parlor Press and WAC Clearinghouse. Retrieved from https://wac.colostate.edu/books/reconnecting.

Berthoff, A. E. (1978). *Forming/thinking/writing: The composing imagination.* Rochelle Park, NJ: Hayden.

Biggs, J. (1996). Enhancing teaching through constructive alignment. *Higher Education, 32,* 347–364.

Biggs, J. & Tang, C. (2011). Teaching for quality learning at university. Maidenhead: McGraw-Hill and Open University Press.

Brandt, D. (1990). *Literacy as involvement: The acts of writers, readers, and texts.* Carbondale: Southern Illinois University Press.

Carillo, E. C. (2015). *Securing a place for reading in composition: The importance of teaching for transfer.* Logan: Utah State University Press.

Flynn, E. A. & Schweickart, P. P. (Eds.). (1986). *Gender and reading: Essays on readers, texts, and contexts.* Baltimore: Johns Hopkins University Press.

Framework for Success in Postsecondary Writing. (2011). Council of Writing Program Administrators, National Council of Teachers of English, and National Writing Project. Retrieved from http://www.wpacouncil.org.

Fulwiler, T. & Young, A. (Eds). (1982). *Language connections: Writing and reading across the curriculum.* Urbana, IL: National Council of Teachers of English.

Gee, J. P. (2007). *Good video games plus good learning: Collected essays on video games, learning and literacy.* New York: Peter Lang.

Graham, S. & Hebert, M. (2011). A meta-analysis of the impact of writing and writing instruction on reading. *Harvard Educational Review, 81*(4), 710–744.

Graham, S. & Hebert, M. (2010). *Writing to read: Evidence for how writing can improve reading.* New York: Carnegie Corporation.

Helmers, M. (Ed.). (2003). *Intertexts: Reading pedagogy in college writing classrooms.* Mahwah, NJ: Erlbaum.

Hillocks, G., Jr. (1986). *Research on written composition: New directions for teaching.* Urbana, IL: ERIC and NCTE.

Hirsch, E. D., Jr. (1987). Cultural literacy: What every American needs to know. Boston: Houghton Mifflin.

Horning, A. S. (2007). Reading across the curriculum as the key to student success. *Across the Disciplines, 4.* Retrieved from https://wac.colostate.edu/atd/articles/horning2007.cfm.

Horning, A. S. (2010). Reading, writing and digitizing: A meta-analysis of reading research. *The Reading Matrix, 10*(2), 243–270.

Horning, A. S. & Kraemer, E. W. (Eds.). (2013). *Reconnecting reading and writing.* Anderson, SC: Parlor Press and the WAC Clearinghouse. Retrieved from https://wac.colostate.edu/books/reconnecting.

Howard, R. M., Serviss, T. & Rodrique, T. K. (2010). Writing from sources, writing from sentences. *Writing & Pedagogy, 2*(2), 177–192.

Jamieson, S. (2013). What students' use of sources reveals about advanced writing skills. *Across the Disciplines, 10*(4). Retrieved from https://wac.colostate.edu/atd/reading/jamieson.cfm.

Kucer, S. L. (1985). The making of meaning: Reading and writing as parallel processes. *Written Communication, 2*(3), 317–336.

Kuh, G. (2003, March/April). What we're learning about student engagement from NSSE: Benchmarks for effective educational practices. *Change*, 24–32.

Levy, S. (2012, April 24). Can an algorithm write a better news story than a human reporter? *Wired*. Retrieved from http://www.wired.com/2012/04/can-an-algorithm-write-a-better-news-story-than-a-human-reporter/.

Lyerly, A. D. & Faden, R. R. (2007, July 6). Willingness to donate embryos for stem cell research. *Science, 317,* 46–47.

Marzano, R. J., Gaddy, B. B. & Dean, C. (2000). *What works in classroom instruction.* Aurora, CO: MCREL.

National Survey of Student Engagement. (2014). Retrieved from http://nsse.indiana.edu/html/about.cfm.

Newkirk, T. (1986). *Only connect: Uniting reading and writing.* Upper Montclair, NJ: Boynton.

Pascarella, E. T. & Terenzini, P. T. (1991). *How college affects students: Findings and insights from twenty years of research.* San Francisco: Jossey-Bass.

Pedulla, J., Abrams, L., Madaus, G., Russell, M., Ramos, M. & Miao, J. (2003). Perceived effects of state-mandated testing programs on teaching and learning: Findings from a national survey of teachers. Boston: National Board on Educational Testing and Public Policy. Retrieved from http://www.bc.edu/research/nbetpp/statements/nbr2.pdf.

Peterson, B. T. (Ed.) (1986). *Convergences: Transactions in reading and writing.* Urbana, IL: National Council of Teachers of English.

Salvatori, M. R. & Donahue, P. (2012). What is college English: Stories about reading. *College English, 75*(2), 199–217.

Sternglass, M. S. (1988). *The presence of thought: Introspective accounts of reading and writing.* Norwood, NJ: Ablex.

Wiggins, G. & McTighe, J. (1998). *Understanding by design.* Upper Saddle River, NJ: Merrill Prentice Hall.

Reading as Transformation

Brian Gogan

WESTERN MICHIGAN UNIVERSITY

Over the past decade, educators have increasingly stressed the importance of providing students with transformative learning experiences. In order to advance a complex notion of the transformative learning that occurs within disciplinary and professional communities, one particular group of educators has built a theory called threshold concept theory. When educators view college reading from the perspective of threshold concept theory as well as from the perspective of the rhetoric and writing studies discipline, educators see reading as transformation. Indeed, interview data collected as part of an empirical study of 75 learners demonstrates that students, likewise, consider reading to be a transformative experience—that is, a receptive, relational, and recursive experience.

Reading and Transformation

In December 2014, the *New York Times* published an op-ed that summarized findings from three research studies, all of which were led by the op-ed's co-authors and each of which examined the experiences of readers reading texts. The research designs of these studies distinguished between readers reading works of fiction and readers reading works of nonfiction (Djikic, Oatley, Zoeterman & Peterson, 2009; Djikic, Oatley & Carland, 2012; Djikic & Oatley, 2014). As such, these studies prove germane to discussions about the Common Core State Standards and their emphasis on the reading of nonfiction and informational texts ("Common Core," 2015). The op-ed, however, failed to mention these standards and it largely avoided assessing the merits of reading one type of text over the other. Instead, the op-ed offered its strongest claim when its co-authors—psychologists Keith Oatley and Maja Djikic—discussed the experience of reading and its psychological effects. Noting that "the idea of communication that has effects of a nonpersuasive yet transformative kind has rarely been considered in psychology," Oatley and Djikic express hope that their "studies encourage others to investigate further this important kind of influence" (2014). In short, Oatley and Djikic's op-ed sought to encourage future research on the experience of reading and reading's transformative effects. This purpose is, not surprisingly, best captured in the title of the op-ed: "How Reading Transforms Us."

Just as it was the focus of Oatley and Djikic's op-ed, the notion that reading is, in its effects, a transformative experience is the focus of this chapter. And while the transformative effects of reading are, according to Oatley and Djikic, rarely considered in psychology, the transformative effects of reading have received a fair amount of attention from individuals in other disciplines, rhetoric and writing studies among them. Examples of rhetoric and writing studies research that consider the transformative effects of reading can be found in the work of Barbara Couture (1998), Marcel Cornis-Pope and Ann Woodlief (2002), and Mary Lou Odom (2013), as well as in my own work (Gogan, 2013).

In *Toward a Phenomenological Rhetoric: Writing, Profession, and Altruism*, Couture observes that reading is often understood as an experience that involves resistance (1998). According to this understanding, "[m]eaningful interpretation results only when readers resist and thus appropriate the alienating contours of the text, transforming them to match their own self-image" (Couture, 1998, p. 40). Although Couture's larger goal is to refigure the experiences of reading, writing, and rhetoric in a way that moves beyond resistance, Couture's point remains that reading is predominantly understood as a transformation involving self and text.

Similarly, Cornis-Pope and Woodlief's discussion of reading, rereading, and the hypertextual affordances of digital technology in "The Rereading/Rewriting Process: Theory and Collaborative, On-line Pedagogy" frames an ideal kind of reading as transformative: "Ideally, the reader should pursue an uninterrupted interpretative process, with an active, transformative rereading already implied in first reading" (2002, p. 155). Understood in the context of Cornis-Pope and Woodlief's argument, the implication is that the transformative effects of reading are not a given; rather, transformation often follows much rereading and is often encouraged by sound pedagogical approaches.

More recently, Odom's 2013 study of the way in which writing across the curriculum methods might be used to redress reading-related problems suggests that, when readers personally engage texts, readers can "transform that initial engagement on the level of feeling to higher order processes such as analysis or focused research" (2013). Odom thus intimates that the relationship between self and text—the same relationship that defines reading in the theories explored by Couture as well as Cornis-Pope and Woodlief—might well constitute a transformative experience that enables readers to complete more complex cognitive tasks.

Likewise, I have emphasized the transformative effects of reading, defining reading as "a dynamic mode of reception that transforms student learning and learners" (Gogan, 2013). In "Reading at the Threshold," I argue that this definition of reading possesses the potential to initiate and sustain cross-disciplinary conversations about reading. My argument—that one common, cross-disciplinary definition of reading might be productive for readers, teachers, and researchers—builds upon Mariolina Salvatori and Patricia Donahue's view that multiple definitions of reading spread across different disciplines can be productive (2013, p. 200). To support my argument, I conducted a three-part, mixed-methods empirical research study of 75 learners enrolled across four sections of a writing-intensive course, and I analyzed the study's data using threshold concept theory—a theory that understands particular concepts as transformative to learning within disciplines and professions. While my study revealed that students associated reading with transformative effects, the study focused on the importance of reading to students as they developed an awareness of genre and, subsequently, left the concept of transformation underdeveloped. This study begs for a rejoinder, a follow-up that probes the implications of viewing reading as transformation by asking: How can educators understand reading as transformation?

In the remainder of this chapter, I offer such a rejoinder by revisiting my earlier study with the goal of more acutely focusing on the transformative effects of reading. In particular, my reevaluation of the study examines the transformative effects of reading by: (1) rereading threshold concept theory to more fully delineate its treatment of transformation; (2) synthesizing work on reading, transformation, and threshold concept theory to better identify the characteristics of reading that make reading a transformative activity; and, (3) reassessing data from my initial study to illustrate students' understandings of reading as transformation. Ultimately, I demonstrate that the receptive, relational, and recursive characteristics of reading activity position reading as transformation.

Threshold Concept Theory and Transformation

Developing a deeper understanding of the concept of transformation and of the way that the college students who were interviewed as part of my study associated reading with transformative effects begins with a reexamination of threshold concept theory. Threshold concept theory was first articulated by Jan Meyer and Ray Land in a 2003 occasional report entitled "Threshold Concepts and Troublesome Knowledge: Linkages to Ways of Thinking and Practising within the Disciplines." The report—which has subsequently spawned over 1100 publications and presentations by academics across the globe (University, 2015)—coins the term *threshold concepts* to denote concepts that are located within disciplines and that are transformative to students' learning (Meyer & Land, 2003). In this initial report, Meyer and Land explain that threshold concepts are requisite for disciplinary progress, in that these concepts mark "a transformed way of understanding, or interpreting, or viewing something without which the learner cannot progress" (2003, p. 1). Indeed, Meyer and Land enumerate five defining characteristics of threshold concepts, arguing that threshold concepts are:

- Transformative, in that learning a threshold concept effects an epistemological, ontological, or ideological shift in learners
- Irreversible, in that the effects of learning a threshold concept cannot be undone
- Integrative, in that a threshold concept exposes hidden interrelatedness
- Bounded, in that a threshold concept marks disciplinary territory
- Troublesome, in that a threshold concept poses difficulty for learners

Of the characteristics that Meyer and Land initially associate with threshold concepts, the first characteristic, which positions threshold concepts as transformative, constitutes the most central characteristic. Meyer and Land focus on identifying, defining, and exploring the transformations that occur in learners as a result of learning a threshold concept. Put differently, their initial report and the impressive amount of research subsequent to it follows from the idea that learning can, indeed, be transformative.

Arguably, the emphasis that Meyer and Land's threshold concept theory places on transformation has grown in strength since the publication of their 2003 report. Meyer and Land frequently employ the nominalization "transformation" as a synonym for the learning associated with threshold concepts. For example, the co-authors state that the purpose of their 2010 collection *Threshold Concepts and Transformational Learning* is to address "the nature and process of this transformation," where "this transformation" refers to learning (Land, Meyer & Baillie, 2010, p. xii). Thus, the transformations effected by threshold concepts seem to overshadow the other four defining characteristics of threshold concepts—so much so, that it might be more accurate to describe the four other characteristics as modifying transformation, where transformative learning is understood as irreversible, integrative, bounded, and troublesome.

Further emphasizing transformation, threshold concept theory has identified three broad categories of transformations that are associated with learning a threshold concept: (1) epistemological transformations, which affect learners' knowledge; (2) ontological transformations, which affect learners' self-perceptions; and (3) ideological transformations, which affect learners' perspectives and worldviews (cf. O'Brien, 2008, pp. 292–293). These three categories are regularly viewed by threshold concept researchers as impacting a learner's relationship with a particular disciplinary community or a professional society. Thus, the transformations in knowledge, self-perception, or worldview that occur in conjunction with learning a threshold concept are bounded by a singular field of study. These transformations are, according to Meyer and Land, manifested in a learner's thought as well as identity (2006, p. 21). Meyer and Land explain that, when an individual comes to an understanding of a threshold concept bounded by a particular community, that individual "acquires new knowledge and subsequently a new status and identity within the community" (2006, p. 23). Prior to learning a threshold concept, the learner is divided from, or uninitiated in, the knowledge, perspectives, or self-awareness that marks the community. Yet, after learning a threshold concept, the learner proves capable of sharing in thought or identity with a disciplinary community or professional society. The learner's thought or identity, therefore, shifts—or, is transformed—in accordance with a change in epistemology, ontology, or ideology.

Regardless of the kind of transformation, the shift in a learner's thought or identity is described by threshold concept researchers as a recursive and oscillatory process. This oscillatory process is aptly captured by Meyer and Land, who use the Latin word for "threshold" (*limen*) to connote a "suspended state" of learning that leaves the learner hovering at or around the threshold, without yet undergoing transformation (Meyer & Land, 2003; Land, Meyer & Smith, 2008, pp. x-xi). Ultimately, Meyer, Land, and other threshold concept researchers recognize that the "process of transformation, and hence movement within these liminal spaces is not unidirectional, yet may 'involve oscillation between stages, often with temporary regression to earlier status'" (Timmermans, 2010, p. 11). Transformation is, therefore, neither a resolutely linear process nor a swift process, especially when transformation involves a learner's regression, oscillation, or suspension in a liminal state.

Yet, in order for a learner to move beyond a liminal state and garner the effects of transformation, a learner's relationship to a disciplinary community or professional society is thought, again, to be crucial: The learner must identify with—that is, share in thought or identity with—a particular community (Meyer & Land, 2006, pp. 23-24). Transformation is, in other words, facilitated by the individual learner's relationship with an established community that is united in epistemology, ontology, or ideology. Threshold concept researchers, including Julie A. Timmermans (2010, p. 13), note that establishing these relationships necessitates both acquisition and loss. Although the learner of a threshold concept gains new thoughts and new identity markers through the learning of a threshold concept, the learner loses an old component of identity or thought not associated with that threshold concept. Accordingly, transformation seems dependent upon the learner's acquisition of thoughts and identity markers that jibe with the community and the learner's simultaneous loss of thoughts and identity markers that clash with the community.

In sum, threshold concept theory advances a complex notion of the transformation that accompanies the learning of threshold concepts across disciplines and professions. The theory holds that transformation occurs in conjunction with a learner's thought, with a learner's identity, and always in relation to a community. The theory also holds that three major kinds of transformations—epistemological, ontological, and ideological—can occur as a result of a learner learning a threshold concept. Transformation, irrespective of the type, is further described as a nonlinear process, in which a learner's thought and identity might come to occupy a liminal state, oscillating somewhere in between acquisition and loss.

Transformation Unbound

Reading enjoys a unique position with respect to the epistemological, ontological, and ideological transformations that are characteristic of learning threshold concepts. As I have argued (Gogan, 2013), reading is crucially important to learning across disciplines—so much, so that reading might be said to be positioned before, at, around, and after the metaphorical threshold invoked by threshold concept researchers. Key to reading's importance is its ubiquity: reading, much like writing, is an activity that extends beyond disciplinary boundaries and informs transformative learning in most, if not all, disciplinary fields and professional associations. Put differently, reading can be viewed as transformation unbound—that is, a kind of activity that leads to transformative effects irrespective of a particular community. When understandings of transformation, as articulated in threshold concept theory, are separated from particular disciplinary contexts and synthesized with understandings of reading and transformation, three characteristics emerge as central to an understanding of reading as transformation. Reading can be understood as bringing about transformative effects in epistemology, ontology, and ideology, because reading is a:

1. Receptive Activity: Reading effects transformation by allowing readers to engage, interpret, and respond to texts. Most fundamentally, reading is understood as mode of reception. According to overly simplistic schemes, reading serves as the rhetorical counterpart to writing. Writers produce texts, while readers receive texts. Reading must, however, be understood as a complex and dynamic mode of reception, in which readers engage, interpret, and respond to texts. Receptive reading empowers readers as active agents in the creation of meaning. As such, reading can be understood as transformation: Receptive reading activity transforms readers from passive receivers to active meaning-makers and thereby changes readers' agency—that is, the degree to which readers contribute to or control the meaning of the text.

2. Relational Activity: Reading effects transformation by enabling readers to relate text to context, self to other, and the singular to the collective. In short, the relationships that reading forges are transformational, as these relationships encourage new, plural meanings for texts and identities. By forging new relationships between texts, contexts, self, and other, reading changes texts and readers. Viewing reading as relational activity challenges reductive understandings of reading that involve one discrete text and one discrete reader, each of which possesses singular meaning and static identity. A relational understanding of reading positions both identity and meaning as contingent upon relationships involving other texts, contexts, individuals, and groups—all of which cause texts and readers to both lose old meanings

and acquire new meanings. Thus, reading can be understood as transformation, in that relational reading activity creates new relationships that alter the meaningful identities of both text and reader.

3. Recursive Activity: Reading effects transformation by encouraging readers to revisit, return to, and literally re-course through text. When reading is conceived of as transformation, the oscillatory and nonlinear aspects of the activity receive emphasis. Subsequently, readers' experiences with texts are understood differently. Instead of understanding readers' experiences with text as linear progressions or straightforward marches through information, a conception of reading as transformation suggests that readers journey within texts, meandering in a more circuitous fashion. Conceiving of reading as a recursive activity positions reading activity as a transformative journey—that is, one that affords readers opportunity for discovery, misdirection, redirection, and reorientation. Thus, reading can be understood as transformation, in that recursive reading activity shifts the direction with which readers approach texts. In short, recursive reading reorients readers.

When discussions of transformation by threshold concept researchers are synthesized with discussions of transformation and reading by rhetoric and writing studies researchers, a general notion of reading as transformation emerges. This general notion of reading as transformation highlights the receptive, relational, and recursive characteristics of reading activity and, consequently, frames reading activity as a significant activity independent of the learning of a threshold concept. In other words, this general notion of reading as transformation attests to reading's position as an activity that results in many types of changes, which extend beyond learning one concept within the boundaries of one discipline or one profession. Unlike threshold concept research, which tends to focus on the kind of transformations brought about by learning a specific concept that is bounded by a particular community, the general notion that the characteristics of reading activity effect transformation positions reading as transformative in and of itself: Reading can be understood as transformation unbound. To demonstrate the way in which reading—as receptive, relational, and recursive activity—brings about transformation, I return to data gathered during a two-year empirical study of 75 undergraduate students (cf. Gogan, 2013).

Review of Study Design

In 2009, a colleague and I began a study of four sections of a required writing-intensive course at Virginia Polytechnic Institute and State University (Virginia Tech). The course served as the second of two three-credit-hour courses that constituted the Composition Program at Virginia Tech and the course emphasized "writing with sources" (George, 2009, p. 6). The four studied sections of this course enrolled 75 students and each section followed identical syllabi and the same assignment sequence—a sequence that focused on the types of reading and writing that learners would encounter in their chosen disciplines. The study attempted to gauge the transformations of the learners and learning that were associated with this course, and one of the study's objectives concerned the role of reading in and beyond the course. More specifically, the study was interested in the role that reading and readers played in the acquisition of rhetorical genre awareness, a concept identified as a threshold concept within the discipline of rhetoric and writing studies by other research studies (Clark & Hernandez, 2011, pp. 66, 76; Pope-Ruark, 2012, p. 243; Adler-Kassner, Majewski & Koshnick, 2012).

To examine the role of reading in the acquisition of rhetorical genre awareness, the study involved three phases, each of which was administered in compliance with Virginia Tech's Institutional Review Board Protocol 10–251. First, the study used in-class observations of student presentations to assess students' performance of disciplinary reading at the course's beginning. All 75 students participated in the study's first phase. Second, the study administered an electronic survey at the course's end. The survey asked students to gauge their abilities in, and preparedness for, disciplinary reading, and it consisted of a mix of multiple-choice questions, multiple-selection questions, open-ended questions, and four-point Likert items. Fifty-three students participated in the study's second phase. Third, the study conducted follow-up interviews with survey respondents, so as to reevaluate the views, understandings, and self-perceptions that students associated with the "Writing from Research" course. Eight students agreed to participate in the study's third phase, consenting to a 30-minute interview one year after the writing-intensive course ended. Part scripted and part artifact-based, the interview prompted respondents to discuss any changes in their knowledge, sense of self, or worldview that they attributed to their reading and writing work in the investigated course.

When data points from the three phases are viewed in aggregate, the study suggests that students perceived the course's first assignment to be important in their acquisition of rhetorical genre awareness and, more significantly, that reading played a transformative role in that assignment for students. The course's first assignment involved a number of interrelated tasks that asked each student to select a scholarly article from his or her discipline, read and analyze that article, present this analysis orally to the class, and submit this analysis as a short paper. Since this first assignment required students to engage exclusively with one source, the assignment reflects the "less-is-more philosophy" described by Sandra Jamieson (2013). This philosophy—which is supported by data collected as part of the Citation Project and which aims to empower students in their understanding of academic texts— suggests that limiting the number of sources from which students write might very well promote student engagement with those sources. Framed in terms of the focus of the present study, this philosophy might be understood as limiting the number of sources used by students in order to promote reading as transformation.

The impact of this philosophy, as it is manifested in the transformative effects of reading, became quite clear over the course of the study's three phases. In the first, observational phase of the study, data revealed little about any transformative effects that might be associated with the reading required for assignment one. Although the student presenters offered 20-minute presentations derived from and dependent upon their reading of a scholarly article, many of the presentations did not in any way indicate that the reading of the article was transformative for the student. A strong possibility existed that the presentations were only loosely connected to the reading of a scholarly article and, instead, either modeled after the presentations of other students or narrowly constructed as a follow-up to previous discussions about different readings (cf. Gogan, 2013). Many of the presentations did not, therefore, exhibit the kind of engagement endorsed by Jamieson (2013), in which students "identify and focus key aspects of what they read" and "engage with [the reading] as a whole." Put differently, many of the presentations did not signal that the student presenter—i.e., the reader—had developed an increased sense of agency over the text, had experienced a change in identity through the text, or had applied an altered orientation to the text. Thus, few of these presentations positioned the activity of reading as transformation.

In the second phase of the study, the students who responded to the survey indicated that the reading conducted in conjunction with the first assignment did, indeed, help prepare them for reading in their discipline. Comments from respondents suggest that, by course's end, a number of students viewed the reading conducted for the first assignment as transformative—that is, as a receptive activity that modified reader agency, a relational activity that altered reader identity, and a recursive activity that shifted reader orientation. For example, one student commented that the reading was a "good idea" because scholarly articles are the articles that students "will be reading and responding to in the future." This comment suggests that the student understands that response accompanies the activity of reading and, as such, this comment positions reading as a dynamic, receptive activity in which readers exercise agency by co-constructing meaning. Two other survey respondents framed reading as a relational activity—one noting that the reading associated with the first assignment prepared him and his classmates "for the rest of their college career and possibly post-college career" and the other noting that the activity of reading established a relationship between her and her discipline that helped her "further understand the career." One final respondent mentioned the reorientation brought about by the reading and, in doing so, this individual gestured toward the recursive activity of reading. He describes a transformation in his orientation to scholarly articles, indicating that he now possesses an ability to pick apart readings "piece by piece" and examine readings "more thoroughly." While these comments from survey respondents suggest that students began viewing reading as transformation, the comments were quite short and lacked the elaboration needed to arrive at a more conclusive finding.

The implication that students were understanding reading as transformation received elaboration in phase three of the study, during which interviews were conducted with eight students. The data gathered from these interviews offer the most conclusive evidence that, one year after completing the first assignment for the writing-intensive course, students viewed the reading component of that assignment as transformative in its effects. In the following section, I reevaluate the interview data from the study's third phase to show the way in which students positioned reading as transformation.

Reevaluation of Interview Data

Student participants described reading as transformation most conclusively in the third phase of the study, during which eight students were interviewed to discuss any changes to their knowledge, self-perception, or worldview that they attributed to their experience with the course as well as with the course's first assignment. The interviews yielded data in the form of eight interview transcripts. While these transcripts revealed much about the students' development of rhetorical genre awareness (cf. Gogan, 2013), these transcripts are further significant for what they reveal about the students' perceptions of reading. During their interviews, students described the reading required for the first assignment as transformative in its effects. The interview questions that elicited the responses, which most conclusively positioned reading as transformation, were:

- What do you remember about the course?
- Which course project did you feel was most beneficial? Why?
- Have you used anything that you learned from the course assignments? How so?

As students responded to the interview questions, the reading that they associated with the first assignment became a receptive activity that increased their agency, a relational activity that altered their identities, and a recursive activity that shifted their orientations to texts. In short, the interview transcripts demonstrate the student's understanding of reading as transformation.

Importantly, most of the students who were interviewed in phase three of the study remembered the first course assignment as a reading assignment. One such student, Angie, recalled reading "a lot of articles" for the first assignment. Although this kind of reading was difficult in the beginning, Angie was quick to note that this reading prepared her for subsequent semesters. Similarly, a student named Zach remembered the first assignment as being particularly reading intensive, but as being beneficial in terms of its preparation for future reading. Zach stated that, for the first assignment, he "read a lot of articles," many of which he found challenging—that is, "hard to read and understand." But Zach also recognized that the exposure to these articles helped prepare him for even more difficult reading in the future. When prompted to discuss the first assignment, both Zach and Angie described the assignment as predominantly focused on the activity of reading. Such reframing of this assignment was not uncommon and it provides perspective into the way in which students understand the experience of reading. Indeed, data from the interview transcripts reveal that students understand the activity of reading as transformative in its effects on their agency, identity, and orientation.

During the interviews, students described the reading associated with the course's first assignment as helping them assume agency as a reader by reading to meet their needs and by co-creating meaning with the text. In doing so, these students outline one transformative effect of reading. Konnor, for instance, explained that the reading conducted for the first assignment gave him practice reading for his own needs. He explained that he developed the ability to process scholarly articles, so that he read according to his own needs and desires. Referring to the change that he experienced in his reading as a result of the first assignment, Konnor stated: "I could look at the parts that I wanted to and search for what I wanted." Here, Konnor implies that he developed agency as a reader and that this agency empowered him. Clearly, Konnor was not a passive recipient of the text. Likewise, another student named Derek described one take-away from the first assignment as knowing how to "interpret" a scholarly article. Derek's use of the word *interpret* to describe reading an article proves significant, for the word *interpret* positions Derek as a co-creator of meaning. Rather than viewing reading as a passive activity, where meaning is transmitted from a writer to a reader, Derek seems to recognize his role as a reader involves interpretation that co-creates the text's meaning. The comments from both Konnor and Derek indicate that the reading they performed for the first assignment proved transformative, for it positioned them as dynamic readers who exercised agency.

Students, in their interviews, further attributed a change in their identities to the reading required by the course's first assignment. Respondents discussed the way in which the reading expanded their ability to forge new relationships between texts, contexts, self, and others. These new relationships encouraged a shift in the understanding of identities. Some students discussed the way in which the reading made them more comfortable around research articles and subject-matter experts. Bryce, for example, noted that, because the first assignment offered him "so much practice" reading scholarly articles, he "feel[s] more comfortable reading." In addition to practice, Bryce figured that his new, more comfortable identity resulted from the way he viewed himself in relation to the article's content, its disciplinary field, and its subject-matter expert writer. Bryce explained that, while he realizes he might not "understand all the material" presented in the article's text by the expert writer, he can still evaluate that text and determine if the article "is pretty solid." The ability to render this evaluation boosted Bryce's confidence. Similarly, Matt found value in "being exposed to different kinds of articles" during the first assignment. Matt felt that the reading allowed him to put himself in relation to the text, the context, and the writer. In particular, reading scholarly articles allowed Matt to get "a better grasp of how engineers think." In general, Matt felt that the exposure to other contexts, which reading enables, makes individuals "better thinker[s]" and gives individuals "more of an open mind." For Matt and for Bryce, reading transforms identities: readers gain openness, reasoning, and comfort, while the identities of expert writers become easier to understand and the identities of their texts become more accessible.

Finally, the interview respondents explained that the reading associated with the first assignment reoriented the way they approach texts. Angie, for one, speculated that the reading influenced the way she "went through the article." Specifically, the assignment left Angie with a sense of the two prominent ways that she journeys through texts. First, she reads "really dense" materials and views "every other line" as extremely important. Second, she traverses the materials to "figure out what's really important." Thus, reading within the writing-intensive course reoriented Angie to texts by distinguishing between the two main ways that she approaches texts. Angie's description of these different approaches further suggests that she understands reading as a recursive activity, or one that requires multiple passes over a text. Other students, such as Bryce, also described the way in which the first assignment encouraged them to practice reading as a recursive activity. Bryce described this assignment as asking him to take an article, "look deeper into it," and "really, really work it over." This kind of reading was something that Bryce "didn't normally do with the articles that [he] read." However, Bryce saw this kind of recursive reading as "play[ing]-in more so than anything [he's] done in [his] classes since." The responses provided by both Angie and Bryce suggest that one of the transformative effects of reading is a reorientation to the activity of reading—that is, reading becomes transformative, when it is practiced as a recursive activity.

Perhaps the most striking account of reading's transformative effects came from a student named Tim. Since completing the writing-intensive course, Tim had taken a number of courses toward a degree in civil engineering. When he was interviewed about the course's first assignment, Tim stressed that the reading portion of the assignment was "the most important," as he learned how to read a scholarly article. To support his view, he told a story of reading as transformation—an anecdote that framed reading as a receptive, relational, and recursive activity. Tim began his story by recounting his experience with the assignment. For the assignment,

Tim selected an article from a peer-reviewed civil engineering journal, he "read the whole article," and he composed a presentation that merely "summarize[d] everything that [he] had read." In retrospect, Tim viewed this indiscriminate summary as problematic. While he firmly believed that reading scholarly articles contributes to disciplinary writing and field-specific work, Tim realized that, during the first assignment, he failed to isolate the crucial information or key points from the article. Tim stated that "looking at an article so that you can use it in your writing is a skill that every civil engineer needs to acquire," yet he clarified this view by explaining that he now knows that the "process of taking out the key points from your article is much more important" than he had previously thought. Tim concluded that the skill of isolating key points and elaborating upon those points was a necessary skill that he "started acquiring" in the writing-intensive course, but it is a skill which he is "still in the process of polishing."

Tim's anecdote captures an understanding of reading as transformation. Tim explains that reading is a receptive activity that requires readers to co-create meaning by prioritizing certain pieces of information over other pieces of information. The more passive reader would indiscriminately summarize an article, while the more active reader elaborates upon crucial pieces of information. Tim also shows that reading is a relational activity that forges new identities. As Tim notes, reading plays a role in the identity formation of civil engineers and reading plays a role in his own identity formation. Tim sees the acquisition of reading skills to be transformative to both identities and to be indicative of a polished professional. As a student, Tim is still in the process of polishing this skill. Finally, Tim demonstrates that reading is a recursive activity that will often reorient or redirect readers. Tim's anecdote captures the way in which he journeys back into his first assignment and maps a different and less linear course through the scholarly article that he chose. Thus, Tim understands reading as inviting rereading and he seizes the opportunity to reorient himself as a reader to a familiar text.

Conclusion

The transformative effects of reading experienced by Tim and his peers demonstrate that educators can understand reading as transformation in and of itself. When practiced as a dynamic mode of reception, reading transforms the agency of the reader, allowing the passive receptor to become an active co-creator of meaning. When practiced as a relational arrangement, reading transforms the identity of the reader and of the text, as it stitches together texts, contexts, selves, and others in novel configurations. And when practiced as a recursive journey, reading transforms the approach or orientation of the reader to the text, affording the reader the opportunity to chart his or her course inside of the text. In these three ways, then, educators can understand reading as transformation and, more to the point, reading as transformation unbound: Whereas the transformation that results from the learning of a threshold concept is bound to a particular discipline or profession, the transformation that results from reading is not bound to one particular community.

The unbound, transformative effects of reading accentuate the importance of pedagogical approaches to reading instruction that, likewise, extend beyond one particular course, discipline, or community. As Ellen C. Carillo stresses in *Securing a Place for Reading in Composition* (2015), reading pedagogy proves crucial in order for students to transfer their knowledge about reading across courses and disciplines. Considering reading's role in first-year writing courses, Carillo argues that college educators "can't expect [students to transfer reading knowledge from writing courses to courses in other disciplines] unless we teach for transfer by framing our teaching of reading in a metacognitive framework that consistently helps students abstract general knowledge about reading from the specific reading practices we teach" (2015, p. 147). From Carillo's perspective, more mindful and more explicit pedagogical framing of reading helps students develop meta-awareness about college-level reading and also promotes the transfer of student knowledge about reading from one context to the next.

Understanding reading as transformation—that is, framing reading as receptive, relational, and recursive activity—constitutes one way in which educators might approach reading pedagogy and, thereby, teach to promote the transfer of student knowledge about reading across courses, disciplines, and communities. Indeed, the interview data from this study suggests as much, for students indicated not only that the reading activity associated with the first assignment transferred from the writing-intensive course to their subsequent courses, but also that the same activity was a transformative experience—one that increased students' agency over the text, altered their identities through the text, and reoriented their approach to the text. Accordingly, the three general characteristics of reading activity that this study has identified might be used by college educators to foster student meta-awareness about reading inside and outside the college classroom. And it is the pedagogical potential of this framework—that is, the affinity between understanding reading as transferable and understanding reading as transformative, between teaching reading for transfer and teaching reading as transformation—that calls for additional research inside disciplines, across disciplines, and beyond disciplines.

References

Adler-Kassner, L., Majewski, J. & Koshnick, D. (2012). The value of troublesome knowledge: Transfer and threshold concepts in writing and history. *Composition Forum, 26*. Retrieved from http://compositionforum.com/issue/26.

Carillo, E. C. (2015). *Securing a place for reading in composition: The importance of teaching for transfer*. Logan: Utah State University Press.

Clark, I. L. & Hernandez, A. (2011). Genre awareness, academic argument, and transferability. *The WAC Journal, 22*, 65–78. Retrieved from https://wac.colostate.edu /journal/vol22/clark.pdf.

Common Core State Standards. (2015). English language arts standards. Retrieved from http://www.corestandards.org/.

Cornis-Pope, M. & Woodlief, A. (2003). The rereading/rewriting process: Theory and collaborative, on-line pedagogy. In M. Helmers (Ed.), *Intertexts: Reading pedagogy in college writing classrooms* (pp. 153–172). Mahwah, NJ: Lawrence Erlbaum.

Couture, B. (1998). *Toward a phenomenological rhetoric: Writing, profession, and altruism*. Carbondale: Southern Illinois University Press.

Djikic, M. & Oatley, K. (2014). The art in fiction: From indirect communication to changes of the self. *Psychology of Aesthetics, Creativity, and the Arts, 3*(4), 498–505.

Djikic, M., Oatley, K. & Carland, M. (2012). Genre or artistic merit? The effect of literature on personality. *Scientific Study of Literature, 2*(1), 25–36.

Djikic, M., Oatley, K., Zoeterman, S. & Peterson, J. B. (2009). On being moved by art: How reading fiction transforms the self. *Creativity Research Journal, 21*(1), 24–29.

George, D., ed. (2009). *Composition at Virginia Tech: Written, spoken, and visual composition*. Boston: Pearson.

Gogan, B. (2013, December 11). Reading at the threshold. *Across the Disciplines, 10*(4). Retrieved from https://wac.colostate.edu/atd/reading/gogan.cfm.

Jamieson, S. (2013, December 11). What students' use of sources reveals about advanced writing skills. *Across the Disciplines, 10*(4). Retrieved from https://wac.colostate.edu /atd/reading/jamieson.cfm.

Land, R., Meyer, J. H. F. & Baillie, C. (2010). Editors' preface: Threshold concepts and transformational learning. In R. Land, J. H. F. Meyer & C. Baillie (Eds.), *Threshold concepts and transformational learning* (pp. viii–xlii). Boston, MA: Sense Publishers.

Land, R., Meyer, J. H. F. & Smith, J. (2008). Editors' preface. In R. Land, J. H. F. Meyer & J. Smith (Eds.), *Threshold concepts within the disciplines* (pp. ix–xxi). Boston: Sense Publishers.

Meyer, J. H. F. & Land, R. (2003, May 4). Threshold concepts and troublesome knowledge: Linkages to ways of thinking and practising within the disciplines. *Enhancing Teaching-Learning Environments in Undergraduate Courses Project*. Retrieved from http://www.etl.tla.ed.ac.uk//publications.html#occasionalpapers.

Meyer, J. H. F. & Land, R. (2006). Threshold concepts and troublesome knowledge: Issues of liminality. In J. H. F. Meyer & R. Land (Eds.), *Overcoming barriers to student understanding: Threshold concepts and troublesome knowledge* (pp. 19–32). New York: Routledge.

O'Brien, M. (2008). Threshold concepts for university teaching and learning: A study of troublesome knowledge and transformative thinking in the teaching of threshold concepts. In R. Land, J. H. F. Meyer & J. Smith (Eds.), *Threshold concepts within the disciplines* (pp. 289–305). Boston: Sense Publishers.

Oatley, K. & Djikic, M. (2014, December 19). How reading transforms us. *The New York Times*. Retrieved from http://www.nytimes.com/2014/12/21/opinion/sunday/how -writing-transforms-us.html?_r=1.

Odom, M. (2013, December 11). Not just for writing anymore: What WAC can teach us about reading to learn. *Across the Disciplines, 10*(4). Retrieved from https://wac.colo state.edu/atd/reading/odom.cfm.

Pope-Ruark, R. (2012). Exploring scholarship of teaching and learning approaches to business communication research. *Business Communication Quarterly, 75*(3), 237–251.

Salvatori, M. R. & Donahue, P. (2013). What is college English? Stories about reading: Appearance, disappearance, morphing, and revival. *College English, 75*(2), 199–217.

Timmermans, J. A. (2010). Changing our minds: The developmental potential of threshold concepts. In R. Land, J. H. F. Meyer & C. Baillie (Eds.), *Threshold concepts and transformational learning* (pp. 3–20). Boston: Sense Publishers.

University College London. (2015, May 10). *Threshold concepts: Undergraduate teaching, postgraduate training and professional development.* Retrieved from http://www.ee.ucl .ac.uk/~mflanaga/thresholds.html.

Creating a Reading-Across-the-Curriculum Climate on Campus

Pam Hollander, Maureen Shamgochian, Douglas Dawson,
and Margaret Pray Bouchard

Worcester State University

In response to a sense on campus that students were not as engaged with their reading as they could be, we asked: "What gets in students' way when it comes to reading?" and "What can professors do to make our students' experience with reading better?

When it comes to reading, there are common problems professors face and there are content-specific issues—both are important aspects of reading-across-the-curriculum. As the conduit for learning, reading is often taken for granted—seen as simply a medium. In this chapter, we will share how we began to build a "reading-across-the-curriculum" climate on our campus. We share what work we, two literacy professors, one science education professor and one biology professor, were doing to advance our goals individually and how we joined forces to produce a more concerted effort. We started by doing research about student reading habits in the discipline of science and by conducting outreach about reading to professors across campus in different disciplines. Our work was grounded in both college-level reading literature and discipline-specific literature. We found through our outreach that other professors on our campus were sincerely concerned about student reading and wanted to know what they could do to help.

If you are a professor who is open to having a frank conversation with college students about their academic reading habits, you may have (as we have) experienced responses such as these: "My professor doesn't expect me to read—she just wants us to know the power points." Or, "I don't buy the book for the course—my professor doesn't cover much of the book." Such comments got us thinking: "What are we communicating to our students directly or indirectly about reading?" In addition, we have been aware for some time that many of our students, both developmental students and students in non-remedial classes, were struggling with the reading they *did* do for classes. Finally, we wondered what other professors on campus thought—what were their experiences with student reading? What kind of reading climate did they think we have on campus? As the conduit for learning, reading seemed like it was often taken for granted—seen as simply a medium and not given the attention it deserved.

We—two literacy educators, one science educator and one biology professor—began discussing our concerns about student reading informally at a Center for Teaching and Learning professional development workshop at our university and decided to form a faculty learning community,[5] which would follow up on our concerns.

Our concerns centered around the lack of support services in the area of reading and the lack of acknowledgment of reading issues on campus. At our university, students request tutoring based on the class they are having trouble with, and there are not any "reading tutors" who are reading specialists. So, for example, a student will sign up for tutoring for Biology and will get a peer tutor who got an A in the class. That student presumably has a good grasp of the content and is probably a good reader, but does not have extensive training in how to support students with reading difficulties. We do have a writing center, but no place where students can get help with reading for classes. In general, there was a lack of attention given to reading as a topic on campus and little data available to us that might help us make our case. We realized that we needed to gather some evidence and spread the word, as well as find other people on campus who might already share our worries.

We decided to begin our work by conducting our own research to gather some data to help us communicate our concerns. Our overarching questions were "What common issues/problems do we as professors face with student reading?" and "What content-specific issues/problems do we as professors face with student reading?" These questions led us to wonder more specifically about our students' experiences with reading, and we asked the following additional questions: "What gets in students' way when it comes to reading?" and "What can we do to make our students' experience with reading better?"

These questions reflect our definition of academic reading at the college level, which highlights, among other things, the active role of students in their reading. College reading has a "constructivist emphasis on human agency" (Spivey, 1997, p. 86), asking students to make connections and actively interact with texts. We conceptualize college reading as a critical process, which students actively engage in as they make sense of complex texts using intertextuality. Texts always exist in relation to other texts and the overlapping nature of the disciplines of college make for a heightened sense of "intertextuality." As Armstrong & Newman (2011) point out, "It is challenging, indeed, to think of a single academic discipline that does not involve intertextual materials and cross-textual synthesis on some level" (p. 2). We align our view of college reading with Horning's 2012 definition, which highlights the complexity and multi-media aspects of literacy:

> Academic critical literacy is best defined as the psycholinguistic
> processes of getting meaning from or putting meaning into print

---

5   Faculty learning communities have been established on many college campuses to formally integrate professors across disciplines and support collaborative research.

and/or sound, images, and movement, on a page or screen, used for the purposes of analysis, synthesis, evaluation and application. . . . (p. 14)

In short, we conceptualize reading as a complex sociolinguistic task that depends on an understanding of how a text relates to other texts and events and involves students in looking critically at subject matter.

After coming up with research questions, we decided to move forward in two ways: 1) by educating ourselves more about the role of reading on our campus and other campuses, and 2) by trying to make reading more of a focus on our campus. Based on our own experiences with teaching, we felt that we needed to research and communicate to other professors about both general reading issues and discipline-specific issues. When we say discipline-specific literacy we mean the reader's ability to understand not only discipline-specific content, but to apply discipline-specific reading practices and "habits of mind"—reading like a scientist, or reading like a historian (Fang, 2012; Fang & Coatoam, 2013).

We began our work by looking at what college-level reading literature and discipline-specific literature has to say about issues in college-level reading. We then narrowed our focus to investigate the effectiveness of assigned reading in several areas of science, hoping to do the same research for several additional disciplines in the future. We collected data by interviewing ten science professors on our campus and found that they also had concerns that were both general and subject-specific. Their responses led us to think more deeply about the quality of student reading and how best to prepare students to read particular genres, such as journal articles and textbooks. Another important result of our interview research was that we now had local data to begin to share with the other faculty to spur conversation about reading on campus. What we *didn't* have was the student perspective. We committed ourselves to design a survey to gather information about student experiences of reading—beginning with science classes.

After reading and interviewing science professors, we felt like one response to our campus's reading problems was best characterized by the idea of "Reading-Across-the-Curriculum" (Horning, 2007, para. 1). There are many common problems we face as professors when we assign reading in our subject areas and also important content-specific issues, and both of these seem to be addressed by the idea of reading-across-the-curriculum. Kim and Anderson (2011) reported how the Fayetteville State University implemented a Reading-Across-the-Curriculum Program, which included professional development for professors, course revisions, workshops for students, and a shared campus text (*Student Health 101*, an online magazine) aimed at increasing student reading. The Fayetteville Program included both a focus on general reading strategies (workshops) and on reading in particular disciplines and classes (course revisions and workshops). They were taught and asked to share their own general reading strategies like "summarizing, reviewing, synthesizing, and outlining passages" (Kim & Anderson, 2011, p. 32), and they were also encouraged to "take the initiative in researching reading comprehension strategies most common to their disciplines . . . " (p. 31). Funds were available to pay stipends to faculty who attended workshops and revised their courses to include more activities that directly focused on improving reading comprehension.

The Fayetteville University Program is reminiscent of writing-across-the-curriculum programs of the 1990s and 2000s, which have helped many students and professors clarify writing goals at many colleges, including our own university. Students need our help with tackling college-level reading as much as they need help with college-level writing. In the rest of this chapter, we will explore what we have found out from others' inquiries into these issues and what we have done to begin the process of creating a Reading-Across-the-Curriculum climate on our campus.

College-Level Reading Issues

There are several factors that seem to contribute to college students' difficulties with college-level reading. First, students receive little direct instruction in how to approach reading after elementary school (Odom, 2013). Second, professors are often at a loss about how best to motivate students to read (Horning, 2013; Odom, 2013). And third, professors either don't realize that they need to provide direct guidance in the art of reading, or struggle to find ways to convey discipline-specific reading strategies (Horning, 2013; Odom, 2013). Students have little experience that prepares them for discipline-specific college-level reading, and while professors in great numbers worry about reading, they feel unsure about what to do about it.

Although many professors assign reading and expect students to comply without any immediate extrinsic reward (besides doing well in class because of knowledge from the reading), others intentionally give quizzes or questions directly linked to the readings, in order to motivate students to read. It has been suggested by research that such assignments need to count 20% or more to have any effect at all on students' reading cooperation (Nilson, 2010).

Unfortunately, questions or writing about reading have not been shown to have universal impact on students' understanding of reading. Odom (2013) reports that writing assignments that acted as "quizzes" did not produce favorable effects. Students' perception of these writing assignments as "quizzes" seemed to hurt their effectiveness. Odom concluded that students were used to seeing these kinds of quiz-like questions and answered them the way they always had in the past—in the most "superficial" way possible (p. 10). Students did not receive any communication about how to approach their reading that gave them any direction about how to interact with the material beyond proving that they had read it.

In the sciences, it is important that students have some training in reading and critically analyzing published information in scientific journals. Whereas undergraduates are accustomed to reading textbooks and taking notes in lectures, they often find it difficult to understand research articles in the basic biomedical sciences. While there is general agreement among scientists that comprehension of scientific papers and communication of scientific concepts are two of the most important skills we can teach undergraduates, few undergraduate biology courses make these explicit course goals, or attempt to teach these skills (Brownell, Price & Steinman, 2013).

Outreach: Cultivating a Reading-Across-the-Curriculum Climate

Before we began collaborating, each of us had been working on our own, bringing awareness to reading issues on campus. Pam had requested to be able to conduct a one-session reading workshop for subject-area peer-tutors during their summer training. Margaret and Douglas had been leading professional development workshops for professors on reading and literacy through the University's Center for Teaching and Learning, and Maureen had been running a Biology book club for Biology students. What changed when we began working together was that we started characterizing the work we continued to do as a concerted effort toward raising consciousness about reading on campus. We started trying to nurture a campus dialogue about reading issues whenever we could. We presented our findings to our Education Department and to a wider group of faculty at an unpaid voluntary professional development workshop through our University's Center for Teaching and Learning.

At the Center for Teaching and Learning workshop we hoped to build momentum for what we perceived as a growing conversation about reading on campus. With the work we had each been doing to make strides, combined with the recent interviews of science professors, we felt like we were moving in a good direction. We also wanted to provide a space for professors to talk about their concerns about reading, and take the opportunity to gather information about their perceptions about students. Since we were planning to do a survey of students' attitudes toward and experiences with reading, we thought their input would help us formulate survey questions.

We ran our workshop with a group of roughly 20 professors over the course of one hour. The group represented faculty from throughout the university. After sharing our concerns and our findings thus far, we opened up the floor to hear what professors on campus had to say. We asked them what their general concerns about reading were *and* what their discipline-specific concerns were.

We found that professors on campus in many different subjects had a lot to say about their students' reading. They were concerned about students' lack of experience with reading college-level texts. This inexperience revealed itself in areas of vocabulary, textual structures, and approaches to reading a particular genre. Professors also worried about students' general lack of strategies for reading, such as identifying key points vs. details and setting a purpose for reading, and expressed a desire for the university to offer workshops to help teach these skills to students. The professors discussed changing societal approaches to and attitudes about reading. There was speculation that technology and social media may be changing people's reading skills and their expectations of how they need to read.

We then asked about disciplinary-specific issues and the professors talked about the detailed nature of reading math textbooks and issues specific to science classes. Science professors talked about the importance of students being able to understand how to read a scientific journal article and praised textbooks that are better constructed to scaffold for student-readers, such as David Klein's (2014) text on Organic Chemistry, which is very visually-oriented. These comments echoed research showing that purposeful instruction in reading particular genres is very useful. Gogan's (2013) study of a "required, writing-intensive course" supports the idea of *direct instruction* as helpful in increasing ability to read in college-level subject area classes (para. 14). Gogan reported that an assignment where students chose a scholarly article in their major and then dissected it using genre study was found to be perceived by 60.4% (marked agree) of students as having "helped me prepare for academic reading in my discipline" and was reported to have great impact a year later by students who were interviewed about the assignment.

To help students approach the challenge of reading research articles in the basic biomedical sciences, Rangachari and Mierson (1995) developed a checklist to guide students in the analysis of different components of a research article. In their study, students were assigned an article (usually a short communication) where techniques were familiar to them, and were asked to use a checklist to help them critically analyze the article. The students were asked to write a paper assessing the article and also to respond to a questionnaire evaluating the experience and their ability to understand the article. Students had positive responses to the questionnaire and rated the experience helpful.

As a result of this conversation, professors also shared some techniques that have been working to improve student reading. For example, responding to student feedback indicating that students often wait until <u>after</u> a lecture to do the assigned reading (in order to get some perspective about what is important), some professors said they now "flip" their classes, meaning that they record lectures and post them online, so that students themselves can make the decision about whether to read before or after the lectures. Flipping classes as a technique also makes class time available for the application of reading material, as opposed to "going over" reading material. This technique is also in line with the finding we mentioned earlier that students will read more if they are asked to apply the reading to an activity.

Odom (2013) found that Writing Across the Curriculum Faculty Fellows who were trying to use writing to improve students' reading were more successful when they very consciously changed the assignments that go along with reading to be more than a "reading check." She alludes to the idea of direct instruction in how to read a particular kind of piece, but spends more time on the areas of personal and real word connections and authentic assignments:

When faculty made changes not just in how they assessed student reading compliance but rather in how they asked students to approach their reading, they found real improvement in students' comprehension of material and their abilities to use what they read to their advantage throughout the course (p. 10).

As their responses showed, the professors were already tuned into students' experiences, but we asked them to focus even more on their students' experiences with college-level reading by asking them, "If you could ask students anything about reading in college, what would you ask them?" Their questions for students conveyed earnest interest in students' feelings about and experiences of reading for college classes. Below were the most frequently articulated questions professors attending the Workshop wanted to ask their students.

Professors wanted to know about student perspectives on reading:

- Why don't you read?
- What is most challenging about reading?
- What difficulties do you experience when reading?

Professors wanted to know what they could do to make a difference:

- What would make you read it?
- What support do you need?
- How can I facilitate your reading?

Professors wanted to gauge how students think about the role of reading in their lives:

- What are you getting out of reading?
- What benefit do you derive from reading?
- What can you find in a good book that you cannot find from any other experience?
- How important do you think reading is to your future success in life?

Professors wanted to inquire about how they read:

- What procedure do you use?
- How do you prepare to read?
- During reading, what else are you doing?
- How aware are you of the author's language choice when you read?
- Do you ever look up words? What do you do when you don't understand?

From the professors' responses and questions for students we see a very current and authentic interest in issues of student reading. The professors are concerned about students' difficulties with the reading for their classes. It has come to their attention that students are struggling. They have also noted the lack of resources on campus set up to address students' reading difficulties. Professors we have talked to are interested in increasing the effectiveness of their reading assignments as teaching tools. They talked about student reading as a shared problem between professors and students.

The professors' questions for students highlighted the active nature of reading we discussed earlier in this chapter. They underscored the time commitment reading takes and the competing demands students face. They are interested in intersections between larger societal forces affecting our approaches to reading and what is happening on our campus. They are not involved in a "blame game." Instead they show a strong interest in making things better by using student feedback and trying new general and content-specific approaches to reading to make student reading more doable and successful. The professors we spoke with are already trying some things and are looking for more organized support for reading on campus.

Moving Forward: Gaining Visibility for Reading

We came away from our first organized "outreach" at the Center for Teaching and Learning Workshop as a Faculty Learning Community feeling energized. We outlined some short and long term goals. We are continuing with our collection of data—this time through a survey reporting on student reading experiences in science classes. That, combined with possible follow-up one-on-one interviews, should give us some interesting complementary data to add to our findings about science professors' experiences. We hope to repeat this model for another subject area; we are planning for history. We will keep sharing out our findings through professional development workshops and our departmental meetings. Uncovering successes and difficulties in reading in classes across campus will give us some concrete concerns to address and to get others interested in addressing.

In the long-term, we think that we need to keep doing the work we have been doing individually, but now as part of a (hopefully growing) network of reading-focused professionals on campus. Whenever we speak publicly now on campus we will link the work we are doing together to show that it is all connected. Workshops for faculty on reading strategies and issues as carried out in the Fayetteville University example sound like a good idea, as do workshops for students. However, collecting data first on professor and student needs seems to make sense.

Perhaps what is particularly challenging for us is that we are trying to amass data to convince stakeholders that there is a problem with reading on campus, while at the same time creating an immediate dialogue to bring reading into the light right now. We see college reading as a complex endeavor, which many students are not prepared to undertake successfully. Because we think college reading is an interdisciplinary issue, we want to create a Reading-Across-the-Curriculum climate now. We don't want to wait. So, we are trying to do that—shift people's thinking about reading—so that reading for classes is not seen as only a delivery method for material, but instead as a complex set of strategies, skills and approaches that need direct and thoughtful attention across the curriculum.

References

Armstrong, S. L. & Newman, M. (2011). Teaching textual conversations: Intertextuality in the college reading classroom. *Journal of College Reading and Learning, 41*(2), 6–21.

Brownell, S. E., Price, J. V. & Steinman, L. (2013). A writing-intensive course improves biology undergraduates' perception and confidence of their abilities to read scientific literature and communicate science. *Advances in Physiology Education, 37*(1), 70–79.

Fang, Z. (2012). Language correlates of disciplinary literacy. *Topics in Language Disorders, 32*(1). http://dx.doi.org/10.1097/TLD.0b013e31824501de.

Fang, Z. & Coatoam, S. (2013). Disciplinary literacy: What you want to know about it. *Journal of Adolescent & Adult Literacy, 56*(8), 627–632. http://dx.doi.org/10.1002/JA AL190.

Gogan, B. (2013, December 11). Reading at the threshold. *Across the Disciplines, 10*(4). Retrieved from https://wac.colostate.edu/atd/reading/gogan.cfm.

Horning, A. S. (2007, May 14). Reading across the curriculum as the key to student success. *Across the Disciplines, 4*. Retrieved from https://wac.colostate.edu/atd/articles /horning2007.cfm.

Horning, A. S. (2012). *Reading, writing and digitizing: Understanding literacy in the electronic age*. Newcastle-upon-Tyne: Cambridge Scholars Publishing.

Horning, A. S. (2013). Elephants, pornography and safe sex: Understanding and addressing students' reading problems across the curriculum. *Across the Disciplines, 10*(4). Retrieved from https://wac.colostate.edu/atd/reading/intro.cfm.

Kim, J. Y. & Anderson, T. (2011). Reading across the curriculum: A framework for improving the reading abilities and habits of college students. *Journal of College Literacy & Learning, 37*, 29–40.

Klein, D. (2014). *Organic chemistry, 2nd Ed.* Hoboken, NJ: John Wiley & Sons.

Nilson, L. B. (2010). *Teaching at its best: A research-based resource for college instructors.* San Francisco: Jossey Bass.

Odom, M. (2013, December 11). Not just for writing anymore: What WAC can teach us about reading to learn. *Across the Disciplines, 10*(4). Retrieved from https://wac.colo state.edu/atd/reading/odom.cfm.

Rangachari, P. K. & Mierson, S. (1995). A checklist to help students analyze published articles in basic medical sciences. *The American Journal of Physiology, 268*(6 Pt. 3), S21–25.

Spivey, N. N. (1997). *The constructivist metaphor.* San Diego: Academic Press.

The Un-Common Read: Perspectives from Faculty and Administration at a Diverse Urban Community College

Jennifer Maloy, Beth Counihan, Joan Dupre, Susan Madera, and Ian Beckford
QUEENSBOROUGH COMMUNITY COLLEGE/CITY UNIVERSITY OF NEW YORK

Maloy et al. discuss the implementation and impact of a Common Read program at Queensborough Community College of the City University of New York, which serves one of the most diverse communities in the country. Instead of following the model at traditional colleges of a Common Read as part of pre-fall orientation, Queensborough has developed a full-academic-year model that encompasses faculty development through a Fall Book Club and planning thematic cross-disciplinary events and assignments that are integrated into spring course curricula. Through their "UnCommon Read" program, the authors define college reading as the construction of an intellectual community, arguing that this is particularly important to create at two-year colleges, where students may face unique challenges. They discuss the impact of three Common Read selections and their campus-wide themes: *The Immortal Life of Henrietta Lacks* by Rebecca Skloot with a focus on issues of race and bioethics; Somaly Mam's *The Road of Lost Innocence* through the lens of global human rights; and *Until I Say Goodbye: My Year of Living with Joy* by Susan Spencer-Wendel, with a theme of empathy. In addition, quantitative research is presented in the form of both student and faculty surveys with results.

Professors have long lamented that their students are poor readers and lack enthusiasm for reading. In 1960, Kingston observed in *The Journal of Developmental Reading* that the typical college reading assigned in classrooms, textbooks and anthologies did little to "develop or improve the students' reading habits." Few of his students at the University of Georgia reported having read a book or a magazine for pleasure or their own interests. Over 50 years later, research indicates that little has changed in terms of college students' reading habits. In 2004, a National Endowment of the Arts (NEA) survey found that 56% of American adults had not read any books in the past year. The resulting report, titled *Reading at Risk*, drew a gloomy portrait of the decline of reading in American life, particularly for those ages 18–24, as only 42.8% claimed to have read a literary text over the course of the year, demonstrating the lowest level of any age group other than individuals over 75. Likewise, the NEA's expansive 2007 report, *To Read or Not to Read: A Matter of National Consequence,* declares the decline in reading both a cultural and national problem (p. 6) and again finds that the decline in reading is most pronounced among Americans ages 18–24, as only 52% reported reading any book outside of school, and 65% of college students claimed that they read for pleasure less than an hour a week.

In response to its initial *Reading at Risk* report, the NEA made a push to increase engagement with the written word through the Big Read initiative in 2006, through which grants were offered to community-based organizations to create book clubs for such works as *Fahrenheit 451.* At colleges around the country, the Big Read has since been adapted into the Common Read. In the past decade, Common Read programs in which students read and discuss a pre-selected book-length text have emerged to engage students in a common intellectual experience and hopefully increase their interest in reading. Traditional Common Read programs often take place at four-year colleges and require all incoming first-year students to read a particular book prior to the beginning of the fall semester. Students then enhance their reading of the book through events that are offered as part of their first-year experience. Identified by the Association of American Colleges & Universities (AAC&U) as a High Impact Practice, the Common Read offers students access to active learning practices and academic engagement. However, essential to the success of such programs is a design that meets the needs of the student population of a particular college. While traditional Common Read programs offer all incoming students a unified first-year experience, we explore in this chapter how our community college has adapted and designed the Common Read in order to meet the needs of a diverse student body while engaging faculty across the disciplines, which we believe is essential at two-year colleges, where students have unique strengths and challenges. We argue that the structure of our Common Read program promotes college reading at our school as it builds an intellectual community of students and faculty across our campus. It posits college reading as a sustained collaborative, intellectual enterprise in which students and faculty critically consider the context and implications of a text across disciplines.

Literature Review: College-Level Reading and the Common Read

In her study, "Literacy Skills among Academically Underprepared Students," Perin (2013) argues that there is almost no research on whether students can apply reading comprehension and writing skills "in the types of holistic literacy practice that signify college readiness" (p. 9). To develop the academic literacy that ensures college readiness, students must overcome "deeply ingrained misconceptions about learning" that position students "as passive recipients of information rather than active constructors of knowledge" (Armstrong & Newman, 2011, pp. 6–7). Armstrong and Newman use Louise Rosenblatt's (1994) schema of transmission and transactional models of reading to demonstrate the need for students to move beyond discrete reading skills and a *transmission* approach to reading in which there is only one—correct—way to understand a text. Instead, they must begin to actively engage in conversations with and about texts, through a *transactional* approach to reading, which develops the critical thinking necessary in college-level work. Likewise, Cheryl Hogue Smith (2012) also emphasizes the importance of a transactional approach in working with students who need to develop college-level reading skills, arguing that students often are so focused on detecting the *correct* reading of a text that they suffer from "inattentional blindness," (p. 59), a term she borrows from Simons and Chabris (1999), in which students read over or through anything in the text that does not correspond to *correctness*. To be successful college-level readers, though, Smith argues students must learn to make intertextual connections, engage with ideas in texts, negotiate multiple understandings of texts, and explore confusion surrounding texts (p. 60).

As Smith (2012) states, this approach to college reading necessitates active questioning and the desire to make connections across texts, and, we would like to argue, across disciplines. Reading in all disciplines, as the following research on Reading Across the Curriculum (RAC) has indicated, has the potential to reinforce active and critical reading throughout students' college careers. Programs and activities that support RAC ensure that faculty in a variety of disciplines have the opportunity and support to apply critical reading strategies in their classrooms (Anderson & Kim, 2011) and continually reinforce a transactional reading model that ensures ongoing development of students' academic literacy. In "Reading Across the Curriculum as the Key to Student Success," Horning (2007) argues for colleges to develop these types of programs in order to ensure that students interact with texts frequently and critically throughout their college careers. She states:

> It seems clear that a refocused emphasis on reading as the process
> of getting meaning from print to be used for analysis, synthe-
> sis and evaluation, in the context of critical literacy across the
> curriculum could potentially address the difficulties of students,
> the goals of teachers and the needs of the nation for an educated,
> informed, fully participatory democratic population. (p. 4)

Common Read programs are one way in which these types of transactional reading practices can be promoted across college campuses, if colleges design their programs to meet the needs of the student population of their particular campus in a way that fosters an academic community for students and faculty. While numerous articles have described the process of book selection and the logistics of program design (Ferguson, 2006; Nadelson & Nadelson, 2012; Straus & Daley, 2002), only recently have Common Read programs been analyzed to determine their effectiveness. Common Read programs have been recognized in a handful of studies as promoting student engagement and retention (Boff, Schroeder, Letson & Gambill, 2007; Daugherty & Hayes, 2012) as well as encouraging students to make connections between their academic and personal lives (Benz, Comer, Juergensmeyer & Lowry, 2013). However, an ongoing debate demonstrates the varying extents to which traditional Common Read programs support community on campus, with some educators and researchers indicating positive results (Benz et al., 2013; Daugherty & Hayes, 2012; Nichols, 2012;) and others indicating negligible results (Ferguson, Brown & Piper, 2014). Nonetheless, Laufgraben (2006), Vice Provost at Temple University, argues that carefully designed Common Read programs are those that are adapted to meet the needs of students, faculty, and community and include "discussion and respect for diverse viewpoints." Such programs, like the one our community college has carefully designed, promote academic literacy and support cross-disciplinary learning for faculty and students as well as an enhanced sense of community across the campus. As we will demonstrate in our description and analysis of our program, when Common Read programs successfully foster a reading community across the curriculum, they combat the "inattentional blindness" that causes students, particularly those at two-year colleges, to struggle in college reading situations where they are required to analyze and synthesize complex ideas and negotiate varying interpretations of texts.

Defining College Reading: Forging an Intellectual Community at Two-Year Colleges

We see the "inattentional blindness" of our students not only as a lack of familiarity with critical literacy strategies but also a hesitancy to see themselves as members of an intellectual community. While community college students bring invaluable life experiences and knowledge to the classroom, they also may also be underprepared for the academic rigor of college, and largely unsure about how to find a place within their campus's academic culture. Community colleges provide opportunity for non-traditional, first-generation, low-income, and minority students, and, in addition, they provide opportunity for students who may not have received adequate academic preparation for the work expected of them in college classrooms and that would make them feel like they belong to an intellectual community. Likewise, community college students often face additional challenges as they try to earn their degree: one quarter of students come from low-income households, one third graduated from high school over a decade ago, half are in danger of dropping out of school because of financial burdens, one third are taking care of dependents while in school, and 15% are single parents. In the face of these realities, less than 40% of students graduate from community college within six years, and two-thirds of students are considered underprepared when they arrive (Bailey et al., 2015, p. 82). Research has demonstrated that community college students require resources to help them develop metacognition and academic motivation (Bailey, 2015, p. 86) and that academic supports, in the form of social relationships and informal interactions with other students and faculty, are invaluable to students' retention and success in college (Schudde & Goldrick-Rab, 2015, p. 37). We believe that unless students are able to become part of an academic community—within which they find support from students and faculty—the challenges that they face may become insurmountable.

Ideally, college calls for an embrace of the luxury to explore the life of the mind in reading, both for information and pleasure. As Carillo (2015) argues as she draws upon Morrow's (1997) topography of reading, college should cultivate a variety of enriched literacy practices such as "reading to build an intellectual repertoire; reading for the unexpected; reading for the play of language; reading for the strategies of persuasion; and reading for genre conventions" (p. 121). Reading is to take center stage in students' academic pursuits: indeed, one of a student's major expenses is textbooks. In practice, college reading is, traditionally, the expectation and assumption by professors that students will do the reading as assigned: highlighting, underlining and glossing the text, taking notes for discussion points, and gleaning meaning, all of which will be supported and enhanced by class discussion. Anecdotally, many students report feeling overwhelmed by their reading load and simply do not do it. At our diverse community college, with students at all levels of academic preparedness, some faculty are explicitly teaching college reading skills but others cannot find room in their packed curriculum for it. Other faculty members find that the more the reading material is contextualized, the better the students are able to comprehend and make connections within and without. Contextual understanding seems to be the key to connect the skills of fluent reading with the pleasure of intellectual inquiry.

With this perspective, our definition of college reading as per our *Un*-Common Read program is that college reading is a collective and holistic enterprise, such as Perin (2013) describes. The Common Read program at Queensborough Community College (QCC), the City University of New York, invites students and faculty to share and participate in the intellectual life of the college, discussing the selected text through investigations of theme, historical and cultural context, and multiple perspectives across disciplines. The value of intellectual life is highlighted as students immerse themselves in the text and in the community of inquiry the Common Read events create and nurture. We seek for students to experience the reading of the chosen texts as "transactional" (Rosenblatt, 1994) and to understand reading to be essential across the curriculum. We hope to move our students closer to viewing college reading as foundational to their identity as college students. The skills of highlighting and note taking are important, yes, and reinforced through our final reflective assignments—but it is the opportunity to experience membership in an intellectual community that truly seeks to shift a student's perspective from resistant or merely dutiful to a fully engaged and conscious satisfaction in developing the life of the mind. As we will demonstrate by providing perspectives on our Common Read from our administrative Common Read Coordinator as well as three Faculty Coordinators, communal intellectual inquiry is fostered each year in our program through faculty and student-facilitated events that are built into the curriculum and model critical thinking of the ideas in a text across disciplines.

Administrative Perspective: Susan Madera, Common Read Coordinator

QCC is nestled in a quiet neighborhood in Bayside, New York. We take pride in knowing that we serve one of the most diverse populations of any college in the United States with over 16,000 students who hail from nearly every corner of the world. Our students come to us from over 143 countries and over 44% of fall 2013 first-year students reported speaking a language other than English at home. Over 64% of first-time, first-year students received some type of grant aid. Similarly to many community colleges across the country, with such diversity and an open-admissions policy come great challenges. Many come to us underprepared. According to the *Queensborough Community College Fact Book* (2014), 68% of fall 2013 first-year students were required to take a remedial math course, 22% remedial writing, and 22% remedial reading. Our mission is to provide quality services that support the intellectual, emotional, and social and vocational development of all our students. To achieve these goals we have created the Queensborough Academies, whose three-pillar approach to success includes academic advisement, technology, and High Impact Practices (HIPs).

At QCC we have identified seven instructional modalities that facilitate student learning skills and competencies, not just content or information, in the form of HIPs. The Common Read is recognized as a Common Intellectual Experience, acknowledged by George Kuh (2008) in *High-Impact Educational Practices: What They Are, Who Has Access to Them, and Why They Matter* as a High Impact Practice that promotes integrative learning across the curriculum. We refer to our program as the *Un*-Common Read as it is poles apart from those offered at other institutions. Student engagement is not relegated only to those who teach first-year courses. It is, instead, a campus-wide responsibility, where reading is the main focus. In lieu of mandatory faculty participation for first-year classes, involvement is voluntary and open to all interested faculty members regardless of discipline or course level. Participation is also offered to students in local high schools and the CUNY Language Immersion Program (CLIP), an immersive program for English Language Learners. Ours is a yearlong initiative that includes one semester of professional development each fall (referred to as the Common Read Book Club), which is led by a team including one administrator who leads and coordinates the effort and one faculty member who facilitates the professional development series. In the spring semester, the chosen text is provided to participating students as a gift from the college. During a three-week period of co-curricular events offered to promote cross-disciplinary thinking, participating students are required to attend at least one event but are encouraged to attend as many as possible. Our program aligns with Laufgraben's definition of a well-planned Common Read as it both promotes reading and supports cross-disciplinary learning. In addition, our program also promotes faculty development opportunities.

The impetus for our Common Read was a grant application for The Big Read, a program of the NEA, which was co-written by a college administrator and a faculty member from the English Department and was submitted but not awarded. Our Office of Academic Affairs recognized the value of the application and offered to support it financially. In its initial offering, during fall of 2011 with the chosen text Cynthia Ozick's *The Shawl* (1990), our program was one semester long. Participants included ten faculty members from five academic disciplines, involving 240 students, and offering three events. That semester, paper surveys were utilized to garner feedback from both faculty and students. Results indicated faculty had a positive experience and felt that it added to their students' understanding of and engagement with core concepts related to their courses. Student responses indicated that they found the events both enjoyable and educational but requested that we consider offering a variety of days and times in the future to accommodate their schedules.

The next academic year we again offered an opportunity for faculty to participate in our initiative, with the chosen text Harper Lee's *To Kill a Mockingbird* (1960, 1988). The number of faculty participants grew, as did the number of academic disciplines, students, and events offered. In surveys collected at the end of the semester, a majority of students indicated that the events offered as part of the Common Read enhanced their understanding of the text and also complemented the learning that took place in their class. In addition, 60% of students who responded claimed that the events they attended helped them to make connections across disciplines.

At the end of that academic year a programmatic review took place and considerable changes were made to improve both the structure and effect of the Common Read. Our Common Read was transformed from a semester-long initiative to a yearlong initiative. Within the year-long model, the Common Read Coordinator performed research prior to the start of the academic year to identify a book that met specific criteria: the text should be available in paperback to maintain affordability, length should not exceed 200 pages (if possible) and the text should be written at a reading level that would accommodate upper high school/early college readers.

Professional development takes place each fall semester with the collaboration of the Common Read Coordinator and a faculty member in the role of Faculty Coordinator. The role of the Faculty Coordinator is to work with the Common Read Coordinator to create the schedule for the entire academic year including professional development in the fall and co-curricular, cross-disciplinary events in the spring. The workshops are redesigned each year to align not only with the text chosen but with the disciplines of participating faculty. This type of faculty-led professional development is crucial in community college settings because it promotes integrating development into classroom practices and ensures "collaborative intradepartmental structures" that support student learning (Bailey et al., 2015, p. 105). Likewise, faculty-driven development is essential to successful Common Read programs. According to Michael Ferguson (2006), former AAC&U senior staff writer and associate editor of *Peer Review*, the Common Read "is most likely to be effective when campuses offer discussion guides or workshops to help faculty integrate the common reading into their classes." The Faculty Coordinator is instrumental in designing workshops which focus on achieving the Student Learning Outcomes associated with the Common Read. Upon completion of participation in the Common Read initiative, students are expected to be able to synthesize meaningful connections between a general education outcome and a co-curricular experience as well as to draw conclusions by combining examples, facts, or theories from more than one field of interest or perspective.

While participants and events vary each year, the Common Read always is designed to promote participation in the intellectual life of college. As we demonstrate in the following sections, each year we focus on new themes and pedagogical approaches in our professional development workshops, and we take unique approaches to teaching the Common Read text in individual classrooms and in campus-wide events. As we demonstrate through the perspectives of three Faculty Coordinators, the benefits of this structure allow us to cater the Common Read to our diverse student body while promoting community across the college.

Faculty Perspective: Joan Dupre, Faculty Coordinator of *The Immortal Life of Henrietta Lacks*, 2012–2013

As I am writing these pages about my Common Read experience using Rebecca Skloot's 2011 bestseller *The Immortal Life of Henrietta Lacks* in an urban community college classroom, the city of Baltimore is erupting into the kind of chaos it has not known since 1968. Thoughtful journalists, after reporting the hard facts about the case of Freddie Gray, the 25-year-old black man who allegedly died from injuries sustained while in police custody, are asking hard questions about social context and history. I wonder along with them about the status of race relations and how neighborhoods so close to Johns Hopkins University can be more mired in poverty and hopelessness than they were in 1935 when 15-year-old Henrietta Lacks, a poor black tobacco farmer, married her cousin and moved from Virginia to Maryland. Lacks died of a virulent form of cervical cancer in 1951, but her cells, taken from her without her knowledge or consent, lived on to help cure disease and generate income for researchers. Her children and grandchildren remained living in the most deplorable conditions, receiving no compensation for the contribution their mother and grandmother made to science until Rebecca Skloot herself set up a scholarship fund for the younger descendants.

Reflecting on my time with the Common Read and *Henrietta Lacks* has led me to consider the role of reading and empathy in our lives and the lives of our students. When it comes to the Common Read, the "others" through whose eyes we may see may be characters (in the case of fiction), real-life figures (in the case of non-fiction), authors, classmates—and professors and students reading the same text from different perspectives in other disciplines. In the instance of *Henrietta Lacks,* some of the other disciplines were nursing, biology and sociology. Louise M. Rosenblatt (1938, 1995), a pioneer of reader-response theory and practice, makes a distinction between what she calls "efferent" and "aesthetic" reading (p. xvii). In the former case, the reader needs to extract information from a text, such as for a biology class. In the latter case, the reader must "permit into the focus of attention . . . the personal associations, feelings, and ideas being lived through during the reading" (p. 292). Many texts, and this is certainly true of *Henrietta Lacks*, require both efferent and aesthetic approaches. Students must take information from the book, but their relationship with the text—and the writer—is complicated by a kind of reciprocity that enriches the reading process, the text, and the reader.

At Queensborough, in what is perhaps the most diverse county in the country, our population is a fascinating mix of ages, ethnicities, colors and religions. This makes it a challenge to follow Rosenblatt's (1938, 1995) dictum that "we must seek to bring to our students at each stage of their development sound literary works in which they can indeed become personally involved" (p. 269). A text like *Henrietta Lacks*, however, makes that personal involvement relatively easy, as it presents both the writer/reporter's journey as well as bringing Lacks' to life.

In opposition to those critics who warned against taking the writer's life and her intentions into account, our class looked at Skloot's life and her intentions in writing *Henrietta Lacks*. In fact, Skloot encourages this by sharing with the reader the relevant parts of her biography and making transparent—at least in general terms—her intentions. One of the things students had to consider was the nature of the journalistic enterprise and if objectivity was a goal—or even a possibility—in the reporting and writing of this book. Skloot establishes trust with her readers when she shares details about her personal involvement with the Lacks family over the ten-year period during which she composed the text.

One of the things students wrote in their reading response journals (a requirement that encourages engaged reading) was what they imagined Skloot intended in a given passage. The sharing of thoughts and feelings about the text and what students imagined were the writer's intentions is the way we began our class discussions. Reading written responses aloud in class and sharing them in groups helped to move students from superficial "canned" responses to more sophisticated readings of the text that consider the unique point of view of each character.

During the semester we read the Skloot text, students participated enthusiastically in the events planned for the Common Read, as part of the required curricula of the course. We viewed a terrific BBC documentary about Henrietta Lacks, *The Way of All Flesh* (1998), directed by Adam Curtis. We also saw *Miss Evers' Boys* (1997), a disturbing but excellent film based on the 1932 Tuskegee syphilis experiments, directed by Joseph Sargent. An engineering professor wrote and hosted a "HeLa" Jeopardy game; a biology class presented on "Cancer, Genes and Viruses"; Nursing students presented research on genetic testing, cloning, healthcare reform, hospice care and patient rights; a physician from Memorial Sloan Kettering Cancer Center gave a talk on "Immigrant Health and Cancer Disparities." The above is a mere sampling of the events the Common Read Coordinator and faculty from several disciplines organized.

With so much media and public attention (and political speeches) paid to the importance of STEM, the chance that the Common Read offers faculty to work across disciplines in the humanities *and* the sciences on a text that reads like a medical detective story is a value beyond measure. *Henrietta Lacks* is the perfect text to use as a jumping off point for a discussion of the relationship between the arts and the sciences; it is an excellent argument for our interdependence as faculty and students—and as human beings. *Henrietta Lacks* allowed us to focus on the connection between bioethics and race relations in a way that today seems all too timely.

As the student surveys we collected at the end of Spring 2013 demonstrate, a large majority of students who participated in the *Henrietta Lacks* Common Read responded positively to this experience. They indicated that reading this book and participating in events allowed them to connect the text to the course material in their classes as well as to their everyday lives. Four hundred and one students responded to a survey regarding their experiences (our study was judged exempt in accordance with CUNY HRPP Procedures: Human Subject Research Exempt from IRB Review). Of those respondents, approximately 98% indicated that this was the first time they were reading the book and 62% of the respondents indicated that they attended events related to the book. Of those students who attended these events over 75% enjoyed these events and found them to be useful. Specifically, over 80% of the respondents indicated that attending the events enhanced their understanding of the reading and subject matter. Over 70% of the respondents indicated that attending an event associated with this book complemented the learning that took place in the students' classrooms. In addition, almost 70% of the respondents indicated that attending an event associated with this text encouraged them to think across disciplines: for example, to think about the text as it refers to history, sociology or biology. Some students indicated the following:

> "The events focused on aspects that I did not focus on while I was reading the text. For example, I mostly focused on biological aspect of Henrietta's cells, but others focused on the impact it had on her family, historical and the significance of African Americans being exploited, and health disparities in United States today."

> "Well the book demonstrates history in the sense that Henrietta Lacks came from a family of slaves. She also lived during the period of industrialization, she like many other people from the South begin moving into the cities in search of work. The book applies to Sociology due to the fact that it shows the racism that existed at this time. For instance, the segregation of hospitals and the unfair treatment African Americans received. It shows the biological side, because it shows how research was done and if it weren't for the development of the HeLa cells science wouldn't have gotten as far as it is today. So, Henrietta's cells were like the starting point for science."

After spending an academic year investigating the book, planning and implementing connected activities inside and outside of the classroom, and integrating themes and issues from the book into course content, a majority of participating faculty members likewise responded positively to their experience in the Common Read. Despite the level of commitment and creativity required by faculty members to design curriculum that connects course objectives to issues and content in the Common Read book, the 28 faculty members who responded to the survey expressed their satisfaction with this process in end-of-year surveys. Over 90% of the respondents indicated that the events offered as part of the Common Read enhanced students' understanding of the text, complemented the learning that took place in their classrooms, and encouraged students to think across disciplines. Likewise, over 90% of respondents said that participation in the Common Read initiative made them feel more connected to the QCC community.

Faculty Perspective: Jennifer Maloy, Faculty Coordinator of *The Road of Lost Innocence*, 2013–2014

In 2013–2014, the Common Read book selection, read by approximately 1300 students, was provocative and controversial: Somaly Mam's (2008) *The Road of Lost Innocence: The True Story of a Cambodian Heroine* is a memoir about a woman sold into sex trafficking in Cambodia that takes on, in graphic detail, the difficult topics of modern slavery and the global sex industry as it ends with a message of perseverance, advocacy, and hope. As we approached our professional development workshops in Fall 2013, the Common Read Coordinator and I wanted to address these issues immediately. Therefore, we designed the Common Read Book Club in a way that encouraged our 35 participating faculty members from across the disciplines to voice their concerns and apprehensions about the book in addition to thinking about both the disturbing and inspiring themes and topics in the book. One way we were able to do this in faculty book club meetings was by contextualizing conversations about the book within issues of human rights. We also encouraged participating faculty to consider how the Common Read could be integrated with other HIPs, particularly service-learning and diversity and global learning. In our meetings, participating faculty discussed how the book could generate discussions not only of human trafficking on a global scale but also an inter-cultural examination of education, tourism, health care, gender, religion, and violence against women. In addition, we discussed how these issues could be explored in the classroom through investigations of particular cultural, historical, and political perspectives in relation to global human rights issues. We worked closely with the Counseling Department throughout the year to ensure that all participating faculty and students were aware of campus resources if they encountered difficulty with the events or themes in the book. As faculty members began planning events and working with students, our Common Read program balanced events specific to human trafficking with those connected to other global issues. (We would like to thank Patricia Devaney, Leyla Marinelli, Margaret McConnell, and Constance Rehor for their tireless dedication to contributing to events and designing curriculum to support the reading of *The Road of Lost Innocence*.)

This gave us an opportunity to develop new curricula from an international perspective and to collaborate with community leaders on related local and global issues. Numerous non-profit agencies, advocates, politicians, and members of law enforcement came to campus to talk with students about the global scale of human trafficking and violence against women. For example, a researcher from Human Rights Watch talked to students about documenting the abuses of migrant women in the United States, and a representative of the non-profit LifeWay spoke to students about supporting human trafficking victims in the US through the creation of safe houses. In addition, faculty members from a variety of departments offered their expertise to connect themes and issues from the book to disciplinary knowledge: A faculty member in the History Department provided an overview of Cambodian history in the second half of the 20th century to contextualize the events in Mam's text. A faculty member in the English Department contextualized the role that Buddhism played in Mam's life as she introduced the Buddhist figure of the Bodhisattva, an individual who devotes her life to selfless service, to illustrate Mam's positioning of herself within the story she tells.

Speakers stressed to students that while human rights issues affect people around the world, human trafficking and violence against women also are present in local communities, allowing students to make connections between events in the book as well as current events in their own Queens neighborhoods. Indeed, New York State Senator Jose Peralta spoke with over 200 students about the prevalence of human trafficking in a Queens neighborhood near campus in which many QCC students live. After the senator spoke, students asked questions that connected Mam's documentation of human trafficking in her text, the senator's description of human trafficking in Queens, and the knowledge they were gaining in a wide variety of classes. One student suggested that the senator try to raise awareness of this issue through community performances and the arts. Another student expressed her desire to address this issue by pressuring elected officials to create legislation to stop human trafficking. Yet another encouraged the senator to reach out to elementary and high school students and educate children about this issue and establish protections for vulnerable populations. Some students even spoke to the senator about events taking place in their own neighborhoods, asking how they can be more aware of who is participating in human trafficking and how they can support victims. Other Common Read events, such as a memoir writing workshop, a forum on global health issues for women, and a student-writing contest, were led by full-time and adjunct faculty from across the campus. Student-designed presentations and activities included quantitative analyses of human trafficking victims around the world, presentations by our nursing students on sexual violence and global health issues, as well as read-alouds by students across campus.

Within my own first-year composition class, I worked to create a balance between addressing the profoundly upsetting reality of human trafficking and critically considering how individuals are complicit in—and capable of raising awareness of—human rights violations across the world. As an introduction to *The Road of Lost Innocence*, students learned about the United Nation's Universal Declaration of Human Rights (1948). As students entered into the book, they had a solid foundation in current human rights violations both inside and outside of the United States. As we began to discuss the book, I focused class discussion on themes throughout the book, including gender, race, socio-economics, language, cultural norms, and cross-cultural interactions. I tried to focus an analysis of the book on Mam's creation of schools and shelters for victims of sex trafficking. I presented Mam's description of her advocacy as a call for action, asking students, as a formal writing assignment, to write a letter to President Obama informing him of a global issue that this book raises, explaining how this issue is relevant to people in the United States, and exploring why and how the United States might work to address this issue. Students also had the choice to write a letter to Mam, who has come under criticism due to inaccuracies that have recently been identified in her memoir. After attending events where they met and conversed with politicians and activists and learned from research conducted by nursing and business students, they were engaged to share their perspective on human rights issues with a public audience.

Despite the difficult subject matter in *The Road of Lost Innocence*, a majority of participating students responded positively to this book, as in the previous year with *The Immortal Life of Henrietta Lacks*. Particularly pronounced in their survey responses were their responses about making connections between the themes and topics in the book and a variety of disciplines. Two hundred and seventy-three students responded to a survey regarding their experiences reading the book. Of those respondents, approximately 80% of the respondents indicated that they were able to meaningfully synthesize connections between their course and an event. In addition, 80% of the respondents indicated that participation in the Common Read helped them draw conclusions by combining examples, facts, or theories from more than one field of interest or perspective. Some of the examples of how these fields of study enabled them to gain additional perspective on the book included the following:

> "Health gave me another perspective on the book because there's a lot of health issues that occur because of sex trafficking."

> "I felt that Psychology was incorporated in 'The Road of Lost Innocence' because Somaly has endured severe mental trauma from the rape and abuse (physical and emotional). Some might feel that Somaly should have been in a mental institution, because how can someone go through the struggles she has endured all her life and stay sane, it seems quite impossible."

> "Within . . . reading this book, one of the disciplines of social studies helped me understand the book better. In the Cambodian history, silence is the main thing for everyone. It's like the saying, 'hear no evil, see no evil.' In Somaly Mam's book, if anyone saw something going wrong, everyone would just bypass it and not say a word. I didn't understand this until I learnt that, in the Cambodian history once you say something you are not supposed to, you would end yourself up in dangerous situations."

The 30 faculty members who responded to the end-of-semester survey made similar claims about students' abilities to connect the book to various disciplines. Eighty-seven percent of the respondents indicated that participation in the Common Read provided an opportunity for students to draw conclusions by combining examples, facts, or theories from more than one field of interest or perspective. Discussing this book posed unique pedagogical challenges as it required faculty to address sensitive and disturbing subject matter as well as investigate the global implications inherent in local events. While participating faculty members certainly had apprehensions throughout this process, they did acknowledge in their surveys that the book provided opportunities for students to make connections across disciplines as well as cultures, promoting global learning at a diverse community college.

Faculty Perspective: Beth Counihan, Faculty Coordinator for *Until I Say Goodbye: My Year of Living with Joy*, 2014–2015

Written in 2011 and published in 2013, *Until I Say Goodbye* is the memoir of *Palm Beach Post* crime reporter and mother of three Susan Spencer-Wendel's choice to "live with joy" despite increasing disability and knowledge of imminent death after her diagnosis with ALS. The book details her travels with family and friends and the metaphorical journey of self-discovery and acceptance of her fate, as Spencer-Wendel died in June 2014. Our college president suggested approaching this Common Read selection not as a rumination on death but from the perspective of empathy—of having compassion for and connecting to the full humanity of others no matter what their situation. This opened up the possibilities to disciplines as diverse as Nursing, English, Biology, Massage Therapy, and Art History as well as to students ranging from those taking credit-bearing courses; to those in CLIP and Academic Literacy classes; to those in our partner high schools, Thomas A. Edison Career and Technical Education High School and Bayside High School.

For the Fall 2014 semester Common Read Book Club, the Common Read Coordinator and I drew on faculty expertise to help frame this theme of empathy. A new faculty member who had written his dissertation on the socio-biological aspects of empathy shared his research and insights with the faculty group, which grounded our reading of *Until I Say Goodbye* and our approach in designing events. Altogether faculty met four times over the fall semester: once for a book club-type discussion, once for the empathy lecture, and twice to meet in small groups to brainstorm events. As faculty members shared their knowledge of such fields as disability studies and palliative care, other faculty were inspired to integrate that perspective in their teaching of the book. It is rare for faculty across disciplines to have time to collaborate in this way but the benefits are great, especially in terms of continued learning of the art of teaching. A particular challenge of community college teaching is that faculty members are forever teaching the same courses in isolation; however, with participation in the Common Read, curriculum, pedagogy, and sense of community are refreshed. Faculty members come away from Common Read planning meetings and feeling revitalized and we hope this transfers to our students.

The Common Read Coordinator and I encouraged faculty to devise final assignments that were reflective about the students' process of reading *Until I Say Goodbye* and the impact of the co-curricular events on their understanding of the book in light of the theme of empathy. Our intention was to explore how participation in the Common Read creates a context for a deeper understanding of students' experience reading the text itself. We particularly wanted students to explore the theme of empathy in a meaningful way. With that in mind, for the Spring 2015 semester, we expanded the reach of the Common Read beyond the 942 participating students and into the greater college community: we devised a Pay It Forward initiative, to spark good deeds across campus and beyond, and collaborated with student government, organizations like NYPIRG (New York Public Interest Research Group), and student clubs to run collections of unwanted eyeglass frames and toiletries for families living in local shelters. Five hundred students and community members participated in these various initiatives.

Indeed, students were highly engaged in the Common Read events, and at each event, students were thumbing through the book, searching for passages, connecting the text to the new learning. A good number of the events were led by students: among others, Introduction to Literature students led a discussion of disability studies; History of Photography students lectured on "Images of Illness and Beauty in Photography;" and Biology students discussed the genetic components of ALS. Attending students reported in the final survey that these student-led events were particularly impactful. Examples of such responses include:

> "Photography gave me another perspective on the book, because through photography I was able to analyze other artists and see how they portrayed the theme of the Common Read as opposed to that of just words."
>
> "Genetics . . . provided scientific insight on what was happening to Susan Spencer-Wendel."

We also invited community partners and activists to campus: 200 students attended a talk by Valerie Estess, the co-founder of Project ALS, who spoke of her group's work and the phenomenon of the "ice bucket challenge," and a representative from the United Cerebral Palsy Association, who came to speak on the subject of disability etiquette. To engage our student community further, we held a poetry contest with the theme of empathy. Thirty percent of student survey respondents actually attended more events than were required, for reasons including "to help improve my listening and reading skills."

For my own experience teaching *Until I Say Goodbye*, I found the book connected well with another of the College's HIPs, service-learning. My Introduction to Literature (EN102) students partnered with CLIP students to discuss both *Until I Say Goodbye* and excerpts from Mitch Albom's 1997 bestseller *Tuesdays with Morrie*, also about ALS, and planned a presentation on "Living the Good Life." At the presentation attended by 70 members of the college community, students shared their own contributions to Spencer-Wendel's "List of Little Things to Love," and I could see the joy on their faces as students from Mexico, Turkey, China, Bangladesh, and Ecuador (to name a few) felt comfortable enough with the language and community to share their thoughts. I also found that by integrating the Common Read events into my curriculum, students experienced a deeper level of understanding of the cultural literacy (Hirsch, 1989) connotations of ALS: they learned not only about Spencer-Wendel's experience but also about Lou Gehrig and Stephen Hawking, baseball and physics, black and white film and the universe.

Every semester that I have taught the Common Read selection (which has been since 2011), I add more to the requirements of a reflective paper I assign to submerge the students as fully as I can in this "common intellectual experience": attending events as a class; requiring students to attend an event of their choice on their own; participating in the events themselves; and, with this semester, doing a presentation themselves. But above all, our focus is on the text itself and always making connections between events and our understanding of the text. The goal throughout the sustained intensity of the Common Read is for the students to have a meaningful deep transaction with the text and we seem to have met that goal: all of the faculty respondents for the Common Read survey indicated that participation in the Common Read provided an opportunity for students to experience deep learning: drawing conclusions by combining examples, facts, or theories from more than one field of interest or perspective.

With this rich across-campus Common Read, both faculty and students benefit from the opportunities to share in the intellectual life of the College. As one student wrote: "the shared experience of reading a book with so many others creates an invisible yet palpable sense of community." From the most idealistic standpoint, our *Un*-Common Read, in which both faculty and students are learners, participants and makers of knowledge at the same time, represents Paulo Freire's (1968, 1998) vision of critical pedagogy in action. As in previous years, students' survey responses to their Common Read experience were very positive, particularly as it allowed them to make connections. One hundred and eighty-nine students responded to a survey regarding their experiences reading *Until I Say Goodbye: My Year of Living with Joy*. Of those respondents 94% of the respondents indicated that they were able to meaningfully synthesize connections between their course and an event. In addition, 91% of the respondents indicated that participation in the Common Read helped them draw conclusions by combining examples, facts, or theories from more than one field of interest or perspective.

Likewise, the faculty surveys for *Until I Say Goodbye* also reflect the pattern that has emerged throughout the years we have offered the Common Read: a vast majority of 31 faculty members who responded to the final survey agree that the Common Read provides students with a unique opportunity to make connections in a variety of fields and to their own personal experiences. In the 2015 faculty survey, all of the respondents indicated that participation in the Common Read provided an opportunity for students to draw conclusions by combining examples, facts or theories from more than one field of interest or perspective. Ninety-seven percent of the respondents indicated that participation in the Common Read provided an opportunity for students to synthesize information and ideas from a required core general education outcome and a co-curricular experience.

Conclusion: Refresh and Spark

As the experiences of the faculty Book Club Coordinators and the analysis of survey data over the years of the program demonstrate, the Common Read at Queensborough provides faculty with opportunities to collaborate and students with opportunities to make connections across disciplines as well as to their own lives. Even though the number of participating faculty members and students may fluctuate from year-to-year and the books chosen each year vary widely in subject matter and overarching themes, each Common Read book provides faculty and students with a unique challenge: to read a book collaboratively and make connections broadly and yet meaningfully. While the topics and issues that the books elicit are rarely easy to approach, faculty must work together to identify accessible approaches to them in the classroom, and students must work together to connect them to specific learning environments as well as to their lives in general. The type of critical work by a community of learners and thinkers is essential to making Common Read programs successful and is at the heart of what we see as college reading. It also is essential to engaging community college students, so many of whom come to college underprepared in reading and/or with a variety of out of school obligations and challenges that threaten their ability to participate actively in our college's intellectual community.

What makes Queensborough's Common Read uncommon is that it is a year-long collaborative experience for faculty participants and a curricular immersive experience for student participants. It provides much-needed community for our faculty and students—most of whom, like so many community college students, commute long distances to the college and are constrained by multiple commitments outside of school. By integrating the Common Read into curriculum, time is carved into participants' lives for an opportunity to slow down and focus on reading and interdisciplinary intellectual engagement. Queensborough's Common Read facilitates what the AAC&U calls "integrative liberal learning": "experiences that cross disciplines, units, and campus boundaries" (2014). Reading is at the core of these experiences. As our survey data suggests, with each Common Read, faculty participants' commitment to developing curriculum and pedagogical approaches is refreshed and student interest in reading and the life of the mind is sparked.

In particular, we believe our student survey data shows promising evidence that successful transfer of such integrative liberal learning is taking place through our Common Read. As educational psychologists Perkins and Salomon (1992) state in their "Transfer of Learning" article, "the transfer of learning occurs when learning in one context or with one set of materials impacts on performance in another context or with related materials" (as cited in Carillo, 2015, p. 103). Each year, a majority of our students indicate, through multiple-choice and write-in comments in our surveys, that they are able to link what they learn in campus events to the Common Read text and that they are able to link what they learn in the texts to various disciplines. They accomplish this through collective enterprise: by interacting with fellow students and faculty members across campus over a number of weeks to read a text deeply and critically from a variety of perspectives. For our diverse community college students, this fosters an intellectual community with the social supports that help our students in their academic pursuits. It also fosters a community in which transfer is enacted and modeled again and again as students, faculty, and community members articulate in our Common Read events how they connect prior knowledge to what they learn from the selected text as well as how they apply themes and ideas from the text to disciplinary contexts. As Carillo (2015) describes in *Securing a Place for Reading in Composition: The Importance of Teaching for Transfer,* this is how successful transfer of learning through reading takes place: by students recognizing a concept, generalizing it to use in a new context, and then applying that concept in a new disciplinary/textual environment.

While we believe that our survey data reveals that participating students and faculty alike are building an intellectual community on campus that successfully facilitates the transfer of learning through college reading, we also see the challenges the Common Read faces as it moves forward. We see the need to be more responsive to some of what our survey data suggests: the Common Read selection with the highest level of student survey responses was *The Immortal Life of Henrietta Lacks*, a bestseller and highly awarded book. Anecdotally, students reported reading it late into the night, not wanting to put the book down. It is difficult, though, to find a book each year that can draw in faculty across the disciplines while being simultaneously academically rigorous and easily accessible for our diverse student body, and each book we choose cannot be equally successful in engaging over a thousand diverse student readers. The selection for 2016, the bestseller *Picking Cotton* (Cotton & Thompson-Cannino, 2009), is the compelling memoir of a man wrongfully incarcerated and the female victim whose eyewitness testimony put him in jail. A record number of faculty and students participated, and we revised our student survey to include questions about students' perceptions of their reading experience and intellectual growth in relation to the text. Preliminary analysis of the responses indicated that an overwhelming majority—92%—of the 1300 participating students who responded to the survey found that participating in the Common Read enhanced their learning and inspired them to learn more. Eighty-five percent agreed that the Common Read experience promoted their intellectual growth. This suggests further research, to follow up with students to see if they did, indeed, pursue an interest inspired by reading *Picking Cotton*. With this encouraging information, the College's Common Read Selection Committee is mindful in the continuing search for the next text that the choice also resonates across disciplines and skill level but also be a great read. In the best of all possible community and senior colleges, college reading is not only an intellectual endeavor but a pleasurable one too.

References

Albom, M. (1997). *Tuesdays with Morrie*. New York: Broadway Books.

American Association of Colleges and Universities (2014). *Liberal arts degrees and their value in the employment market*. Retrieved from https://www.aacu.org/nchems-report.

American Association of Colleges and Universities (Fall 2014/Winter 2015). *Peer review: faculty leadership for integrative liberal learning*. Retrieved from http://www.aacu.org/peerreview/2014-2015/fall-winter.

American Association of Colleges and Universities (2015). *Global Learning VALUE Rubric*. Retrieved from https://www.aacu.org/value/rubrics/global-learning.

Anderson, T. & Kim, J. Y. (2011). Strengthening college students' success through the RAC. *Journal of College Reading and Learning, 42*(1), 61–78.

Armstrong, S. L. & Newman, M. (2011). Teaching textual conversations: Intertextuality in the college reading classroom. *Journal of College Reading & Learning, 41*(2), 6–21.

Bailey, T. R., Jaggars, S. S. & Jenkins, D. (2015). *Redesigning America's community colleges: A clearer path to student success*. Cambridge, MA: Harvard University Press.

Benz, B., Comer, D., Juergensmeyer, E. & Lowry, M. (2013). WPAs, writing programs and the common reading experience. *WPA: Writing Program Administration, 37*(1), 11–32.

Boff, C., Schroeder, R., Letson, C. & Gambill, J. (2007). Building uncommon community with a common book: The role of librarians as collaborators and contributors to campus reading programs. *Research Strategies, 20*, 271–283.

Carillo, E. C. (2015). *Securing a place for reading in composition: The importance of teaching for transfer*. Logan: Utah State University Press.

Cotton, R. & Thompson-Cannino, J. (2009). *Picking cotton: Our memoir of injustice and redemption.* New York: St Martin's Griffin.

Curtis, A. (Director) (1998). *Modern times: The way of all flesh* [Motion Picture]. UK: British Broadcasting Channel.

Daugherty, T. K. & Hayes, M. W. (2012). Social and academic correlates of reading a common book. *Learning Assistance Review, 17*(2), 33–41.

Ferguson, K., Brown, N. & Piper, L. (2014). "How much can one book do?": Exploring perceptions of a common book program for first-year university students. *Journal of College Reading & Learning, 44*(2), 164–199.

Ferguson, M. (2006). Creating common ground: common reading and the first year of college. *AAC&U Peer Review.* Retrieved from https://www.aacu.org/publications -research/periodicals/creating-common-ground-common-reading-and-first-year -college.

Freire, P. (1968, 1998). *Pedagogy of the oppressed.* New York: Bloomsbury Academic.

Greene, H. & Greene, M. (2006). *The liberal arts: What is a liberal arts education and why is it important today?* Retrieved from https://www.purchase.edu/sharedmedia/advising center/greene%20-%20what%20is%20a%20liberal%20arts%20education%20and %20why%20is%20it%20important%20today.pdf.

Hirsch, E. D. (1989). *The dictionary of cultural literacy: What every American needs to know.* Boston: Houghton Miffin.

Horning, A. S. (2007). Reading across the curriculum as the key to student success. *Across the Disciplines: Interdisciplinary Perspectives on Language, Learning, and Writing, 4.* Retrieved from https://wac.colostate.edu/atd/articles/horning2007.cfm.

Kingston, A. J. (1960). College study and reading maturity. *Journal of Developmental Reading, 3*(3), 199–202.

Kuh, G. D. (2008). *High-impact educational practices: What they are, who has access to them, and why they matter.* Retrieved from https://secure.aacu.org/AACU/PubExcerpts /HIGHIMP.html.

Laufgraben, J. L. (2006). *Common reading programs: going beyond the book.* National Resource Center for the First-Year Experience and Students in Transition. Retrieved from http://www.ncrpubs.com

Lee, H. (1960, 1988). *To kill a mockingbird.* New York: Grand Central Publishing.

Liberal Arts Degrees and Their Value in the Employment Market (2014) Retrieved from https://www.aacu.org/nchems-report.

Mam, S. (2008). *The road of lost innocence.* New York: Random House Publishing.

Nadelson, S. G. & Nadelson, L. S. (2012). In search of the right book: Considerations in common read book selection. *Journal of College Reading and Learning, 43*(1), 60–66.

National Endowment for the Arts. (2004). *Reading at risk: A survey of literary reading in America.* Retrieved from http://www.arts.gov.

National Endowment for the Arts. (2007). *To Read or Not to Read: A Matter of National Consequence.* Retrieved from http://www.arts.gov.

Nichols, T. J. (2012). The institutional impact of honors though a campus-community common read. *Honors in Practice, 8,* 175–182.

Ozick, C. (1981, 1990). *The shawl.* New York: Vintage.

Perin, D. (2013). Literacy skills among academically underprepared students. *Community College Review, 41*(2), 118–136.

Queensborough Community College. (2014). *The office of institutional research and assessment fact book 2013–2014, 5.*

Ray, E. J. (2013, July 23). *The value of a liberal arts education in today's global marketplace.* Huffington Post. Retrieved from http://www.huffingtonpost.com/edward-j-ray/the-value-of-a-liberal-arts-education_b_3647765.html.

Rosenblatt, L. M. (1938, 1995). *The literature of exploration.* New York: The Modern Language Association.

Rosenblatt, L. M. (1994). *The reader, the text, the poem: The transactional theory of the literary work.* Carbondale: Southern Illinois University Press.

Sargent, J. (Director). (1997). *Miss Ever's boys* [Motion Picture]. USA: HBO NYC Productions.

Schudde, L. & Goldrick-Rab, S. (2015). On second chances and stratification: How sociologists think about community colleges. *Community College Review, 43*(1), 27–45.

Sigurdson, R. (2006). *Why study the liberal arts?* Retrieved from http://www.umanitoba.ca/faculties/arts/student/why_study_arts.html.

Simons, D. J. & Chabris, C. F. (1999). Gorillas in our midst: Sustained inattentional blindness for dynamic events. *Perception, 28*, 1059–1074.

Skloot, R. (2011). *The immortal life of Henrietta Lacks.* New York: Broadway Books.

Smith, C. H. (2012). Interrogating texts: From deferent to efferent and aesthetic reading practices. *Journal of Basic Writing, 31*(1), 59–79.

Spencer-Wendel, S. (2013) *Until I say goodbye: My year of living with joy.* New York: Harper.

Straus, M. & Daley, J. (2002). *Learning college initiative: Implementing a common book at your college.* Houston: Houston Community College System.

United Nations. (1948). *Universal declaration of human rights.* Retrieved from http://www.un.org/en/documents/udhr/.

High-Profile Football Players' Reading at a Research University: ACT Scores, Interview Responses, and Personal Preferences: An Update

Martha Townsend

UNIVERSITY OF MISSOURI

This qualitative case study examines the reading acumen of a cohort of 26 senior football players at a Mid-western public research university. Data related to three indices—ACT scores, interview responses, and personal preferences—were collected as part of a larger IRB-approved study aimed at determining the factors that led to the entire cohort graduating within their NCAA eligibility period. In general, the players' interview responses and their preferences for recreational reading reveal more about their reading habits than do the ACT data. This feedback, coupled with objective ACT scores, portrays a rich, complex picture of scholarship athletes' literate lives, a picture that defies easy explanation. Overall, the study suggests that college reading and writing instructors may want to reconsider the overwhelmingly negative stereotypes often held about high-profile athletes.

Composition scholars Mariolina Rizzi Salvatori and Patricia Donahue (2012) recently declared that "[f]or those interested in reading, this is an exciting time" (p. 199). Observing that the subject of reading is relevant again, they nonetheless conclude that English Studies' revival of interest in reading after two decades of relative inattention has it emerging as not much more than "an old beast slouching toward a not yet visible destination" (p. 200). Salvatori and Donahue pose a lengthy list of theoretical, programmatic, and institutional questions they believe need to be addressed to move the conversation forward. For her part, Alice Horning has been prodding composition scholars to pay attention to reading for some time, with this edited collection a prime outcome. In her introduction to a special issue of *Across the Disciplines*, Horning (2013) describes what she calls the "don't, won't, can't" problem of today's college students: they don't read in ways that faculty expect; they won't read unless faculty coerce them; and most important, they can't read texts with the critical reading skills educators expect.

This chapter is a case study of one cohort of high-profile football players' reading, athletes who are in a major sports program at a large public university—the kind of athletes and the type of football atmosphere many Americans, college faculty in particular, often call into question. As one set of educational research-ers note, "intercollegiate athletics is one of the significant filters through which the public looks at American postsecondary education" (Pascarella, Truckenmiller, Nora, Terenzini, Edison & Hagedorn, 1999, p. 1). The phrase "dumb jock" is ubiquitous, the amount of money spent on big-time college football programs un-questionably scandalous. At the same time, participation in college sports is at an all-time high. The number of athletes playing on intercollegiate teams in 2008–09 (the academic year this cohort graduated) topped out at 421,000 with 26,104 of them playing football at the elite Division I level (National Collegiate Athletic Association, 2010).

The study offers a detailed look at educational data not available to reporters whose exposés about athletes' academic failures fuel public perception—nor, for that matter, to faculty within academe who uncritically carry forward long-held stereo-types and misperceptions. The data comprise one subset of information collected as part of a larger project titled *The Literate Lives of Athletes: How a Division I Cham-pionship Football Program Graduated 100% of Its Senior Players*. With IRB approval and the cooperation of my university's Intercollegiate Athletics Program, the project attempts to discern the set of factors that coalesced to enable an entire senior cohort of football players to graduate within their NCAA eligibility period.

The "MU 26," as I have come to call them, accomplished this academic feat while simultaneously winning ten of their final season's 14 games, including their divisional championship and a post-season bowl game. Twenty-five of the MU 26 were seniors on the University of Missouri's NCAA Division I football team in the autumn of 2008. One more player, who was actually still a "junior" by NCAA's reckoning, had already received his bachelor's degree and was in the process of completing his master's degree while playing out the remainder of his NCAA eligi-bility. All received undergraduate degrees in 2008–09. (This article uses "student-athlete," "student," "athlete," and "player" interchangeably to refer to the young men on the team.)

The chapter examines three indices of players' reading acumen: 1) ACT read-ing and English scores used in the admissions process, along with grades earned in first-year composition; 2) impromptu responses about reading elicited during players' one-on-one interviews with me; and 3) their personal preferences for rec-reational reading. In general, these indices offer a rich, complex picture of these players' literate lives, a picture that defies simple stereotypes. Overall, the findings from this cohort suggest that college reading and writing instructors may want to reconsider the overwhelmingly negative stereotypes often held about high-profile scholarship athletes. Ameliorating these views could allow for more productive re-lationships with student athletes in and out of the classroom, foster improved aca-demic performance on students' parts, and perhaps result in greater satisfaction on instructors' parts.

Method

The case study approach, according to Robert Stake (1994), is a part of scientific method, but its purpose is "not to represent the world, but to represent the case" (245). This report, then, does not address the many questions that Salvatori and Donahue raise, nor does it resolve the "don't, won't, can't" problem that Horning (2013) poses. But it can, as Stake points out, lead to valid generalizations if modifications are made to fit particular instances. Case studies' utility comes when practitioners and policy makers extend the reported experience to their own situations. The larger *Literate Lives* project, as well as this report of one subset of the data, is a qualitative study indebted to the principles established in Guba and Lincoln's *Fourth Generation Evaluation* (1989). These scholars' constructivist paradigm delineates a step-by-step process, which focuses on hermeneutic dialogue, ethical considerations, and the empowerment of all stakeholders. Using the principles that Guba and Lincoln espouse (though not all of the steps in their elaborate model), I was able to establish a level of trust with the student-athletes such that their one-on-one interviews with me, a relative stranger, reveal a spectrum of self-reported reading habits ranging from "Oh, I don't read at all" to "I read constantly."

Each of the 26 players met with me individually for a video-taped interview, many of which lasted close to an hour, which were later transcribed. I used an IRB-approved, generative protocol of twenty-some questions to elicit players' attitudes and experiences about their academic lives during the three to five years they spent as student-athletes at the university. Each signed a Consent to Participate form, in which I promised not to reveal any information that could potentially embarrass them, a commitment I reiterated at the start of each interview. I had access to their official academic records (transcripts), which enabled me to ask specific questions about courses they had either excelled in or struggled with. Further, as former director of the university's WAC/WID program, I was familiar with many of the professors and courses the athletes referred to, and I was able to follow up with questions about specific assignments or teaching practices.

Acknowledging College Athletics' Worst-case Scenarios

One doesn't have to look far to find examples of literacy problems among high-profile athletes in the revenue-producing sport of college football. One of the better-known examples is that of Dexter Manley, who made it through four years at Oklahoma State University as a functional illiterate (Nyad, 1989). Following a distinguished NFL career with the Washington Redskins, the two-time Super Bowl winner tearfully confessed before a U.S. Senate Subcommittee on Education that until nearly age 30 he could neither read nor write. A less frequently remembered example is James Brooks, who played at Auburn for four years before becoming a first-round draft pick by the San Diego Chargers (Downtown, 2000). Brooks' illiteracy was revealed when he was arrested for failing to pay over $110,000 in child support. In court, Brooks admitted to the judge that he could not read the legal documents ordering him to make the monthly payments. His NFL running back coach later said, "I never put James in a position where he had to show me if he could read" (Downtown, "Maintaining the Veil," para. 9). More recently, *The Chronicle of Higher Education* carried the story of University of Memphis linebacker and defensive end Dasmine Cathey, who is struggling to complete a degree after tutoring himself to read by painstakingly reviewing a secret stash of elementary school learn-to-read books (Wolverton, 2012).

Another example, this one from the college basketball realm, is Kevin Ross who withdrew from Creighton University after three years when it was discovered that he had only elementary school level reading ability (Ross, 1983). His comments about reading in the early grades are particularly poignant: "I always felt self-conscious about my reading, but it didn't seem that I did any worse in school than a lot of others. I never liked to read, and I did it real slow, but so did a lot of other kids." At Creighton, it was a psychology class that revealed the depth of his deficit: "If you can't read, you can't understand," he told a magazine interviewer. Whitner and Myers (1986) cite Ross's story as an example that was used to enable yet another athlete to adjust to counseling he needed to deal with his reading difficulties. By turns shocking and heartbreaking, these stories help perpetuate the perception that underprepared athletes overpopulate our college classrooms.

The case of the MU 26 offers a compelling counterexample to these worst-case scenarios. Dexter Manley's graduation notwithstanding, graduation rates are one of the key indicators of student-athletes' academic achievement. And, the achievement of a 100% graduation rate among a Division I senior football cohort is unusual, particularly at a large, state-supported university where the pressure to win is intense and where athletes are presumed to have more leeway at admission time. The average Graduation Success Rate reported by the NCAA (2013) for entering cohorts in Division I from 1998 through 2001 is approximately 67%, far short of the 100% achieved by the MU 26.

The MU 26 Cohort

The MU 26 are remarkable in their diversity. Their level of achievement in high school and their preparedness for college study vary widely. They come from a mix of rural, suburban, and urban high schools. Fifteen (58%) of the players are white; eleven (42%) are African-American. Some, but not all, have parents who went to college. A few hail from comfortable socioeconomic backgrounds, others fit squarely into the American middle class, some come from economically disadvantaged backgrounds. They graduated from high school in as low as the 27th percentile to as high as the 98th. Ten (38%) finished in the upper quarter of their high school graduation classes; twelve (46%) finished in the lower half. Three were National Honor Society inductees in high school. Twenty-two (85%) are first-time college students; four (15%) transferred from two-year colleges. Twenty-two received athletic scholarships: four were walk-on non-scholarship players. Theirs is a large senior class (the following year's is smaller by a third). More than half come from Missouri; six are from Texas, two from Louisiana, and one each from Kansas, Oklahoma, and California. Most of them chose MU over other similarly competitive big time college football programs.

By the time the MU 26 graduated, their cumulative GPAs ranged from 2.0 (the minimum allowed) to 3.6 on a 4.0 scale. Several cycled on and off academic probation when their semester grades fell below the minimum allowed. All took courses during at least one summer session. They earned degrees in 11 different academic areas, spread across four colleges. In this study, "senior" refers to the players on the team in 2008 who had achieved senior status as defined by the NCAA. It does not refer to a group of student-athletes who entered the university together as a single cohort in the same year. In other words, some players who started with some of the MU 26 did not stay at the university long enough to become seniors. Others came later, as transfer students. Fifteen of the MU 26 took a redshirt year, effectively giving them five years to complete their college degree. Most enrolled in the university in 2004; others came in '05, '06, or '07. All graduated in 2008 or 2009.

ACT Tests / Scores / Findings

The ACT, a standardized achievement test widely used in the college admission process, is administered annually to over 1.6 million students in the United States (ACT, Inc., 2013a). It aims to assess high school students' readiness to succeed in college through multiple-choice subject-area tests in English, reading, mathematics, and science. An optional writing test has been available since 2005, which neither the NCAA nor the University of Missouri requires.

Dating to 1959, the ACT organization—formerly known as American College Testing—has evolved into an integrated, "seamless" system of multiple-choice testing that begins for some students as early as the eighth grade. The most relevant aspects of the system for a discussion of the MU 26 are ACT's College Readiness Standards and Benchmark Scores. ACT, Inc. defines readiness as the acquisition of skills and knowledge students need to succeed in credit-bearing, first-year college courses without the need for remediation (2011). The College Readiness Standards for all four subject areas, plus the writing exam, comprise a detailed 32-page rubric,

14 of which deal with reading and English, all downloadable from ACT's website. Used in conjunction with these standards, ACT's College Readiness Benchmark Scores are established for each of the subject areas and are intended to predict students' success in the corresponding first-year college courses. The benchmark score for reading is 21; for English, 18 (ACT, Inc., 2013c). A high school student receiving ACT's reading benchmark score of 21 could expect a 75% chance of obtaining a C or higher or a 50% chance of obtaining a B or higher in a "reading dependent" course in the social sciences or humanities. A high school student receiving ACT's English benchmark score of 18 could expect 75% chance of obtaining a C or higher or a 50% chance of obtaining a B or higher in English composition.

ACT suggests that "Because no test can measure educational development with absolute precision, it's best to think of . . . ACT scores as a range rather than as a precise point" (2013d). So, a composite score of any number probably indicates a level of educational development at that score, plus or minus one. (Score-range as opposed to precise point score becomes relevant later in the discussion of how the MU 26 are situated relative to the general population of students.) Because of ACT's wide use historically and because the MU 26's scores on it are available, the instrument offers one potentially revealing measure of players' reading acumen.

ACT and the MU 26

Twenty of the MU 26 took the ACT college entrance exam as required for admission to the university. Of the six who did not take the ACT, two took the SAT and four were not required to submit a college entrance exam score because they had already earned A.A. degrees at the two-year colleges from which they transferred. The degree to which any of the MU 26 spent time pouring over test prep books, taking practice exams, or availing themselves of test preparation courses is unknown, although it is safe to assume that their high school counselors—knowing that these athletes were competing for Division I athletic scholarship slots at NCAA institutions that require college entrance exam scores—would have advised the athletes to some degree on how to prepare. ACT acknowledges that one of the most common uses of its assessment is to determine eligibility to play varsity athletics at NCAA institutions (Andrews & Ziomek, 1998).

One of the MU 26 took both the ACT and SAT, perhaps hoping for a scholarship, football or otherwise, at an east or west coast school where SAT scores are used more frequently than the ACT. Taking the exam more than once is common, as students often seek to improve their scores and know that ACT will report only the scores that takers choose to have sent. When retesting, examinees with the lowest scores gain the most, while examinees with the highest scores are most likely to see scores decrease (Andrews & Ziomek, 1998). ACT's website offers a list of reasons why students might want to repeat the exam, noting that 57 percent who retest increase their composite score, while 21 percent stay the same and 22 percent decrease (ACT, Inc., 2013b).

Of the 20 MU 26 students who took the ACT, ten tested once; six tested twice; three tested three times; and one tested four times. Most saw their scores improve with each taking, while a few scores did go down, though not substantially. I use the highest score achieved in the reading and English categories for this analysis. All 20 took the exam between 2002 and 2006, with the majority taking it in 2003 or 2004.

How the MU 26 Scored

- The MU 26 earned composite ACT scores ranging from a low of 12 to a high of 30 (out of 36), for an average of 21—placing the cohort four points below the average of 25 earned by all MU students who entered the university at approximately the same time.
- The MU 26 earned reading ACT scores ranging from a low of 12 to a high of 30 (of 36), for an average of 21, meeting ACT's reading benchmark of 21.
- The MU 26 earned English ACT scores ranging from a low of 11 to a high of 34 (of 36), for an average of 21, or three points higher than ACT's benchmark of 18.

This range of composite, reading, and English scores represents an extraordinarily wide degree of "readiness to succeed" within the cohort, as measured by ACT. Only one of the MU 26 received scores at the low end of the range—a composite of 12, a reading score of 12, and an English score of 11. On the other end of the spectrum, one of the MU 26 scored well above the average of all MU students entering the university at approximately the same time; he earned a composite score of 30, a reading score of 30, and an English score of 34, the latter just two points below the maximum possible 36.

Seven of the MU 26 received composite scores of 24 to 30 (24 being minus one point of the MU general population average of 25 and therefore in the "probable" range of their educational development). In other words, nearly a third of the cohort placed at or above the average of their general population student peers (non-athletes).

ACT Reading Test and the MU 26

ACT's reading test contains four passages, each about 750 words long, from works in the humanities, prose fiction, social sciences, and natural sciences (Ehrenhaft,

Lehrman, Mundsack & Obrecht, 2001, p. 285). Each passage is followed by ten multiple-choice questions. Three categories of reading passages are used: "Uncomplicated Informational," "More Challenging Informational," and "Complex Informational." And five textual elements are itemized in ACT's Reading Standards rubric: 1) main ideas and author's approach; 2) supporting details; 3) sequential, comparative, and cause-effect relationships; 4) meanings of words; and 5) generalizations and conclusions. ACT says the questions require students "to derive meaning from texts by referring to what is explicitly stated and reasoning to determine implicit meanings and to draw conclusions, comparisons, and generalizations" (2006). Test takers have 35 minutes to complete the test.

Of the 20 MU 26 who took the ACT, half received a reading readiness score of 21 or above while half scored below. That is, half achieved the benchmark established by ACT indicating a high probability of success (a 75% chance of earning a course grade of C or better or a 50% chance of earning a B or better) in first-year courses generally considered to be "reading dependent." The half who scored below 21 were presumably not "ready to succeed" in reading-dependent courses. This finding places the MU 26 squarely beside the 51 percent of American students whom ACT's research shows are ready for college and workplace reading (2006). ACT's research is based on the organization's 2004–05 test results, a time line close to when the MU 26 were taking the test.

ACT's research also shows that some groups of students—e.g., males, African Americans, and those whose parents have annual incomes below $30,000—can be as much as 1.5 to 2.5 times less likely to be ready for college-level reading (2006). Given that some of the MU 26 are in this higher risk population, it seems noteworthy that the cohort as a whole still compares favorably to the 51 percent of the overall American college-going population that is "college ready" for reading.

Grades in Reading-dependent Courses

Insofar as the MU 26's grades in first-year reading-dependent courses are concerned, ACT seems to have been an accurate predictor of how these students would perform. Using the same first-year reading-dependent courses that ACT uses to derive its College Readiness Benchmark for reading (history, psychology, sociology, political science, and economics), the MU 26 who scored 21 or above on the benchmark earned a grade point average (GPA) of 2.89 on a 4.0 scale, or fractionally under a B in their reading-dependent courses. The MU 26 who scored 20 or below on the benchmark earned a GPA of 1.71 on a 4.0 scale, or C- in their reading-dependent courses.

To describe these reading-dependent courses more fully, all but one of the MU 26 took a variety of first-year courses in history, political science, psychology, sociology, and both micro- and macro-economics. (The one student who did not take any arrived at the university with a clear focus on a science-based major and enrolled early on in science and foreign language classes.) Approximately one grade point differentiates the above-benchmark scorers from the below-benchmark scorers in each reading-dependent course.

Table 5.1. Average of Grades Earned by MU 26 Student Athletes in First-Year Reading-Dependent Courses

Course/Discipline	Above-benchmark (21 & up) Scorers	Below-benchmark (20 & down) Scorers
History	3.3 (B+)	2.28 (C+)
Economics	3.28 (B+)	1.8 (C-)
Psychology	3.0 (B)	1.83 (C-)
Sociology	2.3 (C+)	1.7 (C-)
Political Science	1.85 (C-)	1.0 (D)

ACT English (First-Year Composition) Test & the MU 26

The English test consists of 75 multiple-choice questions based on five prose passages, and students have 45 minutes to complete the test (Ehrenhaft, Lehrman, Mundsack & Obrecht, 2001, p. 71). The test assesses six elements of effective writing in two broad categories: 1) usage and mechanics, which includes punctuation, grammar and usage, sentence structure, and 2) rhetorical skills, which includes strategy, organization, and style (2006). The MU 26 performed better on the English test than on the reading test: 16 (compared to 10) scored above ACT's benchmark, with four scoring below. According to ACT, then, 16 of the MU 26 should have a 75 percent chance of earning a course grade of C or better or a 50% chance of earning a B or better in first-year composition. Scores from the MU 26 in the above-the-benchmark range from a low of 19 to a high of 34, indicating "readiness" for success in first-year composition. Scores from the MU 26 in the below-the-benchmark are 11 (for one) and 15 (for three).

Grades in English Courses

Overall, the MU 26 earned grades in Missouri's first-year composition course, English 1000: Exposition and Argumentation (itself a reading-dependent course), ranging from F to A-. The cohort's GPA is 2.26 on a 4.0 scale (including D and F grades), or fractionally under a C+. The three who earned F's and D's on their first taking of the course repeated it, since a grade of C- is the minimum that satisfies the university's General Education requirement. All of those whose English benchmark scores are above 18 earned C's or B's in first-year composition, as ACT predicted. One earned an A-. The four whose English scores are below 18 are those who, according to ACT, might have needed "remediation" in English composition. Here the story becomes a little more complex, at least on the local institutional research level. When all students are admitted to the university, the ACT benchmark of 18 is used as a cut-off to recommend placement into either "regular" or "stretch" versions of English 1000. The 16 who met the ACT English benchmark were advised into regular English 1000. The four who scored 17 or below, along with six other MU 26 students (transfers and several who took the SAT), were recommended to take stretch English 1000.

The Sub-story of "Stretch" English

Stretch composition courses date to the early 1990's and are based on the premise that so-called "basic" writers are best served by having access to the same course content required of more prepared students—if longer time is spent on instruction and practice. The regular course is "stretched out," in other words, in some way. Usually, course numbering is the same for regular and stretch versions; tuition is the same; reporting of grades is the same. No penalties accrue for taking stretch versions. (See Glau [1996], for example.) Like these courses taught elsewhere, Missouri's version of stretch English was intended to enroll students who were thought to need additional help to pass the course—precisely those of the MU 26 who scored below ACT's English benchmark of 18.

Theoretically, the regular and stretch versions of English 1000 were similar, with the exception that stretch added one extra day of instruction per week during which an additional one-hour tutorial was taught by stretch instructors to students enrolled in a different stretch section than their own. (The cross tutorials were apparently thought to offer students enhanced benefits by virtue of the instructors' differing perspectives.) However, neither the curriculum for regular nor stretch English was standardized or monitored, so there is no way to know how similar the two versions of the courses may have been.

Moreover, despite longstanding objections from composition studies assessment scholars, local Composition Program professionals never debated using ACT as the screening instrument, according to one person with knowledge of the Program's history. The only issues debated were practical ones related to administering the course: stretch was harder to staff because instructors resisted the extra effort required, less independence was allowed in the curriculum, and no extra compensation was offered. From stretch instructors' point of view, the main advantages were the smaller class size (ten students instead of 20) and the learning community atmosphere that resulted from knowing other instructors' curricula via the tutorial exchanges with one another's classes.

Despite the good intentions of well-meaning supervisors who oversaw stretch English (and no doubt of many of the instructors who volunteered to teach stretch sections), no research was ever done once students enrolled in stretch sections or after they finished the course. No comparisons were made of students' performance in the stretch curriculum *vis-a-vis* regular sections, no studies done to determine whether stretch was, in fact, providing the intended benefits. Worse, there was not even a way to know whether or not students who were recommended to take the stretch version did so. Students were free to ignore the recommendation and enroll in regular English if they wished. Both stretch and regular English 1000 appear on student transcripts without any differentiating marker, and there exists no practical way to determine after the fact which course students took.

At one point, the university's Registration office encountered mechanical difficulty in setting up stretch sections, causing the course to be temporarily suspended. Administrators to whom the Composition Program reported, who funded the course and had been questioning its extra cost, seized the opportunity to quit offering it entirely, and the course passed quietly, almost imperceptibly, out of existence. Whether the MU 26 who were recommended to take stretch English did so, and whether the course helped them or not, is unknown.

Standardized Assessment and the MU 26

For all the attention to—and cost of—students' preparing for, taking and retaking the ACT, and requesting which sets of scores should be reported to colleges, the MU 26's ACT reading and English scores seem to have amounted to very little. It is reassuring to know that nearly one-third of the cohort placed at or above their general population peers. And it's good to know that the cohort lines up precisely with the half of other American college students whom ACT determines are "ready" for college and workplace reading.

But the bottom line is that the university requires a C- or better in first-year composition to pass the university's General Education requirements, to move on to the university's two required writing-intensive courses, and to graduate. And the Intercollegiate Athletics Program, vested as it is in student-athletes' academic success (not least in part due to NCAA regulations), provides academic tutoring for all courses including first-year composition and those that are reading-dependent. Regular study hall time is mandatory for first-year student-athletes as well as for those who fall below given standards. Several of the players report working "hard" to "stay out" of study hall once they finish their first year. The MU 26 accomplished what they had to do to stay in school and on the team.

Two quantitative studies offer further evidence that mitigate the value of standardized assessment for predicting college outcomes in reading and English. A meta-analysis of 109 studies by Robbins, Lauver, Le, Davis, Langley, and Carlstrom (2004) shows that psychosocial and study skills—things like motivation, goals, institutional commitment, social support, and self-concept—are more influential than socioeconomic status, standardized achievement (read: ACT), and high school GPA in predicting college outcomes. And a study by Simons and Van Rheenen (2000) published in Journal of College Reading and Learning points out that, even though NCAA standards rely in part on ACT and SAT scores, non-cognitive factors such as motivation to achieve play a critical role in student athletes' academic performance.

Perhaps the final word on the value of ACT scores for student athletes should go to Peter Smagorinsky, whose research takes a self-described Vygotskian perspective on the teaching and learning of literacy practices. After the prestigious *Educational Researcher* published four studies of standardized reading assessment, the journal's editors invited Smagorinsky to critique the work. His diplomatic reply (2009) finds the research "problematic" and "one-dimensional," not because it reduces data to numbers, but because of "the authors' questionable assumptions about what it means to read and to teach reading" (p. 522). Standardized assessment, he argues, assumes that reading is a self-evident construct, a discrete act, an a-cultural act, and that reading instruction is best managed by policy and assessment experts. As the title of his critique suggests, Smagorinsky believes that standardized reading assessment "collides" with the "incommensurate" cultural practice of reading. Arguing that the assumptions brought to bear by proponents of standardized reading assessment lack sufficient common ground with his own culturally-based assumptions, he says that he cannot compare them. Whereas standardized reading assessment requires that teachers follow standardized practices, he prefers a system whereby teachers hold more authority, autonomy, and judgment "even if such singular instruction defies the assessment apparatus . . ." (526). Smagorinsky's critique resonates with many issues composition scholars have with ACT and similar standardized assessments. Despite the significant impact ACT has on U.S. educational assessment writ large, the following two indices of MU 26's reading acumen may be more revealing of the literacy practices in their day-to-day lives.

Interview Responses about Reading

Because the larger *Literate Lives* study concerns the totality of factors that led to the MU 26 graduating, the IRB-approved protocol of questions concerns their attitudes and experiences of collegiate life broadly construed. Surprising though it may be, the original protocol did not include a question specifically about reading for college courses. Apart from the section below, on players' personal reading preferences, their responses about reading emerged spontaneously in the context of other issues. In general, these responses reflect a range similar to their cohort's diverse profile: the MU 26 claim everything from "I never read" to "I read a lot."

Interviews were conducted in the large facility where student-athletes eat meals, attend study hall, and meet with tutors, coaches, and other athletics personnel—on their own turf, so they would feel at ease. As seniors, these students were long accustomed to being videotaped for practice, games, and press interviews. Additionally, the staff member who processes athletes' scholarship checks assisted with videotaping, so her presence added friendly familiarity to our sessions. And players had met me when I explained the project during their senior-exit meeting with the Athletic Director, at which time I also solicited their consent to participate. All agreed. Conducting the interviews proceeded straightforwardly.

Challenging Courses vs. Reading-dependent Courses

After establishing a comfortable, positive rapport in each interview by first talking about courses the MU 26 had been successful in, the next question I put to each of the interviewees was, "What classes did you find especially challenging and how did you manage them?" Of 23 different classes they cite from the entirety of their three to five years as students, reading-dependent courses are not at the top of the list. In fact, as a category, reading-dependent classes come in third. At the top of the list is the science curriculum—biology, medical microbiology, botany, chemistry, and physics. The second category comprises math—algebra, calculus, and statistics. Only in the third category are classes that ACT defines as reading-dependent—micro- and macro-economics with five mentions, then history, political science, and psychology with one mention each. A final fourth category includes business-related courses—management, accounting, and law.

With regard to managing those challenging courses, players' explanations are as different as the individuals themselves. Replies range from "I set aside study time" to "I did the minimum, got the grade, and got out." Several report simply asking for help from various people—teachers, tutors, various mentors, fellow students, a girlfriend. One athlete, an engineering major, said:

> I spent extra time, pushed myself, and spent extra time with
> [my] teachers. The trick to me is getting the pattern down on
> different things and how they interlock. Basically, just putting
> the time in. Complete silence. Figuring out the patterns and the
> way that you learn.

Another, who chose to forego his goal of becoming a history teacher because practice teaching would have conflicted with the football practice schedule, comments on the 25- to 30-page articles assigned to be read in his history class each week—not because of their length *per se*, but because the quality of the scanning made them difficult to read on a computer.

Parents and Reading

Seven players invoke parental influence as an explanation for their reading habits. "[My parents] were always big into doin' book reports and everything. Still to this day I read quite a lot," notes the would-be history teacher who nonetheless cautions that, "It's what you're into. I've never found a lot of books that other people read to be that exciting [to me]." He acknowledges that he's "got a nice little collection [of reading in progress] goin', but I still think if it's not interesting to you, you're not gonna read it."

Another, who now plays in the NFL, remembers that, "My parents would always encourage me to get my reading done even if I didn't want to. . . . They never pushed me, but they always encouraged me to read . . . my mom reads a lot." And another, who arrived at the university having already earned 21 college credits while still in high school, recalls with fondness the good-natured Sunday dinner-table competitions he engaged in with his overachieving cousins about their various educational pursuits. "My mom wonders how I can go from reading all the books I did when I was in grade school, to not reading too many books lately," he recalls. "I really don't do too much 'fun' reading right now." He is one of several who lament lack of time for reading and needing to prioritize limited time to reading textbooks for classes.

Two others who also invoke memories of parental encouragement tie their interest in reading to their parents' occupations as teachers, one whose mother teaches first grade, the other whose father teaches high school English. The latter offers this example:

> When I was thirteen or fourteen, my dad told me if I could read Moby Dick and explain it and have an intelligent discussion with him by the time I was sixteen, he'd buy me the car I wanted. . . . My number one book of all time would have to be *The Great Gatsby* . . . It's my favorite book . . . The way F. Scott Fitzgerald wrote, you know, the way he developed those characters almost made me feel like you were at, you know, some of those parties that he was throwing . . . that you were in the book. Very few other authors or very few other stories that I've read have ever felt like that.

This player got the car he wanted, which he concedes was never really in question anyway, suggesting a ruse on his father's part to get him to read *Moby-Dick* earlier than he otherwise might have. One player notes that his difficult transition to college life included the absence of parental influence, while simultaneously commenting on the Athletics Department's approach: "You take away all parental guidance—even though this place gives you great academic guidance, they're not hovering. They don't sit there and look down over your shoulder to make sure you're doing this."

Motivations to Read

Beyond parental encouragement, the MU 26 describe multiple motivations for their reading:

- Coaches "breathing down your back" (in reference to reading the playbook);
- Life-long goals (in reference to reading about martial arts and "always wanting to be a samurai");
- Applying lessons learned to the football field (in reference to reading about leadership skills);
- Applying values learned to life (in reference to reading Warren's *The Purpose-Driven Life*);
- Finding yourself (in reference to one player's personal definition of what a "good book" does);
- Interviewing for a job (in reference to Teach for America's required reading list);
- Escaping from the daily pressure to "make yourself a better person" (in apologetic reference for reading "a lot" of fiction);
- Sheer interest in a subject (in reference to the "nifty little facts" to be found in military history books);

This partial list—again, unprompted and in the context of other issues—echoes in part an observation made by Joliffe and Harl (2008) after they studied a similar sized cohort of first-year composition students at the University of Arkansas: "We found students who were actively involved in their own programs of reading aimed at values clarification, personal enrichment, and career preparation. In short, we discovered students who were extremely engaged with their reading but not with the reading that their classes required" (p. 600). While the MU 26 interviews offer no evidence that they were not reading what classes required, a possible explanation for the difference between them and the Arkansas first-year students is the MU 26's senior-class status. Many of them note the maturity they achieved as they progressed through the three to five years of their academic programs. As they got closer to graduation, their motivation to finish their degrees increased. They specifically acknowledge the degree to which they have changed from when they entered college. Their future goals are clarified, the stakes higher, and their investment in their educations more established.

What the MU 26 Didn't Say About Reading

In 500-plus pages of transcribed interviews, there are no references to an active *dislike* of reading, or to problems encountered with reading in elementary or secondary school, or to avoidance techniques applied to required reading for university classes. Of course, that doesn't suggest none exist; it is simply to note they aren't mentioned. Players' lack of complaints about reading could be attributed to my not probing for them; to the larger purpose of the study (which is not on reading *per se*); and to the mostly celebratory impetus for the project itself (the entire cohort graduating), all of which led to generally positive responses overall.

Still, conversation during the interview sessions was reasonably relaxed, and players did openly discuss frustrations encountered along the way toward earning their degrees. When spontaneous negative comments about reading did occur, the context was lack of time imposed by the demands of the sport. "I haven't read a book not for class in I don't know how long," says one. "Mostly now [my time is spent] focusing on school and school books, finance books, real estate . . . ," notes a business major whose degree is in Finance and Banking. Reflecting on the reading he had enjoyed in grade school, one player wistfully notes, "Maybe when I have more free time, that'd be something I'd like to do . . ." his voice trailing off.

Lack of time—and lack of energy at the end of long days filled with classes, meetings, practice, travel, work outs, and games—is a key theme throughout the larger study. While grateful for the scholarship opportunity to play football, many of the MU 26 acknowledge that they haven't been able to focus more on their academic work at the university. That finding is consistent with a survey of over 2,300 student-athletes' experiences in Division I football programs nationally. Potuto and O'Hanlon (2007) conclude:

> [R]esponses showed a generally positive picture of college life. While they regret that their participation in varsity athletics means that they miss out on some aspects of college life, both curricular and co-curricular, they value their athletics participation and believe that it both instills values independent of those derived from other aspects of college and enhances particular skills and their overall college experience. They also report that the trade-offs they make in order to compete are acceptable or more than acceptable. (para. 1)

Three different interview questions were designed to elicit negative responses about their educational experiences (e.g., "Did you face any hardships that 'regular' students don't?"). And the MU 26 do cite a variety of constraints that result from dedication to their sport, such as the rigid schedule, lack of free time, and missing out on things at home. Nearly all, though, attribute their academic success to acquiring time management skills as a matter of necessity. Significantly, they do not report feeling scholastically inferior to their non-athletic peers. They do not report, "I simply did not understand the text that professor assigned" or "I was lost in that class." Rather, when commenting on academic challenges, the typical response is, "Get it done."

A Reading Highlight

Written into the head coach's contract is an expectation that football players will participate in community service and charitable work, and student-athletes know they'll be contributing to the community in some way when they accept a football scholarship. Nine of the MU 26 chose to participate in reading programs for elementary school children; only the "Bowl for Kids' Sake" charity event drew more volunteers. Two of the MU 26 worked with the university's Starlight Reading program, a partnership between Intercollegiate Athletics and the College of Education. Every Wednesday at 10:00 a.m., volunteers connect via satellite with classrooms around the state to read to school children and then engage in an interactive question and answer session. Other MU 26 members went to schools in the city, reading in person to excited youngsters who know these players well through the local media and (the lucky ones) by attending Saturday games with their parents.

These are stories the local press likes to feature, and the university doesn't mind the positive publicity. Chad Bass' fifth-graders at Parkade School are among those who've benefited from student-athlete readers (Braden, 2009). Bass' Friday mystery guest readers include at least two of the MU 26—plus the Athletic Director and several of his assistants. Kids don't know who's coming until the athlete walks in the door. Bass says for some students, guessing who each week's reader will be increases the anticipation. Bass tells me that players read "cold, on the spot," usually from chapter books, picking up unrehearsed from where the last reader left off (Personal Interview). Bass comments, "That was kind of a neat thing for the kids to see. You could tell the athletes were probably reading for the first time in front of kids." Unscripted questions like "Were there any players on the team you didn't get along with?" and "Do you like going to class?" led to candid answers that Bass describes as "very important" for fifth-graders learning about balancing athletics with academics and about life in general.

Reading studies scholar Connie Juel (1991) has documented the benefits of student-athletes working with school children—for both children and athletes. She attributes the success of her pioneering program to: 1) college students' (especially those from minority groups, as three of the nine MU 26 volunteer readers are) ability to serve as role models for young at-risk students; 2) some readers sharing a culture of poverty experienced by some of the students; 3) student-athletes believing the children can learn and succeed; and 4) some readers' own struggle to learn to read.

Not all of the MU 26 reading volunteers fit Juel's four categories, nor did they formally tutor the children on a protracted basis. Nonetheless, their work brought them into contact with scores of impressionable children who observed role models engaging in reading. All nine of the MU 26 describe their volunteer reading in positive terms. This player's interview response is typical:

> It was a nice, humbling experience. It kept a level head on all our shoulders. . . . A lot of us have younger sisters and brothers, and it was just fun. . . . You always felt like this was what we needed to do to show the community and the young kids that we don't just play ball. We are people. We like to share. We like to love. We like to play. We like to joke around and have fun with one another. And it's not always just about football and school. . . . It never felt like we was obligated to do this. It was always something that we knew in our hearts that needed to be done.

Cynics might suggest that mandating community service fails to instill genuine altruism and serves mainly to deliver good press for the football program. Given opportunity to register discontent with this expectation, however, the MU 26 unanimously endorse the concept of "giving back to the community" that supports them. That so many of them choose reading-related activities from among a wide range of possible avenues of involvement speaks to the multiple sides of their literate lives.

A Reductive Understanding of What Reading Is

Just as many students conceive of writing in its most simplistic terms—thinking of only final, formal products, say, while omitting invention, research, and multiple drafts—several of the MU 26, in their off-the-cuff remarks about reading, do the same. The player who staunchly maintains that he "never reads," nonetheless comments on the growth of the Internet and its effect on his age group: "There's so many different ways to read, but I just was never into reading when I was younger." He goes on to acknowledge frequent reading of such texts as Internet sources, newspapers, and sports magazines. Another who claims not to like reading "that much," nonetheless mentions having enjoyed reading excerpts of Levitt and Dubner's *Freakonomics* and wanting to read the whole book. He, too, mentions reading "a lot" of magazines.

Personal Preferences for Reading

Of the three indices examined in this study, personal preference in reading shows the most commonality among the MU 26, along with further evidence of the cohort's diversity. It was one of the players who, as he was leaving the interview room, turned to ask, "Would you like to know what I've been reading?" and began reeling off a lengthy list of books. Unfortunately, the camera was turned off, and I neglected to capture his impressive list; fortunately, he was only the third interviewee and henceforward the remainder replied to the question "What have you been reading lately and is there anything you'd care to recommend to others?"

Sports

A good number of the MU 26 report reading about sports, sports figures, and sports themes. Stories about athletes, biographies, autobiographies, examples of leadership, and lessons they can apply on the football field are high on their radar. Joe Torre's autobiography *The Yankee Years* and Mark Kriegel's biography *Pistol: The Life of Pete Maravich* are seen as examples of "how athletes deal with situations." Jose Conseco's *Juiced: Wild Times, Rampant 'Roids, Smash Hits, and How Baseball Got Big*; Steve Richardson's *Then Pinkel Said to Smith: The Best Missouri Tigers Stories Ever Told*; and *LT: Over the Edge: Tackling Quarterbacks, Drugs, and a World Beyond Football* by Lawrence Taylor and Steve Serby are among the book titles they mention, along with multiple references to sports magazines.

History

Another frequently mentioned category is history, especially martial arts and military history. A Communication major and self-described "big history guy," recalls being particularly moved by a book about the 1911 Triangle Shirtwaist factory fire in New York City. The player who relished competitive Sunday conversations with his cousins cites Civil War and World War II books as central to his reading, even tying social history into his pursuits: "My grandma says she remembers knitting 8" x 8" squares in high school to make blankets [for soldiers]. It's crazy how much military factual stuff there is." Sun Tzu's *The Art of War* and *Samurai Strategies: 42 Martial Secrets from Musashi's Book of Five Rings* by Boye Lafayette De Mente and Michihiro Matsumoto are titles specifically named in this category.

Religious and Inspirational

A third category for personal preference reading relates to religious and inspirational themes. One player, who describes having gotten off to a "rough start" in life but thought he might like to own a business after graduation, reports reading a book suggested by a trusted professor from whom he'd taken a course in Agriculture: "It's called *Let Your Life Speak* [subtitled *Listening for the Voice of Vocation*, by Parker Palmer] and it's pretty much just different situations you go through to get to a certain place, different situations to find yourself, your real self." Another reports being newly focused on the religious aspect of his life and just beginning to acquire his own books on that theme. *In Step With God: Understanding His Ways and Plans for Your Life* by Charles Stanley is the book he cites. A third, who earlier had said, "I haven't read a book *not* for class in I don't know how long," references the Bible along with Rick Warren's best seller *The Purpose-Driven Life: What on Earth Am I Here For?* Continuing, this student says:

> Any time I read something or listen to somebody speak, I try to take at least one point and I try to work it into my life and try to—I won't say change my life—but try to live by that and so that's kind of what I do and just try to take one thing and learn one thing out of each chapter.

The underlying suggestion behind the titles in this category is that these athletes, as well as many other of the MU 26, seem to be actively seeking insight to apply to their future lives and careers. If Jolliffe and Harl (2008) describe the students in their study as connecting texts with "their emerging sense of themselves as adults in the world" (p. 607), the MU 26 could be described as already knowing they are adults in the world who will soon need to make sound decisions about how to proceed. That they might also be talking amongst themselves about this pressing, existential topic—and, given their recent or upcoming graduations, likely receiving advice from their coaches—could be seen in the comment of the player who almost seems to apologize for his reading habits: "I read a lot, but [it doesn't] pertain to sports or making yourself a better person. For some reason, I'm into the fiction books, so . . . they're not the best books to read if you're like . . . they were pretty much like an escape more than anything."

Fiction and Literature

The foregoing categories comprise titles, themes, and habits around which the MU 26 cohere. The *differences* in the MU 26's reading preferences appear in the diverse titles in fiction and literature they report reading, shown here in alphabetical order by author:

- *The Lone Ranger and Tonto Fistfight in Heaven*, Sherman Alexie
- *Angels and Demons*, Dan Brown
- *Da Vinci Code*, Dan Brown
- *The Great Gatsby*, F. Scott Fitzgerald
- *The Pillars of the Earth*, Ken Follett
- *Pelican Brief*, John Grisham
- *The Stand*, Stephen King
- *Time Traveler's Wife*, Audrey Niffenegger
- *1984*, George Orwell
- *Harry Potter* (series), J. K. Rowling
- *The Book Thief*, Markus Zusak

None of the titles represent required course reading; all represent personal reading done for pleasure. Only two of the authors garner citations by more than one athlete—Brown and Rowling. Of the three who mention one or the other of Brown's books, one student who self-describes as "not a big reader . . . [who doesn't] like to read that much" nonetheless notes that he read both of Brown's books quickly and didn't want to put them down. He was "excited" to see Angels and Demons coming out as a film.

One theme from the larger study—the overwhelming tiredness that results from the physical and mental demands of each day—coincides with reading in an unexpected way. One player says, of the coach, "He keeps us so busy . . . to where we're like, 'I don't want to do anything else. I'm just going to go home. Go lay down.' . . . Your body be sore. That's all you're going to do is just go home and lay down and study or read a book." When pressed on what he'd read, though, this player first elicits a promise from me not to laugh at his answer. "I like Harry Potter," he admits.

> It's so much better than the movie . . . it describes more. It puts you there. It describes stuff you see in the movie, but it describes it more. Or there's stuff that you wouldn't pay attention to in the movie.

Another MU 26 Harry Potter fan isn't at all reticent about reading books for a supposedly younger audience, proclaiming Potter his "number one favorite" and noting that he owns the entire series. In fact, he'd bought a supplemental volume of fairy tales that "people in the wizarding world" are reading.

The remaining, eclectic titles are ones that interviewees invoke randomly, with one mention each. The second Harry Potter fan above further notes that he reads "a whole lot of different kinds of books" and reads "quite often . . . poetry books, books on relationships . . . I like having a wide base of information."

All of these examples offer evidence that the MU 26 read often and widely and for more purposes than those who are skeptical of student-athletes might expect.

Even though the study was not designed to elicit information about the cohort's ability to perform the critical task of reading difficult texts assigned in college classes, these athletes nonetheless spontaneously, willingly discuss the "real" reading of their everyday lives. Their remarks constitute examples of literate activity valued within our culture.

Conclusion

Prevailing public perception would likely consign the MU 26 to a much lower educational status than these findings show they warrant. All of these players succeeded in earning undergraduate degrees by the same standards that their general population (non-athlete) peers were held to. At the very least, this cohort demonstrates that high-profile athletes involved in big-time football programs should not be assumed to be deficient in reading ability in ways that will deter them from completing an undergraduate degree. More important, the data show that the MU 26 read a variety of texts for a variety of reasons—and that they do, in fact, have a rich array of reading interests and practices.

We need more studies, though, about both the everyday reading practices of all athletes and about the critical reading skills they bring to difficult texts assigned throughout the curricula. How does this cohort compare with others? How well can student athletes discern an author's underlying assumptions? How well can they evaluate an author's evidence for a claim—or marshal their own to make an argument? Do athletes differ sufficiently from general population students in these tasks to warrant studying them as a separate group? How can we teach student athletes in ways that maximize their college reading and learning?

The findings in all three of these indices are not what I expected going into the *Literate Lives* project. Given the general attitudes and derisive comments so often heard in the halls of academe, I did not anticipate that one of the athletes would have an ACT English score just two points shy of the best possible. I did not anticipate that one of the athletes would have arrived at the university having already completed 21 college credits in high school and go on to complete a Master's degree while still under his NCAA eligibility period. I did not anticipate the diverse list of personal reading they report engaging in. And while I had a general sense that "coaches and, more importantly, student-athletes operate within a complex discursive world," as J. Michael Rifenberg (2012) points out, I did not anticipate the mostly positive comments they would make about reading. I suspect that their reading habits are wider and richer than many others would expect, too.

We stereotype high-profile athletes at our peril—and theirs. Rather than assuming the worst, faculty should ask, care about, and tap into student-athletes' reading interests, as the Agriculture professor did when he gave a lower performing student Parker Palmer's *Let Your Life Speak*. When reading assignments can be tailored to students' interests, we should allow it, knowing their level of engagement will be greater. Most of all, it's time to let go of the old stereotypes and see student athletes as the individual, diverse, richly literate people they are. We shouldn't assume that athletes don't, won't, and can't read. The MU 26 prove otherwise.

Update: Reflections, New Information, and A Look Ahead

Due to the study above having been officially closed, IRB regulations do not allow me to revisit any of the individuals I reported on. In this update to that work, I reflect on the status of high-profile football players in a larger institutional context, add information that was not included in the earlier article, and suggest steps WAC faculty can take to improve our ability to work with high-profile athletes' literacy skills.

In a wholly new development, one arguably related to literacy outcomes, I can report that the current team's players asserted their solidarity with other student groups confronting systemic racism and oppression on campus by threatening to cease "football related activities" including practice and playing an upcoming game (Morrison, 2015). Their groundbreaking action is worthy of more thorough exploration than this brief mention affords. Still, at the very least, the athletes' stance conveys a willingness to look beyond the narrow confines of their sport, to become involved in campus-wide issues of importance beyond the football field, despite risk and uncertain consequences. Many educators, myself included, would argue that these student-athletes put their collective student right of expression ahead of their athletic obligation, to address the institution's problematic history. In doing so, they demonstrated critical thinking, which led to critical action—key outcomes of literate behavior. I can also report that graduation rates for the team's players remain at a high level. Since the MU 26 cohort graduated, more than 90% of each year's seniors have graduated within their NCAA eligibility period. (Maggard, personal communication).

One literacy-related factor not described in the original article is the Athletic Department's Total Person Program (TPP), which provides comprehensive academic services for scholarship athletes. Certified by the College Reading and Learning Association's International Tutor Training Program, TPP maintains a focus on student literacy. For example, incoming athletes complete a 17-page "Learning Success Profile" encompassing six categories: educational history; health and wellness history; family and personal history; language and literacy; writing; and math.

Interestingly, the language and literacy section comprises 13 questions, compared to only seven in the writing section. The former begins by asking what language/s are spoken in the athlete's home and continues with questions about reading, while the latter begins by inquiring about athletes' difficulty organizing and expressing thoughts and ideas and concludes by asking the types of papers they've written. Additionally, athletes compose a narrative about their educational experiences (untimed, but completed in one sitting) describing the approaches they and their families, schools, teachers, and others have taken in creating "an effective learning environment," and they complete a "reading probe" modeled on one from another Division I institution.

The battery of TPP resources also includes an athletics-specific VARK (visual, aural/auditory, reading/writing, kinesthetic) Questionnaire, intended to help athletes understand their preferred learning style. The copyrighted *VARK Guide to Learning Styles* is free and downloadable from the internet. Finally, freshman players who attend the month-long Summer Bridge Program (two days a week) devote four-and-a-half hours over three days to writing a paper that is turned in to a concurrent credit-bearing class.

All of this information helps TPP staff determine whether further testing and what level of assistance is needed, along with what learning strategies to implement with each athlete. Notably, many of the same or similar resources are available to the university's general student population, through a variety of services overseen by the office of the vice provost for undergraduate studies.

Although TPP's resources are based to some degree on a "deficiency model," they reflect, as Odom puts it in her chapter, "the social, disciplinary, and technological forces that shape today's texts and our students' lives." Moreover, they highlight the degree to which Division I athletics operates as a literacy sponsor (Brandt, 1994). The MU 26 indicated throughout their interviews with me that they don't object to hard work. Working hard, after all, is central to their athletic ethos, and they amply demonstrated their ability to transfer that ethic to the classroom. This behavior corresponds closely to their sport-fed tendency to seek improvement week by week. But as Abbott and Nantz point out in this book (and with which the MU 26 would agree), transparency in explaining why the reading is important and showing how it will help students achieve course goals is needed.

Beyond letting go of old stereotypes and seeing student athletes as individual, diverse, and richly literate people . . . beyond assuming that athletes don't, won't, and can't read . . . we WAC practitioners should delve more deeply into the excellent literacy research happening just across the corridor, by our colleagues in education. (I am indebted to Dr. Jonathan Cisco, Assistant Director of Missouri's Campus Writing Program, for introducing me to this body of work.) Some WAC practitioners, Horning among them, invoke the work of such scholars as Shanahan and Shanahan (2008), Moje, Stockdill, Kim, and Kim (2011), and others, whose work in disciplinary literacy could be useful to WAC. But most of us know too little about this parallel work on reading and writing being done by researchers in fields adjacent to, but removed from, our immediate sphere. Neglected, perhaps, because this work is more aligned with teacher education, Moje et al. (2011) point out that for 30 years now "developments in sociocultural theories of literate practice have turned many reading researchers from viewing text as the driver of literacy processes and practices toward understanding who readers are and how contexts mediate text comprehension and production" (p. 453).

Current reading research is focused on disciplinary literacy, say Shanahan and Shanahan (2008), noting that "advanced literacy instruction [is] embedded within content-area classes such as math, science, and social studies" (p. 40). In addition to familiarizing ourselves with the sizable body of research on disciplinary literacy, another underutilized source (again, perhaps because it comes out of Education) is "Writing to Read: Evidence for How Writing Can Improve Reading" (Graham & Hebert, 2010).

There are other steps we can take, as well. I wish I'd asked the MU 26 cohort and their professors more about reading than I did; they would have gladly answered more questions on this subject—a subject I regrettably wasn't sufficiently attuned to at the time. We need to talk more about our students' reading, research more, and present more, at the C's and at WPA conferences than we do. Even in these tight budgetary times, we should be seeking out conferences beyond our comfort zones, where conversations ensue that deal with reading in ways we traditionally haven't. We should design our first-year composition curricula to incorporate a stronger focus on reading than many of us traditionally have done. Last, we might draw inspiration from our colleagues in Education: just as their teacher preparation curricula require every student to take a course titled "Reading and Writing in the Content Areas," so, too, our graduate Composition Studies curricula, whether WAC-focused or not, could include our version of the same.

If the list seems daunting, start small. Just pick one—or find your own reading project, as I did in my first-year composition course last year (Townsend). Perhaps you'll get hooked, like the self-described "not-a-big-reader" MU 26 athlete who nonetheless read Dan Brown's *Da Vinci Code* and *Angels and Demons* back to back "quickly" and then "couldn't wait" for the latter to come out on film. Doing so might just lead you into a research project, and on to a conference presentation, and then to a publication, any one of which could help your students and our field.

Acknowledgments

I am grateful to University of Missouri Athletic Director Mike Alden for endorsing the *Literate Lives* project and to Associate Athletic Directors Brian Maggard and Joe Scogin for serving as Co-Principal Investigators. I thank Cynthia Selfe for suggesting both the larger study and its title *The Literate Lives of Athletes*. Most of all, I am grateful to the athletes for taking time to talk with me during a busy time in their already time-constricted lives.

References

ACT, Inc. (2006). *Reading between the lines: What the ACT reveals about college readiness in reading.* Retrieved from http://www.act.org/research/policymakers/pdf/reading_sum mary.pdf.

ACT, Inc. (2011). *College readiness standards.* Retrieved from http://www.act.org/standard /pdf/CRS.pdf.

ACT, Inc. (2013a). *The ACT test.* Retrieved from http://www.act.org/newsroom/factsheets /view.php?p=160.

ACT, Inc. (2013b). *Using your ACT results.* Retrieved from http://media.actstudent.org /documents/uyar.pdf.

ACT, Inc. (2013c). *What are the ACT college readiness benchmarks.* Retrieved from http://www.act.org/research/policymakers/pdf/benchmarks.pdf.

ACT, Inc. (2013d). *What we do.* Retrieved from http://act.org/about-us/what-we-do/.

Andrews, K. M. & Ziomek, R. L. (1998). Score gains on retesting with the ACT assessment. *ACT Research Report Series 98-7.* Iowa City: ACT, Inc.

Braden, J. (2009, March 19). Reading a mystery for one class. *The Columbia Daily Tribune.* Retrieved from http://www.columbiatribune.com/news/education/reading-a -mystery-for-one-class/article_a88868a3-f95d-5045-92ca-d675488373fe.html.

Domzalski, S. M. (2012). *Crash course for the ACT* (4th ed.). New York: Princeton Review.

Downtown, J. (2000, January 6). The James Brooks illiteracy scandal. *Black Issues in Higher Education.* Retrieved from http://diverseeducation.com/article/432/.

Ehrenhaft, G., Lehrman, R. L., Mundsack, A. & Obrecht, F. (2001). *Barron's how to prepare for the ACT: American College testing assessment* (12th ed.). Hauppauge, NY: Barron's Educational Series.

Glau, G. R. (1996). The "stretch program": Arizona State University's new model of university-level basic writing instruction. *Writing Program Administration 20*(1–2), 79–91.

Graham, S. & Hebert, M. (2010). "Writing to read: Evidence for how writing can improve reading / A report from Carnegie Corporation of New York." Nashville: Vanderbilt University.

Guba, E. & Lincoln, Y. (1989). *Fourth generation evaluation.* Newbury Park, CA: Sage.

Horning, A. S. (2013). Elephants, pornography and safe sex: Understanding and addressing students' reading problems across the curriculum. *Across the Disciplines, 10*(4). Retrieved from https://wac.colostate.edu/atd/reading/intro.cfm.

Jolliffe, D. J. & Harl, A. (2008). Studying the "reading transition" from high school to college: What are our students reading and why? *College English 70*(6), 599–617.

Juel, C. (1991). Cross-age tutoring between student athletes and at-risk children. *The Reading Teacher 45*(3), 178–186.

Martin, C. (2011, July 9). MU class on Harry a big hit. *Columbia Daily Tribune* (p. 14a).

Moje, E. B., Stockdill, D., Kim, K. & Kim, H. (2011). The role of text in disciplinary learning. In M. L. Kamil, P. D. Pearson, E. B. Moje & P. P. Afflerbach (Eds.), *Handbook of reading research* (Vol. IV, pp. 453–486). Mahwah, NJ: Erlbaum/Taylor & Francis.

Morrison, D. (2015, 8 November). MU football players threaten boycott. *Columbia Daily Tribune, p.* 1a.

National Collegiate Athletic Association. (2010). *1981–82 – 2008–09 NCAA sports sponsorship and participation rates report.* Retrieved from http://www.ncaapublications. com/productdownloads/PR2010.pdf.

National Collegiate Athletic Association Research Staff. (2013, October). *Trends in graduation-success rates and federal graduation rates at NCAA Division I institutions.* Retrieved from http://www.ncaa.org/wps/wcm/connect/public/ncaa/academics /division+i/graduation.

Nyad, D. (1989, May 28). Views of sport: How illiteracy makes athletes run. *New York Times.* Retrieved from http://www.nytimes.com/1989/05/28/sports/views-of-sport -how-illiteracy-makes-athletes-run.html.

Pascarella, E. T., Truckenmiller, R., Nora, A., Terenzini, P. T., Edison, M. & Hagedorn, L. S. (1999). Cognitive impacts of intercollegiate athletic participation: Some further evidence. *The Journal of Higher Education 70*(1), 1–26.

Potuto, J. R. & O'Hanlon, J. (2007). National study of student-athletes regarding their experiences as college students. *College Student Journal 41*(4), 947–966.

Rifenburg, J. M. (2012). Fleshing out the uniqueness of student-athlete writing centers: A response to Alanna Bitzel. *Praxis: A Writing Center Journal, 10*(1). Retrieved from http://praxis.uwc.utexas.edu/index.php/praxis/article/view/78/html.

Robbins, S. B., Lauver, K., Le, H., Davis, D., Langley, R. & Carlstrom, A. (2004). Do psychological and study skill factors predict college outcomes? A meta-analysis. *Psychological Bulletin, 130*(2), 261–288. http://dx.doi.org/10.1037/0033-2909.130.2.261.

Ross, K. (1983, February 21). Late in the game, a college athlete learns to read. *People Weekly, 19*(7), 4–5.

Salvatori, M. R. & Donahue, P. (2012). Stories about reading: Appearance, disappearance, morphing, and revival. *College English, 75(2)*, 199–217.

Shanahan, T. & C. Shanahan. (2008). Teaching disciplinary literacy to adolescents: Rethinking content-area literacy. *Harvard Educational Review, 78*(1), 40–59.

Simons, H. D. & Van Rheenen, D. (2000). Noncognitive predictors of student athletes' academic performance. *Journal of College Reading and Learning, 30*(2), 167–182.

Smagorinsky, P. (2009). The cultural practice of reading and the standardized assessment of reading instruction: When incommensurate worlds collide. *Educational Researcher, 38*(7), 522–527.

Stake, R. E. (1994). Case studies. In N. K. Denzin & Y. S. Lincoln (Eds.), *Handbook of qualitative research* (pp. 236–246). Thousand Oaks, CA: Sage.

Townsend, M. A. (2017). A framework-based "no-text/two-text" honors composition course. In N. Behm, S. Rankins-Robertson & D. Roen. (Eds.), *Applications for the Framework for Success in Postsecondary Writing: Scholarship, theories, and practice.* Anderson, SC: Parlor Press.

Whitner, P. A. & Myers, R. C. (1986). Academics and an athlete: A case study. *The Journal of Higher Education, 57*(6), 659–672.

Wolverton, B. (2012, June 7) The education of Dasmine Cathey. *The Chronicle of Higher Education.* Retrieved from http://chronicle.com/article/The-Education-of-Dasmine /132065/.

Reading about Reading: Addressing the Challenges of College Readers through an Understanding of the Politics of P-12 Literacy

Justin Young
EASTERN WASHINGTON UNIVERSITY

Charlie Potter
SPOKANE COMMUNITY COLLEGE

This chapter reviews and analyzes current and competing trends in P-12 literacy research and assessment in comparison to efforts to develop and establish reading instruction at the college level. The authors argue that the current push towards "evidence-based" practices in P-12 education privileges instructional methods that produce measurable, short-term gains in student achievement but conflict with efforts to improve students' college readiness in reading at both the P-12 and college levels. Specifically, this trend contradicts the student-centered approach that will be needed at the P-12 level to enable students to do the complex reading activities required by the "career and college ready" standards of the Common Core. Further, the chapter explores ways that the drive towards producing measurable student improvement via methods such as direct instruction conflicts sharply with concepts of critical literacy that are essential to college reading. The chapter will provide instructional strategies, including metacognitive approaches (i.e., "reading about reading"), for helping students move from a literacy environment focused on short-term gains to a college environment that demands deep understanding and conversation with texts across the disciplines.

Recent efforts to prepare students for college, such as the Common Core State Standards (CCSS), promote the reading of complex texts as essential to success in the college classroom and beyond. Much of the literature surrounding the CCSS suggests that student engagement with the learning process is a crucial step in building college readiness (Conley, 2011). However, this kind of constructivist pedagogical approach has a very complicated relationship to debates in P-12 education over effective reading instruction and the nationwide push towards evidence-based teaching practices. Specifically, the current debate over "balanced literacy" reveals the sharply conflicting epistemological, pedagogical, and ideological perspectives simultaneously at play in the current effort to improve student literacy at the P-12 level, all in the name of increased college and career readiness. The politics of literacy instruction in P-12 classrooms is divisive, and the embattled discussions about P-12 literacy long precede current efforts like the CCSS.

Higher education faculty and administrators seeking to improve student literacy via reading instruction at the college level must proceed with a clear understanding of the wide range of P-12 pedagogical approaches to literacy. Additionally, an analysis of the pedagogical methods employed to achieve P-12 reading outcomes reveals several interesting conflicts with current and prospective approaches to reading and writing instruction for college students. Moreover, an exploration of P-12 literacy pedagogy and theory helps to explain phenomena like patch writing and "tool users," noted by reading and writing scholars like Sandra Jamieson (2013) and Steven Pearlman (2013). By connecting the findings of these researchers with the practices and politics of P-12 literacy instruction, higher education faculty and administrators can more successfully understand, assess, and improve the reading skills of college students at all levels.

Our definition of college reading contradicts approaches that treat literacy as an autonomous, repeatable process that can be detached from context and taught formulaically in order to produce quantifiable results via standard assessments. College reading, as we define it, draws on a long tradition of constructivist pedagogy in literacy and in rhetoric that insists upon the crucial role of the historically situated individual reader, whose unique process of reading can only be examined and understood in relation to shifting cultures, ideological systems, and discourses. Such a definition of college reading draws on theories that insist upon the connection between literacy, reading, and the social, cultural, and discursive nature of knowledge and power (Berlin, 2003; Lea & Street, 2006; Horning, 2012; Pearlman, 2013). College reading, in our definition, is a highly situated process in which students engage deeply with a given text, make connections between text and personal experience, values, other texts—both academic and non-academic—and scholarly, cultural, historical, and ideological contexts of the topic and/or text being explored.

This chapter adds to current scholarship on college-level reading by situating the topic within past and current debates over literacy research, policy, and practice *across* the P-16 continuum. Just as we will argue that college reading must be taught as a culturally and politically situated act, we believe that college reading must be defined in relation to the key contexts that surround it. It is essential that both secondary and post-secondary instructors have an understanding of the ideological and pedagogical contexts that shape reading instruction at each level. High school instructors must have a sense of the assumptions and expectations that college instructors bring to the teaching of reading and writing. Likewise, college instructors must know much more about how the politics of the "reading wars," both past and present, (along with broader shifts in education policy) shape reading and literacy instruction at the P-12 level. To this end, the chapter will explore additional descriptions and definitions of college reading in order to provide context for our own definition. It will then explore the ways that successful college reading (and college reading instruction), as defined above, may be thwarted by current pedagogical and political movements that value and/or promote autonomous and proscriptive approaches to reading instruction. Finally, we provide potential solutions for college-level instructors looking to improve college reading instruction, offering an example of how "balanced literacy," a research-based approach to reading instruction used at the P-12 level, can be implemented at the college level.

Defining College-level Reading Across the Disciplines

Despite current efforts to conduct research on college-level reading, in comparison to the massive amount of literature and theory around developmental psychology and reading in the P-12 environment, relatively few studies and theories have been developed or applied in post-secondary learning. In order to establish our own definition of college reading we will next examine three studies from the Special issue of *Across the Disciplines* on Reading and Writing Across the Disciplines (2013) we believe point to key, specific difficulties faced by college-level readers.

Research college reading indicates that college students, in the effort to produced research-based texts, often fail to adequately comprehend or effectively apply what they have read in academic texts (Jamieson, 2013). Jamieson finds that students do not often cite information from throughout texts they read, instead focusing on brief passages and at times basing entire arguments upon one or two (often misinterpreted) sentences, more often than not found in the first several pages of the cited text. She also observes that students use a strategy Rebecca Moore Howard (1992), the other lead collaborator to their shared "Citation Project," calls "patch writing," whereby students "'borrowed' phrases, patched together into 'new' sentences; they 'borrowed' whole sentences, deleting what they consider irrelevant words and phrases; and they 'borrowed' a hodgepodge of phrases and sentences in which they changed grammar and syntax, and substituted synonyms straight from Roget's" (p. 235).

Unlike Jamieson, Pearlman (2013) explicitly develops an argument about college writing from an understanding of adolescent literacy, pointing to a possible explanation for the widespread use of a patch-writing strategy. He explores the difference between literacy and reading, noting that students turn to patch writing because they cannot contextualize what they are reading within the overwhelming volume of related academic literature. His work points to the need to understand literacy across the P-16 continuum, a notion that is essential to our definition of college reading.

Lynne Rhodes (2013) also observes that much of the struggle for college-level readers involves reading comprehension and lack of disciplinary understanding. Like Pearlman, Rhodes connects the struggles of college reading with P-12 practices, suggesting that elementary and secondary teachers, due in part to the Common Core, teach close reading, meta-analysis, and synthesis but often focus on very simple or creative texts. These strategies, in other words, are not applied to complex texts and do not consider context as a key element of reading. Rhodes also suggests that higher education might benefit from more standardized reading instruction.

Taken together, the articles by Perlman (2013), Rhodes (2013), and Jamieson (2013) suggest that the ability to contextualize, critically engage, and authentically apply what is read are all essential elements of college reading. All three articles point to an understanding of college reading as a contextualized act that requires critical abilities and academic discourse knowledge that beginning college students often lack. The articles also highlight some common areas where more research and understanding are needed in order to improve college reading instruction. Although Pearlman engages with developmental psychology and adolescent literacy, he does not offer ways to connect what is learned in P-12 environments with what is learned in the college environment; instead, he offers an intelligent strategy for engaging students in disciplinary understanding. What is missing, however, is potentially the most crucial piece for student success in college reading: how do college-level faculty build from literacy practices of the P-12 environment in order to ensure that students do not experience gaps in understanding, content, and skill? Like Pearlman and Rhodes, Jamieson observes that success as a college-level reader relies on disciplinary comprehension and cautions that pedagogies must be differentiated for varying levels of skill. Given Rhodes' observations about the need to standardize instruction and expectations, how can college-level instructors best understand and differentiate for student ability without compromising these common outcomes?

The Relationship between P-12 Literacy Practices and College-Level Literacy Practices

One answer to the questions about college reading raised by the above analysis of Jamieson (2013), Perlman (2013), and Rhodes (2013) lies in an understanding of the relationship between P-12 practices and college practices. Without conversation around reading curriculum and outcomes at each level, neither level will adequately achieve goals for reading instruction. Little cross-institution and cross-level conversation occurs between P-12 and college environments, and this lack of communication contributes to a lack of understanding about what and how students are taught. In fact, many of the important details can be community-specific and therefore difficult to determine based on simply reading the Common Core requirements, for example. Further complicating matters is the reality that the political environments of P-12 and college environments are very different, especially when it comes to literacy. Differences in the political, regulatory, and material environments of P-12 and college have led to differing values and instructional practices in literacy education, and even different definitions of reading itself. At the core of these differences is a mismatch between a legislative, policy-driven focus on short-term outcomes on the P-12 level and the kind of deep, critical reading abilities valued at the college level, which must be taught, learned, and assessed over the long term.

In many cases, college instructors teaching reading operate with much greater individual autonomy in comparison with their P-12 counterparts. While an individual college faculty member may be held accountable primarily by a program director or department chair, a high school teacher is held accountable by a federal system of regulations and policies that legitimize pedagogical practices according to a very narrow definition of knowledge—often, practices are validated and funded based only on the "scientific" evidence provided in their support (U.S. Dept. of Education, 2014, para. 2 & 3). Likewise, while college instructors must focus on and are evaluated on the performance of their own students in relation to the university and college as a whole, high school instructors operate within huge state and national systems that seek to measure and compare the performance of students and teachers across the entire country.

The scale of the system in which high school teachers operate is immense in comparison to the environment in which college instructors operate. In a federal education system that involves millions of students and billions of dollars, it should not be a surprise that legislators and education agencies fund only those practices that produce the quickest, most visible learning outcomes. In contrast, college professors have the autonomy to focus on developing students' ability to do the kind of deep, critical thinking that takes time to teach, learn, and assess. In the case of reading, this means that there is often a mismatch between the kind of direct instruction sometimes used to teach reading in P-12 and the kind of reading skills students need to succeed at the college level. Direct instruction can quickly produce measurable improvements in student reading ability (particularly for those reading below grade level). This approach alone, however, is not compatible with the need to teach students to read and analyze deeply, make connections, and synthesize effectively.

The newest of the P-12 reading wars—between the proponents of a particular version of close reading versus those who advocate a brand of balanced literacy—is a related, more specific version of the general mismatch between approaches to reading instruction at the P-12 and college levels; this discussion is particularly pertinent to the transition from high school to college and the issue of college readiness.

Reviewing the Politics and Practices of P-12 Literacy Education

In addition to the general observations offered in the previous section, a summary of P-12 literacy theory and practice is helpful for understanding the context for our exploration of the relationship between P-12 reading instruction and our definition of college reading. The conversations around literacy in the P-12 environment are regularly described as "wars" or "battles," with teachers, school districts, and faculty often endorsing one theory or practice at the expense of others. Debates about scientifically proven practices, direct instruction and phonics, whole language instruction, and balanced literacy all contribute to the political climate in P-12 literacy education. This context is important for instructors of college-level reading and writing as well as reading across the disciplines; depending on the type of practice endorsed in a school district, by a particular administrator, and/or in a specific classroom, a student entering college might have been taught using a dramatically different reading pedagogy.

Approaches to Literacy Instruction in P-12 Environments

Common pedagogical practices in P-12 literacy instruction include phonics, direct instruction, whole language, constructivism, and balanced literacy. Each strategy is contentious. None has emerged as the preeminent best practice in instruction, and the strategies are not always mutually exclusive. Conversations around these strategies, as well as their scientific value, are what comprise the conflict described as the "reading wars." Exhaustive bibliographies have been assembled on each of these methods.[1] For this reason, we will provide only a basic overview of the practices and arguments in this chapter.

Direct instruction is a pedagogical practice that involves explicit demonstration and practice of skills in a learning environment. Typically, direct instruction practices are counter to constructivist or discovery models of learning. The What Works Clearinghouse (2007) describes direct instruction practices as "teaching techniques that are fast-paced, teacher-directed, and explicit with opportunities for student response and teacher reinforcement or correction" (p. 1). In the case of literacy, the teaching of phonics is often synonymous with direct instruction practices. National Institution for Direct Instruction (NIFDI, 2015), which publishes the Reading Mastery direct instruction program, outlines several key tenets of direct instruction, which include:

---

1   *Approaches and Methods in Language Teaching* by Jack Richards and Theodore Rodgers (2014) offers a comprehensive overview of whole language and its relationship to phonics, and the *Handbook of Research on Reading Comprehension* (2009) by Susan Israel and Gerald Duffy explores each method thoroughly. A broad look at issues and trends in reading instruction today can be found in *What Research Has to Say about Reading Instruction* by S. Jay Samuels and Alan Farstrup (2011).

- Low performers and disadvantaged learners must be taught at a faster rate than typically occurs if they are to catch up to their higher-performing peers.
- All details of instruction must be controlled to minimize the chance of students' misinterpreting the information being taught and to maximize the reinforcing effect of instruction (para. 2).

These two tenets cause constructivists and whole language proponents to take issue, some going as far as calling direct instruction "factory learning" (Wheatley, 2015a). Unlike direct instruction, whole language approaches to learning reject the notion that knowledge can be packaged and delivered to students. In fact, some whole language researchers reject the notion of "instruction" altogether, suggesting that education is instead authentically "learner-initiated but teacher-supported" (Wheatley, 2015b, p. 37). As Richards and Rogers (2014) note, whole language is sometimes called a philosophy or belief rather than a method.

It is important to note that those who favor whole language do not necessarily think direct instruction or phonics instruction are "bad." From the point of view of proponents of whole language or constructivism, direct instruction can be used effectively in specific classroom contexts, and phonics instruction is understood to be an essential component of the process of learning to read. However, whole language suggests that humans learn language as a "meaning-making" system, emerging out of the language acquisition research of Noam Chomsky (2006), and context, semantics, syntax, and meaning are as crucial to language learning as are phonics.

Whole language is one example of a constructivist strategy for literacy instruction. Generally, constructivist methods for teaching reading, according to Brian Cambourne (2002), follow five principles. First, classroom culture should allow for demonstrations of strong or effective reading behavior. Additionally, attempts to teach are explicit, systematic, mindful, and contextualized. Cambourne also suggests that learning is related to "continuous intellectual unrest" (p. 30). Reflection and metatextual understanding of reading processes must be developed. Finally, assignments and assessments should be authentic. Here, Cambourne refers specifically to P-12 practices; as we will suggest, many of these practices can be extrapolated for the college-level reading environment. Constructivist strategies focus heavily on the role of context and self-reflection in comprehension (Kamii et al., 1991; Wilkinson & Silliman, 2000). This type of pedagogy is most closely aligned with common practices in composition and rhetoric (Young & Potter, 2013).

Foundational research in the field of literacy suggests that a balanced approach, which brings together elements from direct instruction/phonics and constructivism/whole language, is necessary (National Reading Panel, 2000).[2] Overall,

---

2   Beginning in 2000, the National Reading Panel Report, *Teaching Children to Read*, sought to end the so-called reading wars by promoting a balanced literacy approach (Kim, 2008). The report

however, current research suggests that specific instructional approaches consistent with whole language and constructive pedagogy have the support of more experts. "A Focus on Struggling Readers: A Comparative Analysis of Expert Opinions and Empirical Research Recommendations" (Jones, Reutzel & Smith, 2011) attempts to compare expert consensus on effective and ineffective practices to recommendations derived from empirical research studies on reading instruction. The study examines and compares strategies advocated by the proponents of constructivism with strategies advocated by those in favor of direct instruction. Modeling and scaffolding, approaches consistent with a constructivist approach, are clear winners in this study, as are integrated approaches to literacy that incorporate speaking, writing, and reading. This study also emphasizes the importance of student engagement. Further, Jones, et al. delineated as "ineffective" strategies like "Isolated Instruction," "Skill Drill and Mastery," and "Exclusive Teacher Control" (Jones et al., 2012, pp. 278–279). This classification suggests the importance of contextualization and student-centered instruction in teaching reading. Although not at the complete exclusion of approaches that are more direct, we argue that whole language and constructivist approaches offer a level of contextualization and engagement that best prepares students for the work they will do in the college environment.

Research-Based Practices: The Demand for Scientific Education Solutions

While much of the political furor over the Common Core State Standards and the continued push back towards No Child Left Behind (NCLB) has focused on testing-related issues, another major shift in U.S. education policy and practice has occurred with less outcry or concern. This shift is important, as it is currently leading to the devaluation, at the P-12 level, of the kind of reading instruction that is consistent with approaches advocated by researchers at the college level. No Child Left Behind mandates funding and support of demonstrably "scientific" educational practices (U.S. Dept. of Education, 2014, para. 2 & 3). Classroom activities must be "scientifically based" or "research-based," supported by multiple comparison group studies and cost-benefit analyses (U.S. Dept. of Education, 2014, para. 2 & 3). Such requirements can delegitimize qualitative forms of research, while forms of research that can most explicitly— quantitatively— demonstrate the benefit of an educational practice are privileged. On the federal and state level, an educational practice or approach will not be supported (i.e., with funding) unless that practice

---

indicated that students must be provided instruction in their early years that addresses phonemic awareness, phonics, fluency, vocabulary development, and comprehension. These approaches are widely accepted in P-12 education as foundational to effectively teaching children to read.

or approach has been shown to produce demonstrable outcomes in student learning. Student learning growth is quantitatively measured via testing and value-added modeling; meta-analyses of research studies focused on particular classroom practices are then produced, showing the effect size of a given practice on overall student learning growth. Such analyses are often combined with cost/benefit analyses to show the overall practical benefit to the state of the implementation (expressed in tax revenue and/or increased earnings) of a particular practice.

The drive towards scientifically proven instruction is illustrated by Hattie's book *Visible Learning* (2012), a meta-analysis of thousands of meta-analyses of instructional practices. Hattie seeks to evaluate and rank according to effect-size (that is, impact on student learning) all forms of P-12 instruction. The book compiles and analyzes meta-analyses in order to determine and compare the impact on student learning of everything from tutoring to extended learning to professional development. The book endeavors to promote only those instructional practices that promote visible learning, while exposing common practices that show little scientific evidence of effectiveness.[3]

Unsurprisingly, the scientific approaches to reading instruction that are validated and promoted within this paradigm are those that readily produce short-term, easily measured results. For example, in a particularly telling comparison, the method of direct instruction is one of the most highly ranked practices covered by Hattie. It is shown to produce more significant impacts on student learning than many of the hundreds of practices analyzed in the book (Hattie, 2012, pp. 205–206), and many pages of the book are devoted to this practice.[4] Constructivism, in contrast to direct instruction, does not fare well in Hattie's book. The entire educational paradigm of constructivism is given little coverage, and it is poorly—even misleadingly—defined as a paradigm of pedagogy that involves "minimal guidance" and contrasts teachers who deploy the "current fad" of constructivism as less effective "facilitators" with the more effective teachers who are "activators"

---

3   In the case of reading/literacy instruction, this approach is illustrated by the large-scale studies funded by the U.S. Department of Education and distributed through the aforementioned What Works Clearinghouse site. The Clearinghouse website compiles reports on specific approaches to literacy instruction such as instruction on phonics, vocabulary, or comprehension and ranks them according to their scientifically proven impact on student learning. The site provides reviews of particular practices but often focuses on proprietary reading "programs."

4   As discussed earlier in the chapter, direct instruction is a form of behaviorism that can sometimes involve rote activities like call and response, memorization, and recitation in unison. It's important to note that research does suggest that direct instruction can have positive impacts on student learning, and that, from a constructivist viewpoint, it is a strategy that can be deployed effectively within the context of a classroom that involves a range of different strategies designed to meet the diverse needs of different students. It is not, however, generally the kind of instruction endorsed by college composition teachers, and, when deployed on its own, it is not a form of teaching that enables critical thinking.

(Hattie, 2012, pp. 243–244). Constructivism, as a whole, is thereby abruptly dismissed as having little impact on student learning. This should be a problem for those conducting research on reading instruction at the college level: the instructional approaches advocated by scholars such as Horning (2007), Pearlman (2103), and Jamieson (2013) are, broadly construed, constructivist. Further, the kind of critical academic literacy valued by college reading researchers and instructors is less likely to be taught at the P-12 level if direct instruction is privileged as a scientific teaching method over student-centered, constructivist approaches.

While the reasons for constructivism's dismissal in *Visible Learning* (2012) are arguably arbitrary and certainly ideological, they are by no means definitive. Direct instruction is celebrated, and constructivism dismissed, on the basis of Hattie's algorithm for what constitutes a scientifically proven practice. However, other summaries of the scientific value of a practice like direct instruction might be found, conversely, to be negative, as is the case with the review of direct instruction by the What Works Clearinghouse (2007). These conflicts contribute to the overall climate in literacy education: what, exactly, *is* a scientifically proven practice?

Balanced Literacy, the Common Core, and Ideology: What Does It Mean for College Reading?

The future of P-12 reading instruction and college reading preparedness may hinge on whatever side prevails in what might be the 21st century version of the reading wars, which can be represented as a battle between Lucy Calkins and David Coleman. Both figures are high-profile public proponents of the Common Core but advocate for and represent differing approaches to reading instruction. Calkins is perhaps the leading public educator touting a balanced literacy approach as a means to enable students to meet the Common Core State Standards for English Language Arts (ELA). She argues that the Common Core must be "protected from the documents surrounding it, that are people's interpretations of it" (Wall, 2014). Calkins is referring to the curricular materials developed by David Coleman, the chief architect of the Common Core, and his foundation Student Achievement Partners, which produced curricular models designed to illustrate the central principles of the Common Core and effective approaches to instruction aligned with those principles. On one side of this debate over policy and practice in literacy education and the teaching of reading is Calkins, who argued in a January 2014 speech that the materials designed by Coleman and his foundation "violate principles valued by 'experienced educators'" (Wall, 2014, para. 31). On the other side of the debate are Coleman and Susan Pimentel, two of the key founders of the Common Core.

Representative of this debate is the controversy over a model reading lesson focused on the Gettysburg Address, designed by David Coleman himself (Student

Achievement Partners, 2013). In Calkins speech she proclaims that the lesson "basically represents horrible teaching." Calkins criticized the emphasis on completely decontextualized close reading, which forced students to "'rely exclusively on the text'" (Wall, 2014, para. 31). Calkins takes issue with the lack of student choice, student voice, and contextualization reflected in Student Achievement Partner's curricular models, typified by this lesson. The analysis of a New York City public high school teacher of this exemplar for instruction adds additional depth to Calkins' critique:

> [The lesson] gives students a text they have never seen and asks
> them to read it with no preliminary introduction. This mimics
> the conditions of a standardized test on which students are asked
> to read material they have never seen and answer multiple-choice
> questions about the passage. Such pedagogy makes school wildly
> boring. Students are not asked to connect what they read yester-
> day to what they are reading today, or what they read in English
> to what they read in science (Jeremiah Chaffee, qtd. in Strauss,
> 2013).

Key to the balanced literacy approach promoted by Calkins is the principle that students acquire the ability to read most effectively if they are encouraged to engage with what they are reading. This engagement, which resembles what we describe as college reading, is promoted by giving students some manner of choice in what they read, and the opportunity to respond in personal ways to what they have read. The balanced literacy approach holds that, in order to learn to comprehend, internalize, and synthesize what is being read, reading material must be contextualized; students must be provided the tools and knowledge to make connections between what they are reading and the various contexts that surround that reading.

In contrast to this approach, the "Gettysburg" model lesson plan begins, "The idea here is to plunge students into an independent encounter with this short text. Refrain from giving background context or substantial instructional guidance at the outset" (Student Achievement Partners, 2013, p. 3). This exemplar for instruction runs counter to all of the pedagogical principles just described, as it focuses on the reading and analysis of an *explicitly* decontextualized text. While the lesson eventually does allow for (minimal) discussion of context around the text, such an approach runs directly counter to what would best prepare students for college reading, at least according to current research on the skills students need to be successful college readers. If the focus of this lesson is on prepping high school students for college-level reading, why emphasize decontextualized reading, given the choice?

While those behind the development of the Common Core are obviously committed to the task of producing college-ready students, the curricular approaches they advocate for reading have more in common with the principles, purposes, and limitations of direct instruction than the kind of critical reading and associated pedagogies advocated by scholars engaging with the issue of college reading. The approach to close reading articulated by Coleman and the Student Achievement Partners focuses on the careful analysis of text to the exclusion of anything that might surround that text: historical or cultural context, the purpose or goals of the text, and reader's own personal experience or perspective. Such an approach to reading instruction, like direct instruction, may produce more effective test takers in the short term. Jeremiah Chafee, the teacher quoted above (in Strauss, 2013) suggests that this kind of reading activity is similar to the conditions of standardized tests themselves: students are asked to read and answer questions about decontextualized passages of text, which are given to students without any introduction. While students may be taught under this close reading model to carefully parse individual pieces of text, they are not taught many of the other skills needed for success in the kind of reading valued at the college level.

The elements of reading instruction absent from both general direct instruction methods and from this specific close reading method are essential parts of the definition of college reading. These missing elements provide insight into the specific weaknesses of beginning college readers (and writers). Students must be able to read individual complex texts deeply and critically; additionally, they must be able to synthesize what they are reading by making connections among a given text, other related texts, historical and cultural contexts, and their own experience and perspective. In this way, reading is essential to participation in any academic discourse community, wherein reading and writing are done in order to engage in scholarly conversations. Students who are taught to read via the kind of functionalist, decontextualized pedagogies of direct instruction and close reading described above will struggle when confronted with college reading tasks. Such students are also likely to struggle when confronted with reading tasks outside of the educational environment.

It is unsurprising, then, that students enter college unable to complete many reading and writing assignments. As Pearlman (2013) suggests, students recognize that they cannot meaningfully engage in the college-level reading necessary to complete researched writing. They therefore resort to using strategies like patch writing in order to complete assignments. Such students may lack practice in engaging with, and making connections among a range of difficult and unfamiliar texts, as Rhodes (2013) suggests. Jamieson's (2013) observations and analysis of the weaknesses common in the reading and research writing behaviors of students correspond with the weaknesses and limitations of direct instruction/close reading pedagogies. Further, Jamieson's research indicates that students write entire arguments on the basis of decontextualized, often incorrectly interpreted sentences, rather than developing claims on the basis of entire texts, understood in relation to a range of other related texts. This suggests that such students do not have practice with finding ways to connect one text to others, or with strategies for independently developing an understanding of the various contexts that surround a given text.

These descriptions of the common weaknesses of underprepared college readers all point to another crucial missing element in the direct instruction/critical reading approaches used at the P-12 level: personal engagement. Pearlman (2013) and Jamieson (2013) both note, for example, that students resort to patch writing in part because they haven't been able to engage in a deep way with the texts they encounter in the course of completing a research project. In order to meet basic expectations, students use new concepts and terms only as tools to complete an assignment, rather than as building blocks toward greater understanding and skill. Jamieson's work aligns with this analysis, as it demonstrates that students conducting research projects skim for sentences that they believe are important and build entire arguments upon those sentences; she notes those sentences are, more often than not, taken from the first one or two pages of cited articles and chapters. These observations suggest a picture of students who are not personally invested in what they are learning and writing. This may not mean that such students don't care; this portrait of the college reader and writer suggests that such students have not developed the habit of making connections between what is being read in the classroom and what they might actually care about in their individual, personal lives outside of school.

Reading About Reading: Balanced Literacy at the College Level

Herein lies a key advantage that constructivist, whole language/ balanced literacy approaches have in preparing students to succeed across the college curriculum as readers and writers: all of these approaches hold as essential the role of student engagement as central to the learning process. Interestingly, the documents that make up the official text of the Common Core State Standards for English Language Arts are prefaced with what is termed a "portrait of students who meet the standards set out in this document" (National Governors Association, p. 7). This portrait describes a set of students that are "engaged and open-minded" and who "demonstrate independence," qualities that seem to be aligned with a constructivist, balanced literacy approach to the teaching and learning of reading (National Governors Association, p. 7). The question is: how will students be prepared at the P-12 level so that they match up with the CCSS "portrait" and enter college with the habits of mind that they need to succeed as readers and writers at the college level? As David Conley (2011) notes about the CCSS, "if implemented poorly . . . the standards and assessments could result in accountability on steroids, stifling meaningful school improvement nationwide" (p. 16). In order to truly meet the standards of the Common Core, Conley argues, educators must "move classroom teaching away from a focus on worksheets, drill-and-memorize activities" towards a pedagogy that promotes active student engagement, through the cultivation of key "cognitive strategies" and habits of mind (p. 16).

This kind of epistemological and pedagogical perspective is also reflected in the *Framework for Success in Postsecondary Writing*, a report jointly produced by the Council of Writing Program Administrators and the National Council of Teachers of English (2001). The report details the habits of mind that successful college writing students possess in relation to the rhetorical skills taught and valued at the college level. Four of the habits of mind listed by the report are particularly pertinent here:

- Curiosity—the desire to know more about the world.
- Openness—the willingness to consider new ways of being and thinking in the world.
- Engagement—a sense of investment and involvement in learning (p. 1).
- Metacognition—the ability to reflect on one's own thinking as well as on the individual and cultural processes used to structure knowledge.

Students who are taught primarily through a direct instruction and/or close reading model while in P-12 may not, when they get to college, have the habits of mind needed to connect to and explore a range of unfamiliar and difficult academic texts, particularly when working in a discipline that is not their major. According to constructivist pedagogy, learning can only truly occur via a process of internalization within the individual student; students must be taught to connect *and practice connecting* to whatever it is they are learning in school. Students also must learn to reflect meta-cognitively upon how they have learned and how they are currently learning in order to better take personal ownership of the learning process.

In order to achieve success in teaching college reading, college-level instructors must ask students to reflect on the ways they have been taught to engage with language. This kind of approach could be understood as *an extension of balanced literacy into the college classroom*. Such a pedagogy requires students themselves to understand the politics of literacy they experienced in the P-12 environment and to engage with the politics of literacy that inform their college experience. College students (and even high school students) must read about *how* they were taught, engage with their experiences in the classroom, identify the gaps in their learning, and plan for remediating those gaps. Reading about the politics of literacy, learning about direct instruction, whole language, and constructivism as well as the political structures that determine what content is taught and how it is delivered is an important step toward bridging student understanding of college-level expectations.

At the authors' institution, an example of a balanced literacy approach to college-level reading and writing instruction is currently implemented as a unit of the university's first-year writing program. The unit is focused on teaching students to read and respond in an exam setting to a range of academic and popular texts focused on the themes of literacy, education, and power. (The content of the unit originated in the University of Oklahoma Composition Program; while the original unit was primarily intended to teach the writing abilities needed to successfully complete a college-level essay exam, the unit has been revised with a central focus on reading skills.) This current curriculum establishes a balanced literacy approach to the teaching of reading and application of academic discourse at the college level. Classroom activities focus on applied strategies for reading, analyzing, retaining and applying complex academic material, along with a focus on engaging students' personal experiences with literacy and classroom learning.

This approach balances the need to teach the functional and critical reading (and writing) skills that are key to success in the college discourse community, with a focus on engaging students' individual personal experiences and encouraging the development of effective habits of mind. For example, activities require students, in preparation for an eventual exam, to annotate articles, find key words and define them. In the classroom, students are engaged in a discussion of key claims and concepts from assigned articles, and guided through an activity that requires the synthesis and application these keywords, claims, and concepts. In this way, students are taught the functional reading skills they will need in order to be successful at the college level. Additionally, these skills are taught within the context of a common college-level assignment—the essay exam; in this way, reading is taught as an applied skill essential to success across the college curriculum. On the other hand, to ensure that students are connecting what they learn to their own personal, diverse experiences, they are asked to read a variety of academic articles that explore literacy as a contested term, dependent upon the goals of those in power who seek to define it (e.g., C.H. Knoblauch's [1990] "Literacy and the Politics of Education," Robert Yagelski's [2000] "Abby's Lament," from his book, *Literacy Matters,* and Lynn Reid's [2015] "The Politics of Remediation"). The students also read about the contested cultures and processes of the institution of education itself (e.g. excerpts from Kozol's [2012] *Savage Inequalities)* as well as the role that language and literacy can play in creating individual identity (e.g., an excerpt of Gloria Anzaldúa's [1987] *Borderlands*).

An effort is made to connect these readings with student experiences. Some of the students at our institution can identify with Abby, the disaffected high school student who doesn't think that she or literacy itself matters much at all in a world where many young people feel powerless. Our institution has a significant population of Chicano migrant workers who may be able to identify with Anzaldúa's struggle to find herself in an American culture that defines literacy narrowly in terms of functionality and performance. All of the reading that students do in this unit, while it is mostly academic, is connected in one way or another, to the position and experience of the college student him/herself.

When college instructors ask students to have a meta-awareness of the types of literacy instruction being offered (and that students have experienced), those instructors will better be able to assess the types of pedagogies with which students are comfortable and familiar. Once both students and instructors understand this familiarity, they can begin to challenge it with new methods of learning. Students and faculty must both acknowledge the cognitive moves associated with a student moving from a classroom where direct instruction was the primary strategy for relating to texts to a classroom where critical academic literacy is expected.

Conclusion

The observation that P-12 and college-level faculty need to understand the practices, politics, assumptions, and outcomes of both P-12 and college environments is not a revolutionary one. In fact, this argument seems quite obvious: how can we ensure the success of students-as-students and students-as-citizens if we do not look at the big picture of how they are taught and what they are expected to learn? Nevertheless, communication between the two groups is not common or easy.

One way to address the issue of college readiness collaboratively (in terms of reading or otherwise) is through efforts to establish regional cross-sector professional learning communities that include representatives from the P-12, community college, and university levels. Examples of such initiatives are found in two current Washington State College Spark Grant programs. These efforts, the "Successful Transitions to College" project and the "The Bridge to College" project, seek to bring together educators across the P-16 continuum to collaboratively address the common challenges students face in making the transition from the high school to college level. The Successful Transitions to College initiative is focused on a specific region in the state, bringing together high school teachers from a number of districts, community college instructors, and college faculty together. The group first identifies and defines specific transition to college barriers. Then, the group designs and implements interventions that address those barriers to student success. Participants work in cross-sector teams to develop, class test, and assess these interventions, using the CCSS as a common framework for discussing, defining, and evaluating college readiness. This project provides an alternative to "top-down" and siloed systems of professional learning in education. Instead of the usual hierarchical and static model of professional development, which involves "experts," often from higher education, delivering knowledge to P-12 teachers, this professional learning community operates as an open network of engaged and supportive K-12 and higher education professionals working collaboratively across sectors and institutions towards the common goal of improving the college readiness of local students. The "Bridge to College" project operates on a similar, collaborative model, bringing together regional, cross-sector "communities of practice" to develop, implement, and assess a new statewide Grade 12 transition-to-college course designed to support students struggling to meet college readiness standards. The need for these kinds of cross-sector collaboration have become increasingly evident, given the scrutiny that issues like college readiness, success, and retention are receiving from education practitioners, policy-makers, and researchers. The existence of these initiatives, and the enthusiastic participation in them from across the K-16 continuum that we have witnessed, highlight the current disconnect between P-12 and higher education practices, and the desire of teachers, professors, and policy-makers to find innovative ways to bridge these divides.

However, groups of students are not homogenous; even with such professional learning efforts in place, individual instructors may be unprepared to recognize and teach according to the literacy background of every student. While a curious professor might be able to learn about literacy practices and reading wars or even collaborate directly with local P-12 educators, that professor will still not necessarily know whether particular students come from a background favoring direct instruction over whole language. When students become a part of this conversation and are asked to read about and understand the meta-processes shaping their relationship to learning, we are opening a new dimension in this conversation.

Most importantly, we argue that literacy instruction is an example of how the literacy "medium is the message." If students are taught methods that yield short-term outcomes like direct instruction, students learn to accommodate the direct instruction model. They do not know *how to learn* via other instructional methods without being introduced to them as such and asked to reflect upon the ways they were taught the things they know. If students are taught via direct instruction, they learn discrete literacy behaviors but not critical thinking and engagement. If they learn via whole language, the inverse may be true. In order to bridge the gap between P-12 and college reading expectations and abilities, each member of the academic conversation must understand that the modes of instruction differ greatly across environments. An understanding of those differences and their politics, both by student and instructor, is the first step in creating an effective system for college reading instruction.

References

Anzaldúa, G. (1987). *Borderlands: La frontera*. San Francisco: Aunt Lute.

Berlin, J. A. (2003). *Rhetorics, poetics, and cultures: Refiguring college English studies*. Andersen, SC: Parlor Press.

Cambourne, B. (2002). Holistic, integrated approaches to reading and language arts instruction: The constructivist framework of an instructional theory. In A. Farstrup

(Ed.), *What research has to say about reading instruction* (pp. 25–47). Newark: International Reading Association.

Chomsky, N. (2006). *Language and mind.* Cambridge: Cambridge University Press.

Conley, D. T. (2011). Building on the Common Core. *Educational Leadership, 68*(6), 16–20.

Council of Writing Program Administrators, National Council of Teachers of English, and National Writing Project. (2011). *Framework for Success in Postsecondary Writing.* Retrieved from http://wpacouncil.org/framework.

Hattie, J. (2012). *Visible learning for teachers: Maximizing impact on learning.* Oxford: Routledge.

Horning, A. (2007). Reading across the curriculum as the key to student success. *Across the Disciplines, 4.* Retrieved from https://wac.colostate.edu/atd/articles/horning2007.cfm.

Horning, A. (2012). *Reading, writing, and digitizing: Understanding literacy in the Electronic Age.* Newcastle upon Tyne: Cambridge Scholars Publishing.

Howard, R. M. (1992). A plagiarism pentimento. *Journal of Teaching Writing, 11*(2), 233–245.

Institute of Education Sciences (U.S.) & National Center for Education Evaluation and Regional Assistance (U.S.). (2015). *What Works Clearinghouse.* Washington, DC: National Center for Education Evaluation and Regional Assistance, Institute of Education Sciences, U.S. Dept. of Education. Retrieved from http://ies.ed.gov/ncee/wwc/.

Israel, S. E. & Duffy, G. G. (2014). *Handbook of research on reading comprehension.* New York: Routledge.

Jamieson, S. (2013). Reading and engaging sources: What students' use of sources reveals about advanced reading skills. *Across the Disciplines, 10*(4). Retrieved from https://wac.colostate.edu/atd/reading/jamieson.cfm.

Jones, C., Reutzel, D. & Smith, J. (2011). A focus on struggling readers: A comparative analysis of expert opinion and empirical research recommendations. In R. Flippo (Ed.), *Reading researchers in search of common ground* (pp. 274–303). New York: Routledge.

Kamii, C., Manning, M. M. & Manning, G. L. (1991). *Early literacy: A constructivist foundation for whole language.* Washington, DC: National Education Association.

Kim, J. S. (2008). Research and the reading wars. *Phi Delta Kappan, 89*(5), 372.

Kozol, J. (2012). *Savage inequalities: Children in America's schools.* New York: Broadway Books.

Knoblauch, C. H. (1990). Literacy and the politics of education. In A. A. Lunsford, H. Moglen & J. Slevin (Eds.), *The Right to Literacy* (pp. 74–80). New York: Modern Language Association.

Lea, M. R. & Street, B. V. (2006). The "academic literacies" model: Theory and applications. *Theory into Practice, 45*(4), 368–377.

National Governors Association Center for Best Practices & Council of Chief State School Officers. (2010). *Common Core State Standards for English Language Arts.* Washington, DC: National Governors Association Center for Best Practices & Council of Chief State School Officers.

National Institute for Direct Instruction. (2015). *Direct Instruction*. Retrieved from http://legacyoflearning.co/direct-instruction/?doing_wp_cron=1447445958.0298969745635986328125.

National Reading Panel, National Institute of Child Health & Human Development. (2000). *Teaching Children to Read*. Retrieved from http://www.nichd.nih.gov/publications/pubs/nrp/documents/report.pdf.

No Child Left Behind (NCLB) Act of 2001, Pub. L. No. 107–110, § 115, Stat. 1425 (2002).

Pearlman, S. J. (2013). It's not that they can't read; it's that they can't read: Can we create "citizen experts" through interactive assessment? *Across the Disciplines, 10*(4). Retrieved from https://wac.colostate.edu/atd/reading/pearlman.cfm.

Reid, L. (2015). The politics of remediation. In L. C. Lewis (Ed.), *Strategic discourse: The politics of (new) literacy crises*. Logan: Computers and Composition Digital Press/Utah State University Press. Retrieved from http://ccdigitalpress.org/strategic.

Rhodes, L. A. (2013). When is writing also reading? *Across the Disciplines, 10*(4). Retrieved from https://wac.colostate.edu/atd/reading/rhodes.cfm.

Richards, J. C. and Rodgers, T. S. (2014). *Approaches and methods in language teaching*. Cambridge: Cambridge University Press.

Samuels, S. J. & Farstrup, A. E. (2011). *What research has to say about reading instruction*. Newark, DE: International Reading Association.

Strauss, V. (2013, November 19). Common Core's odd approach to teaching Gettysburg Address. *The Washington Post*. Retrieved from https://www.washingtonpost.com/news/answer-sheet/wp/2013/11/19/common-cores-odd-approach-to-teaching-gettysburg-address/.

Student Achievement Partners. (2013). The Gettysburg Address. Retrieved from http://achievethecore.org/page/35/the-gettysburg-address-by-abraham-lincoln.

U.S. Department of Education (2014). NCLB/Proven methods: Questions and answers on NCLB. Retrieved from http://www2.ed.gov/nclb/methods/whatworks/doing.html#2.

Wall, P. (2014, April 24). How Lucy Calkins, literacy guru and Fariña ally, is fighting to define Common Core teaching. Retrieved from http://ny.chalkbeat.org/2014/04/24/how-lucy-calkins-literacy-guru-and-farina-ally-is-fighting-to-define-common-core-teaching/.

Wheatley, K. F. (2015a). Factors that perpetuate test-driven, factory-style schooling: Implications for policy and practice. *International Journal of Learning, Teaching and Educational Research, 10*(2), 1–17.

Wheatley, K. F. (2015b). Questioning the instruction assumption: Implications for education policy and practice. *Journal of Education and Human Development, 4*(1), 27–39.

Wilkinson, L. C. & Silliman, E. R. (2000). Classroom language and literacy learning. *Handbook of reading research* (Vol. III, pp. 337–360). New York: Routledge.

Yagelski, R. (2000). *Literacy matters: Writing and reading the social self*. New York: Teachers College Press.

Young, J. A. & Potter, C. R. (2013). The problem of academic discourse: Assessing the role of academic literacies in reading across the K-16 continuum. *Across the Disciplines, 10*(4). Retrieved from https://wac.colostate.edu/atd/reading/young_potter.cfm.

Part 2. Disciplinary Approaches to Theory and Practice in College Reading

Utilizing Interdisciplinary Insights to Build Effective Reading Skills

William M. Abbott and Kathryn A. Nantz
FAIRFIELD UNIVERSITY

In team-teaching a first-year undergraduate Honors course, we (an economics professor and a history professor), have found that even well-motivated students complain of "too much reading." When they find reading assignments difficult to master quickly and easily, students often want professors to summarize the readings in class, and when professors rightly refrain from such simplification, students' frustration can lead to a lack of motivation. In this chapter we will explore student attitudes towards reading assignments that span a variety of disciplinary boundaries—including economic monographs, historical texts, and an historical novel, among other materials. Given this variety of assignments, we exploited interdisciplinary pedagogies that melded diagrammatic economic methods with extensive historical prose. In doing so we found it necessary to construct tasks and provide incentives that help students read in a more organized and productive manner and then use those readings to produce written work and oral class presentations. When, at the close of the course, we asked our students to discuss their most significant mental breakthroughs ("ah-ha" moments), many of their "ah-ha"s combined historical with economic perspectives, confirming our expectation that asking students to engage deeply with texts across interdisciplinary lines can generate extraordinary learning and creativity.

Introduction

When in the summer of 2013 we were putting the finishing touches on our team-taught, first-year Honors course, "Ideas that Shaped the West," we were aware of many of the undergraduate reading problems outlined by Alice Horning (2007), Judith and Keith Roberts (2008), and John Bean (2011). Such research indicates that while expert reading is required in order for college students to generate the kinds of writing that reflect critical and analytical thinking, there is evidence that students are not developing these expert reading skills.

Many authors have described the characteristics of expert, or "college-level," reading. Roberts and Roberts (2008) describe the term as follows:

> A good reader forms visual images to represent the content being read, connects to emotions, recalls settings and events that are

similar to those presented in the reading, predicts what will happen next, asks questions, and thinks about the use of language. One of the most important steps, however, is to connect the manuscript [they] are reading with what [they] already know and to attach the facts, ideas, concepts, or perspectives to that known material. (p. 126)

Writing assignments can encourage students to do this sort of close reading. As Horning (2007) has pointed out,

The side-by-side integration of reading and writing has been firmly established by research reported by Linda Flower and her colleagues in the 1990s. Their study of reading-to-write as the cognitive work of college students makes clear that new college students face the challenge of moving beyond simple comprehension of texts and response to them in writing . . . Flower's findings show that students need to move beyond simple comprehension and beyond simple response to "adapt, restructure, or synthesize knowledge in order to answer complex questions. . . ." (Defining reading, para. 4)

Perhaps the richest description of what we mean by college-level reading is provided by Ken Bain (2012), in his book *What the Best College Students Do*. He says, "Reading can take many forms, and how it is done makes a huge difference" (p. 232). For Bain, creative and critical thinkers do all of the following: they read with deep intention, they make predictions and look for arguments before they begin and then test those predictions as they go, they examine the reading before engaging it, they make connections as they read, they look for arguments in the text, they evaluate the quality and nature of the evidence, they read any text against others they have read, and they engage in all cognitive activities at the same time (pp. 233–238). Bain says, "They remember, understand, apply, analyze, synthesize, and evaluate as they read" (p. 237) and they "read as if they plan to teach" (p. 238). These activities often require multiple readings of any given text, and allow the students to then use what they have learned to create their own ideas in writing.

Though aware of many of these issues, we approached our fall Honors course with great confidence. Our students had been selected from the top of our entering freshman and sophomore classes; their reading and writing skills were surely first-rate. We had taught this course twice before (in 2005 and 2008) and had received good reviews from the students. Prior to 2005, we had taught clusters as well as team-taught courses, combining our two disciplines of economics and history, and had found a host of benefits in such interdisciplinary instruction (Abbott & Nantz, 1994, 2001, 2012).

Once we were into the semester, our confidence continued. We were working harder than ever to provide a range of student reading and writing experiences. In class, we frequently broke the students into small groups and had them report orally on the reading assignments. Every week a group of four or five students would give a formal oral report on the week's readings. We gave our students written questions on the reading, which were discussed in class. We gave them outlines, study guides, and glossaries. We gave them diagrams and charts to help them visualize textual elements, including double-entry drafts, cause-effect matrices, and simple concept maps. Our writing assignments included short "brainstormer" essays along with longer polished papers. The students appeared to be enjoying the class and, to judge from the mid-semester assessment and from end-of-semester reflection essays, learning a great deal.

Imagine our surprise, then, when the student evaluations placed us, and our course, among the bottom 10% in our university and in the entire IDEA database (IDEA is our university's student evaluation-of-teaching instrument, see http://www.ideaedu.org). We had both won teaching awards in the past, and our student evaluations, both for the team-taught Honors course and other courses that we had taught separately, had never been this low for the economist, and seldom if ever for the historian. Although we knew that the instructors in the other section of this Honors course had given higher grades for a similar or lighter workload, and that some of our students might therefore have rated us lower out of a sense of unfairness in grading, we knew that there had to be more to it than that, particularly inasmuch as the majority of the student complaints had to do with reading. There was too much of it; it was not organized; it was not covered adequately in class.

We thus subjected our entire course to a painstaking review. We explored student attitudes towards our reading assignments; we explored the connections between reading, writing, and speaking that our students made as they completed the assignments. We examined student artifacts, including term papers, short writing assignments, and final portfolio reflections, in which students responded to our questions, which of the course readings had made the biggest impact upon their thinking, and what their most significant mental breakthroughs ("ah-ha" moments) were.

The results of our research, which we present in this chapter, confirmed many of the advantages that interdisciplinary instruction has for the development of expert, "deep" reading in undergraduates. Many of our students' "ah-ha"s combined historical with economic perspectives, showing the creativity that can result from reading economic monographs, historical texts, and a historical novel all in the same course. We believe that interdisciplinary tools can be used in *any* course to make it easier for *all* students to do the kind of deep reading that leads to critical thinking as well as to effective written and oral work. We also learned that in some respects interdisciplinary courses and clusters need particular care if reading-skill goals are to be reached.

Our challenge, as we see it, is twofold. We need to help students build the skills they need to become deep readers: readers who can use what they have learned through reading to think and write in sophisticated ways. We also need to establish incentives that motivate students to read our assignments carefully and productively. These challenges are related, but they must be addressed separately if students are to attain our learning outcomes.

Description of the Course and the Students

Fairfield University is a comprehensive, Jesuit-founded school located in southwestern Connecticut, with a population of around four thousand undergraduates. We attract students with strong academic backgrounds, primarily from the northeast. The course we describe here, "Ideas that Shaped the West," is the first course in our university's Honors program. It is team-taught, in this case by an economist and a historian; some of the main goals are to introduce students to the kinds of interdisciplinary inquiry that are featured in our Honors program and to engage first- and second-year students intentionally in seminar-style learning, which depends on student preparation for class and close reading of texts. Students are concurrently taking other classes to satisfy core curriculum and often major program requirements.

Students who selected our section (as opposed to another section taught by a literature professor and a psychology professor) tended to have majors in business, nursing, and other social sciences, and had a wide variety of interests and backgrounds. We were teaching this course for the third time; this class had 29 students, the 2008 class had 28, and the 2005 class had 18. According to the catalog: "This team-taught lecture/seminar course examines selected ideas or themes from Western intellectual history, focusing on developments in philosophy, society, science, and the arts." In our section, students explored the theme of Empire using a historical lens and an economic perspective. We only briefly touched on the ancient empires so that we could spend most of the semester in the modern era. We did provide an introductory week on current-day empires, which allowed us to introduce the notion of economic rather than territorial empire building. Our hope was that we could then hook historical events onto this "imperial" scaffold and allow students to make connections between the past and present.

In September 2013 we enthusiastically introduced the course and started working our way chronologically through the key western ideas, in a manner similar to the two previous times we had taught this course. We assigned three texts that addressed the course themes and which introduced material at a variety of levels; Fusfeld's (2001) *The Age of the Economist* provided a history of economic thought, Ferguson's (2004) *Empire: The Rise and Demise of the British World Order and the Lessons for Global Power* traced the rise and fall of the second British Empire, Lal's (2001) *Unintended Consequences: The Impact of Factor Endowments, Culture, and Politics on Long-Run Economic Performance* provided a cultural explanation for economic growth, and

Clavell's (1966) *Tai Pan*, a historical novel set in Hong Kong during the 1840s, described the tea-opium trade between Britain and China. We also cobbled together an extensive "Course Reader," which included additional readings (excerpts from Adam Smith's (1776) *The Wealth of Nations* and Karl Marx's (1848) *The Communist Manifesto*, and a variety of short readings), maps, organizers, and class discussion questions.

We expected that our students would use all of this material to engage with class themes and to complete course writing assignments. It was never our intention that they would intensively read every piece; some were for illustrative purposes while others were more central to class discussion and assignments. Because our Honors program brings together students from every program and school at the university, we included a wide variety of readings so that every student could find subjects that fit his or her particular interests. We did not, however, distinguish carefully enough between the illustrative and the central, which led to some of the motivational problems described below. We have since learned of Alice Horning's advice, to highlight "particular reasons that any of us uses a reading selection: Is the text being read for content, as part of a process, or to illustrate a structure?" (Rhodes, p. 7). This is particularly necessary in an interdisciplinary course such as ours, inasmuch as economists' reading habits and styles can differ somewhat from those of historians. As Lynn Rhodes points out: "We must explicitly share our expectations with students about performances that we identify as good reading in our classrooms . . . If we want students to read strictly for content, we must teach strategic summary skills. If we want students to analyze genres, we must explicitly direct analysis and interpretations" (p. 7).

Our problem was that we wanted to achieve all of these goals with our reading and writing assignments. Unlike English composition courses, where reading assignments can be selected primarily as a means of modelling good writing (Bunn, 2013), we were responsible for content: for covering historical and economic data and themes in a first-year honors course. Hence, as we show below, we alternate between the teaching of "reading" as process and the selection of "readings" as course content, because the selection of those readings has multiple goals. Sometimes we want the students to summarize the text; sometimes we want them to mine it for specific data and then analyze it; sometimes we want them to do both. We found that the quality of student reading, as well as their motivation to do good reading, was clearly related to their understanding of our goals.

Overcoming Challenges: Motivation

Susan Ambrose (2010) and her co-authors have outlined three types of value that students attach to their work: attainment value, which is the sheer satisfaction of having completed a difficult task; intrinsic value, which comes from interest in the subject itself, and instrumental value, which "represents the degree to which an activity or goal helps one accomplish other important goals, such as gaining what are traditionally referred to as *extrinsic rewards*" (p. 75). Even in an Honors course, the third type of value is likely to be the most common. As Ambrose, Bridges, DiPietro, Lovett, and Norman (2010) have shown, further, students can have positive or negative "outcome expectancies": the belief either "that specific actions will bring about a desired outcome" or that "specific actions have no influence on a desired outcome" (p. 77).

Negative outcome expectancies are a particular problem in history reading, inasmuch as it is difficult to test students on all of the information covered in 60 or 70 pages of a historical monograph or novel, let alone the entire work. Unlike a mathematics text, which presents a logical progression from simple to more complex, a history text too often comes across as a sea of detail, a small part of which will be on the exam or be expected to be used in an essay. Students who come to the reading asking only "What is going to be on the test?" or "What parts of the reading do you want us to cover in our essay?" are only expressing a logical desire not to waste time and effort on something that will not pay off in the form of a higher grade. Thus, extensive reading assignments by their very nature are often frustrating, because the student does not know how much, and which parts, of the reading are going to provide an immediate reward. One can and should explain to students that a purpose of extensive reading is to give them mental exercise in organizing information by differentiating specific from general points and figuring out cause-and-effect chains: skills that are useful in any career. However, for instrumental-value students, these explanations can be insufficient to prevent frustration, resentment, and a consequent lack of motivation. We must show them how to conduct these mental exercises, teaching reading as process AND as content mastery.

Here is where a combination of history and a mathematically-oriented social science such as economics can be helpful. In having students write essays on readings that covered both disciplines, we found that more of the reading could be made "instrumentally" relevant to the assignment than in a straightforward history essay assignment, because the questions asked could be conceptually broader. There is greater variety not simply of readings, but of reading goals and of the methods that are possible to pursue.

Certainly effective and thorough "mining" of readings for information is one important goal. There are, however, different kinds of mining. Less productive assignments encourage students to look for specific, isolated facts and discard the rest of the reading as useless. If, however, the mining entails the drawing of connections between two or more readings, from different disciplines, in an illustrative, comparative, argumentative, and/or problem-solving mode, the student has to read each of the various sources *actively, keeping information from the other sources in mind* as he/she does so. By improving students' connection-making skills, this variety, together with the above-cited writing assignments, actually make the exercise of reading easier by making it more interesting. There is a focus and a purpose to the readings, beyond simply a search for miscellaneous facts.

A related issue concerning motivation was raised in a recent article by Naomi Baron (2015) titled, "The Plague of tl;dr" ("too long, didn't read"). Baron explores the ways that reading has changed as a result of new technology, as we have moved from reading print to digital screens. She says, "When reading on-screen, we can rapidly click or scroll our way from page to page within a document. We are able to connect with the outside world, to hop from site to site, to multitask. Sustained concentration, analysis, and rereading are not encouraged" (para. 4). Students use word searches, find-functions, and other digital tools to perform a sort of "scavenger hunt"; our tech-savvy students seek out answers in the text by searching on a single word or phrase that might provide an immediate answer to a question, rather than truly engaging with the text. Baron concludes, "When we give students ever-shorter reading assignments (in the hope they will be completed), we imply that substantial or complex texts aren't worth the effort" (para. 21). As we work harder to help students build reading skills, they spend their lives in a digital world that sends the message that close reading and deep, reflective pondering are lost arts. Baron quotes research from the University College London that concludes, "It almost seems that [readers] go online to avoid reading in the traditional sense" (para. 12). Thus our task is even more daunting than it may have been ten or 20 years ago: How do we provide incentives for students to value deep reading as a worthwhile skill? How can we draw them into the processes of reading, pondering, and constructing meaning that college-level work requires? These are the challenges we take up in what follows.

Building Reading Skills Through Writing Assignments

Taking these deep reading characteristics as our reading goals, we chose to begin with relatively straight-forward but creative writing assignments that required particular reading skills. We built upon these assignments through the semester with increasingly challenging problems. We assigned four short essays, which we called brainstormers; the goal was to get students to mine readings, make connections (particularly between economic and historical concepts), and put down conclusions on paper without worrying about grammar and spelling. We also assigned two longer essays ("polished papers") in which formal grammar rules were included in the rubrics, and integration of course themes was required. Our overarching goal in all of these writing assignments was to replicate Joan Didion's experience: "I write entirely to find out what I'm thinking, what I'm looking at, what I see and what it means." (1976).

Though similar in that they melded economic with historical problems, the four brainstormer assignments each focused on different reading goals. The four grading rubrics, which we handed out with the assignments, were thus different for each paper. The first assignment, which was based upon the concept of empire, emphasized creativity in imagining all aspects of the human experience: political, economic, religious, social, technological, and geographical. Students were to create their own empire, describing all the characteristics that would make it both sustainable and conducive to the greatest good. We purposely did not emphasize reading for content in this introductory assignment. We wanted students to summarize the reading assignments, take a few concepts from them, think hard about the basics of the human condition, and as Roberts and Roberts (2008) describe, connect what they were reading with what they already knew. Hence, the rubric asked: (1) Were all the characteristics of your empire (political, economic etc.) described clearly? (2) Was the notion of the "greatest good" defined and explained? (3) Did you clearly explain HOW each of the characteristics of your empire will lead to the "greatest good"? (WHY, in other words, is each of these characteristics superior to the alternatives?) (4) In explaining bullet 3, do you draw upon factual knowledge? (5) What makes you believe that this empire is sustainable, and why? (6) Were you able to present your ideas in a creative but understandable way? Each requirement was assigned the same number of points, so actual mining of the readings for information was only one sixth of the grade. The class scored an average of 67.14% on this part of the rubric.

The second brainstormer assignment included more of what Flower, Stein, Ackerman, Kantz, McCormick, and Peck (1990) suggest, that students "adapt, restructure, or synthesize knowledge in order to answer complex questions" (p. 249). Students were asked to read from a complex economic text, Deepak Lal's (2001) *Unintended Consequences*, and also from a historical novel, James Clavell's (1966) *Tai Pan*, and explain how the latter illustrated the former's concepts. Here the mining of information from both texts was given a high priority—two-thirds of the available points—but it was not simply a treasure hunt; students needed to keep the Lal concepts in mind as they read the Clavell and apply them to that novel. This connection-making task was simplified by being confined to two sources, by our summary of the Lal concepts in the assignment prompt, and by our simply calling for illustrative examples out of the *Tai-Pan* novel. Here the average results for the extent to which students mined the readings for information took a big jump, to 72.21%. The other third of the rubric assessed coherency and connection-making: the actual describing of how the *Tai-Pan* information illustrated Lal's concepts. For this portion of the rubric, the score was 69.2%.

The third brainstormer assignment moved from illustration to advocacy, thus requiring many of the processes outlined above by Bain (2012). It asked the students to argue the economic pros and the economic cons of the 18th-century slave trade and

New World slavery, using the relevant economic principles that had been presented in the course readings and by the economics professor (Nantz) in class, along with the historical accounts of slavery and the slave trade. In the prompt this time we did not describe the relevant economic concepts; students had to search both the economic and the historical sources and connect them via a cost-benefit assessment. The rubric here had only two parts: mining of the reading and coherency. Whether because the assignment involved argument instead of illustration, or because the students were becoming more familiar with our standards for utilization of the reading material, the average score for mining the readings went up to 76.12%.

The fourth brainstormer combined the skills required in the first three: imagination, illustration, and argument, while dealing with a broader range of subjects than 18th-century slavery. Students read Karl Marx's (1848) *Communist Manifesto* and, pretending that they were writing in 1945, argued whether the events of the period 1883–1945 had done more to bear out his views (economic, political, social) or to disprove them. As before, the rubric included the thoroughness of the historical information, but it also included the accuracy with which the student understood and applied Marx's views. Despite the larger amount of historical information required than in the previous assignments, the "mining" score dipped only slightly, to 73.85%. It would appear that, as the complexity of the assignment increased, the students' reading efforts rose to match it. Whether their reading analysis grew more sophisticated is unclear, as the scores for organizational effectiveness on these essays declined as the essays became more complex. Nevertheless, the constructive nature of economics pedagogy, which starts from simple concepts and builds an increasingly complex structure from them, is clearly useful for history instructors, whose readings are too often the same in quantity and complexity over the course of a semester.

The first polished paper utilized the concept of interdisciplinary inquiry, and followed Ambrose et al.'s (2010) recommendation to "Provide Authentic, Real-World Tasks" (p. 83). Students pretended that they were advisors to Secretary of State John Kerry and used the historical and economic knowledge that they had acquired to suggest a course of action to maintain peaceful relations with China amidst the ongoing disputes in the South China Sea. Here our students were expected to draw upon all of the course readings, from the Clavell (1966) novel to the history monographs to the economics texts, but in a real-world problem-solving mode rather than the more theoretical and academic exercises of the brainstormers. Every element of Bain's (2012) rich description of the reading process was required if students were to write a good paper. We were pleased by the results; the average scores for mining of information and for the logic of the arguments were higher than in any of the brainstormers: 89.87% for the former, and 81.58% for the latter.

At the very end of the course, each time we have taught it, we have assigned a haiku. Students must, in 17 syllables, describe the ideas that they found most important in this course. This was a low-stakes assignment; there was no grading rubric to measure student use of course material, and every student who completed the assignment earned an A. Its main purpose was to help students pull together the major themes of the course in a creative way. Each time we have taught this course many of the student haikus have revealed an effective integration of course themes. Here are some examples:

Wal-Mart slavery
stream of trade and intellect
pass the eggrolls please
(Colleen Gibson, 2005)

Growth, property, apps
Make it last—adapt! Survive!
Compete till you win
(Lily Savage, 2013)

I dream of peace, bread
To truly have all men fed
But Marx is still dead.
(Michael Spiller, 2013)

In promoting haiku as a means of teaching economics, Stephen T. Ziliak (2011) praises its interdisciplinarity, writing that "Poetry can fill the gap between reason and emotion, adding feelings to economics" (p. 1). We did not adopt Ziliak's "haiku economics" in any of the complex metaphorical ways he outlines in his seminal 2009 article, and we did not get any written student evaluation of the assignment since the haikus were due on the last day of class. To judge from the class discussion, however, reciting their poems and listening to everyone else's efforts in a friendly environment (we professors had to write haikus too) was clearly an enjoyable way to summarize the semester's work. In the end, we were left with the question: How can we better provide students with the deep-reading tools they need to produce the sort of integrative thinking shown by these examples?

Helping Students Read More Efficiently

Although our students' reading abilities appear to have improved with these written assignments, the students often complained that the class sessions did not sufficiently organize the reading for them. Such complaints put us in mind of the early 20th-century efficiency experts Frank and Lillian Gilbreth, who, with their pioneering studies of human motion, earned praise from factory workers for making it "easy for a man to work hard" (quoted in Cooper, 1981, p. 171). Because our students could not master all of the readings quickly and easily, they wanted us to "make it easy" for them by lecturing on the readings and discussing all of them in class, a practice criticized by Bean (2011) and Roberts and Roberts (2008). Although we agree with Bean that we as instructors can do too much of the work that students need to be doing, we realized that, in an interdisciplinary course such as ours, the reading material needs greater coordination than we gave it, precisely *because* of that interdisciplinarity. As instructors, our job is to provide some of the integrative tissue that students need to see readings—to see the authors' perspectives and content—as related to one another.

In exploring the move in K-12 education from "learning to read" (K-5) to "reading to learn," Lee and Spratley (2012) state, "We call this more advanced form of literacy required of adolescent readers 'disciplinary literacy' because each academic discipline or content-area presupposed specific kinds of background knowledge about how to read texts in that area . . . " (p. 2). This is even more true of college-level reading, which requires moving beyond "reading to learn" to reading to learn *across disciplinary boundaries*.

Our two disciplines provide excellent examples. With regard, first, to processes of reading, economics readings tend to be relatively short as measured by absolute page count. Students often assume they can buzz through 20–30 pages per week from their economics course text with ease as compared to their history courses, which may require over 100 pages from a variety of primary and secondary sources. What they often fail to realize is that several pages of complex economic arguments and graphical analysis might take considerable time to master. The historical reading, on the other hand, must be skimmed and organized around themes rather than consumed word-for-word. By the same token, economics and history courses assign different types of writing assignments; economists focus attention on applying economic concepts and analyzing data to improve understanding of economic outcomes or to forecast future outcomes while historians, as we have seen, ask students to process large amounts of information to identify support for positions or to describe connections among events, ideas, and/or source documents. Each discipline calls upon students to utilize the skills outlined by Horning (2007) and Bain (2012), but in different ways.

Second, with regard to content, there is the mastery of discipline-specific vocabulary. As Young and Potter state:

> Students identified vocabulary as one of the biggest challenges in their effort to successfully read academic material. Moreover, students appear to need help dealing strategically with the new and—to them—strange words that they frequently encounter in college

level reading assignments. It is essential that students be taught to identify key terms that hold particular disciplinary value in texts that are filled with unfamiliar, difficult words. We cannot expect students to identify and understand disciplinary-specific academic terminology without instruction on doing so . . . (pp. 16–17).

Students must understand the importance of such specialized languages—and practice the skill of mastering them—if they are to build the kind of reading skills that will allow them to access the content of a particular discipline.

Although we selected readings for content overlap (Ferguson [2004] and Clavell [1966] both deal with Chinese-British relations; Lal [2001] and Fusfeld [2001] both cover economic systems), our students frequently complained that the course readings took off in all directions and did not wrap up sufficiently in a general summary. One student, asked whether the interdisciplinary combination of economics and history contributed to his/her learning, replied:

Yes, in some ways. It helped that money tends to be a heavy influence throughout history, and the Economics perspective helped to explain some of the actions and reactions. However, it did not contribute when it added on additional knowledge that seemed distinct from the history, considering that it was difficult to understand.

Another student stated:

It was rather overwhelming to have many multiple assignments from many different books all at once for a few readings . . . I felt as though I was supposed to be able to find a connecting theme between all the readings and sometimes I was unable to and it was rather frustrating.

In a Midsemester Assessment of Teaching (MAT) performed by our university's Center for Academic Excellence, students complained that the readings were "too long" and "unconnected."

Like Jolliffe and Harl (2008), therefore, we found that our students needed more help in making thematic connections among the course readings (pp. 612–613). Because reading facility in any subject depends upon knowledge of context and familiarity with the subject (Haswell, Briggs, Fay, Gillen, Harrill, Shupula & Trevino, 1999), we found outlines, discussion questions, study guides, and glossaries useful (pp. 12–13, 17–18). Here the diagrammatic methods of economics helped students comprehend more loosely-connected historical narratives. (See Figures 1A and 1B.) We used matrices and other visual methods to accustom students to different patterns of prose, giving them practice in what Nancy Spivey (1990) calls the "reorganizing" of unfamiliar texts so as to make them "conform to [the students'] own schemata" (p. 264). The historian (Abbott) began constructing topical reading charts, which encouraged students to lay out all of their sources in front of them and read by topic, rather than simply reading through one source at a time. (See Figure 2.)

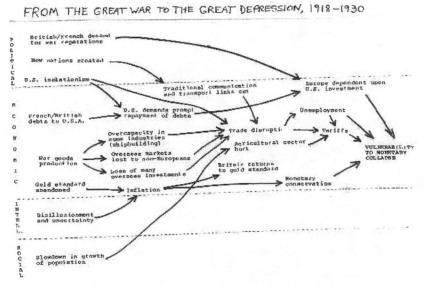

Figure 1A: Cause-Effect Matrix, from World War I to the Great Depression

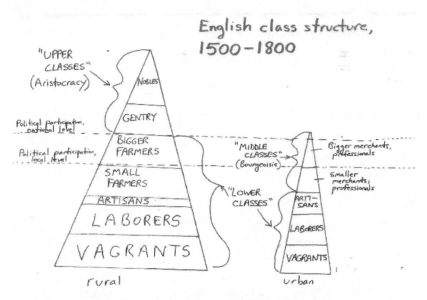

Figure 1B: Social Classes in Early Modern Britain

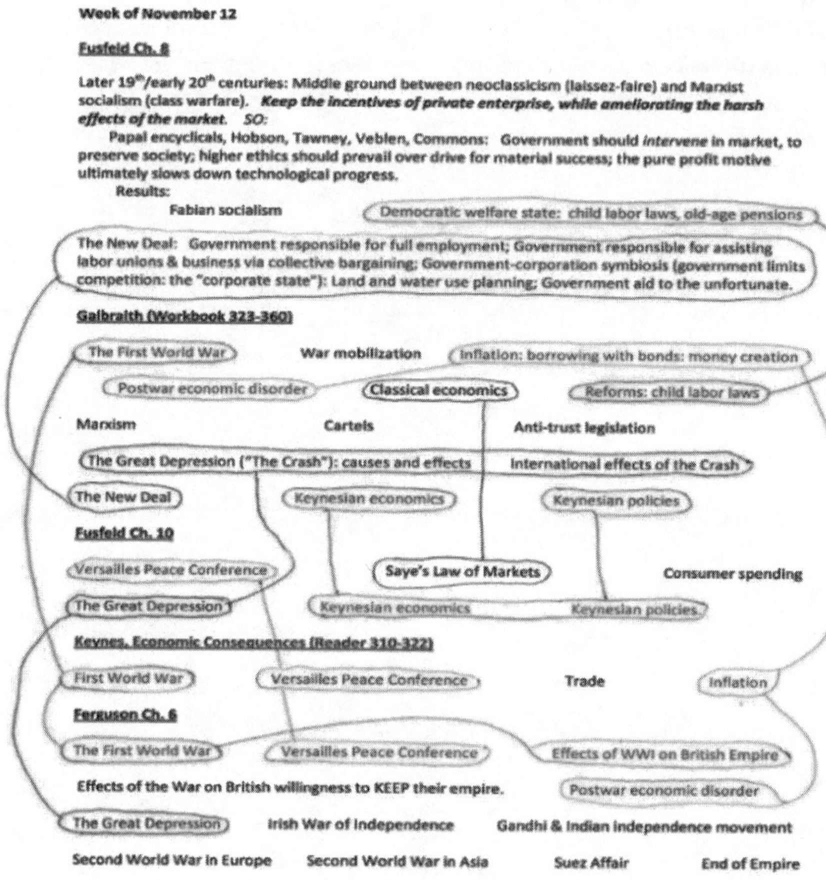

Week of November 12

Fusfeld Ch. 8

Later 19th/early 20th centuries: Middle ground between neoclassicism (laissez-faire) and Marxist socialism (class warfare). *Keep the incentives of private enterprise, while ameliorating the harsh effects of the market.* SO:

Papal encyclicals, Hobson, Tawney, Veblen, Commons: Government should *intervene* in market, to preserve society; higher ethics should prevail over drive for material success; the pure profit motive ultimately slows down technological progress.

Results:

Fabian socialism   Democratic welfare state: child labor laws, old-age pensions

The New Deal: Government responsible for full employment; Government responsible for assisting labor unions & business via collective bargaining; Government-corporation symbiosis (government limits competition: the "corporate state"): Land and water use planning; Government aid to the unfortunate.

Galbraith (Workbook 323-360)

The First World War   War mobilization   Inflation: borrowing with bonds: money creation

Postwar economic disorder   Classical economics   Reforms: child labor laws

Marxism   Cartels   Anti-trust legislation

The Great Depression ("The Crash"): causes and effects   International effects of the Crash

The New Deal   Keynesian economics   Keynesian policies

Fusfeld Ch. 10

Versailles Peace Conference   Saye's Law of Markets   Consumer spending

The Great Depression   Keynesian economics   Keynesian policies

Keynes, Economic Consequences (Reader 310-322)

First World War   Versailles Peace Conference   Trade   Inflation

Ferguson Ch. 6

The First World War   Versailles Peace Conference   Effects of WWI on British Empire

Effects of the War on British willingness to KEEP their empire.   Postwar economic disorder

The Great Depression   Irish War of Independence   Gandhi & Indian independence movement

Second World War in Europe   Second World War in Asia   Suez Affair   End of Empire

Figure 2: Topical Reading Chart: Galbraith, Fusfeld, Ferguson

By modeling this method of integrating the reading across authors and texts, our hope was that students would begin using this reading strategy themselves. (We did not ask them do this task; upon reflection, we should have done so as an in-class or homework exercise.) Young and Potter (2013) suggest an initial classroom exercise: "annotation and discussion of an assigned academic article, to find key words and define them." Then, discuss "key claims and concepts in another article," and finally "synthesize and apply these keywords, claims, and concepts through the creation of indexes and study guides" (p. 6). When the students themselves identify terms common to both historical and economic readings (capitalism, socialism, Karl Marx, J.M. Keynes, the Great Depression), they can more effectively make mental connections between the disciplines, to the enhancement of their reading skills.

Pursuing Bain's goal of having students "read as if they plan to teach," we also used oral group-reporting assignments, which were designed to encourage both understanding of weekly assignments and connection-making between the different readings. Student panels pulled together common themes from the readings and related them to their own life experiences. Our rubric included the following elements: balance (each presenter to have equal time), clarity, originality (encouraging and rewarding creativity in the presentation of material), and connection-making between student life experiences and current world events. Students were put in permanent groups (mixed by gender and major), and each group made two presentations during the semester. The grades on these presentations were mostly As with a few Bs, as students came up with creative slides, provided maps and other visuals, created games to illustrate important concepts (like the Prisoner's Dilemma and how capitalism creates winners and losers), and found wonderfully aligned video clips and online material to share. We gave each group extensive feedback on their work within hours of their presentations.

Student Comments and Opportunities for Improvement

Predictably, the extent to which we reached our reading-skill goals varied with individual students. However, in addition to the IDEA student evaluation forms, handwritten evaluation forms, a mid-term assessment, and a questionnaire, we also had students write a fifth brainstormer, a reflective, end-of-semester assignment, which asked them to assemble all of their course writing in a folder and then craft a one-page reflection on how their writing and thinking had changed and evolved over the course of the semester. These reflection papers revealed both positive and negative student perceptions of our interdisciplinary course.

Notable among the positives were the mental connections that most of our students were able to make between the two disciplines, thereby creating more of Ambrose et al.'s (2010) "intrinsic value" as a motivator (p. 75). Mixing historical with economic readings clearly provided more of those "ah-ha" moments of discovery that make the reading interesting. One student stated: "I learned about international economic relations and strategy. I didn't realize how many things are mutually advantageous and necessary between nations and that they impact more than just the economy (ex. Social or political relations). I learned SO much this semester." Another student wrote that her biggest "ah-ha" moment involved learning how the world "acts as a multi-faceted machine: connections between historical events and economics." Further, about her writing process, she noted, "the importance of using all the sources and not rushing into the writing process . . . [You need to] take time to digest and illustrate the connecting factors and relevant examples." Each of these examples reflect Ambrose et al.'s definition of intrinsic value: " . . . the satisfaction that one gains simply from doing the task rather than from a particular outcome of the task" (p. 75).

Another interesting result came from student reading preferences. No single source received all negative or all positive reviews: the class divided fairly evenly in preferring the Lal (2001), the Fusfeld (2001), the Ferguson (2004), the Clavell (1966), or the Course Reader. Thus we conclude that by providing different genres of reading, and not just similarly-written texts on a variety of subjects, our interdisciplinary course stood a better chance than single-discipline courses of catching all of our students' interests. Commenting on the second brainstormer, one student stated:

> I read each text (Tai-Pan and Lal) carefully, and highlighted the important quotes. From there the paper seemed to write itself. I think this ease of writing was due to the fact that I enjoyed Tai-Pan the most of the readings. It illustrated the concepts we were learning with a rip-roaring good yarn, applying them to a real-life situation and showing how they unfolded in the real world.

Another student commented:

> Chapter 4 in the Lal was my favorite read within the class. The ideas regarding Promethean growth in the West and cosmological beliefs helped me draw connections to other empires we have been discussing throughout the semester. Lal had me thinking like no other. With each of the Lal readings I adapted to his views and would begin to think like an economist, as we got further into the course. In my opinion, Lal provided me with an understanding in which I would then be able to draw connections and ideas from Lal to the other readings: Ferguson, Clavell and Fusfeld.

Yet another student stated: "A lot of my sources for [Brainstormer #3] came from Fusfeld, which was my favorite book to read. This is because it was not too hard and he looked at events in an economic perspective, which I usually do not do; so it was very interesting to me and made me think differently." Clearly, our interdisciplinary instruction and reading helped achieve Ambrose et al.'s (2010) goals of "connecting material to student interests," "providing authentic, real world tasks," and "showing relevance to students' current academic lives" (pp. 83–84). In so doing, it also fulfills Bain's (2012) and Horning's (2007) definitions of good college reading.

Students responded positively to the various visual organizers and reading guides we provided. They enjoyed breaking down the historical outcomes by using matrices that connect social, political, economic, technological, religious, and other factors. (See Figure 1A.) One student commented,

> With each assignment I learned to firstly analyze the categories that we have been using throughout the semester to understand the historical forces that make up an empire: economic, political, social, cultural, intellectual, and technological. I felt that this was critical to my writing and how it has improved over the course of the semester. This technique enabled me to present my ideas in a much more understandable way and draw connections when comparing and contrasting authors and empires.

Another student said, "The maps and diagrams in the reader were very helpful, as I am a visual learner and was able to draw a lot of connections through viewing timelines and flow charts." Next time we teach this course, we will make sure to align assignments to these sorts of tasks, asking students to create their own visual organizers. Use of concept mapping software, and other kinds of online apps for creative graphical representations, might be easy and fun for students to use for these tasks.

Our students liked readings that were, in their words, "not too hard," or written in "simple English." This brings up another issue: the effectiveness of the prose in our reading assignments. While increasing the sophistication of our students' reading material is an important goal, sophisticated readings need not be difficult to follow. One student praised the Fusfeld (2001) by saying: "Every fact had information to support it and help make it more understandable." Here economics has an advantage over history in that its readings are more concise and coordinated; again, the one discipline can assist the other in this context. When next we offer the course, the historian (Abbott) will remember that brilliant historians can often write turgid prose, and will select readings accordingly.

In addition to responding positively to writing assignments that addressed common themes, students appreciated texts that helped tie other texts together. "I liked reading the course reader," said one student, "because it gave a lot of background info on historical topics that I thought the other books were lacking in." When we next teach this course, we plan to assign a brief, concise western civilization text that the students will read first and master its basic vocabulary; we will then build our other readings around that summary.

While some students preferred that professors lecture on the reading rather than having the weekly oral panel presentations by peers, one student commented that having to produce an oral presentation "forced me to think of the material in less conventional ways." Thus it seemed as though *constructing* the presentation encouraged deep reading. However, students became passive audience members rather than engaged co-learners when they were not presenting. In the future, we need to make class engagement a bigger part of the presenting group's overall grade while at the same time reminding the audience members that their participation, too, will be graded.

Another suggestion from some students was that we give quizzes or tests on the material. In an Honors course such as ours, we thought we would not need to use such ordinary assessment methods, but it is possible that such exams would increase our readers' motivation and morale by providing a greater variety of assessments. It is one task to mine readings for information relevant to an essay assignment; it is another to summarize a reading for a review; it is yet another to organize the reading mentally into general categories and subcategories so as to complete a quiz. Other students opposed quizzes and exams, stating that they would reduce student incentive to read. Bean (2011) provides support for this position: "Quizzes encourage students to extract 'right answers' from a text rather than to engage with the text's ideas, and they don't invite students to bring their own critical thinking to bear on a text's argument or to enter into conversations with a text's author" (p. 168). The latter, Bean apparently assumes, is impossible to test in a quiz, but Nilson (2010), citing research on the pros and cons of reading quizzes, suggests that if they are to be used they should focus on major points and concepts rather than details (p. 220), and Young and Potter, as we have seen, propose "teaching students to read and respond in an exam setting to a range of academic and popular texts" (p. 6). Balancing these alternative motivational and de-motivational factors is difficult in any class, but particularly so in an interdisciplinary course where students are not held responsible for a body of content knowledge specific to a particular major or minor. Our students needed to internalize enough of the course content to successfully engage in class discussions, and to write meaningfully about concepts and ideas. We are uncertain whether or not regular reading quizzes would help or hinder our course goals.

Understanding Evaluation Scores

Despite the weaknesses in our course, we would have expected the abovementioned strengths to have resulted in better student evaluation scores than we actually received, particularly given the more favorable results of 2005 and 2008. In comparing the syllabi from those two classes with that of 2013, we note that, although the reading load was similar and many of the texts were the same, a new aspect of our 2013 version was the course Reader, in which we included more short articles than we had given out previously. As we were putting the Reader together we may have fallen into the old trap of including a reading simply because it looked interesting to us or was a favorite of ours, not because it supported a specific learning goal.

This larger *number* of individual readings may have been a reason behind student complaints that the course reading should have been better coordinated.

A breakdown of our IDEA scores, moreover, indicates that we were more successful in achieving learning goals than in winning student satisfaction with us and our course. The IDEA Diagnostic Report breaks down instructor performance into three categories. Twenty-five percent of the score is the average of answers to the question "Was this an excellent course?" Twenty-five percent is the average of answers to "Was this an excellent instructor?" Fifty percent of the score is the average of answers to the question "How much progress did I make?" on three or four learning goals selected by the instructor from IDEA's list of 12 goals. Although our scores on the first two questions were in the bottom 10% of the entire IDEA database, our score in the third was much closer to the IDEA average.

That we had greater success with learning goals than with student satisfaction is further suggested by the positive comments in the fifth, reflective-essay brainstormer, some of which are quoted above. By asking not simply what basic concepts students had learned with each of the earlier assignments, but also (1) whether there were any "ah-ha" moments when different ideas seemed to connect together in a mental breakthrough, and (2) which readings or authors made the biggest impact on their thinking and why, such a reflective essay gave us a more complete picture of student achievement than did the more general and standardized learning goals on the IDEA form. We hope, too, that a reflective essay written over several days is more thoughtful, and hence more reliable, than standardized forms filled out in 20 minutes or so.

In our case, too, a reason for the lower IDEA scores may well have been the differing perceptions of what constitutes a "fair" grade. Grade inflation has been well-documented among U.S. universities, and Fairfield is no exception (Abbott, 2008). As at other universities, also, grading patterns at Fairfield vary widely from department to department: there is little to no consensus on what an A, a B, a C, or a D means, or what constitutes "fairness." Most students use their own life experience to construct their expectations with respect to grades; in our case, half of our students, as first-semester freshmen, had no basis for comparison to college-level standards. With the grade point average of *all* of Fairfield's first-year students hovering around 3.1, many Honors students, even first-year students with no previous experience of college-level work, have logically come to expect something considerably higher in their Honors classes. Our average in this Honors course was only a 3.27. This contrasts with the 2008 class's 3.45 and the 2005 class's 3.63 averages. It is possible that the lower evaluations of 2013 may in part be explained by the lower grades.

In this context, we should probably have been more explicit as to how many hours per week we expected our students to spend on their reading. According to John Bean, as we have seen, one of the challenges students face in doing deep reading is "failure to commit time on task." As suggested by the above-cited student recommendation to "take time to digest," entering first-year students often do not realize that they are expected to put in, at a minimum, two hours outside of class for every hour spent in class, or that, as affirmed by Young and Potter (2013), re-reading is a normal and expected part of college-level work.

Conclusion

It is clear from our analysis that interdisciplinary pedagogy can provide effective tools to improve undergraduate student reading, as long as the problems inherent in such disciplinary combinations are clearly understood. On a broader level, interdisciplinary insights can be of help in any undergraduate reading context, particularly in light of efforts to promote what Horning (2007) calls reading across the curriculum. As a result of our research, we have the following suggestions for instructors who want to capitalize on interdisciplinary methods to build college-reading skills:

- Select readings that satisfy specific purposes, and clearly organize those readings so that students recognize these purposes. This does not mean that you have to reduce your course reading load. Simply ask yourself: How will the students use this reading to achieve course goals? If you cannot answer the question, perhaps the reading does not belong in the course.
- Assign a variety of readings (different genres, authors etc.) so that students with diverse backgrounds and interests can find authors and ideas that engage them. Some enjoy a "rip roaring good yarn" like Tai Pan; others prefer writers that speak in "plain English"; still others enjoy thumbing through a reader, looking for short and interesting articles.
- If you include readings whose primary purpose is illustrative, follow Alice Horning's (2007) method and allow students to choose different readings from a list and write reviews of them (Strategies for reading, number 3). Such flexibility improves "intrinsic" motivation, which comes from interest in the subject itself.
- Select those readings for topical and thematic coordination. Instructors struggle with this selection process in all the courses they teach, but tight coordination of class materials is even more important for interdisciplinary courses, both because of their topical variety and because of the varying interests of the students.
- Model the kinds of work that must be done while reading (creating graphic organizers, for example) but also make clear to students that they should use these same techniques as they are reading. If students do not understand that they should use the same strategies that you use to unpack a difficult text, you miss an opportunity to help them build their own skills.

- Apropos of the above point, conduct in-class reading exercises that require students to summarize, apply, or diagram specific readings. Have students debate specific issues, using the course readings. Explaining a reading is clearly not the same as discussing it.
- Be as transparent as possible in explaining why the reading is important and how it will be useful in helping students to achieve course goals. Is it, as Alice Horning asks, "being read for content, as part of a process, or to illustrate a structure?" (Rhodes, p. 7). The why and the how might seem obvious to you, but students may need help making the kinds of connections between readings and assignments that are important to success.

When all is said and done, our experience illustrates that at the very heart of our students' positive reading experiences is the "ah-ha" moment of connective discovery. However, while we should try to create such moments in class as well as outside of it, such moments come only from the hard work involved in integrating ideas from complex texts. Although instructors can try to make it "easy for students to work hard," they must also motivate them to work hard. Students must recognize the meaningful payoff they experience when they do deep reading.

References

Abbott, W. M. (2008, January–February). The politics of grade inflation: A case study. *Change*, 32–37.

Abbott, W. M. & Nantz, K. A. (1994). History and economics. *College Teaching 42*(1), 22–26.

Abbott, W. M. & Nantz, K. A. (2001). The uses of economics in an integrated cluster. *History Teacher, 34*(3), 447–457.

Abbott, W. M. & Nantz, K. A. (2012). Building students' integrative thinking capacities: A case study in economics and history. *Issues in Integrative Studies, 30*, 19–47.

Ambrose, S. A., Bridges, M. W., DiPietro, M., Lovett, M. C., Norman & M. K. (2010). *How learning works: Seven research-based principles for smart teaching.* San Francisco: Jossey-Bass.

Bain, K. (2012). *What the best college students do.* Cambridge, MA: Belknap Press.

Baron, N. S. (2015). The plague of tl;dr. *The Chronicle of Higher Education.* Retrieved from http://search.proquest.com/docview/1658735797?accountid=10796.

Bean, J. C. (2011). *Engaging ideas: The professor's guide to integrating writing, critical thinking and active learning in the classroom* (2nd ed). San Francisco: Jossey Bass.

Bunn, M. (2013). Motivation and connection: Teaching reading (and writing) in the composition classroom. *College Composition and Communication 64*(3), 496–516.

Clavell, J. (1966). *Tai Pan.* New York: Dell Publishing.

Conley, D. T. (2015). A definition of college readiness. On AdLit.org. *All About Adolescent Literacy.* Retrieved from http://www.adlit.org/article/31527/.

Cooper, G. (1981). Frederick Winslow Taylor and scientific management. In C. W. Pursell (Ed.), *Technology in America: A history of individuals and ideas*. Cambridge, MA: MIT Press.

Didion, J. (1976). *Why I write*. Regents' Lecture, University of California at Berkeley, CA.

Ferguson, N. (2004). *Empire: The rise and demise of the British world order and the lessons for global power*. New York: Basic Books.

Fusfeld, D. R. (2001). *The age of the economist* (9th ed.). Englewood Cliffs: Prentice Hall.

Flower, L. Stein, V., Ackerman, J., Kantz, M., McCormick, K. & Peck, W. (1990). *Reading-to-write: Exploring a cognitive and social process*. New York: Oxford University Press.

Haswell, R. H., Briggs, T. L., Fay, J. A., Gillen, N. K, Harrill, R., Shupula, A. M. & Trevino, S. S. (1999). Context and rhetorical reading strategies: Haas and Flower (1988) revisited. *Written Communication, 16*(1), 3–27.

Horning, A. S. (2007). Reading across the curriculum as the key to student success. *Across the Disciplines, 4*. Retrieved from https://wac.colostate.edu/atd/articles/horning2007.cfm.

Jolliffe, D. A. & Harl, A. (2008). Texts of our institutional lives: Studying the 'reading transition' from high school to college: What are our students reading, and why? *College English* (70), 599–617.

Lal, D. (2001). *Unintended consequences: The impact of factor endowments, culture, and politics on long-run economic performance*. Cambridge, MA: MIT Press.

Lee, C. D. & Spratley, A. (2010). *Reading in the disciplines: The challenges of adolescent literacy*. New York: Carnegie Corporation. Retrieved from http://carnegie.org /fileadmin/Media/Publications/PDF/tta_Lee.pdf.

Marx, K., Engels, F., Moore, S. & McLellan, D. (1992). *The Communist Manifesto*. Oxford: Oxford University Press.

Nilson, L. (2010). *Teaching at its best: A research-based resource for college instructors* (3rd ed.). San Francisco: Jossey-Bass.

Rhodes, L. A. (2013). When is Writing Also Reading? *Across the Disciplines, 10*(4). Retrieved from https://wac.colostate.edu/atd/reading/young_potter.cfm.

Roberts, J. C. & Roberts, K. A. (2008). Deep reading, cost/benefit, and the construction of meaning: Enhancing reading comprehension and deep learning in sociology courses. *Teaching Sociology, 36*, 125–140.

Smith, A. (1776). *An inquiry into the nature and causes of the wealth of nations* (C. J. Bullock, Ed.). The Harvard classics (Vol. X). New York: P. F. Collier & Son.

Spivey, N. N. (1990). Transforming texts: Constructive processes in reading and writing. *Written Communication, 7*(2), 256–287.

Young, J. A. & Potter, C. R. (2013, December 11). The problem of academic discourse: Assessing the role of academic literacies in reading across the K-16 curriculum. *Across the Disciplines, 10*(4). Retrieved from https://wac.colostate.edu/atd/reading/young_potter.cfm.

Ziliak, S. T. (2009). Haiku economics: Little teaching aids for big economic pluralists. *International Journal of Pluralism and Economics Education 1*(1), 108–129.

Ziliak, S. T. (2011, January 3) Haiku economics: Money, metaphor, and the invisible hand. *Poetry Magazine*.

Getting to the Root of the Problem: Teaching Reading as a Process in the Sciences

Laura J. Davies
SUNY Cortland

This chapter examines how reading can be taught in high school and undergraduate science courses. Teaching reading in the content areas is important because students' reading skills are intrinsically connected to their writing skills and their subject-specific content knowledge. In order to improve students' reading abilities, the act of reading needs to be a more visible and frequent part of high school and college courses. The chapter defines college-level reading as acquiring genre- and discipline-specific "reading processes" that have recursive stages of pre-reading, reading, and revised reading. The extended examples in this chapter demonstrate how high school and college science teachers can teach students particular reading processes that can help them comprehend and analyze three common genres assigned in science courses: the popular science trade book and magazine article, the science textbook, and the empirical research article. The reading activities suggested emphasize the rhetorical nature of these scientific texts. This chapter argues that science teachers need to rely on frequent modeling and direct instruction in order to make the process of reading scientific texts more transparent to students.

I don't mind dandelions. In contrast to my neighbors' yards, deep-dark green swaths of grass, unmarred by weeds, my yard is speckled yellow. As anyone who's tried knows, it's a pain to get rid of dandelions. A dandelion's taproot buries quickly into the ground, making it nearly impossible to rip the plant out with your bare hands. You have to get down on your knees, trowel in hand, and dig the dandelion out—flower, stem, root, and all.

And this work takes quite a bit of effort. Some people get around that effort by dousing their lawns in herbicides; others, like myself, just mow down the dandelions when they turn scraggly and bald. But mowing is a temporary solution. Just days later, the taproots left just under the surface of the soil sprout anew, and the dandelions repopulate my yard.

I'm talking about dandelions here because I find them a useful metaphor when I talk with faculty across the disciplines about the connections between our students' reading skills, their writing skills, and their subject-specific content knowledge. The faculty conversations I hear in offices and hallways often fail to take into account the deeply rooted *reading* issues that contribute to problems in students' content knowledge and writing, problems that range from papers riddled with grammatical errors, exams or in-class discussions that demonstrate incomplete understanding of course material, written arguments that lack or misrepresent evidence, and plagiarism. Because students' underground reading issues aren't addressed, the "solutions" to student content knowledge and writing problems that are often discussed, from textbook pop quizzes and grammar drills to plagiarism detection software systems such as SafeAssign and Turnitin.com, are as temporary and ultimately ineffective as mowing down a lawn full of dandelions.

As the editors explain in the introduction to this collection, high school and undergraduate students have difficulty reading disciplinary texts. Part of this difficulty can be traced to students having ineffective or no *reading processes*, processes that are nuanced and flexible enough to use in a variety of rhetorical situations. Without these processes, students read shallowly and narrowly, miss important genre cues, and cherry-pick facts contained in individual sentences rather than comprehending whole-text arguments (Jamieson, 2013; Horning, 2011; Howard, Serviss & Rodrigue, 2010). These unsophisticated reading processes, coupled with the sophisticated writing prompts that faculty in the disciplines assign their students, can lead to poor student performance or student writing that might not accurately reflect students' knowledge of and engagement with the subject matter. What I'm arguing is that in some cases, a student's error-ridden or plagiarized writing, or that student's lack of content knowledge, can be symptoms of a much larger reading problem. Faculty members in all disciplines need to develop pedagogical strategies that will treat the problem—our students' lack of sophisticated reading processes—not the symptoms.

In this chapter, I explain how faculty in the sciences can teach students reading processes that can help students decode, analyze, and discuss disciplinary texts. I first define college-level reading by naming and describing stages of reading. In order to read complex, discipline-specific texts, students must learn strategies for what I term the *pre-reading, reading*, and *revised reading* stages. These stages are not linear or discrete. Rather, the stages of a sophisticated reading process overlap. Expert readers are recursive in how they move through these stages, circling back as they read and re-read a text for different purposes. Then, I describe activities that science teachers can use to teach students how to read the three genres high school and undergraduate students most often encounter in their science courses: 1. the popular science trade book or magazine article, written for a general educated public audience (including collections such as *The Best American Science and Nature Writing* and articles from publications like *Scientific American, Popular Science*, and *Wired*); 2. the science textbook; and 3. the empirical research article (published in peer-reviewed scientific journals such as *The New England Journal of Medicine, Science*, and *Chemical Reviews*). All the activities I describe underscore the rhetorical and contingent nature of scientific knowledge. Too often, students regard scientific texts as collections of facts about biological, chemical, or physical processes. When students think of scientific texts as merely content, they miss out on discovering how these texts can help them participate in the larger scientific process of posing hypotheses, collecting and analyzing data, making claims and conclusions from that data, and considering and challenging alternate methods and conclusions. The activities and assignments I suggest in this chapter show how emphasizing stages of the reading process (*pre-reading, reading*, and *revised reading*) can open up scientific texts to high school and undergraduate students, introducing them to the ways in which scientific knowledge is created, communicated, and circulated. If students understand the nature of the texts they read, they can read the texts with more alacrity, distinguish a text's key claims and information more easily, and write about the texts with more sophistication.

Definition of the Reading Process

All faculty—not just those in English departments or first-year writing programs— need to teach undergraduate students how to read. Rhodes (2013) makes this point and uses the assessment data from her first-year writing program to show that, contrary to what many faculty expect, students come into college with weak reading skills. In response, Rhodes argues that faculty across the disciplines need to "explain explicitly why and how we want students to address the texts we assign." (Rhodes, 2013, para. 6) Rhodes' argument here—that faculty must clearly explain to students the *purpose* of reading assigned texts—also draws on Horning's (2007) research on undergraduate students' weak reading skills. Rhodes explains that students who are not "good readers" are lacking "reading processes." (para. 2; para. 22) One of the primary reasons students come to college with poor reading skills is that they do not have sophisticated reading processes that help them comprehend, analyze, and interpret complex texts. College-level reading processes are "recursive," Rhodes argues, "requiring dialogue and feedback, along with revisions of perceptions and readjustments" (para. 22). Reading, Rhodes argues, is not a simple, one-step activity. It requires complex, critical thinking skills. In her description of reading processes—processes that depend on dialogue, feedback, and revision— Rhodes uses similar language as scholars who have described the writing process. This parallel between a concept of a *reading process* and the concept of a *writing process* is helpful for developing a reading pedagogy that is useful for faculty across the disciplines.

Writing process theory fundamentally changed how teachers teach writing and faculty's expectations for student writing. The advent of writing process theory in the 1960s, 1970s, and 1980s, and then the arguments for writing across the curriculum programs that quickly followed (including theories developed by Nancy Sommers [1980], Frank D'Angelo [1987], Susan McLeod [1989], and David Russell [1992]) shifted attention from the product of student writing to our students' writing processes. The writing process movement gave faculty and the discipline of writing studies a language to talk about what writers *do* while writing. Research about writers' writing processes helped scholars dig under the surface to unveil the work that goes into producing a piece of written text. The research that helped develop theories and practices of writing across the curriculum named and described the rhetorical complexities of disciplinary-specific genres, which require different kinds of writing and writing processes. Writing process and writing across the curriculum theories changed faculty expectations for student writing: faculty within writing studies and many outside the field now expect that students will go through multiple stages in their writing process and that these stages will take time and look differently for different genres and students. Most faculty also understand the recursive and reflective nature of the writing process and the role of dialogue, conferencing, and workshops in this cyclical process. Some faculty build in overt instruction of the writing process, teaching students how they might develop an idea, outline an argument, and revise for a particular audience.

Defining and discussing *reading processes*, as the field of writing studies has done with *writing processes*, can change how faculty teach reading across the disciplines and faculty's expectations for student reading. The definition of a reading process that I outline below shares some of the theoretical assumptions that describe the writing process, and it builds from Rhodes' (2013) argument about the importance of direct reading instruction, Horning's (2011) explanation of the reading skills and habits of advanced or "expert" readers, and Freedman's description of a pedagogical model to teach reading skills to multilingual students (2013). Freedman's (2013) model consists of nine specific reading strategies that were taught to students dually enrolled in an East Asian Studies course and the English Language Learning (ELL) program at the University of Toronto. Though her case study focused on these ELL students, Freedman points out that these "methods were presented as techniques that can assist nearly every reader or writer, whether one is working in an additional or native language" (para. 10). The reading techniques presented to the students included previewing texts, skimming texts, using context to decode vocabulary, analyzing how a writer used sources and evidence in their argument, and making a visual map of the argument (Freedman, 2013). What is important about the strategies Freedman explains is that these techniques, coupled with low-stakes reading quizzes to test students' comprehension, help students treat reading as a deliberate, tangible process. The methods gave students a focus for their reading, and having multiple goals for reading (reading to analyze evidence, reading to distinguish a writer's argument from the argument of a cited source) encouraged students to do multiple re-readings of a text, which in turn helps increase comprehension.

One way to help our students think of reading as a process is to name and describe, as Freedman did in her case study, the specific strategies expert readers use when reading a complex text. These strategies can be loosely divided among three stages: *pre-reading*, *reading*, and *revised reading*. As with the terms used to describe the writing process (*pre-writing/drafting*, *writing*, and *revising*), the stages are neither linear nor prescriptive. Rather, this process is recursive (Gogan).

In the *pre-reading* stage, readers sketch out the general purpose, genre, and scope of the text. The goal of pre-reading is to begin placing the text in a larger context, doing the meta-textual and meta-contextual awareness work Horning (2011) describes. Some of the work readers do while pre-reading includes noting the organizational pattern of the text, referencing the table of contents to see the large-scale structure and moves of a book-length text, researching the publication and author(s) of a text to understand the disciplinary conversations that the text might participate in, quickly glossing the text's headings and subheadings, and glancing at the works cited to note familiar sources that this text cites. Pre-reading might include writing work: writing down general impressions of the text's genre, purpose, and audience, jotting down questions the reader might have developed from the preliminary pre-reading research, and listing terms and concepts that are repeated in the text's title, headings, and subheadings.

In the *reading* stage, readers read the text with a specific, genre- and discipline-specific strategy. For example, when reading an empirical research study, experienced readers do not read the article straight through: instead, they read the abstract first, then the conclusions and discussion, and then the methods, data, and literature review. Knowing how to read during the reading stage depends on work done in the pre-reading stage. Reading does not necessarily have to be close and precise in the reading stage; in fact, skimming and scanning texts quickly is a strategy often deployed by expert readers in all stages of reading (Horning, 2011). During the reading stage, readers often annotate a text, marking interesting and important claims, circling key words, and asking questions in the margins. A reader may read a text several times in the reading stage, and this reading may happen collaboratively. Readers may read out loud with a partner or in a whole class, or do "stop and reads," where they read a paragraph or passage, and then stop and discuss its meaning with one another before moving on.

Finally, during the *revised reading* stage, readers shuttle between a close analysis of the text and reflecting on the implications of that text's argument and findings. Some of the strategies that Freedman (2013) describes, such as differentiating between the central argument and the arguments of the sources cited, belong in this stage. This analytical and reflective work is what distinguishes the reading stage from the revised reading stage. Revised reading means that the reader sees the text anew, through new angles and for new purposes. Some of this revision work is local and small, such as noting and analyzing patterns of diction throughout a text's claims and sub-claims. Other revision work is larger and more involved, such as moving on to read a major cited source and then re-reading the original text to understand more fully how the text interpreted and relied on the source. Revised reading also can ask students to make connections across a range of interdisciplinary texts, as described by Kathryn Nantz and William M. Abbott in their chapter in this collection. Nantz and Abbott describe several "brainstormer" assignments they used in their undergraduate Honors course that helped students read economics and history texts for particular purposes (p. 13). The revised reading stage unlocks the quiet, underground moves and implications of a text that may be missed in cursory readings.

Although I make a case in this chapter for teaching students rhetorical reading processes, Huffman's chapter in this collection offers an important caveat about the efficacy of emphasizing rhetorical reading. Huffman collected assessment data over three semesters from students in a newly redesigned developmental reading course at her university. Her study showed that students' reading comprehension did not improve through learning how to rhetorically analyze texts, which includes marking claims, identifying biases, and distinguishing content from purpose. As Huffman explains, the results of her study were surprising to her. She argues that students' continued struggles with comprehension even after being taught how to rhetorically analyze texts may be connected to the kinds of rhetorical reading strategies they were taught and how often these strategies were reviewed. My description of multi-stage readings processes and the reading activities I suggest below are offered with Huffman's findings in mind. Teaching rhetorical reading is not a magic bullet that can solve students' weak reading skills. What is more important is that students are introduced to a wide range of reading processes, that faculty are given adequate support to develop appropriate reading pedagogies for their courses, and that reading itself becomes a frequent and visible component of courses across the disciplines.

Teaching Students Reading Processes in the Sciences

In this section, I describe activities faculty in the sciences can use to teach high school and undergraduate students how to read scientific texts more critically. This section focuses on three commonly assigned genres in high school and undergraduate science courses: 1. the popular science trade book and magazine article; 2. the science textbook; and 3. the empirical research article published in a peer-reviewed journal. The activities I describe guide students towards thinking of reading as a recursive process that includes stages of *pre-reading*, *reading*, and *revised reading*, stages explained in the section above. My recommendations in this section build on Mary Lou Odom's suggestions in her chapter in this collection, in which she advises faculty to carefully consider how they can teach students ways in which students can navigate the complex, often multimodal texts that are assigned in courses across the disciplines.

The examples below derive from my work as a writing program director at both a national military service academy and a regional state college as well as my work as a graduate writing fellow at a large public university. My conversations with my science colleagues at all of these institutions, as well as my discussions about science reading and writing pedagogy with Margaret M.P. Pearce, assistant professor of biology at University of the Sciences, have helped me understand the particular challenges of teaching students how to read popular science trade books, science textbooks, and empirical research articles in ways that will help students more fully understand and participate in scientific discourse communities. Science faculty members, like many faculty across the disciplines, may feel underprepared to teach reading and writing, a worry addressed in writing across the curriculum scholarship (Bean, 2011). Also, many faculty are concerned about the limited class time they have to cover large amounts of content in their courses. Often, teachers worry that spending time in class teaching students specific reading or writing strategies will take too much time away from the course's content (Patton, Krawitz, Libbus, Ryan & Townsend, 1998). However, I and others argue that integrating assignments that target the development of students' reading processes help students move beyond superficial understanding and engagement with the content they read and learn in lectures and labs (Kalbfleisch, 2016; Morris, 2016).

Teaching students reading processes in their high school and undergraduate science classes can be a way to introduce students to the rhetorical nature of scientific discovery. Including philosopher Thomas Kuhn and rhetoricians Alan G. Gross and Charles Bazerman, scholars who study the rhetoric of science have long argued that scientific writing and scientific research are neither "objective" nor "detached" (Kuhn, 1962; Gross, 1990; Bazerman, 1988). Rather, scientific knowledge is produced through persuasion and shifting social structures and relationships. When scientists write up their findings, or make an argument about a specific hypothesis to a lay but educated audience, they are making claims, not listing facts. Students may not understand the contested, situated nature of scientific texts, and thus may perceive the knowledge presented to them in scientific trade books, textbooks, and empirical research articles as objective truths explained by unbiased writers. Students who hold onto this perspective (seeing science as a disinterested or neutral endeavor) miss out on participating in the scientific process because they do not understand how scientific knowledge is constructed, contested, circulated, and changed over time.

This concept of texts as situated, dynamic arguments is a threshold concept. Threshold concepts are ideas that are fundamental to understanding disciplines and acquiring knowledge. Once someone learns a threshold concept, they do not forget that concept (Adler-Kassner, Majewski & Koshnick, 2012). Although threshold concepts were originally described as tied primarily to disciplinary bodies of knowledge, others, such as the Council of Writing Program Administrators in their WPA Outcomes Statement for First-Year Composition 3.0 (2014) and the Association of College & Research Libraries in its 2015 Framework for Information Literacy in Higher Education, take a more interdisciplinary approach, describing threshold concepts that are shared across disciplines. Because the idea that texts are rhetorically constructed and situated is a threshold concept—not an idea that most students come to the high school or college classroom understanding—reading texts rhetorically is not something faculty should assume their students can master while reading on their own, outside the classroom. Teachers must bring the practice of reading inside the classroom.

Popular Science Trade Books and Magazine Articles: Teaching Reading in a High School Physics Class

One positive outcome of the Common Core State Standards Initiative is its insistence that "reading, writing, speaking, and listening should span the school day from K-12 as integral parts of every subject" ("Key shifts," 2016, para. 13). In other words, English language arts teachers do not bear sole responsibility for teaching students critical literacy skills and practices. Rather, students need to be reading, writing, speaking, and listening in all their content classes, and all K-12 teachers need to teach students how to read, comprehend, interpret, and analyze the complex, content-specific texts they assign in their classes. In grades 6–12, the Common Core State Standards (CCSS) expects that students will be learning how to read informational texts and literary nonfiction in their history, science, and technical classes. These specific "Literacy in History/Social Studies, Science, and Technical Subjects" standards ask teachers to venture beyond the course textbook and ask students to read increasingly complex texts in a range of subject-appropriate genres. The literacy standards expect that students will be able to work with these texts in specific ways, such as being able to name the text's central ideas, figuring out domain-specific vocabulary terms, analyzing a text's structure, and evaluating a text's evidence and conclusions ("English language arts standards," 2016). The CCSS's Appendix B includes a list of grade-specific "text exemplars" that teachers may use in their courses to meet these standards. The informational text exemplars for science, mathematics, and technical subjects at the high school level include government documents (reports from the U.S. Environmental Protection Agency and U.S. Department of Energy), primary texts (Euclid's *Elements*), technical descriptions and definitions that use both text and images, procedures and instruction sets, and various selections from popular science trade books and magazine articles ("Appendix B," 2016).

The CCSS, which have been adopted by 42 states as of July 2016, are not alone in promoting the value of assigning popular science trade books and magazine articles to high school students. The National Science Teacher Association (NSTA) also recommends using high-quality, current science trade books in K-12 science courses and publishes a list of the best science trade books published each year. Trade books, the NSTA argues, can engage students on a deeper level than traditional textbooks: "they pull students into a story-like presentation of scientific information. The topic becomes more real, more understandable, and more personal" (Schlichting, 2002, para. 6). Because many of these texts are written with strong narrative elements (a distinct authorial point of view, a reliance on description, anecdote, and metaphor), they can be more familiar to student and lay audiences. Popular science trade books and magazine articles are also powerfully influential in constructing students' and adults' scientific literacy, or their understanding of scientific and technical topics. In fact, rhetorician Heidi Scott explains how well written popular science trade books can sway the public to subscribe to a scientific theory that is widely contested among professional scientists, such as Stephen Jay Gould's evolutionary theories, just because the arguments are so compellingly written (Scott, 2007).

Even though popular science trade books and magazine articles often have strong narrative elements that make them more "readable" than science textbooks or empirical research articles, students still need to be taught how to read these texts. In other words, popular science trade books and magazine articles require a particular reading process. Below, I describe activities designed to teach high school students a reading process they can use to critically read popular science trade books and magazine articles. I use one of the CCSS text exemplars for grades 11 and 12, Gordon Kane's article, "The Mysteries of Mass," as the basis for these reading process activities. Kane is a leading physicist who studies particle physics and string theory, and his article was published in 2005 in *Scientific American*. Because the reading activities I describe ask students to examine the article's layout and the relationship between the article's visuals and texts, it is important that students read a PDF copy of the original version of the article, with the layout intact.

Kane's article, which would be appropriate for older high school students in a physics class, does more than explain how mass is calculated and the potential impact of the Higgs field and Higgs boson on scientists' understanding of the nature of the universe. Kane's article demonstrates how a writer takes up a research question and explores that question methodologically through research and descriptions of scientific theories and experiments. What is particularly interesting—and may be perplexing to many high school students—is that Kane does not arrive at an answer to his research question at the end of the essay. His two-part question—"How do elementary particles acquire mass?" and "Why do they have the specific masses that they do?"—is a question that is addressed in part by the theory of the Higgs field, but not entirely (Kane, 2005, p. 34). Kane's research question is genuine: he is explaining to the general, educated audience of *Scientific American* readers the phenomena that his fellow physicists are currently working on and flummoxed by. The uncertainty that Kane admits to emphasizes that science is an open-ended process, with far more questions than conclusive answers. Another reason the Kane article is a good example to use for teaching reading processes is that it is a manageable length for the older high school students: at seven pages long—longer and more sophisticated than the short *Buzzfeed* articles students read, post, and share through social media, yet short enough to read in class. As I argue above, it is essential that students read in class so that the work of reading is made visible in the science classroom. Students need to be taught through modeling, direct instruction, and discussion *how* they should read the texts they are assigned in their science courses.

It is important to interrupt the students' impulse to immediately start reading the article linearly, like they might do with a fictional narrative like a short story. It is also crucial to call students' attention to the fact that this article, like other popular science trade books and magazine articles, does more than define and describe facts. Instead, the writer is making an argument with this article. One *pre-reading* activity that can circumvent both these default instincts is asking students to "map" Kane's article onto the rhetorical triangle. Doing this visual mapping work helps students notice Kane's rhetorical situation: his context, his content, his purpose, and his audience. Teachers can ask students to draw a large triangle surrounded by a circle on a piece of paper, labeling the circle *context* and the three sides of the triangle *audience, content,* and *purpose.* The circle for *context* represents the larger rhetorical situation of the article: who the author is, when the article was written, the larger scientific conversation that this article participates in, and the larger global economic and sociopolitical context. The *content* side of the triangle is concerned with the "what"— the key terms, claims and evidence that the article is discussing. The *audience* side of the triangle addresses "who," both who this article was originally written for and the other stakeholders who are interested in this topic and argument. Finally, the *purpose* side of the triangle tackles the all-important question of "why"—why did the writer write this article, and what is that writer's ultimate objective?

Students can work with each other and the teacher in class to find this information online and within the article. Students can fill the map with words, phrases, bullet points, quotes, dates, and statements that answer these (and other) questions:

- "When did Kane write this? What do you know about what was happening in the world then?
- "Where was this published? What do you know about this publication? What kinds of people might read and subscribe to this magazine?"
- "Who is Gordon Kane? What is he an expert of?"
- "Who is writing to? How do you know?"

- "Who else might be interested in this topic and this article?"
- "Who or what was Kane responding to? How do you know?"
- "What kinds of examples and evidence does Kane use in his essay?"
- "Why, do you think, Kane wrote this article? What is your prediction? How did you make this prediction?"

Mapping this article may take one or two 40-minute class periods, or a full 75-minute block. Every student should have a copy of Kane's article that they can refer to, either printed out or on a tablet or laptop. The teacher can focus the activity by drawing the rhetorical triangle map on the board and filling it in with the students, asking the students to go back to the text and name the sentence, the paragraph, and the page that supports their analysis of Kane's argument and rhetorical situation.

This mapping activity is a powerful in-class *pre-reading* activity for several reasons. First, it compels students to slow down and revisit a text again and again, not to evaluate the evidence or claims but to focus on the text itself. There is a time for evaluation, but it is premature at the *pre-reading* stage—*pre-reading* is about getting a handle on the text and its general scope and trajectory. Second, mapping asks students to read for the general structure of the *argument*, not for content knowledge. The questions above frame the text as piece of responsive discourse, not a collection of statistics, quotes, and points. Third, the activity of drawing and mapping, much like graphic organizers students use in K-12 to plan their writing, makes apparent the kinds of cognitive work expert readers do while reading. As stated above and in this collection's introduction, expert readers are neither linear nor passive readers: they read recursively and with a purpose. By introducing students to mapping early in the course, teachers can come back to this exercise throughout the academic year, asking students to map the texts they read throughout the semester in whole-class discussions, in small groups, with partners, or by themselves.

After this pre-reading exercise, the teacher can ask students to read the article in its entirety. It is important that this reading happens in the classroom, as students need to be able to ask questions, discuss their reading with their teacher and peers, and see their teacher modeling how to read. A helpful classroom activity for the *reading* stage is asking students to write short summaries after they read the article once. Summary writing is a skill that many students lack, as demonstrated in Howard et al.'s 2010 research on student source use. With the Kane article, the teacher can ask students to write a one-sentence summary of Kane's central point, using both his essay and their map of his argument. After students write this one-sentence summary individually, they can write their summary on the board or several large sheets of paper around the room, not labeling their sentence with their name. These one-sentence summaries will probably be wildly different, as students usually focus on the content the writer is explaining (the definition of the Higgs field or the use of particle accelerators to determine the mass of the Higgs boson, in the case of Kane's article) rather than the writer's central purpose or argument. When all the one-sentence summaries are displayed, the teacher can lead the class in discussing the similarities and differences among the sentences, noting what key words and concepts are repeated across the summaries.

Although the one-sentence summary activity looks on the surface like a writing activity, I consider it part of the *reading* stage of the reading process I named above. It is another form of active reading or annotation; students shuttle between their *pre-reading* map and the text itself to write the summary. The one-sentence summary activity also illustrates how readers read and interpret texts differently. Each reader's uptake of the text is impacted by his or her own contexts and purposes. For example, students who have a shallow understanding of the physics of atomic structure will read Kane's article differently than students who might have explored topics such as dark energy, cosmology, or the Big Bang on their own. What makes the one-sentence summary activity so powerful is that it helps students distinguish between what the writer is *doing* within the text as a whole versus what the writer is *saying* or *talking about* at any particular place in the text, an important rhetorical distinction explained by Bean (p. 170).

When students read popular science trade books and magazine articles, they usually have an easier time discussing the writer's examples, evidence, and definitions than the writer's central argument. The one-sentence summary activity does not take much class time, yet it invites students to read the article multiple times and begin to notice genre elements. One important genre characteristic of the popular science trade book and magazine article is that the writer's main claim evolves, or becomes more sophisticated, over the course of the argument. A teacher can demonstrate how Kane posits increasingly specific questions over the course of the article by displaying the article on a projector and underlying Kane's claims and inviting students to name how the claims are related to each other. The concept of the evolving thesis is sometimes discussed in writing textbooks (Rosenwasser & Stephen, 2015), yet students often assume texts have the same basic construction as a five paragraph essay: an introduction with the thesis, three points of evidence, and a conclusion that re-states the thesis. A teacher can show students how Kane's central purpose does not appear until the conclusion of his essay: the essay was the work of the argument, not a report of an argument already conceived and settled.

After students read the Kane article and determine its central purpose, one *revised reading* activity they can do is analyze in more depth how the article is organized visually and structurally. In the original version of the article published in *Scientific American*, diagrams, sidebars, and illustrations, which in total constitute about half the length of the seven-page article, surround the main body of the text. Teachers can point to each of these sidebars and diagrams and ask students to discuss or write why Kane might have included each of these elements. What do they *do* for the reader—define a term, give background information, summarize the main points, offer an analogy, illustrate a complex process? This activity can open up a conversation about the interplay between text and image: how does Kane's main text benefit from these visuals? How might the reader's understanding of the scientific concepts he describes in the main text be changed if there were not these sidebars and diagrams?

Another corollary *revised reading* activity that teachers can lead students in doing is asking students to compare and contrast the information they learned in the Kane article with the material they are learning through their textbook and through their hands-on lab work. Compared to course textbooks, popular science trade books and magazine articles like the Kane article are more narrowly focused and often include more detail about specific scientific processes or the history of a scientific discovery. Kane's article on the Higgs field and Higgs boson explains an active research field awash with different theories about how particles acquire mass and interact with each other. After reading the Kane article in the context of a unit on atomic and subatomic physics, a physics teacher can ask his students these (and other) questions to extend students' reflection and critical thinking:

- How does reading the Kane article change how you understand the material you have been learning in class?
- What information is new to you?
- What is surprising to you?
- Where do you see contradictions? What do you make of these?

Science Textbooks: Teaching Reading in an Undergraduate General Chemistry Course

Research in college-level science pedagogy has shown that textbooks account for at least half of the required reading for undergraduate science courses (Wambach, 1998). Although these texts seem straightforward, students have difficulty engaging with content material from their course textbooks because of weak reading skills, which can be compounded by overall density of science textbooks, the absence of a "story line" to engage students and link facts and chapters together, and science's specialized language and vocabulary (Crow, 2004, para. 6). As Linda Crow argues in her analysis of undergraduate introductory biology textbooks, "biology textbooks are faced with dual purposes of teaching the foreign language of biology with teaching the content of biology" (Crow, 2004, para. 4). Her point resonates with all the sciences, not just biology. High school and undergraduate science students need strategies for navigating their course textbooks because for many students, textbooks are not readily accessible depositories for content. Textbooks also call for a particular reading process.

Content-rich textbooks are not context-free delivers of information. Just like popular science trade books and magazine articles, textbooks are arguments, rhetorically structured for a particular purpose and audience. As researchers in the history of the book and scientific communication have shown, current scientific knowledge and theories are not always accurately and adequately represented in science textbooks. Rather, the science textbooks can be a hub where scientific research, the market, social movements, religious arguments, and government regulations all meet, creating a text which presents a calculated worldview (Shapiro, 2013; Vicedo, 2012, p. 85). Teaching students that the textbooks they read are more than "passive receptacles of the bounties of scientific creativity and research" changes how students read the textbook (Vicedo, 2012, p. 83). Instead of memorizing facts, students can begin to question and critically examine the claims that hide behind the passive voice, nominalizations, and objective tone that characterize science textbooks (Dimopoulus & Karamanidou, 2013). When teachers challenge the textbook's presentation of science as "ahistoric, beyond doubt, universally applied knowledge," they have the potential to not only change how students approach a textbook reading assignment but also how students understand the scientific process (Dimopoulus & Karamanidou, 2013, p. 61).

The activities I describe below can help students read their textbooks more strategically and rhetorically. I use Raymond Chang and Kenneth A. Goldsby's general chemistry textbook, *Chemistry*, as my example text. Published by McGraw Hill, *Chemistry* is now in its 12th edition (2016), and it is a popular and well-regarded textbook used in undergraduate chemistry courses for students who are both chemistry majors and non-majors.

The first thing students probably notice about *Chemistry*, besides its hefty price, is its size. The 12th edition of *Change* and Goldsby's *Chemistry* is nearly 1,200 pages long, divided among 25 chapters, 4 appendices, and copious amounts of front matter and back matter, including a lengthy preface, glossary, answers to chapter questions, and an index. A helpful pre-reading activity early in the course can be to call students' attention to the textbook's rhetorical situation and its organizational principles. Here are questions faculty can ask students to answer as they begin to browse through their textbook:

- When was this published? What does this text's publication date tell you?
- Who are the authors? What do you know about them from the text, and from what you can find through a quick Internet search? How does this information affect how you think about and how you might read this textbook? What stake do they have in this book?
- Glance at the "contents in brief": What are key terms that appear here among in the chapter titles and subtitles?

- Read through the more detailed "contents": What is repeated in the chapter titles and subtitles in the table of contents? What is missing? What surprises you?
- What are the connections or relationships between the chapter topics? Why might the chapters be organized in this way?
- How might the appendices be useful for you?
- What terms are confusing to you?
- What supplementary materials (digital ebook, animations of chemical processes and reactions) are included, and how do you access them? How might these change how you read this text?
- What do the authors want you (as the student) to learn through this book? What are their priorities? What do they explain as their purpose in their preface?

Many science teachers may already assign students an activity like this; science faculty I've worked with sometimes give students a similar "textbook scavenger hunt" to complete within the first few weeks of the course. However, there is a key difference between that assignment, which is often completed for homework and never talked about in class, and the activity I am suggesting. The above pre-reading activity requires the faculty member to spend time in class discussing what students discovered about their textbook. Again, reading must be brought into the classroom in order for students to learn how to read discipline-specific texts such as their science textbook. The discussion does not have to be long. What is important is that the teacher has a conversation with students early in the course that identifies the course textbook as a rhetorically constructed text, not just a chronicle of facts. When students see the textbook this way, how they read the course textbook can shift: no longer do they merely skim chapters for facts, as novice readers might, but they can also begin questioning, as expert readers do, how the textbook presents scientific knowledge and why it privileges some theories over others.

A reading activity science faculty can do with their students is modeling annotation techniques for textbook reading. In high school, students may have been given study guides, concept maps or other graphic organizers to guide their reading of textbooks (Diep, 2014, para. 5). However, they still may not have an effective reading process for college-level textbooks, a process that helps them focus on the most important information in dense, lengthy textbooks like *Chemistry*. Research has shown that students who annotate while reading their science textbooks have an easier time remembering the information that they read (Zywica & Gomez, 2008). Both faculty and teaching assistants who may lead discussion sections of large introductory science classes can demonstrate how they annotate a textbook by sharing their annotations with their students, either by distributing photocopies of annotated pages, displaying an PDF of annotated pages on an overhead projector or smart board, or simply passing their annotated textbook among a group of students during class. The teacher can suggest a system students can use to either digitally or physically annotate their textbook, such as circling headings and sub-headings, highlighting key vocabulary terms, boxing difficult or confusing words, underlining key terms and claims, and writing short notes in the margins about connections between the content on that page and other knowledge they have from other chapters, lab work, or other classes. This modeling activity can be repeated throughout the semester, as even a short five-minute demonstration of a teacher's annotations for a particular chapter can emphasize the importance of annotation. This activity shows students that for expert readers, annotation is an inseparable part of the reading process for reading college-level textbooks, not something done in addition to reading (Zywica & Gomez, 2008, p. 163).

A science textbook's formidable length and dense, informational style can inhibit students from taking the time to re-read and reflect on the theories, knowledge, and arguments the text presents. For instance, an undergraduate student who may or may not be a chemistry major would find it challenging to read and fully digest all 1,200 pages in *Chemistry*, even if that textbook was their primary text in a two-semester introductory chemistry sequence. One revised reading activity that can encourage students to revisit key sections of their textbook is asking students to "translate" a particular passage for a younger high school or middle school audience. This is a variation of the "speaking for science" activity described by Cary Moskovitz and David Kellogg, where students write a press release for a general audience after reading a primary scientific text (Moskovitz & Kellogg, 2005, p. 327). For example, Chapter 2 of *Chemistry*, entitled "Atoms, Molecules, and Ions," gives a historical and theoretical overview of the chemical and physical properties of atoms and elements, explains how elements interact with one another, and describes the organization of the periodic table, molecular models, and chemical formulas.

Within this chapter, which contains eight sub-sections, the textbook authors offer this definition of the term "molecule": "A molecule is an aggregate of at least two atoms in a definite arrangement held together by chemical forces (also called chemical bonds)" (Chang & Goldsby, 2016, p. 50). The paragraph-long definition goes on to state that molecules have a neutral charge and may be formed from atoms of the same element or atoms of two or more elements. This textbook definition contains jargon-laden terms that could be confusing to younger students (e.g. "aggregate" or "definite arrangement.") When undergraduate science students revise this definition of a molecule for a particular audience, such as an eighth grade student, they have the opportunity to see their textbook anew. This revised reading activity invites students to re-read their textbook and use it for a new purpose, as a research source. Through the work of revising this textbook definition, students can think in more depth about the concept of a molecule as well as discuss how different words, shorter sentence lengths, and images might make the concept clearer for younger science students.

Empirical Research Articles: Teaching Reading in an Upper-division Microbiology Course

Recently, scholars of science education have argued for an increased emphasis on reading and discussing primary research in undergraduate courses as a way to introduce students to the values, practices, habits of mind, and discourse of the professional scientific community (van Lacum et al., 2012; Robertson, 2012; Wenk & Tronsky, 2011). Alberts (2009) argued against textbook-centric science teaching, contending that "rather than learning how to think scientifically, students are generally being told about science and asked to remember facts" (para. 1). Textbooks, unlike research articles, are written primarily for students and with the overarching purpose of delivering content. Research articles, on the contrary, are written for scientists in the field. Faculty who want to move away from textbooks in their undergraduate science courses, however, cannot just assign research articles to their students. They must also take the time during class or in small-group discussions and workshops to model a reading process for scientific research articles.

Another advantage of using primary research articles in an undergraduate course such as microbiology is to introduce emerging areas of inquiry that are not yet canonized in scientific texts. One of the recent vigorous developments in microbiology research is the role of gut flora, or gut microbiome, in human health and disease. Drawing on Robertson's (2012) explanation of using journal clubs to teach students reading strategies for scientific articles, below I describe activities to help undergraduate students read a recent study of gut microbiome through stages of *pre-reading, reading,* and *revised reading.* This article, Suez et al's "Artificial Sweeteners Induce Glucose Intolerance by Altering the Gut Microbiota," was published in October 2014 in *Nature,* a top international science research journal.

An important *pre-reading* activity is discussing the purpose and structure of the scientific research article. Understanding the purpose of the genre is part of an expert reader's metatextual awareness (Horning, 2011). The scientific research article is a manifestation of the scientific process: it names (albeit not in this order, which is key to point out to students) the researchers' observations, hypotheses, methods, data, and conclusions. Robertson (2012) suggests creating with students a checklist or worksheet that lists these attributes of the scientific process. Students can then use the checklist as a reading guide. Instead of reading "passively," Robertson argues, the worksheet encourages active, purposeful reading (p. 28). Asking students to bring printed copies of the text or using an overhead projector to display the article is one way to encourage active reading. Having a tangible, visible object to discuss and manipulate helps focus students on the text and facilitates making moves tethered to the text instead of making vague generalizations.

A short but effective *pre-reading* activity for scientific research articles is making predictions for the text based only on the title. Scientific research article titles name the key variables and research findings of a study, and students can be taught to use the titles as summaries to prepare them to read and interpret the study. For example, the title of Suez et al's (2014) study, "Artificial Sweeteners Induce Glucose Intolerance by Altering the Gut Microbiota," gives the reader—even a relatively novice reader—important clues about the study. Faculty can ask students to paraphrase the title, define the key terms in the title (artificial sweeteners, glucose intolerance, gut microbiota), make connections between those terms and their previous experiences and knowledge of microbiology, and predict the methods, assumptions, and possible limitations on the study. A related *pre-reading* activity is previewing the figures, often included in the appendices, and developing interpretations about the study and its findings based on the charts, tables, and figures alone.

Research articles are relatively short (the Suez et al., 2014 study has six pages of text and 11 pages of figures and data), yet they are often densely written with domain-specific vocabulary. In the *reading* stage, it's not necessary to ask students to decode each sentence. Rather, it's more useful to direct students' attention to the most critical parts of the research article for undergraduate students (the abstract, the conclusions, and the discussion) and model how to read. For example, the abstract for the Suez et al. (2014) study is 134 words, thus making it a feasible passage to tackle during class. Faculty can ask students to read the abstract out loud, sentence by sentence, stopping after each sentence to paraphrase, discuss, and look up unfamiliar or confusing terms. Slowing down the reading process within the key sections of a scientific research article, like the abstract, demonstrates to students how sophisticated readers decipher complex texts and how closely texts must be read.

One way to give students contextual awareness (Horning, 2011) for a scientific research article is to introduce them to tracing citations as a method for revised reading (Horning, 2011). Faculty can direct students to the references section of the article, discuss the citation method used in the sciences (Council of Science Editors, or CSE) and its rhetorical implications, and ask students to locate and read another recent article about gut microbiome published from a different lab. This revised reading activity emphasizes the ongoing inquiry work of scientific research: scientists across the world are engaged in similar research, whose relationships can be either cutthroat or collaborative, and they use different methods and variables to solve similar problems. Asking students to compare and contrast two scientific research articles focused on the same general research inquiry sheds light on the dialogic nature of science research and highlights the role of the scientific research article as a mechanism for extending that conversation.

Conclusion

Conversations about student writing issues and/or students' lack of content knowledge at an institutional level need to be reframed and focused on students' reading practices. More often than not, these issues, ranging from shallow understanding of course content to student plagiarism, are symptoms of students' weak reading skills. Confronting these issues without addressing student reading skills is futile as mowing down a lawn full of dandelions. The dandelions—and the problems that emerges from weak reading skills—will keep popping up. In order to help students become better readers of the complex texts faculty across the disciplines assign, faculty need to model the reading processes for expert readers use and design in-class activities that can help students acquire these processes.

The three examples of reading process pedagogy that I described above illustrate a few strategies high school and college science faculty can use to help their students read three discipline-specific genres: the popular science trade book and magazine article, the science textbook, and the empirical research article. Through these examples, I hope to give science teachers an adaptable model for how they can talk with their students about what it means to read these genres, how they can demonstrate the reading processes of skilled readers, and how they can support their students' emerging reading processes. One benefit of teaching reading in science courses is that it gives faculty an opportunity to teach students the dynamic, rhetorical nature of science texts. Faculty in other disciplines can modify these particular pre-reading, reading, and revised reading activities for other subjects, genres, and levels of students. Through these activities, students can begin to imitate the recursive processes expert, college-level readers use as they decode and analyze texts.

All high school and college faculty need to reframe how we think about reading. Reading is far from a basic skill mastered in elementary school or in a first-year writing class. Reading processes students learn in other classes, grades, and contexts are not easily transferrable. This problem of transfer has been discussed in writing studies research (Carillo, 2015), and Chris Anson's study of how even expert writers struggle to transfer their writing knowledge and writing skills should give pause to faculty and administrators who may claim that students should "already know how to read" (Anson, 2016). Even when a student is a good reader in one class or one context, that does not necessarily guarantee that he or she will read well or read critically in another class or context. Every text is different, and so teachers need to continually model and talk about how to read the genres in their discipline. Although faculty members are often expert readers, they might not be experienced at teaching students how to interact critically with texts. In order to help students acquire college-level reading skills through the stages of pre-reading, reading, and revised reading, faculty need to be supported by their institutions as they develop ways to teach discipline-specific reading strategies. It will take time for students to learn how to read, and it will take time for faculty across the disciplines to learn how to teach reading. Yet, this investment of time and energy is worth it. Just as teaching writing across the curriculum helps students learn the values and practices of specific disciplines, teaching reading across the curriculum can also help students understand and participate in the disciplines they are studying.

References

Adler-Kassner, L., Majewski, J. & Koshnick, D. (2012, Fall). The value of troublesome knowledge: Threshold concepts in writing and history. *Composition Forum, 26.* Retrieved from http://compositionforum.com/issue/26/troublesome-knowledge -threshold.php.

Alberts, B. (2009). Redefining science education. *Science, 323*(5913), 437.

Anson, C. M. (2016, June). The Pop Warner chronicles: A case study in contextual adaptation and the transfer of writing ability. *College Composition and Communication, 67*(4), 518–549.

Appendix B: Text exemplars and sample performance tasks. (2016). *Common core state standards for English language arts & literacy in history/social studies, science, and technical subjects.* Retrieved from http://www.corestandards.org/assets/Appendix_B.pdf.

Association of College & Research Libraries. (2015, February 2). *Framework for Information Literacy for Higher Education.* Retrieved from http://www.ala.org/acrl /standards/ilframework.

Bazerman, C. (1988). *Shaping written knowledge: The genre and the activity of the experimental article in science.* Madison: University of Wisconsin Press.

Bazerman, C., et al. (2005). Rhetoric of science, rhetoric of inquiry, and writing in the disciplines. In C. Bazerman, et al. (Eds.), *Reference guide to writing across the curriculum* (pp. 66–84). West Lafayette, IN: Parlor Press and the WAC Clearinghouse. Retrieved from https://wac.colostate.edu/books/bazerman_wac/.

Bean, J. C. (2011). *Engaging ideas: The professor's guide to integrating writing, critical thinking, and active learning in the classroom.* (2nd ed.) San Francisco: Jossey-Bass.

Carillo, E. C. (2015). *Securing a place for reading in composition: The importance of teaching for transfer.* Logan: Utah State University Press.

Chang, R. & Goldsby, K. A. (2016). *Chemistry* (12th ed.). New York: McGraw Hill.

Council of Writing Program Administrators. (2014, July 17). *WPA outcomes statement for first-year composition (3.0).* Retrieved from http://wpacouncil.org/positions/outcomes. html.

Crow, L. (2004, January 30). The good, the bad, and the ugly: Introductory biology textbooks. *Journal of College Science Teaching.* Retrieved from http://www.nsta.org/pub lications/news/story.aspx?id=49013.

D'Angelo, F. (1987). *Aims, modes, and forms of discourse.* In G. Tate (Ed.), *Teaching Composition: Twelve Bibliographic Essays* (pp. 131–154). Fort Worth: Texas Christian University Press.

Diep, F. (2014, June 11). Reading techniques help students master science. *Scientific American*. Retrieved from http://www.scientificamerican.com/article/reading-tech niques-help-students-master-science/.

Dimopoulus, K. & Karamanidou, C. (2013). Towards a more epistemologically valid image of school science: Revealing the textuality of school science textbooks. In M. S. Khine (Ed.), *Critical analysis of science textbooks: Evaluating instructional effectiveness* (pp. 61–77). Dordrecht, Netherlands: Springer Science+Business Media.

English language arts standards: Science & technical subjects: Grade 11–12. (2016). *Common Core State Standards Initiative*. Retrieved from http://www.corestandards.org /ELA-Literacy/RST/11-12/.

Freedman, L. (2013, December 11). "Reading to write" in East Asian studies. *Across the Disciplines, 10*(4). Retrieved from https://wac.colostate.edu/atd/reading/freedman.cfm.

Gogan, B. (2017). Reading as transformation. In A. Horning, D. Gollnitz & C. Haller (Eds.), *What Is College Reading?* Fort Collins, CO: The WAC Clearinghouse and University Press of Colorado. Available at https://wac.colostate.edu/books/college/.

Gross, A. G. (1990). *The rhetoric of science.* Cambridge, MA: Harvard University Press.

Horning, A. S. (2007, May 17). Reading across the curriculum as the key to student success. *Across the Disciplines, 4.* Retrieved from https://wac.colostate.edu/atd/articles /horning2007.cfm.

Horning, A. S. (2011, October). Where to put the manicules: A theory of expert reading. *Across the Disciplines, 8*(2). Retrieved from https://wac.colostate.edu/atd/articles/horn ing2011/index.cfm.

Howard, R. M., Serviss, T. & Rodrigue, T. (2010). Writing from sources, writing from sentences. *Writing & Pedagogy, 2*(2), 177–192.

Huffman, D. (2017). Examining a rhetorical approach to teaching developmental reading. In Horning, A., Gollnitz, D. & Haller, C. (Eds.), *What Is College Reading?* Fort Collins, CO: The WAC Clearinghouse and University Press of Colorado. Retrieved from https://wac.colostate.edu/books/college/.

Jamieson, S. (2013, December 11). What students' use of sources reveals about advanced writing skills. *Across the Disciplines, 10*(4). Retrieved from https://wac.colostate.edu/atd /reading/jamieson.cfm.

Kalbfleisch, E. (2016, January). Imitatio reconsidered: Notes toward a reading pedagogy for the writing classroom. *Pedagogy, 16*(1), 39–51.

Kane, G. (2005, June 27). The mysteries of mass. *Scientific American, 293,* 40–48.

Key shifts in English language arts. (2016). *Common Core State Standards Initiative.* Retrieved from http://www.corestandards.org/other-resources/key-shifts-in-english -language-arts/.

Kuhn, T. S. (1962). *The structure of scientific revolutions.* Chicago: University of Chicago Press.

McLeod, S. H. (1989). Writing across the curriculum: The second stage and beyond. *College Composition and Communication 40,* 337–343.

Morris, J. (2016, January). A genre-based approach to digital reading. *Pedagogy, 16*(1), 125–136.

Moskovitz, C. & D. Kellogg. (2005). Primary science communication in the first-year writing course. *College Composition and Communication, 57*(2), 307–334.

Nantz, K. & Abbott, W. M. (2017). Utilizing interdisciplinary insights to build effective reading skills. In A. Horning, D. Gollnitz & C. Haller (Eds.), *What Is College Reading?* Fort Collins, CO: The WAC Clearinghouse and University Press of Colorado. Available at https://wac.colostate.edu/books/college/.

Odom, M. L. (2017). Multiliteracies and meaning-making. Writing to read across the curriculum. In A. Horning, D. Gollnitz & C. Haller (Eds.), *What Is College Reading?* Fort Collins, CO: The WAC Clearinghouse and University Press of Colorado. Retrieved from https://wac.colostate.edu/books/college/.

Patton, M. D., Krawitz, A. Libbus, K., Ryan, M. & Townsend, M. A. (1998, October). Dealing with resistance to WAC in the natural and applied sciences. *Language and Learning Across the Disciplines, 3*(1), 64–76.

Rhodes, L. A. (2013, December 11). When is writing also reading? *Across the Disciplines, 10*(4). Retrieved from https://wac.colostate.edu/atd/reading/index.cfm.

Robertson, K. (2012, July/August). A journal club workshop that teaches undergraduates a systematic method for reading, interpreting, and presenting primary literature. *Journal of College Science Teaching, 41*(6), 25–31.

Rosenwasser, D. & Stephen, J. (2015). *Writing analytically* (7th ed.) Boston: Cengage Learning.

Russell, D. R. (1992). American origins of the writing-across-the-curriculum movement. In A. Herrington and C. Moran (Eds.), *Writing, teaching and learning in the disciplines* (pp. 22–42). New York: Modern Language Association.

Schlichting, K. (2002, August 26). Promoting science literacy at home. *Science Scope.* Retrieved from http://www.nsta.org/publications/news/story.aspx?id=47360.

Scott, H. (2007). Stephen Jay Gould and the rhetoric of evolutionary theory. *Rhetoric Review, 26*(2), 120–141.

Shapiro, A. R. (2013). *Trying biology: The Scopes trial, textbooks, and the antievolution movement in American schools.* Chicago: University of Chicago Press.

Sommers, N. (1980, December). Revision strategies of student writers and experienced adult writers. *College Composition and Communication, 31*(4), 378–388.

Suez, J. et al. (2014, 9 October). Artificial sweeteners induce glucose intolerance by altering the gut microbiota. *Nature, 514*, 181–186.

van Lacum, E., et al. (2012, August). First experiences with reading primary literature by undergraduate life science students. *International Journal of Science Education, 34*(12), 1795–1821.

Vicedo, M. (2012, March). Introduction: The secret lives of textbooks. *Isis, 103*(1), 83–87.

Wambach, C. A. (1998, Winter). Reading and writing expectations at a research university. *Journal of Developmental Education, 22*(2), 22–25.

Wenk, L. & Tronsky, L. (2011, March/April). First-year students benefit from reading primary research articles. *Journal of College Science Teaching, 40*(4), 60–67.

Zywica, J. & Gomez, K. (2008, October.) Annotating to support learning in the content areas: Teaching and learning science. *Journal of Adolescent and Adult Literacy, 52*(2), 155–165.

"Reading to Write" in East Asian Studies

Leora Freedman

UNIVERSITY OF TORONTO

A reading-writing initiative called "Reading to Write" began in 2011–12 at the University of Toronto as a partnership between an East Asian Studies (EAS) department and an English Language Learning (ELL) Program. In this institution, students are expected to enter into scholarly discussions in their first year essays, yet many (both native English speakers and non- native speakers) did not seem to adequately comprehend or to complete the assigned reading. With a large number of multilingual students enrolled in its courses, EAS was seen as the ideal site to pilot integrated support for English language proficiency. Language-teaching methodology related to reading comprehension, vocabulary expansion, and academic writing was adapted to the disciplinary material and embedded in the curriculum of weekly tutorial (small group) sessions led by TAs. The initiative has resulted in a rapid development in TAs' teaching ability as well as a rise in EAS department morale. Although a formal study has not been undertaken, the perception among TAs and faculty is that the quality of students' reading and writing has also improved.

Cultural Changes in the University

In Canada, "college reading" is not necessarily synonymous with the reading done at four-year universities. Colleges have traditionally focused on vocational education, so "college reading" is more likely to consist of textbooks rather than scholarly material. On the other hand, the reading at four-year universities emphasizes the critical comprehension of peer-reviewed texts and includes oral and written engagement with this disciplinary scholarship. Even for students with English as their first language (L1), this university reading presents challenges. The situation is further complicated by the relatively recent growth of a "multilingual majority" (Hall, 2009) in our university population. The difficulties multilingual students may have with scholarly reading are often compounded by gaps in their educational backgrounds as well as by disruptions that have occurred in their lives (Johns, 2005). . . . The four-year university system in Canada is currently engaged in an extensive process of change in order to develop adequate social and pedagogical strategies for integrating so many students with English as their second (or third etc.) language (L2).

Given these deep cultural changes in the makeup of our student population, teaching methods are rapidly evolving. This article will discuss the development of "Reading to Write," a pedagogical experiment launched four years ago in two large introductory East Asian Studies (EAS) courses at the University of Toronto (UT). EAS focuses on the study of East Asian history, languages, literature, philosophy, and religion; and students can earn either an undergraduate major, "specialist," or minor (these terms have somewhat different meanings in Canada). The department offers mainstream, credit-bearing courses which were previously not in any way specially geared for L2 students, though they attracted a large percentage of L2 undergraduates. EAS courses also continue to include many L1 students. English language instruction, in which primacy was given to fostering academic reading ability for both L1 and L2 students, has now been integrated into three EAS gateway courses through a collaborative initiative with the English Language Learning Program (ELL) http://www.artsci.utoronto.ca/current/advising/ell. As of 2016, "Reading to Write" has been running for five years, but the focus of this chapter will be on the initiative's first and most formative academic year, 2011–12.

The 23,702 undergraduate students in UT's Faculty of Arts and Science, to which EAS belongs, come from 140 countries ("About Arts & Science" 2012). Many (40–50%) are first generation university students. UT has a policy of "guaranteed access," in that financial means are arranged for all accepted students, and the institution serves many Toronto residents, 40% of whom were born outside Canada. There is also a large cohort of multilingual international students. The university has a well-developed system of writing centers and a Writing Across the Curriculum (WAC) program, both of which provide support to this initiative. The ELL Program also offers non-credit courses and drop-in activities for multilingual students. However, for all undergraduates across this university there is no required English or composition course, and there are no credit-bearing English as a Second Language (ESL) courses. There are also no general education requirements of the type seen in US (and some other Canadian) institutions. Given the scale of the need to address English language development, the goal of the initiative was to create a model that could be exported from EAS to other departments. In order to achieve this, it has been necessary to work toward a significant cultural shift around multilingualism, to build what Zamel (2004, p. 7) terms "the model of possibility."

Raising Awareness about Multilingualism

Several years of preparatory groundwork preceded the EAS initiative. During this period, individual sessions were given by the ELL coordinator to groups of TAs across the disciplines, in cooperation with the WAC and TA Training programs. Topics included the function of languages in students' layered identities (Ferreira &

Mendelowitz, 2009; Hafernik, 2012), teaching multilingual students (Freedman, 2012b), and marking papers in a multilingual environment (Freedman, 2012b). Resources for faculty and teaching assistants were disseminated on the Writing at UT website http://www.writing.utoronto.ca/faculty and at new faculty orientation sessions. The non-credit Intensive Academic English course offered to students by the ELL program had also generated curricular models and "content based" materials (Song, 2006; Stoller, 2002) that could be adapted to credit courses. When funding became available for a larger project, it was apparent that the most fruitful place to start was with a reconsideration of the role of reading in the academic lives of students. Initial sessions on how to incorporate reading strategies instruction into the discussion of a disciplinary text (Freedman, 2012c) had been given for faculty and TAs, and the strong responses—both positive and negative—indicated that this topic touched a nerve.

In just a few years, the initial surprise at the suggestion that students in a university requiring a very high GPA for entry might need reading instruction has begun to give way to acceptance of this fact and enthusiasm for integrating methods of reading support. (For a detailed survey of research establishing the critical importance of directly teaching university-level reading, see the "don't, won't, can't" section of the editors' Introduction to this book). It has been helpful to expose TAs and faculty to recent research on reading comprehension among university students, which explores the reasons for non-compliance with reading assignments (Hoeft, 2012) as well as the gap between students' perceived level of comprehension vs. their actual understanding (Manarin, 2012). Instructors and TAs now see that "ESL" issues are intertwined with issues of migration, class, and educational background, and that our native-speaker population also benefits from the attention to English proficiency.

Creating an Instructional Model

The goal of the "Reading to Write" initiative was to integrate language instruction with the regular curriculum (Cox, 2011) of two large first-year East Asian Studies courses which attract many international and multilingual students and are required for a major in this discipline. (This department was not involved in the university's WAC program, and there were no previous interventions. It was also determined that it was not necessary to obtain approval for this project from the Institutional Review Board). Reading was seen as the most fundamental area to address, underlying the difficulties many of the students have with research, writing, vocabulary, and speaking. At initial meetings with the EAS department, the ELL coordinator discussed the "reciprocity" between reading and writing (Leki, 2001) and the need to address the more visible writing issues through the disciplinary reading that informs writing (Grabe, 2001; Matsuda, 2001). EAS had the advantage that its faculty and TAs had first-hand experience with attaining a high level of literacy in an additional language, either English or an Asian language, since knowing an Asian language is an important part of the discipline. As well, EAS undergraduate students and Ph.D. candidates are required by the department to study one of the Asian languages; therefore, attention to language learning was already part of the departmental culture. For many faculty members, both reading in a foreign language and translation are regular aspects of their scholarship.

Although these are large lecture courses with about 200 students per class, the students also have a weekly 50-minute session or "tutorial" with a teaching assistant, in groups of about 25. Most TAs at UT teach tutorials that are attached to larger courses taught by a faculty member, though some TAs work only as markers (graders). These tutorials have traditionally been seen as a site for reviewing and—at their best—critically discussing and applying course concepts. However, the TAs are usually given minimal teacher training, and the planning of tutorial sessions is often left up to the TA. Some departments or courses do have a distinct curriculum for tutorials, but criticism is often leveled at the many other departments in which the tutorial is merely a repetition of ideas from the lecture or the readings in easier, more digestible terms.

In EAS, the more general problem of reading comprehension was compounded by the department's emphasis on teaching history as an exercise in critical thinking from the very beginning of students' involvement in this discipline. This means that contrary to the expectations of many EAS students, the learning of historical chronology and facts is subordinated to the critical examination of historiography. In some instances, faculty are attempting to "un-teach" the monolithic official histories students have absorbed in their previous educations. It is likely that this process of challenging the way students have been taught to think about East Asian history makes reading in English even more difficult, as the schemata necessary for the task are not already ingrained.

It was decided by EAS that all 12 weeks of the TA-led tutorial sessions would be reshaped to include the teaching and practice of strategies for scholarly reading and writing. These would be designed to be useful to both L1 and L2 students. Both the faculty and the Lead TA wanted to address the problems of past iterations of these courses, in which students had relied on TAs to summarize points from the professors' lectures and from the readings. The initiative was seized as an opportunity to make the tutorials a more active learning environment, to scaffold readings without replacing them, and to support students' writing.

One of the primary goals of the "Reading to Write" initiative was to improve the training of TAs as a path toward assisting students. In this goal, we benefited from the experience of the university's WAC program, which provided a ready-made TA development model. In the WAC program, departments choose a Lead

TA who receives intensive training in writing pedagogy. In turn, the Lead TA trains the TAs in particular courses to deliver writing instruction as part of one or more tutorials ("Writing Instruction"/WIT, 2011). In this pilot phase of the ELL initiative, the Lead TA was largely trained one-to-one with the ELL coordinator. In the 2011–12 "Reading to Write" initiative, the EAS Lead TA held four developmental workshops with the course TAs each term, in which TAs simulated some of the tutorial activities they were expected to lead. In some of these training sessions, the materials used to demonstrate methods of teaching reading strategies were taken from the literature on multilingual learners, so that TAs were simultaneously introduced to the ideas of Vivian Zamel, Ilona Leki, and other researchers.

During this preparatory period, the ELL coordinator did not encourage EAS faculty members to change readings they traditionally assigned or to lessen the amount of required reading. The faculty members reflected on their choices of reading and made some changes, but generally the initiative has emphasized helping students rise to the expected level of achievement in their reading and writing. The essay assignments in both courses were redesigned to reflect the structures common in EAS literature. Students were explicitly asked to make decisions about essay organization that mirrored those made by scholars in this discipline. For example, students structured their analytical content either chronologically, discussing a point related to a particular time and moving across cultures, or spatially (geographically), analyzing a point related to a particular location and moving through time. As well, six shorter, "low-stakes" writing assignments were designed and added to each course. In addressing the needs of language-learners through faculty development, the "Reading to Write" initiative reflected the CCCC position statement on Second Language Writing and Writers (2009).

Redesigning EAS Tutorials

As a first step in preparing tutorial materials, the ELL coordinator produced a series of short handouts describing various reading and language-learning strategies. The approach is similar to what might be used in an advanced English language course in which students are learning to read scholarly texts. Some of the methods were adapted from the ELL coordinator's experience abroad teaching English as a Foreign Language to advanced undergraduates as well as MA and Ph.D. candidates. These methods were presented as techniques that can assist nearly every reader or writer, whether one is working in an additional or a native language.

The reading, vocabulary building, and writing strategies presented in the handouts in the first term were: (1) previewing (see Appendix A); (2) skimming and scanning; (3) active reading; (4) learning vocabulary from context clues; (5) summarizing, and (6) distinguishing an author's opinion (as opposed to the opinion of a cited source). In the second term, some of these earlier strategies were applied in new ways, and additional handouts were developed on: (7) distinguishing between information and argument; (8) how information is used in an argument, and (9) the visual mapping of an article (Freedman, 2012a). All of these handouts are posted in the Resources for Students section of the ELL website: http://www.artsci.utoronto.ca/current/advising/ell/resources-for-students.

Using these ELL handouts as a basis, the Lead TA created six online "low-stakes" writing assignments for each course, a plan inspired in part by Khoo's (2007) use of short assignments for critical reading/writing practice by English-language students. In the Fall EAS course, an introduction to pre-modern East Asian history, these brief assignments fell into two categories. The first few were accounts of the students' own experiences with these strategies, as applied to the collection of primary historical documents that formed the bulk of the Fall course reading. The last few assignments introduced a method for summarizing and also required an informal account of the student's observations and questions about the text. We called this informal response "active reading" and described it as the first stage of formulating a critical reading response. These assignments were reflective and personal, yet they were also linked to the disciplinary material—a combination well-suited to students transitioning from high school. We thus built into the course design the expectation that students would experience for themselves the "reciprocity" between reading and writing and would see how practice in each reinforced the other. We wanted them to become conscious of their individual approaches to reading. In addition to this, we realized they needed a comparatively long time to get used to the idea—totally foreign to many—that their own views of a reading could be significant.

In each tutorial during the Fall EAS course, students were introduced by their TAs to a particular strategy or aspect of the reading/writing process. Students were then expected to apply these principles independently to new texts, and the results would become the basis for the following week's tutorial discussion. The TAs were encouraged to use these strategies recursively throughout the semester and also into the spring course. Beginning the reading of a text with in-class previewing or skimming made reading into a social activity. This group attention to reading also gave opportunities for the TAs to define major terms that are not necessarily explained by the readings and cannot be learned through a dictionary definition (e.g. "modernity"). These tutorials were thus supporting students' learning but in a more sophisticated way than before, one which gave them tools they could apply to other situations.

For the spring course, which is an introduction to modern East Asian history and for which the Fall course is a prerequisite, the Lead TA designed more complex "low-stakes" assignments that required a combination of summary and critical response. The reading load in the spring course is heavier and more theoretical. Thus, the emphasis in the tutorials and writing assignments gradually shifted toward the elements of argument. The TAs read over the students' reading responses prior to the tutorial session in which that reading was to be discussed, so they came to tutorial knowing what students had not grasped. It was clear that "forcing" reading compliance through the reading responses as well as the expectation of verbal contribution to discussions did make the groups more prepared. Across the first year of the initiative, it was apparent to the experienced TAs that students were better able to participate and more engaged with the course material than in past iterations of these courses. Attendance at tutorials remained high even though attendance was not part of the grade.

During this spring course, new methods were introduced, such as visually mapping an author's argument (see Appendix B), which the TAs demonstrated in tutorial and students then practiced independently with a different reading. (See Grabe [2012] for a discussion of this strategy). It became apparent that some of the work on argument that was planned for this term could not be fit into the schedule, since the students needed more time to practice grasping the basics of an author's message. Students were introduced to the concept of how the selection of evidence functions to frame a historical argument, for example, but did not appear ready to formulate their own full critiques of authors' arguments. The requirements for the essay, while aiming at developing critical thinking, were centered on the thoughtful synthesis of course concepts. It was planned that in the second year of this pilot, the initiative would extend into a second-year theory course in which students would be introduced more fully to methods of argument and would be expected to critique sources in a more sophisticated manner.

Focus on Writing in EAS

By the time students in both courses were asked to write the research essay, which was based on a group of pre-selected readings, they had already submitted and received comments on many low-stakes writing pieces. This early practice in articulating the course concepts appeared to bear fruit in their essay-writing. In their meetings with the ELL coordinator, the experienced TAs, professors, and the Lead TA have commented consistently on the virtual disappearance of "patch-writing," or attempts at paraphrasing in which students have used segments from sources with minimal alterations, and a significant lessening of plagiarism, as well as the evidence of students' increased familiarity with course readings. The writing practice was enhanced by having students write a short paragraph at the end of each tutorial about what they had learned or what remained confusing to them. In meetings, the TAs reported that their students' writing on these short pieces (for which no TA response was given) was often the best they did in the course.

The process of writing the essay was scaffolded in both semesters, beginning with the reading responses, which could be used as the basis for an essay if the student wished to do so. In addition, three to four tutorial sessions were set aside for the discussion of the writing process and for in-class work on the essay, which involved free writing, peer exchange, and informal feedback from the TA. The Writing at UT website (http://www.writing.utoronto.ca/advice) provided a number of ready-made materials that TAs could adapt for teaching essay organization (Plotnick, n.d. [a]), quoting and paraphrasing (Plotnick, n.d.[b]), and the documenting of sources (Procter, 2012). One of the most direct ways in which the courses addressed language-learning was in the activity around thesis statements. In an early stage of the writing, students brought to tutorial a trial thesis and a list of evidence from sources in note form. In small groups, they then shared the thesis statement and also explained orally how they planned to draw from the sources to support the thesis. Since the essay sources were restricted to a pre-selected group of course readings, a discussion could then develop around which ideas or facts from these sources would best support each student's central concept.

In giving students a chance to talk through their synthesis of the readings at an early stage in the writing, the courses exemplified a pedagogy that recognizes the strong and complex links among critical reading, writing, oral ability, and listening comprehension which need to be fostered for ELL students' academic success. (Grabe, 2001; Williams, 2008; Yang, 2010). It is clear to researchers that discussion of difficult, complex topics orally as well as in writing helps students make linguistic progress (Casanave & Sosa, 2008), and that literacy proceeds most rapidly when language learning is embedded in "real" tasks which are meaningful to the student (Zamel, 2004). Students also participated in a peer exchange of drafts, through a guided activity prepared by the ELL coordinator (Freedman, 2012a), and they were required to revise and resubmit their essays after receiving a grade and comments from the TAs.

Responses to the Initiative

Although a formal study of this initiative has not yet been undertaken, the frequent meetings among the ELL coordinator, the Lead TA, faculty members, and the course TAs led to detailed discussions that focused on the perceived results of this intervention. (Internal assessments for the purpose of revising the program design have been done, with the Lead TA periodically reviewing random samples of students' writing, as well as distributing student surveys to capture students' own perceptions of their progress. These results are not included in this article). Some TAs noted that students they observed in their tutorials still seemed to focus primarily on the readings used in the low-stakes writing assignments, and they were often not as well prepared to discuss other readings in class. In other discussions about their tutorials with the ELL coordinator, TAs pointed out that during tutorial discussions it seemed to them that students had done a significant amount of the reading, if not all of it, since they were able to respond to questions and comments from both the TA and other students about the assigned reading—a type of interaction that was rare in these tutorials prior to this initiative.

In reflecting on the reading responses they had marked, as well as on the essay assignments that often developed from these short responses, the TAs also felt that their students had benefited from articulating some of the course concepts prior to writing the research essay. Participants in this teaching initiative told the ELL coordinator that department morale had been raised, since teaching the tutorials was no longer a monologue by the TA for students who hadn't done the reading, and TAs' attempts to start discussions were more often rewarded with student participation. The EAS department was also energized by the interest and admiration of its pedagogical experiment among the university's administration and other departments, as well as the use by other departments of materials generated by the initiative. The significant drop in plagiarism cases contributed to this aura of success. At the end of the year, the Lead TA was nominated by students and faculty in EAS for the university's TA teaching excellence award, which she won.

Another source of pride was the knowledge that we were experimenting with a pedagogically challenging goal: to support L2 students while also helping L1s. Another TA wrote to the ELL coordinator: "I have definitely noticed that the quality of the written responses has greatly improved, particularly for our non-native English speakers, of whom there are many. The program is definitely of use for our students, and I certainly hope that we are able to continue it in the future [. . .]" It is interesting to note that the TA perceived the program as helpful to both L1 and L2 students and that no sense of conflicting needs between the two groups is expressed. In their discussions with students, TAs have repeatedly discovered with great surprise that what they considered to be the most basic, unarticulated procedures necessary for scholarly reading (e.g. giving oneself permission to scan chapter titles or headings; looking first through an index; reading with greater or lesser focus on certain passages)—were revolutionary ideas for their undergraduate students.

There was also a perception among the TAs and faculty that the most negative student outcomes had been avoided, with a significant drop in failures that were previously linked to non-compliance with reading assignments and misperceptions about the reading material. The department's acting chair reported: "Everyone involved is in agreement that the program is critically needed and should definitely continue—we just need to have more discussions on how to adapt it given what we have learned [. . .]." The main area addressed in subsequent discussions about adapting and improving the initiative was the need to retain sufficient tutorial time for the teaching of course content. Faculty and TAs differed as to the percentage of time they felt should be given to language instruction. It seems likely that the success of this "integrative" instruction also depends on the relative skill of the TA: The more experienced TAs seem to find it easier to fuse language instruction and course content into a more seamless whole. This aspect of the initiative has continued to be a focal point for discussion in these group meetings, even as techniques for training the TAs in this challenging goal have become more consciously articulated and more sophisticated.

A Work-in-Progress

The "Reading to Write" initiative is a work-in-progress, in which the approach is still the subject of ongoing assessment, discussion, and debate. The questions include, but are not limited to:

1. What is the relationship of this initiative and its broader application across departments, to the WAC program and the writing centers?
2. Does this approach also address the needs of both L1 and L2 students who have advanced English language proficiency?
3. How will language instruction be balanced with course content, especially in courses that rely more heavily on tutorials to deliver new content?
4. Will these methods accelerate English language proficiency in this largely multilingual student population?

Of these questions, the relationship of the ELL methods to the WAC program and writing centers will likely be the easiest to determine, since the approaches naturally complement one another. Writing instructors have long been aware of the interrelatedness of reading, writing, speaking, and listening. Writing center pedagogy also supports the approach of addressing more than one modality (e.g. speaking, writing, and listening are part of most sessions). Also, our writing centers have recently begun to partner with ELL to address the reading issue. The ELL coordinator has been repeatedly invited to speak to writing center directors and instructors about how support for academic reading can be integrated with the centers' work. As of Fall 2016, 1:1 sessions focused on helping students with their academic reading will be offered for the first time as a pilot project in one of the writing centers. In this area, too, a cultural shift at the university appears to be taking place. Many of these writing instructors have become versed in techniques for teaching reading comprehension that until recently were more familiar to foreign language teachers.

The question (b) of how well this approach can serve the needs of advanced students is entwined with the question (c) of how to balance language instruction with course content. The answers need to be crafted course by course as the methods are disseminated, since the ideal balance will vary with the student population taking the course as well as with the course content and level. TAs should be consulted in these decisions, since they are the ones primarily experiencing the results of the intervention in the tutorial classroom, which is the locus of reading and writing support activities. At the same time, faculty members, the Lead TA, and the ELL coordinator can provide concrete suggestions for addressing the full range of needs in the tutorial—from the linguistically advanced students who need a forum for trying out sophisticated arguments, to the less advanced students who need a clear definition of terms at the heart of the discipline. To some extent, this balance is what teaching always involves; the initiative simply causes more of these dilemmas to be articulated and provides opportunities for discussion. Feedback from students on the quality of the tutorials and the uses they make of the strategies has also been sought and will help to determine future directions.

These inquiries will also provide some answers to the question of (d) how helpful these interventions are for the multilingual population. It is important, however, that faculty, administrators, and TAs maintain the perspective that achieving high levels of literacy in a transnational, multilingual world is a lengthy and complex process. Linguistic development, like students' intellectual development in general, is often uneven and non-linear. Students need to understand that successful performance in academic writing, which may be a more immediate goal, is linked to efforts in other areas, such as reading, which are often invisible to the people marking their papers. (For example, a grader may comment on an overly general sentence, identifying it as a writing problem, but the same grader may not comment on or even perceive the student's vague grasp of the reading material; the grade is given officially for the quality of the writing).

Finally, students need to develop the self-discipline to continue working independently toward a higher level of English proficiency, since the university does not require continuous instruction in English. Bensoussan's (2009) study showed that English as a Foreign Language (EFL) students read in English mainly for information and academic purposes but rarely for pleasure, while Upton & Lee-Thompson (2001) have documented the extensive use made by many students of mental translation through the medium of their first languages. These researchers' observations help to explain the laborious progress students often make through their assigned texts; the joylessness with which many of them approach reading in English or in any language, and the reasons they are "too busy" (Hoeft, 2012, p.13) to complete assigned reading.

The pedagogical contribution of "Reading to Write" is that it intervenes during the students' first university year to draw attention to the imperative for students to read and develop strategies for scholarly reading, and as well, to give students a gradual introduction to the sophisticated analytical writing tasks that will become more common as they progress to higher-level courses. The set of strategies it provides for reading, building vocabulary through engagement with texts, and improving academic writing skill can be applied in a variety of linguistic situations, throughout the undergraduate years and beyond. All students stand to benefit from an educational environment in which English proficiency is emphasized through the dissemination of methods that acknowledge multilingualism and can also be used to attain proficiency in other languages.

It is nevertheless important to recognize that we cannot instantly overcome the effects of many formative years spent "not-reading" or reading only superficially even in the L1 (see Editors' Introduction to this volume). There are also risks inherent in explicitly teaching students as "strategies" the actions that good readers learn to perform instinctively through repeated engagement with written texts. For example, when teaching skimming and scanning we found it necessary to repeat that these strategies are not intended as substitutes for thorough reading. As Grabe (2012) points out, a strategy is not exactly the same as a skill, and before our students can become skilled readers, most of them will need many more years of practice in recursively using these strategies in individualized combinations with a variety of materials. In "Reading to Write," we are beginning what will ideally evolve into a longer process for which the student will take responsibility.

Current Developments

The "Reading to Write" initiative has been continued and expanded over the past four years, contributing to further pedagogical innovations. Many of the TAs have repeatedly returned to teach in the introductory courses, already comfortable in their role and familiar with our methodology. These factors have resulted in a smooth, unobtrusive integration of the language-based instruction with the EAS course content. This disciplinary integration is a challenging task, but it is necessary if the enhancements to the courses are to avoid seeming too remedial for university students. TAs report feeling more competent in these tasks, and they also work more collaboratively with each other to plan their sessions. Significantly, several EAS faculty members have decided for the first time to integrate the modeling of scholarly reading into their lectures, too.

In the spring 2013 term, the initiative expanded into a second-year EAS course focused on theory. In addition to the recursive use of many of the reading strategies introduced in the 100-level courses, emphasis was placed on strategies for close reading (Freedman, 2015). The analytical reading of targeted passages with an eye toward theoretical tendency, authorial perspective, tone, and other elements of argument was modeled by the professor during lectures. Students then practiced close reading with guidance from TAs, who collaboratively developed critical questions to address in tutorials. The course also included several reading quizzes, or written demonstrations of analytical reading. On the whole, the students, many of whom completed all three EAS courses in this initiative, seemed more reflective about the content of their reading and their own reading practices as well as better able to deploy academic language. One TA commented that by the end of this term, "they [the students] were actually discussing the texts in the language of the texts."

This shift into not only comprehending disciplinary texts but also gaining facility with their language is highly significant for students. Sandra Jamieson (2013) has documented the often superficial use students make of disciplinary sources in their writing. Both Steven J. Pearlman (2013) and Brian Gogan (2013) recommend addressing this gap through a focus on close reading of disciplinary texts. However, multilingual students do not necessarily perceive or absorb the phrases common to an academic discipline which may seem obvious to a native English-speaker (Cortes, 2004), or even the more general academic phrasing (Adel & Erman, 2011; Nekrasova, 2009). Unless the instructor calls particular attention to these phrases—many of which also contain the grammar students need to learn (Lewis, 1997)—students may not take notice of or absorb them. As such, our TA training has begun to focus on teaching students to find these phrases and to distinguish phrasing common to a discipline from the distinctive phrasing of individual writers which needs acknowledgment. We explore how TAs can "give" students the language they need, woven into a discussion of a topic or into the comments on their writing.

These current developments are already being shared with the 18 departments in our WAC program, through training as well as invited presentations. A number of the WAC Lead TAs and course professors in departments like Religion and Anthropology have begun to experiment independently with the integration of reading instruction. As of Fall 2016, similar initiatives have been developed in the Linguistics, Contemporary Asian Studies, Philosophy, and Statistics departments. It is anticipated that this shift in the culture of the university's approach to teaching writing will continue to gain momentum, and that new methods will emerge as these techniques are filtered through an increasing number of disciplinary curricula.

This approach acknowledges that writing cannot be addressed in isolation from students' engagement with reading. In turn, university or college reading represents a leap into critical scholarly discourse that students will not necessarily make on their own, whether English is their L1 or L2. There is now more understanding in our institution that reading tasks often need as much scaffolding as those involving writing. For a large part of our student population, university reading means reading extensively for the first time in English. Thus, language teaching methods are increasingly important tools for instructors who want their students to be able to take an active part in class discussions and to make critical use of readings in their writing. By integrating language teaching methodology focused on reading comprehension with some common WAC approaches, the "Reading to Write" initiative provides a model for future developments in this area. It also suggests that college reading must be defined at least partially as a language-learning process.

Note

The author warmly thanks these individuals in the East Asian Studies Department, University of Toronto: Ms. Sara Osenton; Dr. Graham Sanders; Dr. Thomas Keirstead; Dr. Ken Kawashima, Dr. Janet Poole, and the course TAs. This article is dedicated to Ms. Deborah Knott and Dr. Margaret Procter, with gratitude for their extensive work developing and supporting the English Language Learning Program at the University of Toronto.

References

"About Arts & Science." Faculty of Arts & Science/ University of Toronto. Retrieved from http://www.artsci.utoronto.ca/main/about.

Adel, A. & Erman, B. (2012). Recurrent word combinations in academic writing by native and non-native speakers of English: A lexical bundles approach. *English for Specific Purposes, 31*, 81–92. http://dx.doi.org/10.1016./j.esp.2011.08.004.

Bensoussan, M. (2009, November). Reading preferences and expectations of multilingual Israeli university students. *Journal of Multilingual and Multicultural Development, 30*, 465–480. http://dx.doi.org/10.1080/01434630903071957.

Casanave, C. P. & Sosa, M. (2008). Getting in line: The challenge (and importance) of speaking and writing about difficult ideas. In D. Belcher & A. Hirvela (Eds.), *The oral-literate connection: Perspectives on L2 speaking, writing, and other media interactions* (pp. 87–109). Ann Arbor: The University of Michigan Press.

Conference on College Composition and Communication (CCCC). (2009). *Statement on second language writing and writers*. Retrieved from http://www.ncte.org/cccc/resources /positions/secondlangwriting.

Cortes,V. (2004). Lexical bundles in published and student disciplinary writing: Examples from history and biology. *English for Specific Purposes, 23*, 397–423. http://dx.doi.org /10.1016/j.esp.2003.12.001

Cox, M. (2011, December 21). WAC: Closing doors or opening doors for second language writers? *Across the Disciplines, 8*(4). Retrieved from https://wac.colostate.edu /atd/ell/cox.cfm.

Gogan, B. (2013, December 11). Reading at the threshold. *Across the Disciplines, 10*(4). Retrieved April 23, 2015, from https://wac.colostate.edu/atd/reading/gogan.cfm.

English Language Learning Program. University of Toronto/Faculty of Arts and Science. Retrieved from http://www.artsci.utoronto.ca/current/advising/ell.

Ferreira, A. & Mendelowitz, B. (September, 2009). Creating a dynamic contact zone: An undergraduate English course as multilingual pedagogic space. *English Teaching: Practice and Critique, 8*(2), 54–79.

Freedman, L. (2015). Using close reading as a course theme in a multilingual disciplinary classroom. *Reading in a Foreign Language, 27*(2), 262–271. Retrieved from http://nflrc .hawaii.edu/rfl/October2015/articles/freedman.pdf.

Freedman, L. (2012a). Previewing; Skimming and scanning; Active reading; Learning vocabulary from context clues; Summarizing; Distinguishing between information and argument; How information is used in an argument; Distinguishing an author's opinion; Visual mapping; Guide for revision or peer exchange of drafts. In *Resources for Students*. English Language Learning (ELL) Program/ Faculty of Arts & Science, University of Toronto. Retrieved from http://www.artsci.utoronto.ca/current/advising /ell/resources-for-students.

Freedman, L. (2012b). Teaching multilingual students: An overview for course instructors and TAs. Grading multilingual students' papers: What are the issues? Grading multilingual students' papers: A practical guide. In *Resources for faculty/ Multilingual students*. Writing at University of Toronto. Retrieved from http://www.writing .utoronto.ca/faculty/multilingual-students.

Freedman, L. (2012c). Teaching reading comprehension. In *Resources for faculty*. Writing at University of Toronto. Retrieved from http://www.writing.utoronto.ca/faculty.

Grabe, W. (2012). *Reading in a second language: Moving from theory to practice.* Cambridge: Cambridge University Press.

Grabe, W. (2001). Reading-writing relations: Theoretical perspectives and instructional practices. In D. Belcher & A. Hirvela, (Eds.), *Linking literacies: Perspectives on L2 reading-writing connections* (pp. 15–47). Ann Arbor: University of Michigan Press.

Hafernik, J. J. & Wiant, F. M. (2012). *Integrating multilingual students into college classrooms: Practical advice for faculty.* Toronto: Multilingual Matters.

Hall, J. (November, 2009). WAC/ WID in the next America: Redefining professional identity in the age of the multilingual majority. *The WAC Journal 20*, 33–49. Retrieved from https://wac.colostate.edu/journal/vol20/index.cfm.

Hoeft, M. E. (2012). Why university students don't read: What professors can do to increase compliance. *International Journal for the Scholarship of Teaching and Learning, 6*(2), 1–19.

Jamieson, S. (2013, December 11). What students' use of sources reveals about advanced writing skills. *Across the Disciplines, 10*(4). Retrieved April 23, 2015, from https://wac .colostate.edu/atd/reading/jamieson.cfm.

Johns, A. (2005, May 15). Guest editor's introduction: The linguistically diverse student. *The Linguistically Diverse Student: Challenges and Possibilities across the Curriculum* [Special Issue]. *Across the Disciplines 2*. Retrieved from https://wac.colostate.edu/atd /lds/index.cfm.

Khoo, E. (2007). *Beating the odds: Success stories of students overcoming English language challenges.* (Booklet.) University of Toronto Scarborough, The Writing Centre, Teaching and Learning Services. Retrieved from http://ctl.utsc.utoronto.ca/eld/sites /default/files/beating_the_odds.pdf.

Leki, I. (2001). Reciprocal themes in ESL reading and writing. In T. Silva & P. K. Matsuda (Eds.), *Landmark essays on ESL writing* (pp. 173–190). Mahwah, NJ: Lawrence Erlbaum Associates.

Lewis, M. (1997). *Implementing the lexical approach: Putting theory into practice.* Boston: Heinle Cengage Learning.

Manarin, K. (2012). Reading value: Student choice in reading strategies. *Pedagogy, 12,* 281–297.

Matsuda, P. K. (2001). Reexamining audiolingualism: On the genesis of reading and writing in L2 studies. In D. Belcher & A. Hirvela, (Eds.), *Linking literacies: Perspectives on L2 reading-writing connections* (pp. 84–105). Ann Arbor: University of Michigan Press.

Nekrasova, T. M. (2009). English L1 and L2 speakers' knowledge of lexical bundles. *Language Learning, 59*(3), 647–686.

Pearlman, S. J. (2013, December 11). It's not that they can't *read*; it's that they *can't* read: Can we create "citizen experts" through interactive assessment? *Across the Disciplines, 10*(4). Retrieved April 23, 2015, from https://wac.colostate.edu/atd/reading/pearlman.cfm.

Plotnick, J. (n.d. [a]). Organizing an essay. In *Advice/ Planning and organizing.* Writing at the University of Toronto. Retrieved from http://www.writing.utoronto.ca/advice/planning-and-organizing.

Plotnick, J. (n.d. [b]). Using quotations; Paraphrase and summary. In *Advice/ Using Sources.* Writing at the University of Toronto. Retrieved from http://www.writing.utoronto.ca/advice/using-sources.

Procter, M. (2012). Standard documentation formats. In *Advice/ Using Sources.* Writing at the University of Toronto. Retrieved from http://www.writing.utoronto.ca/advice/using-sources.

Song, B. (2006). Content-based ESL instruction: Long-term effects and outcomes. *English for Specific Purposes 25,* 420–437.

Stoller, F. L. (2002). Promoting the acquisition of knowledge in a content-based course. In J. A. Crandall & D. Kaufman (Eds.), *Content-based instruction in higher education settings* (pp. 109–123). Alexandria, VA: TESOL.

Upton, T. A. & Lee-Thompson, L-C. (2001). The role of the first language in second language reading. *Studies in Second Language Acquisition 23*(4), 469–495.

Williams, J. (2008). The speaking-writing connection in second language and academic literacy development. In D. Belcher & A. Hirvela, (Eds.), *The oral-literate connection: Perspectives on L2 speaking, writing, and other media interactions* (pp. 10–25). Ann Arbor: The University of Michigan Press.

Writing at the University of Toronto. Advice on Academic Writing. Retrieved from http://www.writing.utoronto.ca/.

Writing instruction for teaching assistants (WIT) project: A description. (2011). University of Toronto. (Internal document received from Dr. Andrea Williams, WIT Coordinator, November 29, 2012).

Yang, L. (2010). Doing a group presentation: Negotiations and challenges experienced by five Chinese ESL students of commerce at a Canadian university. *Language Teaching Research 14,* 141–160. http://dx.doi.org/10.1177/1362168809353872

Zamel, V. (2004). Strangers in academia: The experiences of faculty and ESOL students across the curriculum. In Vivian Zamel & Ruth Spack (Eds.), *Crossing the curriculum: Multilingual learners in college classrooms* (pp. 3–37). Mahwah, NJ: Erlbaum.

Appendix A. Reading to Write: About Previewing

It is common for students to dive into an academic text and begin reading in a hurry, which is often counterproductive. When reading for academic purposes, it is preferable to read with certain goals in mind. This will enable you to place your focus on the proper elements of the reading and to avoid wasting time on elements which aren't important for your purposes.

Your professors and TAs may read with their research goals in mind. As a student, your primary purposes in reading are shaped by the course you're taking and/or the papers you're writing. Spend a few minutes previewing a text before starting to read, in order to orient yourself toward what is important for *you* in this reading. Here is a basic method which can be applied to many texts. Not every question will be relevant for all texts, and you may find additional questions to ask yourself.

1. Read the **title**—don't skip over it! Titles are chosen to orient the reader and should give a sense of the central concepts in the text.
2. Think about the **subject matter**: Have you read about this topic before?
3. Where and when? What do you already know about it, or what might you guess? Is it linked in some way to your personal experience? Do you already have opinions about some aspect of this topic?
4. **Who** wrote this text? What information do you have about this **author**? Does any information about the author appear anywhere on the title page or elsewhere in the text? If the author is an historical figure, what do you already know about him or her?
5. **Where** was this text originally **published**? What type of publication is this, and where does it fit into this field of study? Who would be the **audience** for this kind of writing? What would the audience expect to find in it?
6. When was this text originally published? What is the significance of this time period in this field of study? Is the text historical? Current? Or is it possibly outdated? What were the major events or theoretical trends around the time the text was written or published?
7. Read the chapter titles or the headings that break up the chapter or article. What seems to be the general progression of ideas here?
8. Why has your professor assigned this text? Where does it fit into the course as a whole? What kinds of facts and ideas are you expected to retain from this reading?

Appendix B. Reading to Write: Visual Mapping

Many people find it easier to absorb reading material by creating a visual map of an article, book chapter, or an important section of a piece of writing. A visual representation of concepts has the advantage of showing on a single page the complex logical relationships that an author may develop in many pages of writing. The map can provide a useful reminder of these relationships to refer back to as you move through a text. Additionally, it can function as a study tool, reminding you of key concepts that you've read and heard lectures about in greater detail. Depending upon your personal learning style, a visual map may be a superior means of memorizing material for tests and can also aid in the writing of longer papers. The map may be drawn by hand or made on the computer; sophisticated "mind-mapping" software programs also exist for this purpose. Here are some examples of visual mapping:

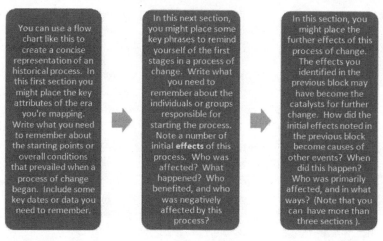

Figure 1

Note that this chart could also be added to in any way you find helpful. If you need to keep events that occurred in several regions or countries clearly separated, an individual chart could be made for each region. Alternatively, you might organize your chart to show the causes and effects that occurred across regions and countries. Quick flow charts made by hand during a lecture may also make your class notes more understandable when it's time to review them.

Here is another type of visual map which might be used to help distinguish between an overarching idea or thesis that runs through an entire article or section of a work, and the smaller details, examples, or points which help explain and illustrate that central concept.

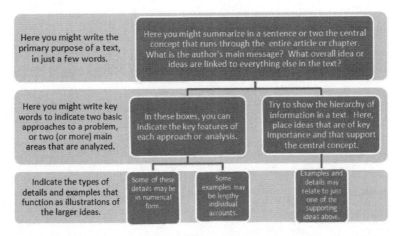

Figure 2

The two examples above were made using "Smart Art," which appears under the "Insert" button in Word 2007. However, even a simple Word table like the one below can become a valuable visual aid. (This is made by clicking on "Insert Table," and then specifying the number of rows and columns you want). Many students find that the time taken to create a table is worthwhile, as it helps in keeping track of ideas in a complex reading and can also allow a comparative look at several readings.

Examples in Table Form

(Example 1)	(1a)	(1b)
Here, you could place a summary of one author's point of view on a subject.	The centre column might hold the areas common to both the author and the sources cited by him or her.	Here, place contrasting evidence or ideas which the author may refer to or critique in the article.
(Example 2)	(2a)	(2b)
Another way to use a chart is to use each column for some key area you're comparing across texts. Here, name the area.	This column could contain the relevant ideas from Article A which relate to the key area you're comparing.	This column could contain the relevant ideas from Article B which relate to the key area you're comparing, and so on. There may be many more columns and rows added.

Examining a Rhetorical Approach to Teaching Developmental Reading

Debrah Huffman

INDIANA UNIVERSITY PURDUE UNIVERSITY, FORT WAYNE

This chapter discusses assessment of curricular changes made to a first-year reading course required of students who do not meet the minimum score on at least one of three standardized reading exams.[1] The curriculum moved from a basic-skills, objective-testing model to a rhetorical-analysis, writing-based model. The theory driving the changes was that a rhetorical approach to developmental reading may foster better comprehension as well as critical thinking through better engagement with the material. Data examined from the first three semesters—36 sections and 633 students—includes pretest and post-test essays, final grades, and student evaluations. Results suggest inconsistent gains in identification of main idea, primary points, and bias. Course pass rates and evaluations showed more improvement. An unexpected result was that student writing about the assigned reading changed significantly, with 91 percent of post-tests at least twice as long as pretests and 71 percent having more paragraphs. Implications are that students using the rhetorical analysis, writing model may be more engaged and satisfied by the course, and the reading they learn to do may make them more engaged writers, but the approach may not improve comprehension. This study speaks to what may promote effective learning and assessment of reading.

One of the most significant areas of college reading scholarship is developmental reading pedagogy, significant not for abundance as much as duration. Developmental reading pedagogy has a very long history in the United States and is still one of the most common types of stand-alone reading courses outside of literature. Preparatory departments were common in mid-19th century colleges and universities and included special classes for the underprepared, reading and writing skills being prevalent areas of concern (Wyatt, 1992). For over 150 years now, the "problem of poor reading" continues to be addressed by developmental reading courses, and those courses continue to meet with varied levels of success.

Despite numerous scholarly articles proposing solutions and a pool of K-12 reading research theory that has trickled up to postsecondary education, we have yet to find a satisfactory way to address the reading needs of developmental college students as they begin their experiences reading across the curriculum. The deficit,

---

1   The study was IRB approved and granted exemption, protocol #1305013619.

transmission, and skills-based models still used by many college developmental reading courses are criticized practices (Newton, 1999; Tierney & Pearson, 1994 [1981]), both for lack of practical effectiveness and deflation of student commitment and enthusiasm for their higher education. Experiences with such a standard approach at my university seemed to bear this out and led to the renovation discussed here.

This chapter does not claim to offer the new best way to teach first-year or developmental reading. It offers part success story and part cautionary tale as it describes a reading course renovation and subsequent study. I survey the previous course to acquaint readers with a common curriculum for college developmental reading courses and put into context the rather radical departure I took in its redesign. Following a description of the changes made, most of the chapter is devoted to the issue of assessment of the new course to provide readers some important considerations for implementing or gauging the effectiveness of similar curricular changes.

Reading Instruction, Study Skills, and First-year Orientation

The existing reading course at my university was a common incarnation of college developmental reading, an amalgam of teaching reading skills as well as study skills and freshman success initiatives. It was housed in the campus Centers for Academic Success and Achievement (CASA) and designed by its director, who had a doctorate in literature. The roughly 25 sections per semester were taught predominantly by part-time instructors in that division. The staffing was also typical. Developmental reading courses are often overseen by the campus academic support unit and taught by part-time faculty with little or no academic specialization in reading. Unlike some developmental college courses, this one did earn three credits and a letter grade.

Many students began the course frustrated. If they were not already discouraged that insufficient test scores[2] made the course mandatory for most of them, they took a Degrees of Reading Power (DRP) test in class on the first day that could exempt them from having to take the course if they scored high enough (most did not). The DRP requires students to select the most plausible sentences to fill in blanks within paragraphs of a short passage. This initial exam did not count toward the final grade, but another DRP test given as the final exam was worth 20 percent of the grade, so the second test was high stakes as well as stressful. A "hold" was placed on the students' registration until successful completion of the course (above

---

2   Students needed to score at least one of the following: above 450 on the SAT Critical Reading test, above 19 on the ACT Reading Test, or a score of 001 or 002 on the IPFW Reading Placement (Accuplacer) test.

a C-), and quite a few students ended up having to retake the course to achieve a successful grade.

Frustration mounted with the reading coursework. The reading-across-the-curriculum textbook was also a common approach, focused on basic reading concepts such as vocabulary, inference, and patterns of organization. However, in addition to the 17 short-answer and multiple-choice quizzes (comprising about half of each chapter), an accompanying online component was required with numerous practice and "mastery" multiple-choice tests. Add a midterm and a final exam, and students were taking tests every week in class as well as on their own. The course also assigned additional thematic material on global issues for five short essay responses and 17 annotations of readings based on explicit directions. Although these additional assignments were arguably effective ones, students often ended up either not completing them or giving them only cursory attention.

The course also had additional components designed not for reading instruction but for new student orientation and success. Students attended and occasionally completed short assignments for 10 "community hours" and "campus connections" usually led by an undergraduate senior who focused on study skills, career identification, and involvement in campus organizations and events, often through playing games. The community hour was a fourth hour required every week in addition to the three weekly class hours. Attending all these hours with my students (some instructors did not), I noticed more apathy than frustration, although a few students complained about the relevance and the extra hour required for the three-credit course.

Separately any part of this course could have been effective, but the course was trying to do too much and serve too many purposes. Student engagement suffered, as did their grades. Many just quit coming to class or doing the required work and activities. The course did not have a good reputation, among students or their advisors. When the CASA director, who had asked me to help revise the course, left the university and my Dean moved the course to the English department and my leadership, the charge was simple: improve the D/F/W (grade of D, F, or Withdraw) rate. Certainly I wanted the new course to keep the students engaged enough to complete the course with above a D; however, I had broader and more meaningful goals for student learning.

It was midterm Spring as I was teaching my first semester of the previous course when I learned I would be taking over the course for the coming Fall. I had worked closely with the CASA director to understand the course, and I had talked with others who had been teaching it, so I understood some difficulties. As a teaching scholar of reading and of composition for over 15 years at the time, I had well-informed ideas about what to change. The greatest challenge was developmental pedagogy, which was not a familiar area for me; however, as I quickly began cramming on developmental scholarship I quickly learned that engagement and motivation are critical components.

Rhetorical Reading in the Writing Program

Moving the reading course to the Department of English and Linguistics, to be coordinated by a soon-to-be associate professor specializing in reading and composition (I was tenure-track at the time) and taught by part-time instructors in English, immediately gave the course some disciplinary clout. The community hours were eliminated, as was the hold restriction that had been requiring the attention of a full-time employee. I assigned outcomes that enabled the course to meet a new general education requirement, and I eliminated the DRP tests. These moves were all made to address procedural obstacles and stigmas that hindered student persistence in the course. To more clearly distinguish this course from the previous one, it was also renamed. COAS-W111, Critical Inquiry, became ENG-R190, Rhetorical Reading.

The new name identified perhaps the most significant change. Rhetorical analysis, one of my specializations, had been an important part of our introductory composition courses. In my own writing classroom research over multiple semesters I had observed how teaching rhetorical analysis—of purpose, audience, genre, and appeals—seemed to have led students to write better. From pretest to post-test, most showed improvement not only in content treatment but also in elimination of error, even when the writing class did not give sustained attention to grammar and spelling. My research into developmental reading pedagogy indicated that a rhetorical approach is unique, courses typically focusing on basic comprehension activities. Most developmental reading examined word choice by using suffix or prefix to help define it, not discussing the importance of using particular wording, or identifying main points, not discussing how well they are supported. My theory was that reading rhetorically could engage developmental reading students just as it did those in regular composition courses and open up the texts in a way that students would treat the content with more awareness and comprehension as well as critical thinking. In short, engagement was my primary goal, believing that if students were more intrigued by what they were reading they would give more attention to it.

As I read about common developmental approaches that worked from a re-mediation or deficit model, as I reflected on my own experiences of how first-year composition students could grasp rhetorical analysis and exhibit attention to detail, and as I considered scholarship on critical pedagogy, I decided to turn the new (developmental) reading course on its head. Instead of working from what students lacked and focusing on trying to re-teach that, I wanted the new course to work from what they were capable of considering and build learning from that point. I tried to foster what Young and Potter in this collection refer to as a balanced literacy approach where the rhetorical way of reading had students orient the text in terms of situation, audience, and purpose in order to better comprehend or understand it.

My experience teaching COAS-W111 had shown me that its students were strong in many aspects of learning and reading, and I believed rhetorical reading could be their zone of proximal development.

Following Freire's concept of the pedagogy of the oppressed, developmental students could be the oppressed of the oppressed, relegated to vocabulary lessons and a cognitivist-based search for the main idea (Klenk & Kibby, 2000). Shaughnessy, a pivotal scholar for defining basic writing, argues that the problem with basic writers is one of inexperience, not incapability or deficiency (1979), and the same could be said for basic readers. Klenk and Kibby state, "It is generally accepted that most children who struggle to read do not require instruction that is substantially different from their more successful peers; rather, they require a greater intensity of 'high quality instruction'" (p. 668). Being treated as inferior isn't lost on college students, who silently or vocally resent the back-to-basics approach of many developmental reading programs (one college reading textbook even titles its first chapter "Back to Basics"). As several authors in this collection and other reading scholars have showed (Guthrie & Wigfield, 2000, 2006; Ruddell & Unrau, 1994; Vacca & Padak, 1990), student motivation, engagement, and self-confidence are critical for student readers.

Considering recent research on the difficulty most college students have reading, referred to in the introduction to this collection, I also wanted to make this course beneficial for any student, not just the so-called developmental one, hence the rhetorical considerations taught could be new and beneficial for all. Underlying this broader appeal is scholarship critical of the use of standardized tests such as the SAT, ACT, and Accuplacer exam still used (per academic regulation) to place students in ENG-R190 (Behrman, 2000; De Fina, Anstendig & De Lawter, 1991; McDonald, 1965; Robinson, 1950; Simpson & Nist, 1992; Smagorinsky, 2009; Tierney & Pearson, 1994 [1981]; Valencia & Pearson, 1987). Numerous scholars have taken issue with using test scores to draw conclusions about student reading ability, which is also why I chose not to use the DRP exam that had been used for testing out and as the (heavily weighted) final exam in the previous course.[3]

Numerous scholars over decades have recommended teaching rhetorical reading (Haas & Flower, 1988; Lamb, 2010; Simpson, Stahl & Francis, 2004; Warren, 2012). Haas and Flower (1988) observed how rhetorical observations worked with understanding content in their study of rhetorical reading, stating "It makes sense that readers who are trying to make inferences about author, context, purpose, and

---

3   In one of the preparatory workshops I conducted for new instructors of the course, experienced instructors and graduate students, I had them take a section of the DRP exam, which provides an excerpt of text to read and multiple-choice questions that require the test taker to fill in a blank at the end of a paragraph with the most appropriate option. Only one of the eight got all correct answers, and many expressed dismay and concern that the questions and options were difficult and confusing. I had a similar experience taking a sample Accuplacer reading test online.

effect . . . would be more likely to recognize the claims—both implicit and ex-plicit—within a text" (p. 181). Warren (2012) promotes it as especially relevant for disciplinary literacy as a practice and "habit of mind" more than a strategy or skill. Indirectly, Ruddell and Unrau (1994) advocate it when they suggest student read-ing difficulty may be more a matter of attention to content and interest than in-ability to recognize or understand it. Deighton (1956) suggests it when he charges that "If [the reader] ignores the manner, tone, and purpose of the writer, he is in danger of being victimized by rhetoric" (p. 65). Not entirely breaking new ground, I also had as precedent a developmental reading program that took a critical literacy approach (Lesley, 2001).

McCormick (2003) and Haas and Flower (1988) in particular ask questions that are especially provocative for adopting a rhetorical reading curriculum for a developmental reading course. McCormick asks "Is it possible to create processes of reading such that allegedly weaker students can become actively engaged in and succeed at and may in fact excel over conventionally 'good' students?" (p. 36). Haas and Flower ask "Is rhetorical reading a strategy students could easily adopt if cued to do so?" (p. 181). Trying to answer both of these questions guided development of the R190 curriculum.

Writing replaced objective testing as the vehicle showing learning. Two required written assignments reflected the importance of using authentic and relevant texts of the student's individual choice (Guthrie & Wigfield, 2000; Nist & Simpson, 2000; Rhoder, 2002; Simpson & Nist, 1992). The first, the Decision Making as-signment, required rhetorical reading and comparison of two public texts on an issue and was designed to teach awareness of claims and evidence as well as rhetori-cal techniques of argument. Using popular culture texts showed students how what they were learning could be applied outside of academia and let them use some-thing more familiar first in order to scaffold (McCormick, 2003; Rhoder, 2002) for the last assignment, the Academic Text Analysis. The latter required rhetorical analysis of reading the student had been assigned in another disciplinary course compared with two other texts students found on the subject (either academic or mainstream) and was designed to teach them awareness of difference in exposition as well as how "informative" texts can also be rhetorical ones. The two writing assignments, along with a more basic introductory assignment given before those two, were designed to give practice with increasingly complex texts and deeper reading for meaning as well as surface facts.

That reading and writing are mutually supportive is well known among com-position scholars and encouraged by reading scholars (Shanahan & Lomax, 1988; Simpson & Nist, 1992). The major writing assignments in R190 were a way of mak-ing visible that reading, like writing, is a process (Flower & Hayes, 1994; Tierney & Pearson, 1994 [1981]; Vacca & Padak, 1990). Requiring multiple drafts of each as-signment allows for revision and continual improvement, as in composition courses, instead of one-shot, high-stakes objective tests. Part of the process also included self-assessment to develop students' metacognitive awareness of their own reading ability. In keeping with our Writing Program's practice for introductory composition courses, I did not require the use of a common rubric for evaluation, but the assignments used across sections required particular treatment such as summary and discussion of main points. I was firm that instructor feedback always be on the students' treatment of reading content, not the structure or correctness of the writing.

Teaching reading as a process helps students develop the ability to interpret and analyze, additional skills beyond comprehension. Davies in her chapter in this collection discusses the importance of teaching this multifaceted aspect of reading and discusses how writing pedagogy can inform a reading pedagogy, with an eye to teaching reading in different disciplines. Strategies we covered in R190 addressed all the process stages Davies describes: prereading, reading, and rereading. In her first-year writing course, Davies also begins reading pedagogy with rhetorical attention, valuing it for the way it opens students to the analytical and interpretive aspects as well as comprehension.

To support teaching reading rhetorically and as a process, I had a wide range of reading strategies described over years of reading and writing research. To be effective, strategy instruction needs to be given ample instructional time, use real texts with appropriate level of challenge, and be offered as a range of choices instead of mandates (Nist & Simpson, 2000; Simpson, Stahl & Francis, 2004). The strategies taught in R190 varied across sections of the course but incorporated what Simpson and Nist (2000) identify as key to effective reading strategies that promote transfer to reading in other courses and disciplines: question creation and answer (such as specific questions about appeals and claims), summary writing, making connections (such as with reading log prompts about student knowledge of subjects and comparison questions), and organizing strategies (such as concept map drawing of a text and says/does columns).

Over the course of three semesters assessed, 15 instructors new to teaching a reading course but familiar with composition pedagogy taught 36 sections and 633 students. We assigned and collected numerous measures of student learning: drafts of essays, surveys, midterms, reading logs, and pretests and post-tests. Much could be analyzed from this study, but the remainder of this chapter focuses on the pretest and post-test as measures of student reading ability.

Assessing the New Course

Using writing as a method for teaching and assessing reading in the course, instead of objective tests, could be regarded as less valid due to its subjective nature. Different instructors would grade a written response differently and possibly evaluate improvement as well. However, the issue of how accurately "objective" tests indicate learning notwithstanding, using writing has construct validity because it will likely be a common method of assessment used in other college courses. Although final copies of the two required assignments were collected and could be used for assessment, using something produced without instructor input and guidance seemed a better measure of what students might be able to do beyond R190 in other courses. For this reason students were given a pretest reading assignment at the beginning of the semester and a post-test assignment at the end.

Both required a written response to an identical prompt, and instructors who assigned the tests in their classes were asked not to require a particular length or give guidance beyond the prompt questions. The link to the text used for each was provided to the students in advance. Instructors may or may not have provided a print version of the text, although it was encouraged. Most instructors assigned the pretest as the first reading log assignment, and students typically completed it outside of class. The post-test was completed in class as an exam during the two-hour time assigned for the final exam and was typically handwritten in an exam booklet provided for the student. I was not inclined to make the pretest a true "test" given on the first day that would be allotted a grade or points that could negatively affect student morale and course engagement (and grading on effort would have been superficial). Having it as a short or log assignment seemed a way to compel students to complete it without stress and frustration about a test situation or grade. However, the fact that the post-test was treated as a traditional exam may have affected responses, as discussed later.

My intention for the test was to see what students were capable of saying about a reading before and after R190 instruction. The hypothesis was that at the end of the semester they would be better able to notice main idea, primary points, and bias that each text contained as well as other features they had not commented on before. My experience with pretests and post-tests in my writing courses suggested their initial responses at the beginning of the semester would be mostly simple summary or personal opinion on the topic.

The prompt was the same for the pretest and post-test each semester, with one exception. In the first semester the prompt was "What do you understand about this text? How did you come to that understanding?" A cursory review of the first pretest responses suggested the prompt may be too vague, and the post-test question was revised to "Given that to understand means to comprehend, figure out, and know, what do you understand about this text? How did you come to that understanding?" The prompt was also revised in subsequent semesters. In the second semester the prompt was "Reading this text, what do you think is important to know and consider? Why?" to avoid the word "understand" and to try to elicit attention to main points ("to know") and rhetorical elements ("consider"). Again based on responses not showing enough attention to specifics about the texts, in the third semester the prompt was revised to be very specific and direct: "What do you notice about this text, its content, and the way it is written? What are the main points the text wants to communicate to the reader?" The "What do you notice?" could elicit rhetorical attention while the "main points" question clearly asked for significant concept recognition. The difficulty formulating the prompts themselves reflected the difficulty we would see evident with establishing reading comprehension.

The texts used for the pretests and post-tests were selected for particular commonalities. All were ostensibly expository and could be located and accessed through a public search engine such as Google. Each conveyed information about its subject in a similar public readability level and was approximately the same length. The pretest text used for the first two semesters was one titled "The Black Death, 1348," and the post-test used for the first two semesters was "An Overview of Stem Cells." The pretest text for the third semester was "The Economic Case for Raising the Minimum Wage," and the post-test was "Hydraulic Fracturing."

Although subject matter differed, each text contained four distinct points along with a discernable main idea. For example, I determined the main idea of the stem cell text used in the first two semesters to be that stem cells, and embryonic stem cells in particular, have potential and are an important area for research. The four main points are the properties and differentiation of stem cells, the potential of embryonic stem cells, the limitations of adult stem cells, and the need for further research. Although the readings were informational, the subject information was limited to one predominant view, so each text had a bias. The stem cell article focused on advantages and barely referred to controversy. The bubonic plague reading was comprised of reflections on certain aspects of the disease as written by an author who lived at the time, Boccaccio. The readings used for the last semester of the study were the most obviously biased, especially if one looked at the source. The pretest text was an exposition on benefits of raising the minimum wage from the Obama administration's White House site, and the hydraulic fracturing, or fracking, text was a promotion of the benefits from a website produced by the Society of Petroleum Engineers.

A different reading and subject matter were assigned for each test in the course for three reasons: 1) so students would not respond differently simply because they recognized the reading from the pretest assignment and presumed they would be expected to respond differently, 2) so the focus was on application of reading ability and not on particular subject matter, and 3) so the instructor could use the pretest reading for instruction after the pretest assignment was completed. Trying to avoid certain problems, however, often raises others, as discussed below.

While I had planned a coding process that involved multiple raters and a common rubric for evaluating the pretests and post-tests, I had to alter the process. In the final semester of data gathering, I was appointed Director of Writing and given charge of employing and evaluating the part-time and teaching assistant faculty, many of whom had been teaching R190. Although it meant losing inter-rater reliability, I decided to code the tests myself. Scott and Brannon (2013) problematize the likelihood that meaningful consensus is possible in evaluating essays, even with multiple raters, especially given differences in status. I was afraid that any instructors I could solicit assistance from for the coding would either feel compelled to participate or compelled to give me assessment they thought I wanted to see, thinking that to do otherwise might jeopardize their employment preferences. I was also concerned instructors of the course would feel pressure to be too generous with assessing the post-tests, desiring to see improvement from their efforts. I had to trust my own efforts not to be inclined to do the same.

To be as objective as possible, I chose to use a very basic coding of whether students simply identified (mentioned) or elaborated (discussed in more detail) the main idea and main points in the text. Points, I believed, were clear to an attentive and moderately skilled reader, especially because many points had only one focused paragraph or a designated section. I did not count as identification simple listing of subheadings that corresponded to the points. The same coding was used for whether students recognized the bias in each reading by at least mentioning the source or using a term like "argues" (identified) or more directly discussing how the information was not objective or complete (elaborated). Eliminating pretests and post-tests that were unreadable, ones that were not part of a pair from the same student, and ones from a section where the similarity in how the students responded suggested they were given a format for response by the instructor, I had 369 pretest/post-test essay sets, comprising 58 percent of the overall student work.

Later on I initiated a second coding analysis of a selection of pretests and post-tests, to gain a different perspective and if possible triangulate the findings. In 2015, I taught a graduate level seminar on reading and asked four students, none familiar with R190, to help develop a rubric and code 30 of the pretest/post-test combinations, five randomly selected from six sections of the third semester of R190. The rubric used a four-point scale, with one score set for comprehension and another for analysis. Given the context of studying reading scholarship, the seminar students determined that evidence of comprehension should include paraphrasing (not using statements verbatim), identifying the main idea, not getting lost or off-track in disassociated thoughts, and not being repetitive. They determined that evidence of analysis should include recognizing bias, thinking critically about content, correctly identifying the audience, explaining significance or interrelation of content, and seeing purpose. They examined both the minimum wage text and hydraulic fracturing text and "normed" practice student essays to calibrate their scoring, which was very close if not identical, achieving inter-rater reliability.

The four seminar students scored the pretest set in one class session and the post-test set in the next. A score of 1 indicated no treatment or less than minimally acceptable. A score of 4 indicated exemplary treatment of all the evidence elements. The scorers were mindful that their scoring of the rubric elements should take into consideration what freshmen students (not necessarily developmental students) should be able to comprehend and analyze. I considered 2 to be a benchmark of minimal ability. Two scorers scored each pretest and post-test, and where they disagreed by more than one point a third scorer was added. I averaged the two (or three) sets of scores.

This second assessment method conducted with the seminar students is what I had originally planned, with a more holistic consideration of what comprehension and analysis look like, although it is notable that the scorers did not consider treatment of all points necessary for comprehension. The concerns I had about my position as their instructor influencing the scores was minimal because the context was a seminar and the task was a very reasonable one given the seminar content. The scoring was not part of their grade and, as I repeatedly told them I saw problems as well as merit in what I had constructed for R190, they assured me they would not let any knowledge of my investment in the new curriculum affect their scoring. Although they examined only 8 percent of the 369 test combinations, their results would help in analysis of the data overall by providing an additional analytic lens.

Results

Table 1 shows the results of my coding for student treatment of main idea, and Tables 2 and 3 show the results of coding for identification and elaboration of main points respectively. Students were able to identify the main idea better at the end of all three semesters, and they elaborated better on the main idea for the first two semesters of the revised course; however, the third semester, which used the fracking text, saw a decrease in ability to discuss the main idea in more depth. This could have been due to the website (multi-page) format of that text, which did not resemble a more traditional essay like the other texts had. While identification and elaboration of the first main point saw some slight and some significant increases, and the second point saw an increase in elaboration, the other points were identified and elaborated less in the post-test than in the pretest. This raises an interesting question as to whether a multi-page website allows for more neglect of content (not clicking to read the next section) than does text fully contained in one place and illustrates one of the problems in the choices for pre- and post-tests. For all the pretests, only 30 students (8%) covered all four points, and 49 students (13%) covered all points across all post-tests. The lack of full coverage could indicate that students have difficulty reading and comprehending long texts, but it could suggest that coverage of all four points may be a problematic way to gauge comprehension.

Table 1. Percentage of Students Treating Main Idea on Pretests and Post-tests

	Pretest		Post-test	
Semester	Identified	Elaborated	Identified	Elaborated
First (*N*=199)	16%	28%	**37%**	**36%**
Second (*N*=27)	15%	33%	**44%**	**48%**
Third (*N*=143)	3%	69%	**23%**	48%
Total (*N*=369)	11%	44%	**32%**	42%

Note. Identified indicates the main idea was stated in the response. Elaborated indicates the main idea was discussed. Boldface indicates increase from pretest to post-test.

Table 2. Percentage of Students Identifying Supportive Points on Pretests and Post-tests

	Point 1		Point 2		Point 3		Point 4	
Semester	Pre	Post	Pre	Post	Pre	Post	Pre	Post
First (*N*=199)	22%	18%	25%	5%	43%	4%	16%	6%
Second (*N*=27)	4%	**11%**	37%	11%	26%	7%	—	4%
Third (*N*=143)	8%	**31%**	27%	**31%**	4%	**24%**	27%	15%
Total (*N*=369)	15%	**22%**	26%	15%	27%	12%	19%	9%

Note. Boldface indicates increase from pretest to post-test.

Table 3. Percentage of Students Elaborating on Supportive Points on Pretests and Post-tests

	Point 1		Point 2		Point 3		Point 4	
Semester	Pre	Post	Pre	Post	Pre	Post	Pre	Post
First (*N*=199)	24%	25%	20%	29%	32%	27%	23%	9%
Second (*N*=27)	30%	59%	37%	44%	56%	44%	30%	19%
Third (*N*=143)	15%	29%	43%	31%	3%	24%	34%	15%
Total (*N*=369)	21%	29%	30%	31%	22%	27%	28%	12%

Note. Boldface indicates increase from pretest to post-test.

Table 4 shows the results of coding for bias, whether students recognized the inherent singular view promoted by each text. The results indicate an increase of identification and elaboration on the bias of the texts for the post-test. That the third semester did not show an increase in elaborated bias treatment may not be surprising, providing a caveat for those who might devise a similar assessment. Recognizing bias on the Obama administration website may have been easier for students who have grown up in a "red state" such as mine, where conservative politics dominate. That only about a quarter of the students recognized that the fracking text came from petroleum engineers who have a vested interest in selling hydraulic fracturing could also be influenced by context. We might expect more awareness of this text's bias among students living in states such as Virginia or Oklahoma, where the issue is much more visible and contentious. Interestingly, Melis in this collection describes results of a survey of community college students that indicated they believed bias is the easiest aspect of a text to determine.

Table 4. Percentage of Students Treating Bias on Pretests and Post-tests

	Pretest		Post-test	
Semester	Identified	Elaborated	Identified	Elaborated
First (N=199)	5%	14%	**14%**	12%
Second (N=27)	7%	15%	**11%**	**37%**
Third (N=143)	10%	53%	**20%**	26%

Note. Identified indicates the main idea was stated in the response. Elaborated indicates the main idea was discussed. Boldface indicates increase from pretest to post-test.

Along with aggregate results, I also examined whether individual students showed improvement. Table 5 shows gain and loss for individual students regarding main idea, points, and bias. That is, coding included how many points students were able to identify or elaborate at beginning and end of semester. For example, one student identified the main idea and three of the main points in the pretest but identified the main idea and only one point partially in the post-test. Another student identified the bias, the main idea, and all four points in the pretest but identified only two points fully and one point and the main idea partially in the post-test. Therefore, both students' results suggested a loss of recognition. Aggregate results are mixed and inconclusive. Although students gained in main idea treatment for the first two semesters, they lost treatment in the third semester. Although they lost treatment of points in the first two semesters, they gained slightly in the third. Finally, students gained more than lost in the treatment of bias, with the exception of the third semester. It could be that the third semester's post-test fracking text led to a gain in points treatment because it had clear subdivisions that aided readers in identifying key points in the structure of the text. The loss in main idea treatment of this text could indicate that students were "fractured" in their cohesive thought about the text by the multiple web pages and sections on the site.

The low gains shown in treatment of the main idea, primary points, and bias recognition could also be attributed to text difficulty and structure. The texts used at the end of the semester may have simply been more difficult, which is certainly true for the first two semesters, when students moved from a simpler style and engaging subject matter to a more scholarly article; however, in the third semester students were still able to make post-test gains at least for the main idea and first two points, and both post-test texts clearly designated subtitles for their primary points. The third semester's fracking text was taken from a website and included numerous visuals, so it may have been easier and more engaging to read. The pre-test text for the third semester, on minimum wage, was the only text that did not have subsection titles and likely made point recognition more difficult. Again, a caveat for researchers: select pretest and post-test material that is truly as compara-ble as it can be.

Table 5. Percentage of Students Showing Gain and Loss in Treatment of Main Idea, Points, and Bias from Pretest to Post-test

	Main Idea		Points		Bias	
Semester	Gain	Loss	Gain	Loss	Gain	Loss
First (*N*=199)	44%	23%	25%	55%	23%	16%
Second (*N*=27)	52%	22%	41%	45%	37%	11%
Third (*N*=143)	18%	33%	43%	37%	16%	44%

Table 6 suggests what students might have learned and been able to apply regarding rhetorical awareness. Coding noted where students wrote about credi-bility, audience, support, and wording or whether the actual rhetorical terms were used. This coding was used only for the post-tests because rhetorical concepts were introduced in the course and the post-test could gauge how much students applied that knowledge. A few students noted rhetorical principles (not by their Latin terms) in the pretest, but not enough to warrant their attention for the pre-test, so any pretest/post-test comparison would have naturally weighed in favor of post-test results.

Table 6. Percentage of Students Treating Rhetorical Elements in Post-tests

Semester	Ethos/ Credibility	Pathos/ Audience	Logos/ Support	Style/ Wording
First (*N*=199)	49%	45%	14%	12%
Second (*N*=27)	33%	19%	—	7%
Third (*N*=143)	50%	27%	13%	23%
Total (N=369)	48%	36%	12%	16%

In post-tests, nearly half the students in the first semester treated ethos, matters of credibility that included discussion of author, publisher, and sources, and exactly half treated it in the third semester. Pathos, including discussion of emotional ap-peals and likely or intended audience, was treated by 45 percent of the students in the first semester but by far fewer students in the third semester. Logos, matters of strength of claims and support, got the least treatment consistently. These results suggest that matters of ethos or credibility are easier for students to treat than matters of pathos and logos. This better attention to credibility could be due to its emphasis for research writing in both secondary and postsecondary education.

The results of the seminar students' scoring, in Table 7 reflect some of the mixed results seen in the coding I used, with individual gains and losses, but overall the results of their scoring indicate slight gain in analysis and greater gain in comprehension from pretest to post-test. Their scoring indicates that 40 percent of the 30 students scored at least a point higher in comprehension and/or analysis, but it also shows that 33 percent of the students lost a point in one or both areas. When I compared my coding for main ideas, points, and bias for the same 30 students, the seminar students' scoring for comprehension and analysis on the pretest was very similar, disagreeing on only four pretests; however, their scoring and mine differed on 11 of the 30 post-test responses. Their higher scores could reflect a subconscious influence to score higher when they realized the post-test set was from the end of the semester, or, conversely, they could reflect that their rubric for comprehension and analysis is a more accurate one than simple counting of main idea and points treatment.

Table 7. Scoring of Pretest and Post-test for 30 Students Using a Rater-Generated Rubric

	Pretest	Post-test
Average comprehension score	1.4	2.2
Average analysis score	1.6	1.8
Percentage showing no change		10% (n=3)
Percentage showing .5-point increase		33% (n=10)
Percentage showing 1-point increase		40% (n=12)
Percentage showing 2-point increase		20% (n=6)
Percentage showing 1 point or less decrease		33% (n=10)
Percentage showing both loss and gain		17% (n=5)

Note. The pretest and post-test for the 30 students were randomly selected from multiple instructors in the third semester. The rubric used a four-point scale, 4 being highest.

One unexpected difference between pretests and post-tests quickly became apparent in my coding. Students were clearly writing more at the end of the semester. Of the 369 students, 91 percent increased word count in their post-tests, and 22 percent wrote four times as much or more. The average number of words in the post-test essay responses doubled in the third semester and more than doubled in the first semester. While in the third semester this could have been due to the fracking text being about 35% longer than the minimum wage pretest, the texts used for the pretests and post-tests in the first two semesters were of comparable length (about 1650 words and about 1750 words respectively); therefore, increased student writing about the readings does not seem attributable to the length of the assigned texts.

Of course, one plausible explanation is that what the students learned about reading in the course enabled them to feel they had more to say about it. However, a very influential fact was that students were sitting in a classroom completing the post-test as a final exam. A captive audience, or captive authors in this sense, they may have felt more compelled to use the two hours than they had the out-of-class time given for the pretest. Nonetheless, I saw one of the same results I had in my writing classroom research, that structure also changed, with students composing in more paragraphs at the end of the semester instead of one long stream of thought evident at the beginning. Table 8 shows the average number of paragraphs almost doubled every semester, with 71 percent of the students using more paragraphs and 23 percent using four times as many or more. Further study of pre- and post-tests written under identical conditions and using highly comparable texts could help to clarify the possible significance of this length difference.

Table 8. Average Number of Paragraphs and Words on Pretests and Post-tests

Semester	Paragraphs		Words	
	Pretest	Post-test	Pretest	Post-test
First (N=199)	2.3	4.9	190	472
Second (N=27)	3.2	5.1	252	505
Third (N=143)	2.5	4.3	244	461

Two more assessments collected for this study are purely quantitative. One is the student course evaluation, completed in class anonymously by each student without the instructor presence at the end of the semester and shared with instructors after final grades are posted. The evaluations address the course and the instructor, but for this study I collected data only for the six questions that pertained to the course. The questions asked whether the student thought the course had clear goals, whether the course met its goals, whether it was organized, whether the student had sufficient opportunity to be evaluated, if he or she learned in the course, and if the course was worthwhile. Each student marked one score on a five-point Likert scale for each question, with 1 being the lowest score (indicating disagreement) and 5 being the highest (indicating agreement). Using our department means for writing courses for comparison, I determined that a score of 4 would be the benchmark.

As Table 9 indicates, with the exception of one question in one semester, the benchmark was met (the average student score for whether the course was worthwhile was 3.90 in the first semester). The overall average rating of the course across all the semesters for the six questions was 4.24, securely in the "Agree" category and within standard departmental parameters. The high mark is noteworthy especially because the benchmark of 4 that I set could be steep considering the course was a new one and mandated by test scores. It is interesting that students felt they learned from the course but still showed more reserve on the course's usefulness, suggesting that instructors need to be more verbally and pedagogically clear about how what students learned to do could transfer to other reading situations across disciplines and outside academia.

Table 9. End-of-Semester Anonymous Student Evaluation Scores for the Course

Semester	Clear Goals	Met Goals	Organized	Sufficient Evaluation	Learned	Worthwhile
First (N=280)	4.25	4.18	4.09	4.24	4.10	3.90
Second (N=39)	4.33	4.36	4.29	4.48	4.25	4.25
Third (N=198)	4.34	4.27	4.38	4.40	4.20	4.05

Note. Student evaluations used a five-point Likert scale with 1 being Strongly Disagree and 5 being Strongly Agree. Questions asked if students agreed with the following: course goals were clear, the course met its goals, the course was well organized, they had sufficient opportunity to be evaluated, they learned in the course, and the course was worthwhile.

Like the students in Gogan's study, in this collection, ours indicated by their scoring of the course that they felt they had learned more than the assessment suggests they had. This may be tapping into what Gogan discusses as receptive activity, where readers gain agency over what meaning they derive from a text. Hence, students in R190 may feel empowered by doing something to the text, hunting for rhetorical moves and evaluating points, instead of just feeling they should receive the main points from it.

Another quantitative measure, course final grades, directly addresses my Dean's charge to improve the successful pass rate, and here the results are significant. Table 10 shows the final student grades for the course for the three semesters and the two prior, before the course was revised. Failing grades (F) dropped from 22 percent in the semester prior to the course change to a high of 12 percent in the third semester of R190. The overall no-pass rates for the course, determining whether students needed to retake it, dropped from a high of 30 percent to a high of 20 percent. Grades in the D range remained similar. Grades in the C range decreased in R190, and grades in the A range increased. This could be argued as grade inflation on the part of the R190 instructors; however, it could also be argued as the result of qualitative assessment and teaching reading as a process where improvement could be recognized.

Table 10. Student Course Grades Before and After the Course Renovation

	Previous Course		Renovated Course		
Course	Fall 2012	Spring 2013	Fall 2013	Spring 2014	Fall 2014
Grade	(*N*=396)	(*N*=73)	(*N*=341)	(*N*=49)	(*N*=243)
A range	11%	5%	35%	31%	30%
B range	32%	36%	33%	29%	35%
C range	34%	32%	15%	24%	19%
D range	7%	5%	6%	6%	4%
F	15%	22%	10%	10%	12%
Unsuccessful	24%	30%	18%	18%	20%

Note. Range includes plus and minus grades. Unsuccessful refers to those students receiving a C-, D range, or F final course grade.

Reflecting on the Curriculum and Study

Certainly one explanation for the less-than-striking gains and even losses in rec-ognition of main idea, primary points, and bias could be that a rhetorical reading approach is not effective for teaching reading. What McCormick (2003) warned may have come to pass, that "[W]hen one gets into specific classroom settings, many theories, particularly if they have not been tested on a wide cross section of students, simply fall apart" (p. 28). Instruction in rhetorical analysis may dis-tract students from comprehending primary material instead of promoting more attention to it, as I had hoped. Low gains in attention to rhetorical elements could indicate that determining the more concealed argument of an "informational" text may have been asking too much of the students, although I tend to disagree based on my experience teaching rhetorical analysis, which was a new concept to many freshmen at least in my first ten years of teaching.

Another possible explanation for the low gains and losses is that the strategies being taught need improvement. Some, such as concept maps that can visually represent main points, emphasis, and relationships within the text content, may need to be emphasized and done repeatedly to try to encourage students to use them in other contexts. How much we emphasize active reading strategies that ask students to mark the text may need re-evaluating because much of what students read is electronic and does not easily allow marking, and students will likely not print off such texts unless they are asked to do so by an instructor. Students need to be shown that taking notes or making visual representations of what they read is useful to aid in comprehension and critical thought. One strategy I do believe would benefit from less attention may be previewing that pertains more to text structure than it does generating ideas about content. Many students were content on the post-tests to simply describe what they saw on the text instead of discussing it in ways that illustrated comprehension and analysis.

The tendency for first-year college students to just describe and summarize (or use quotations) is a powerful one to overcome. These students have almost certainly taken tests in high school that covered detail from nonfiction texts, but much of that treatment could have been in the form of multiple-choice exams, which allows students to recognize and select what is correct or accurate from a given set of responses instead of extracting it themselves and applying it, the latter more likely what will be asked of them by college tests. Furthermore, while rhetorical analysis of nonfiction has become more popular in college composition classes, many high school language arts classes practice interpretation of fiction and personal reflection on it much more. If students do not grasp rhetorical analysis they can revert to simple description and summary.

I do believe that the change in the length of student writing from pretest to post-test is important when considering reading ability. Students clearly had more to say about what they were reading for the post-tests than for the pretests. Although they knew their post-tests would be graded, they knew writing quality was not the focus and length was not a grading factor, and they wrote more and paid greater attention to structuring their responses in the post-test. Some students were also taking the introductory composition course at the same time, so the attention to writing may have been more natural. Nonetheless, it is reasonable that they were thinking more about their reading and feeling more confident in expressing what they read.

Limitations of this Study

In drawing any conclusions, factors that inhibit accurate assessment need to be identified and addressed. One very obvious limitation regarding the use of pre-tests and post-tests as the primary measure of learning is that the texts used for the two were different in subject matter, format, and style. The conditions under which they were completed also varied. The level of student familiarity with the subject and regard for the activities' value could have easily skewed results. Standardized reading tests, the other and more common assessment, present text excerpts that also could be familiar or unfamiliar subjects for the students, but the format and style are generally the same. Those tests also get serious regard from most students (perhaps too much). While making the post-test used in this study a final exam was designed to foster serious regard and avoid the possibility of skipping it that could have happened if it were just a reading log assignment, it complicates comparison to the pretest, which was not given as much weight in the overall course grade.

Analysis of the two course assignments and reading log responses could have also yielded important results that limit conclusions drawn from this study. If we are trying to teach reading as a process, and I argue that we should, the products of that process are worth considering, even if they were guided by instructor and peer feedback. If we regard reading, like writing, as a social and collaborative activity, then we should look at what students are able to do in that context as well as what they do on their own on a "test." Another limitation is coding structure and the lack of inter-rater reliability. The seminar graduate student coding of 30 pretest/ post-test combinations illustrates that reliable coding of a qualitative measure is very important for drawing conclusions. One person's perspective on assessment is almost always less desirable than the consensus of a group.

Perhaps the greatest limitation to this study is lack of a control group and the related limitation of instructor differences in teaching. The sudden move of the reading course to my department disrupted my plan to initially introduce the rhetorical reading approach in one section only. The problem with the pass rate and stigma attached to the course also made it imperative to "do something now" for all students instead of introducing changes gradually to control for variables. Essentially it became an intervention study. The fact that multiple instructors taught the course in multiple ways in their classrooms is an unavoidable critical limitation. To decide whether or not rhetorical reading is a good vehicle for teaching reading, the way it is taught is crucial.

Future Research and Curricular Change

Based on the results and their interpretation, I plan changes to R190, and as of this writing have already piloted some of those. The rhetorical approach will remain for the immediate future, but elements of the curriculum need adjustment, especially to more specifically address comprehension. The use of writing as the primary grading method will remain, but other measures of course effectiveness will be introduced.

Instructors need to give more sustained attention to recognition and explanation of primary points a text makes. Instructors need to make clear how rhetorical analysis can help uncover those points and think critically about them, especially in other courses across the disciplines. I have also asked instructors to redirect students away from strategies that enable focus on describing the text to ones that require thoughtful consideration. I have already rewritten the two required assignments to promote more attention to purpose and support of claims.

A common rubric for evaluating the two required assignments will also be created, collaboratively among the R190 instructors. This will allow for better understanding of how to grade the assignments, especially for new instructors, and it will provide a more reliable assessment measure. The rubric created and used by my graduate seminar students shows this need not be an onerous task. Not every instructor likes using a rubric, but for initial norming purposes, it could help different teachers with different styles feel on the same page, at least when it comes to evaluation of student work.

Study of the course will also continue, with changes. I plan to use an objective test, something similar to the DRP or Nelson-Denny, taken in class at the beginning and end of the semester, to add a more objective measure of comprehension. The results will not be discussed, so when students see the same exam again they will not know if they answered correctly the first time and may respond the same or differently. The multiple-choice test results will be an interesting comparison to the qualitative measure of the students' written responses. A more traditional final exam will also be required, one with multiple-choice answers, short answer, and short essay based on a provided text.

Another added measurement of learning will be longitudinal. At the end of the semester following that in which R190 is taken, an anonymous online survey will be sent to the students who took it, asking such questions as whether they used in other courses what they learned in the reading course. It would be interesting to see if what Odom found and discusses in this collection is true, that students think the writing helps their reading. Odom found that over 85 percent of students thought a writing assignment helped them better understand the text but, interestingly, also found less agreement among the faculty of this benefit based on their assessment. The survey will allow students more reflection on the practical application of what was learned than does the end-of-semester evaluation and could be a good indicator of transfer. Young and Potter in this collection, while they emphasize measurable improvement, warn not to focus on short-term gains at the expense of instruction that promotes transfer. Developmental reading researchers (Caverly, Nicholson & Radcliffe, 2004; Holschuh & Paulson, 2013; Simpson, Stahl & Francis, 2004; Tierney and Pearson 1994 [1981]) also call for more longitudinal evaluations of developmental programs and policies but caution against trying to capture the complexity of transfer. Using grades made in other courses, GPA, or just persistence cannot be reliable indicators of the reading course's success due to many other variables that can affect such measures.

The results of this study seem to indicate that the rhetorical analysis approach did not consistently lead to better comprehension, but neither do the results suggest it is a failed approach. The improved grades and completion rates and the high evaluation marks given by students are important measures, especially considering the course in the context of a higher education environment that increasingly emphasizes retention and persistence. Results indicate the rhetorical analysis approach engaged the "developmental" students and that they were able to achieve better grades through it than had students in the previous course.

Two problematic considerations give pause in considering rhetorical reading for reading pedagogy, developmental or otherwise. One is that getting "the main idea" and "the main points" are debatable concepts—and as Gogan discusses in this collection should not be treated as the most important elements for reading that make the most difference for students—but rhetorical elements can also be treated too rigidly. McCormick writes, "Much work that is done in 'critical thinking,' for example—a site in which one might expect students to learn ways of evaluating the 'uses' of texts and the implications of taking up one reading position over another—simply assumes an objectivist view of knowledge and instructs students to evaluate texts' 'credibility,' 'purpose,' and 'bias,' as if these were transcendent qualities" (1994, p. 60).

A related problem made clear by this study in particular is how we define comprehension. What does it mean, and how do we know it has happened? Words used to describe comprehension, such as understanding or knowing, are equally as ambiguous. Does comprehension mean correct fact extraction and explanation, or critical thought about what fact really is, or both? Were the R190 students who did not list each of the four primary points made by the pretest and post-test text truly not comprehending the text?

These questions and the value I place on rhetorical awareness are what lead to my definition of college reading. Haas and Flower's definition of reading, "A process of responding to cues in the text and in the reader's context to build a complex, multi-faceted representation of meaning" (1988, p. 169), is apropos for college. However, based on my findings from this study, I extend that definition to try to capture other aspects I find necessary: a self-aware process of engaging texts that involves being able to identify, reason with, and apply important stated and unstated content and consider the significance of the content, the text's context, stated and possible purposes, and effect on audiences. This definition is not as elegant in simplicity as that of Haas and Flower but is complex, as may be the way we define (and delimit) what developmental means.

References

Bean, J. C., Chappell, V. A. & Gillam, A. M. (2014). *Reading rhetorically*, 4th ed. New York: Longman.

Behrman, E. (2000). Developmental placement decisions: Content-specific reading assessment. *Journal of Developmental Education, 23*(3), 12–18.

Caverly, D. C., Nicholson, S. A. & Radcliffe, R. (2004). The effectiveness of strategic reading instruction for college developmental readers. *Journal of College Reading and Learning, 35*(1), 25–49.

De Fina, A. A., Anstendig, L. L. & De Lawter, K. (1991). Alternative integrated reading/writing assessment and curriculum design. *Journal of Reading, 34,* 354–359.

Deighton, L. C. (1956). New approaches to reading. *College Composition and Communication, 7*(2), 63–67.

Flower, L. & Hayes, J. R. (1994 [1981]). A cognitive process theory of writing. In R. B. Ruddell, M. Rapp Ruddell & H. Singer (Eds.), *Theoretical models and processes of reading,* 4th ed. (pp. 928–950). Newark, DE: International Reading Association.

Furman, J. & Stevenson, B. (2014). The economic case for raising the minimum wage. *The White House, President Barack Obama.* Retrieved from https://www.whitehouse.gov /blog/2014/02/12/economic-case-raising-minimum-wage.

Guthrie, J. T., Wigfield, A., Humenick, N. M., Perenevich, K. C., Taboada, A. & Barobsa, P. (2006). Influences of stimulating tasks on reading motivation and comprehension. *The Journal of Educational Research, 99*(4), 232–246.

Guthrie, R. & Wigfield, A. (2000). Engagement and motivation in reading. In Kamil, M., Mosenthal, P. B., Pearson, P. D. & Barr, R. (Eds.), *Handbook of reading research, Vol. 3* (pp. 403–422). Mahwah, NJ: Lawrence Erlbaum Associates.

Haas, C. & Flower, L. (1988). Rhetorical reading strategies and the construction of meaning. *College Composition and Communication, 39*(2), 167–183.

Holschuh, J. P. & Paulson, E. J. (2013). *The terrain of college developmental reading.* College Reading and Learning Association.

Hydraulic fracturing. (n.d.). *Energy4me Essential Energy Education.* Retrieved from http://energy4me.org/hydraulic-fracturing/.

Klenk, L. & Kibby, M. W. (2000). Re-mediating reading difficulties: Appraising the past, reconciling the present, constructing the future. In M. L. Kamil, P. B. Mosenthal, P. D. Pearson & R. Barr (Eds.) *Handbook of reading research, Vol. 3* (pp. 667–690). Mahwah, NJ: Lawrence Erlbaum Associates.

Lamb, M. (2010). Teaching nonfiction through rhetorical reading. *English Journal, 99*(4), 43–49.

Lesley, M. (2001). Exploring the links between critical literacy and developmental literacy. *Journal of Adolescent and Adult Literacy, 45*(3), 180–189.

Matthews, K. (n.d.). An overview of stem cells. *Openstax CNX.* Retrieved from https://cnx.org/contents/32b0b61a-6ad4-44fc-a636-9060e2c9cb07@1.1.

McCormick, K. (1994). *The culture of reading and the teaching of English.* Manchester: Manchester University Press.

McCormick, K. (2003). Closer than close reading: Historical analysis, cultural analysis, and symptomatic reading in the undergraduate classroom. In M. Helmers (Ed.) *Intertexts: Reading pedagogy in college writing classrooms* (pp. 27–49). Mahwah, NJ: Lawrence Erlbaum Associates.

Newton, E. (1999). "Josh": Case study of an underprepared college student in a response-centered composition classroom. In B. Martin Palmer (Ed.) *College reading: Perspectives and practices* (pp. 3–19). Carrollton, GA: College Reading Association.

Nist, S. & Simpson, M. L. (2000). College studying. In M. Kamil, P. B. Mosenthal, P. D. Pearson, and R. Barr (Eds.), *Handbook of reading research, Vol. 3* (pp. 645–666). Mahwah, NJ: Lawrence Erlbaum Associates.

Rhoder, C. (2002). Mindful reading: Strategy training that facilitates transfer. *Journal of Adolescent and Adult Literacy, 45,* 498–512.

Robinson, H. A. (1950). A note on the evaluation of college remedial reading courses. *Journal of Educational Psychology, 41*(2), 83–96.

Ruddell, R. B. & Unrau, N. J. (1994). Reading as meaning-construction process: The reader, the text, and the teacher. In R. B. Ruddell, M. Rapp Ruddell & H. Singer (Eds.) *Theoretical models and processes of reading*, 4th ed. (pp. 996–1056). Newark, DE: International Reading Association.

Scott, T. & Brannon, L. (2013). Democracy, struggle, and the praxis of assessment. *College Composition and Communication, 65*, 273–298.

Shanahan, T. & Lomax, R. (1988). A developmental comparison of three theoretical models of the reading-writing relationship. *Research in the Teaching of English, 22*, 196–212.

Shaughnessy, M. P. (1979). *Errors and expectations: A guide for the teacher of basic writing.* New York: Oxford University Press.

Simpson, M. L. & Nist, S. L. (1992). Toward defining a comprehensive assessment model for college reading. *Journal of Reading, 35*, 452–458.

Simpson, M. L. & Nist, S. L. (2000). An update on strategic learning: It's more than textbook reading strategies. *Journal of Adolescent and Adult Literacy, 43*, 528–541.

Simpson, M. L., Stahl, N. A. & Francis, M. A. (2004). Reading and learning strategies: Recommendations for the 21st century. *Journal of Developmental Education, 28*(2), 2–32.

Smagorinsky, P. (2009). The cultural practice of reading and the standardized assessment of reading instruction: When incommensurate worlds collide. *Educational Researcher, 38*, 522–527.

The black death, 1348. (2001). *Eyewitness to History*. Retrieved from http://www.eye witnesstohistory.com/plague.htm.

Tierney, R. J. & Pearson, P. D. (1994 [1992]). A revisionist perspective on "Learning to learn from text: A framework for improving classroom practice." In R. B. Ruddell, M. Rapp Ruddell & H. Singer (Eds.) *Theoretical models and processes of reading*, 4th ed. (pp. 514–519). Newark, DE: International Reading Association.

Tierney, R. J. (1994[1981]). Learning to learn from text: A framework for improving classroom practice. In R. B. Ruddell, M. Rapp Ruddell & H. Singer (Eds.) *Theoretical models and processes of reading*, 4th ed. (pp. 496–513). Newark, DE: International Reading Association.

Vacca, R. T. & Padak, N. D. (1990). Who's at risk in reading? *Journal of Reading, 33*, 486–489.

Valencia, S. & Pearson, P. D. (1987). Reading assessment: Time for a change. *The Reading Teacher, 40*, 726–732.

Warren, J. E. (2012). Rhetorical reading as a gateway to disciplinary literacy. *Journal of Adolescent and Adult Literacy, 56*, 391–399.

Wyatt, M. (1992). The past, present, and future need for college reading courses in the U.S. *Journal of Reading, 36*(1), 10–20.

"O Father of Education, You Come with a Book in Your Hand": The Ambivalent Status of Reading in a Two-Year Tribal College

Ildikó Melis

BAY MILLS COMMUNITY COLLEGE

This chapter defines college-level reading from the perspective of two-year community colleges, and claims that college-level reading should be redefined as a spectrum concept that incorporates institutional diversity. Research data from a small TCU (Tribal Community College) illustrate how the decline of reading affects a particularly vulnerable student population disadvantaged by geographical isolation, low socio-economic status, and a cultural heritage of ambivalence about formal education. The last part of the chapter presents teachers' voices from a TCU. Some of these responses to the reading crisis show alarming signs of submission, which are supplemented with more resistant suggestions for intervention. The chapter argues that TCUs and other similar venues of higher education need to start bringing reading back from the cold and adopt reading across the curriculum, by articulating their expectations and by incorporating in their curriculum creative reading assignments of increasing complexity.

The title of this chapter is a line from a 19th century poem whose author is not known. The poem has been passed down by generations of educators, and it illustrates the ambivalence of indigenous people towards one of the grand narratives of modernization, education, and towards one of its technologies, the book, which in the mid-1800s was as enigmatic as computers are today. The line, like the rest of the poem, expresses some concern that the book will become a harsh tool and will eradicate other more traditional forms of teaching and learning (See full text in Appendix B). Yet, the poem also expresses some awe about the unprecedented power of books and book learning.

Almost two hundred years later, as I am making an attempt to define the nature and the state of college-level reading from the perspective of a two-year tribal college, my feelings are similar to those of the anonymous 19th century Native American. However, the power relations between the technologies of education have significantly changed. My fear today is that the once powerful book is vanishing as my students' eyes are glued to flickering pages of texts and images, which they seemingly manipulate so skillfully with the rapid movement of their fingers on electronic devices. I am worried that the once modern, but now traditional "print literacy" as I knew it is on the way out, yet I am also hopeful that technology perhaps will bring something in that is just as or even more powerful.

This chapter is a contribution to the definition of college-level reading in a particular and perhaps atypical setting of higher education. Hoping that others in this collection and elsewhere have provided enough evidence of an alarming decline in both the quality and the quantity of reading on a national scale (Davis in this volume; Hollander et al. in this volume; Horning, 2011; Horning, 2007; NCEE, 2013), I wish to supplement the larger scale of these trends with a miniature local variety, which, in some ways, is a microanalysis similar to Martha Townsend's microanalysis of football players' reading experiences in this volume.

Survey data from 2010, 2014 and 2015 involving a small number of students (30–50) and 12 full-time instructors from a geographically isolated two-year tribal college (with a student body of approximately 500) are analyzed and interpreted. These data highlight the growing gap between pre-college reading experiences and college expectations, the corrosion of these expectations, and the ambivalence of responses to the situation. In two-year colleges, more specifically, there is a definite shift in the definition of college-level reading with growing stress on what Rosenblatt (2005/1985) called efferent reading (focused on information retrieval). The decline or move away from more complex texts and reading practices started earlier (Holbrook, 1986) and was recently confirmed as almost final and irreversible (NCEE, 2013; Tinberg and Nadeau, 2010). The trend can also be interpreted in terms of transformative learning, or rather, the lack of it, as the concept is elaborated in Gogan's article in this volume and elsewhere (Gogan, 2013). The data from my surveys as well as the interviews I had with students and instructors show alarming signs that the decline of reading is accepted without resistance along with (perhaps a bit unfounded) optimism that technology will bring about a revival.

This chapter argues that the trends shown in the analyzed student and instructor surveys are not new and are the outcome of a combination of factors, such as the emergence of young adult literature, the pressure towards fast and measurable ways of teaching/learning, or the course book publishers' cost cutting efforts. Due to the constantly changing targets of texts and reading levels, the definition of college-level reading should incorporate institutional diversity, and institutions of higher education should determine their own specific mixture of what Louise Rosenblatt called the efferent (information oriented) and aesthetic (explorative, interpretation oriented) continuum (Rosenblatt, 2005). In other words, I propose that college-level reading is a spectrum concept rather than a single and static one. Finally, it should be recognized that what we perceive as negative trends or imbalances in our college-age students' reading experiences can be reversed by intervention. The 2013 executive summary of the National Center on Education and the

Economy, which focuses on two-year colleges and acknowledges that "The bulk of serious technical and vocational education takes place in the U.S. below baccalaureate level" also suggests that incorporating complex texts, and complex reading practices in two-year college curricula are crucial (NCEE, 2013, p. 6). At the end of this paper, classroom practices that help students move along the spectrum of reading skills are suggested, and it is proposed that colleges should continue (or, if not yet, start) exposing students to meaningful reading experiences across the curriculum.

Shifting Concerns, Moving Targets: The Definition of College-Level Reading

The definition of college-level reading is complicated by several factors. One of them is the diversity of colleges ranging from small, two-year colleges, to large four-year flagship universities. Two-year colleges, in spite of their recent growing enrollment and political attention, once started out as "junior colleges," under a name that suggested a status between high school and "real college." As such, community colleges have often found themselves caught between two, occasionally conflicting missions: One was to prepare students for (re)entering the job market (vocational training); the other was to create a pathway to four-year colleges (preparation for transfer). Thus, two-year colleges show a great deal of variety in how they combine these two major elements of their mission, which has an effect on the role and definition of reading, just as the mission of preparing students for scientific research or public school teaching affects the role and definition of reading in other institutions of higher learning.

College instructors generally assume that learning to read takes place at pre-college levels of education, yet it is not clear what they mean by "reading." Just as Ede and Lunsford (1991) pointed out that "writing" can mean anything from forming letters on a page, typing up a handwritten manuscript or drafting a novel, when "reading at college level" is taken for granted, the complexity of the act of reading is not duly acknowledged. Those who claim that reading instruction does not belong to college level are most likely not fully aware that at advanced levels, reading comprises a broad spectrum of cognitive layers beyond comprehension. This spectrum of cognitive processes involves analysis, interpretation and critical evaluation of print and electronic texts as well as their attached visual or numeral elements that, in our electronic age, increasingly accompany words. At college level, and at the high end of the reading spectrum, students need to become expert or meta-readers, who understand how texts work and can navigate them for meaning (Horning, 2011).

The above definition of college-level reading, however, may be less clearly articulated in addition to being slowly eroded in two-year colleges. Due to the combined effect of economic and social factors, two-year (community) colleges have been shifting their emphasis away from academic toward vocational training, which has led to a shift along the spectrum of preferred reading practices. Being typical college professors, Howard Tinberg and Jean-Paul Nadeau took it for granted that reading and discussing challenging texts are valued in college, but they found that community college students "do not inhabit well" the texts that are considered staple items in a college anthology (Tinberg & Nadeau, 2010, p. 8). To put it more bluntly, while colleges, in general, emphasize analysis, interpretation, evaluation and critical or rhetorical reading, community colleges tend to be more comprehension centered in their instruction (Carillo, 2015; Tinberg & Nadeau, 2010).

In another approach, the shift evokes Louise Rosenblatt's much earlier, but still relevant, work on reading as a meaningful transaction between reader and text. Rosenblatt published a series of articles since after World War II, in which she explained the difference between efferent and aesthetic reading (Rosenblatt, 2005). As she stressed, all reading is a combination of these two ends of a spectrum of transactions between reader and text. However, when a student reads a text with the purpose of finding pre-determined answers to questions or as if he or she was reading a TV-guide to find show times, we talk about efferent reading. Aesthetic reading, on the other hand, is the type of reading that creates meanings through a productive transaction between the reader's and the writer's personal knowledge and experience represented in the form of text on a page. The outcome of this transaction is not pre-determined and can be unpredictable.

Yet another way of approaching the shift in the definition of reading that is characteristic of two-year colleges is through the role of fiction and non-fiction reading in the curriculum. In many two-year colleges, there has been an increasing emphasis on reading non-fiction, or science texts at the expense of literature. Rosenblatt's articles show that the pendulum swings between literary texts and other, more utilitarian readings have been going on for decades, without much realization that perhaps seasoned readers need experience in both types of texts, and perhaps it is not so much the texts that determine the reading experience, but the kind of transaction between readers and texts that is fostered (Graff, 2009). In other words, Rosenblatt already in the early 1980s pointed out that literary texts, be that young adult literature or Shakespeare, can also be turned into an efferent reading experience if students are expected to answer multiple-choice questions only. Similarly, if students analyze complex works by formulaic, pre-determined categories, like "setting," "characters," "conflict," instead of being encouraged to create personal meaning, to make inferences about or to question the writer's intentions, and to interpret the literary conventions followed in the work, there is no deeper (aesthetic) transaction between the text and the reader.

Needless to say, some kind of analysis or systematic separation of elements of texts (e.g., setting, characters and conflict) is necessary for effective reading, but it should not be exclusive and perfunctory. The secret probably is in finding the balance that allows students to gain experience in multiple ways of interacting with multiple genres of text. This concept is consistent with theories of transformational learning (Gogan in this volume), which emphasize that effective reading is a "receptive, relational, and recursive experience" that ultimately changes the reader's knowledge, self-perception and worldview (Gogan, in this volume, p. 8). In less theoretical and more practical terms, the National Center on Education and the Economy pointed out that processing, retaining and synthesizing large amounts of information without support, or understanding non-verbal data in graphs, charts and other visuals are essential in preparing students for any vocation (NCEE, 2013, p. 7). And there is plenty of evidence to show that even business experts are aware of the various cognitive and interpersonal advantages of good reading (Hyatt, 2015). Yet, it looks like especially in the less privileged institutions of higher education, the students' reading experiences tend to be more limited.

Before we would look at the data that show these signs, it would, perhaps be helpful to highlight a few, lesser known facts about a small sub-group of two-year colleges, the TCUs or tribal colleges and universities, where small sets of data used in this chapter were collected.

Introducing the Tribal College

Within the category of two-year colleges, tribal colleges represent a small (35–38 schools),[1] but culturally and politically significant group. The first TCUs were founded during and after the civil rights era with the purpose of creating a more supportive and culturally more positive learning environment for Native American students, who have been conspicuously underrepresented in the U.S. college educated population. In addition to the typical dual function of vocational training and academic preparation in two-year colleges, tribal colleges also endorse the mission of preserving the Native American cultural tradition and language. TCUs vary in size and location, but they all share a few characteristics: The majority of students come from low-income families and are first generation college students; the schools often struggle for funding from a variety of public and private sources; similarly, their small but dedicated faculty enjoy fewer privileges, lower pay and more extensive teaching and administrative work load compared to other, non-tribal two-year colleges. In the small tribal college where the reading surveys reported in this chapter were conducted, out of the 191 students who between 2008 and 2011 responded to the student profile questions attached to their admission tests, 56% reported their annual family income under $20,000, and 48% said

---

1   The actual number of TCUs varies due to suspended or pending accreditation.

they were unemployed. Eighty-four percent on the admission test survey claimed that neither of their parents has a bachelor's degree, and 65% said neither of their parents has an associate degree (Melis, 2013). Geographical isolation often adds to the disadvantage: According to the admission test student profile survey, 46% of the responding students travel between 10–25 miles, 20% between 25–50 miles, and 8% more than 50 miles daily to get to school. Considering the severe winter weather during most of the school year in Michigan's Upper Peninsula, these students literally have to go extra miles to achieve success in college (Melis, 2013).

Faculty in TCUs are also in a somewhat marginalized position. In accordance with the culturally appropriate egalitarian spirit, faculty in many TCUs are addressed by first names, work under the same contracts as college staff, and are "instructors," not "professors." A 2003 report commissioned by the American Indian College Fund concluded that with all adjustments for inflation, "current annual salaries at mainstream, public 2-year colleges are likely to exceed TCU salaries by almost $10,000" (Voorhees, 2003).[2] Only 11.3% of TCU faculty have earned a Ph.D., compared to 20% in public two-year colleges, 72.6% in public comprehensive four-year colleges and 84.8% in public research universities (U.S. Department of Education data cited in Voorhees, 2003, p. 4). In a small TCU like the one I conducted the reading survey in, several faculty fulfill multiple functions of advising students, administering programs and grants, supervising charter schools, or running some program related project or facility (e.g., fitness center, cultural events, on-campus internet and computer technology, or sustainable farming) in addition to teaching a full load of classes (minimum 15 credits), often with overload or online classes added to supplement income.

Faculty in two-year colleges, in general and compared to four-year college faculty, seldom engage in theoretical discussions or rely on published research in decisions related to their daily work as Tinberg and Nadeau (2010) reckoned. Faculty meetings are rare, and typically are dedicated to the goal of serving the student population more efficiently rather than to the discussion of pedagogical or theoretical matters (Tinberg & Nadeau, 2010). There is rarely, if ever, time to do research on any matter, and research, when it is done, is limited to gaining comparable data (cut-off scores on admission tests; caps on class sizes) from other institutions for administrative purposes.

---

2   Although these data are dated, there are no more recent surveys available. The current President of the American Indian College Fund, Cheryl Crazy Bull, confirmed in personal communication that efforts have been made to call attention to this situation after the 2003 study, yet, the author has plenty of anecdotal and personal experience to testify that TCU faculty still work under very harsh circumstances compared to other, non-tribal two-year colleges, and are not even close to enjoying some of the benefits of faculty in four-year colleges (e.g., tenure; release time when taking administrative responsibilities; support for conferences or publication; closeness of research libraries).

This sketchy background was necessary to put the rest of this paper in context by stressing that neither the student nor the teacher survey was created to address some institutional need; its results were not shared beyond personal (but often passionate and involved) discussions with individual faculty members. In addition, because of the small number of participants in the survey and the outlier character of the school, the findings should be viewed as testimonial, illustrative examples with very low level of generalizability.

Participants in the Surveys

Since the students taking the surveys were all students in a two-year tribal college, it would be assumed that they are Native Americans. However, the definition of Native Americans is not a simple task.[3] To receive federal funding, TCUs are typically required to maintain a 51% Native American enrollment. For reporting purposes, Native Americans are those who possess a valid ID card as members of a federally recognized tribe. Since tribal card ownership entitles the owner to access various health, education and other social services, most students who are eligible own a card. In Michigan, there are 13 federally recognized tribes, but in the tribal college, there are many students who do not have a tribal membership card for a variety of reasons: The student could not document Native American ancestry or failed to meet some of the administrative membership requirements; the student is affiliated with bands or tribes that are not federally recognized, or they are affiliated with bands or tribes residing on Canadian territory on the other side of the St Mary's River.

Native American identity is loosely defined by locals as following the traditional lifestyle, being involved in cultural events (ceremonies, powwows), or, as they often say, "walking the red road." Individuals in the community qualify for these criteria to varying degrees irrespective of whether they own a tribal card or not; some who own a card self-identify as Native American (or, more specifically, Anishiinaabe); other card owners don't. In spite of heroic efforts to revive the native language (Anishnaabemowin), very few speak it fluently, and among the younger college students almost none. Decades of forced assimilationist policies and divisive distribution of benefits lead to the situation today that best can be characterized by fragmented indigenous identity with hopes for moderate cultural revival. Under these circumstances, it would be difficult to say that the small set of data presented here is representative of "Native American" tribal college students; more realistically, the data are representative of a small tribal-college with a geographically isolated, low-income, rural student population.

---

3   A report on Native Americans published by the U.S. Commission on Civil Rights in 2003 was titled "A quiet crisis," and Native Americans were called the "invisible minority."

The 2010 Reading Survey

In 2010, the author of this chapter was the honored recipient of the American Indian College Fund's Mellon research grant, which is typically awarded to science oriented projects, or to faculty working on a doctoral degree. The grant made it possible to design and process 4 small surveys and a focus group interview with the help of two part-time work-study students and to write up a 90-page report while I was teaching only one writing class for a semester. One of the four surveys was the *Reading Survey 2010*. Forty-nine students from a small tribal college in Michigan's Upper Peninsula responded to a paper and pencil survey in their college writing class. In spite of the small size of the sample, it represented quite well the total population of the college: almost equal number of both genders; majority of respondents were younger students (82%[4] under 30; 48% 21 or younger); 33(67%) of the respondents were tribal members, 15 (30%) non-tribal; one (2%) did not answer the question). Four aspects of the survey findings will be highlighted here: The responding tribal college students' not school related readings (Table 1); the students' self-reported use of textbook reading strategies (Table 2); the students' self-reported difficulty with various aspects of reading (Figure 1), and their most memorable reading experiences.

Table 1. Non-school-related Readings of Surveyed Tribal College Students

Most typical non-school related readings	Percentages of mention (answers n=92; students n=49)
Local newspapers	23%
Entertainment magazines about celebrities, fashion etc	18%
Sports magazines	16%
Fiction	14%
News magazines (Time, Newsweek)	9%
Tribal news or information	8%
Gardening magazines	4%
Non-fiction	2%

Note. Numbers do not add up to 100 due to rounding.

Table 1 summarizes 92 responses from 49 responding students, with an average of 1.8 types of reading selected from a list or added under "other, specify." The most popular choice was the local newspaper, which strongly suggests that the

---

4   Because of the small size of the sample, percentage data are added for easier interpretation. These percentage data often do not add up to 100, an inevitable rounding error in percentages gained from small base numbers.

reading served efferent, practical purposes of finding a contractor in the classified ads section, or was driven by curiosity for events (births, deaths, weddings) in the community, but this choice can also indicate vigorous interest in local tribal politics typical of the region. The local newspaper also often covers environmental issues, such as the protection of endangered animals, or the hazards of oil pipelines. Next to local news, national entertainment and celebrity news was found as the second most popular reading material. Although high interest in celebrity news usually suggests superficiality, my conversations with students convinced me that reading celebrity news is, in a way, closest to my students' pre-college experience with critical thinking because celebrity news teaches them to separate truth from falsehood and perceived image from reality. This hypothesis, however, needs to be tested because there is also evidence that many students fail to recognize celebrity news as manipulative and fictional discourse.

Table 2. Surveyed Tribal College Students' Use of Textbook Reading Strategies

Textbook Reading Strategy	Percentage of all Selected Reading Strategies
Previewing chapters and scanning for general idea	17%
Underlining or highlighting important concepts	15%
Making notes on the margin	11%
Making notes in a notebook	10%
Reading the text out loud	10%
Looking up words in dictionary	9%
Guessing word meanings from context	7%
Writing questions on the margin	6%
Discussing the text with other students	6%
Making notes after reading the textbook	5%

Note. N students=49. N strategies selected=173. Numbers do not include the five students who said they do not read textbooks.

The second set of survey findings is related to the surveyed tribal college students' textbook reading experience. Since it was reasonable to assume that these students' most typical encounter with expository prose is through reading their textbooks, the survey used the textbook reading situation as an example to find out what reading strategies these students commonly use. All students who responded to the survey were enrolled in one of the four English/writing classes offered at the time (two at pre-college level; two first-year college composition). Around 30% of the students had taken pre-college level English classes at the TCU, where reading strategies are covered in detail and practiced regularly. The 49 tribal college student respondents mentioned 173 strategies from a list of 10, which means they all use an average of 3.6 strategies, while five (3%) of the respondents claimed that they do not read their textbooks.

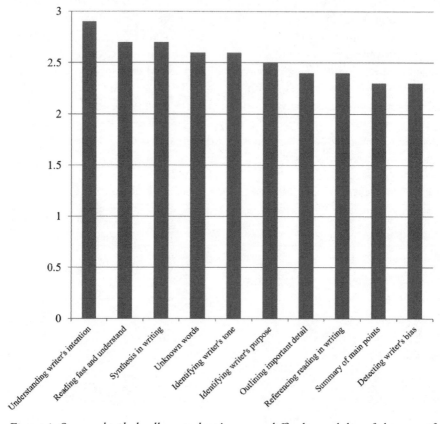

Figure 1. Surveyed tribal college students' average difficulty rank list of elements of reading on a scale of 3 (n=49)

Noticeably, the reading strategies that assume deeper engagement with the text, such as writing questions on the margin, discussing the text with others, or writing after reading were the least frequently mentioned in the sample. We know from experience that these students heavily depend on the expected cash from the end-of-semester resale of their textbooks; therefore, it is no surprise that they typically stay away from "pencil and book" reading strategies. The popularity of highlighting, however, seems to contradict this assumption unless highlights reduce the re-sale value of textbooks less significantly than copious marginal notes. Another problem with highlighting texts is that it often turns into a mechanical habit with little or no mindful selection involved, whereas writing annotations or questions on the margins cannot be done without some engagement with the text.

It is also noteworthy that the surveyed tribal college students do not frequently use dictionaries probably because print dictionaries are not readily available anymore, and textbook reading often takes place away from computers. Textbook reading out loud was a strategy of choice for 10% in the sample. The explanation is that many students with dyslexia or attention deficit (mostly undiagnosed among these students for lack of access, high cost and shame associated with diagnostic labeling) find that reading out loud is the only way they can focus on the text. In the small study area outside my office, I often encounter two or three students, huddled together around the round table and taking turns reading their science, "sosh"(=sociology), or health and fitness course books. This technique may help readers stay on task, but unless discussion ensues, reading textbooks out loud does not involve analysis, interpretation, evaluation or reflection.

One question in the *Reading Survey 2010* asked students to mark on a Likert scale ranging from "very easy" to "very difficult" how difficult the listed elements of reading are for them. Because of the small size of the sample, scores for each element were averaged and a rank list of difficulty was generated. It is worth noting that none of the elements of reading rated below 2. In other words, no element of reading was found easy, not even the lowest in the rank list (see Figure 1). Follow up conversations with students were used to resolve the contradiction that "understanding the writer's intention" was found most difficult while "detecting the writer's bias" earned the lowest average difficulty score. The interviewed students explained that bias is easy to see. In fact, they consider everything that is not factual "just an opinion," therefore, biased, which is a common oversimplification learned somewhere perhaps in high school. Similarly, students explained that understanding the writer's intention is difficult because no one can tell what another person has in mind. They did not seem to have acquired the idea that readers can make fairly reliable inferences from textual clues. It does not take the supernatural ability to read minds, just the learnable ability to recognize metadiscursive markers, statements of purpose, and other textual clues. With all the limitations of self-reported data considered, these findings suggest a mismatch between the surveyed students' articulation of "bias," "understanding the writer's intention" and that of most college English textbooks. This gap or mismatch would deserve more analysis followed by an adjustment in teaching materials that would acknowledge the need for elaboration, models and practice to support underprepared readers.

Finally, one more outcome of the *2010 Reading Survey* was the responses to the question that asked students to list the three most memorable books in their life. Fifty-seven percent mentioned three or more books, 14% mentioned only two books, 16% mentioned one book, and 7% mentioned no book. These data were not worse than the Pew Research Center's comparable national data on the decline of book reading between 1978 and 2014 (Weissmann, 2014). The students' mixed or missing reading experiences are also consistent with national data on the decline of reading in high school and middle school (Jolliffe & Harl, 2008; "What kids are reading," 2014). It was more alarming to find out, however, what those memorable readings were and also that 7 (14%) of the readers mentioned books that they hated to read in high school (one student just saying "I hated them all."). The list of 97 books mentioned by the respondents from the tribal college included some staple high school readings (*The Diary of Anne Frank, To Kill a Mocking Bird, The Old Man and the Sea*); showed signs of young adult literature (YA) rapidly making its way into high school reading lists; but most of the books students fondly remembered were for much lower age level (e.g., Roald Dahl, Dr. Seuss, the Berenstein Bear books etc.). The mention of these titles and authors suggests that these students had memorable reading experiences in elementary and middle school, which is wonderful, but reading in high school was not equally memorable or pleasant (some students did not remember names or titles and wrote references, such as "Lenny and George," presumably referring to Steinbeck's *Of Mice and Men*). The Renaissance Learning Center's study on what young people read also recognized the spread of young adult literature while Cunningham and Stanovich (2001) provided evidence that if young people do not read more challenging books and watch television or movies instead, they accumulate a deficiency in their decoding skills, vocabulary development, and, in general, will lack practice in dealing with complex reading materials or life situations. Reschly (2010) reported data that connect limited early reading experiences with accumulated academic disadvantage in later schooling that also correlates with dropout rates. In other words, the surveyed students entered college with a gap between their reading experiences and the expectation of more complex reading (at least of their textbooks) in a two-year tribal college.

Five Years Later: Is the Downturn Ending?

After an article from the Mellon research grant project was published (Melis, 2013), I designed a small, online survey that 33 students from my College Composition II: Content Area Research class took. The purpose of this small survey was to see if there is any change in students' reading experiences five years after the *2010 Reading Survey*. The College Composition II class focuses on preparing students for writing college papers, and the typical first assignment is to read a non-fiction article and write a summary-response essay to acquire the basics of correct paraphrasing, citing, and source attribution. Since the students were reading Mitchell Stephens's "The Death of Reading" article (first published in 1991), it seemed a good idea to conduct the electronic survey and share and discuss the results in class.

This time I was more interested in finding out whether these students perceive a shift in reading habits and skills and if they consider a presumed decline to be a problem. We had a short discussion about reading and other forms of learning.

The term "avid reader" was defined as describing a passionate reader; oral learning or learning from listening to elders was mentioned as valuable source of knowledge comparable to books; and e-reading was defined as the reading of the future, with a virtually unlimited number of books stored on one small device at affordable prices, accessible for everyone. After these discussions, the survey showed that 14 students (44%) consider themselves avid readers while 18 (56%) do not read much, learn by listening, read only for school or only online (See Table 3). Nobody thought that not reading is a good thing even though traditional, oral or hands-on learning were mentioned as equally valuable sources of learning. While students are aware of the oral tradition and value their interaction with elders, they don't think that these traditional forms can fully replace, instead of just supplementing, modern print or electronic literacy.

Table 3. Students Self-perception as Readers in a TCU, 2014–2015 (n=33)

Which description fits you best as a reader?	Number of responses (n=32)	Percent of responses
I consider myself an avid reader	14	44%
I read only for school	4	12%
I don't even read for school. I learn by listening	2	6%
I read only online	2	6%
I am not much of a reader, but I should be	10	31%
I am not that much of a reader, but it's ok	0	0%

Note. Only 32 responses were recorded for this question. In computer surveys, some responses do not get recorded; respondents may miss the question or forget to submit their answers. Percent data do not add up for 100 due to errors caused by rounding.

Looking at the written answers about one book that affected these tribal college students as readers and that they would like to pass on to their children, again, it was found that the majority of memorable readings come from middle school; many respondents did not remember titles or authors, ten (34%) mentioned a title only, without explaining the effect of reading; those who explained the significance of the book predominantly mentioned emotions, reinforcement of family values, or perfunctory reasons like "It is taught in most high schools and I would appreciate if my children read this book." Most remarkably, books from such nationally and internationally respected Native American authors as Sherman Alexie, Scott Momaday, Joy Harjo, Leslie Silko, or especially Richard Wagamese, Thomas King and Louise Erdrich, who all are of Anishinaabe/Ojibwe origin, are conspicuously missing from the memorable books list of both the 2010 and the 2015 surveys. This inexplicable absence of these culturally most relevant readings from these tribal college students' reading experiences is a symptom of a much deeper crisis of reading that would deserve immediate attention of those who make decisions about high school reading curricula.[5] Three characteristic answers to the question "Name one book that had a memorable effect on your life and that you would like your children to read" are quoted in Figure 2.

> *I cannot remember the title of the book, but I remember reading a novel when I was in middle school that greatly affected me. It was about a mother who lost her child in a jet-ski accident. It was so sad. I remember how happy they were before the accident and how depressed the mother was after. It really showed me that life is short and one never knows when their life will end. It taught me to appreciate my loved ones because time is limited. I would really like my child to read this book in middle/high school. For the sheer purpose of teaching my child to value family and loved ones.*

> *Knight. It's a book about the Holocaust and it had my attention though out the whole book. I normally don't read books but this book had my full focus and i could not put the book down for anything.* [sic]

> *The Silmarillion was probably the one book that had the most effect on me. I read the book my senior year of high school and haven't encountered a reading of such great magnitude yet. I also feel that if children pushed them selves to read more books like the Silmarillion would be an easier read and would be a great read.*[sic]

Figure 2. Three typical answers of surveyed TCU students to the question, "Name one book that had a memorable effect on your life and that you would like your children to read."

After reviewing these responses, one is inclined to raise the questions why students do not read more, and why don't they read texts that would have more memorable and more clearly articulated effect on their thinking. One typical answer usually is that technology (texting), social networking and television or movies crowd out the books, but this small survey did not confirm this common sense assumption, contrary to what many teachers believe[6] (see Appendix A: Teachers' Voices). Ten students (32%) said that their biggest challenge is to find interesting books to read; twelve (37%) blamed time-consuming hobbies for taking up most of their free

---

5   One explanation is that the two-year tribal college surveyed, in an effort to emphasize vocational training and employable skills, eliminated all literature classes. There is one Native American Literature class, however, that the school started offering, but it would require stronger administrative support to maintain consistent enrollment.

6   The college has Internet access, but we have no information about the students' home access. In general, the students participating in the surveys have cellphones, and some have smart phones, too, which are mostly used for games, music, texting, but not reading. Classrooms are equipped with laptops for all students, and so is the Library and the Learning Center.

time. These hobbies, most probably, are the numerous video games that glue tribal youth to screens instead of books. Not finding interesting books sounds almost absurd in an age when all the world's classics are available free of charge online in the Gutenberg Galaxy; when books for all ages and interests are available at a relatively affordable price on Kindle or through Amazon, not to mention the small, but very responsive public library on campus that serves both students and the community. The library has access to interlibrary loan, ebooks, and other electronic resources and uses its small budget quite effectively to order good quality contemporary fiction and non-fiction. In addition, they also have a very good (although not very well organized) Native American collection. It is true, however, that finding scholarly or academic resources, especially ones that are at an accessible reading level, is very difficult in this location because most of the scholarly or professional electronic data bases that are taken for granted in four-year colleges are forbiddingly expensive and not even cost-effective for a small, geographically isolated tribal school.

> I try to read when I get the time too, I definitely would like to read more. I find it hard to find the time to read. My mother reads about 2 books a week though and loves to read. [sic]

> My mother reads every night; where my dad, on the other hand, hardly ever reads. I feel as though I am right in the middle, I read often, but not every day. I have the feeling most people my age aren't like this though, less and less students seem to read for enjoyment, they'd rather play video games or watch tv.

> My reading habits are vastly different than those of my parents' generation. My parents read for fun. This generation feels as if reading is a chore. I can't speak for everyone in this generation tough, because some truly enjoy reading [...] I am a more 'hands-on' learner, or if I listen to someone explain a certain subject that will help me more than reading the instructions. I have a very short attention span and if I must read it has to be in completely quiet. I have a very hard time concentrating.

Figure 3. Three typical answers from surveyed TCU students to the question "Briefly explain how your reading habits are different (if they are) from those of your parents' generation."

Suspecting cultural influence or negative motivation coming from the environment, one question asked the respondents to compare their reading habits to those of their parents. Typical responses appear in Figure 3. The respondents, with a few exceptions, admitted that the parents (mothers, in particular, were more frequently mentioned than fathers) read more. Access, motivation, and special learning needs or disabilities came up most frequently as reasons for not reading more or more often. Perusing more among these answers would reveal more boredom, lack of interest or joy in reading, as well as conflict with television, video games (but not so much with computers), awareness of easy electronic access and of the need for change. The "hands-on" learner represents a small, but quite reticent group of tribal college students who would need help to overcome a fixed mindset of dichotomy between "hands-on" and book learning often reinforced by various rigid theories of learning styles.

In spite of these alarming numbers and voices, students overall appear to be optimistic about the future of reading (mostly presuming that technology is the key), and want their children to be good readers. These students confirm Mitchell Stephens's observation that "Ironically, but not coincidentally" reading is "fading from our culture at the very moment its importance is . . . established" (Stephens, 1991, para 5). When asked about their overall evaluation of the future of reading, 25 (78%) of the 32 respondents chose the answer "Reading is still alive; it just moved on to Kindle and other electronic devices"; two (6%) selected "Reading books is no longer important. We can learn all we need from the Internet," not realizing, perhaps, the contradiction since most information on the Internet also requires reading. (This assumption may not be fully accurate as students frequently report using YouTube sources to learn anything from changing a tire to using semicolons). Optimism about the future was voiced in positive comments in responses to the question "Briefly explain what kind of readers would you like your children to be." See three typical examples of responses in Figure 4.

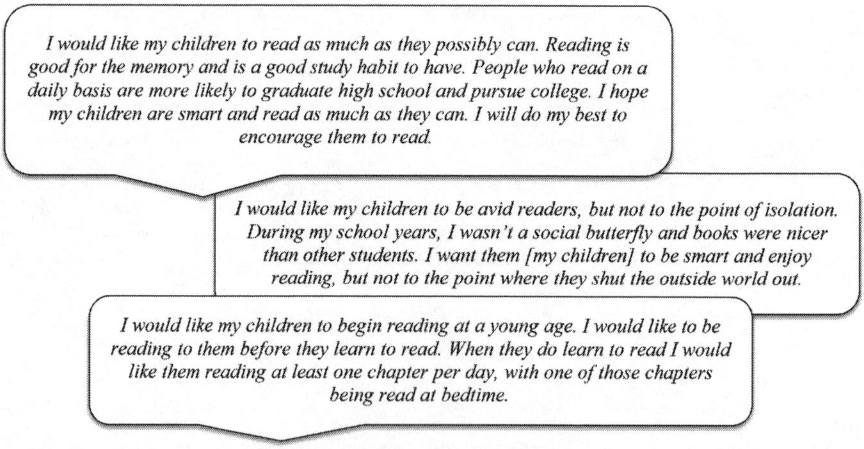

> I would like my children to read as much as they possibly can. Reading is good for the memory and is a good study habit to have. People who read on a daily basis are more likely to graduate high school and pursue college. I hope my children are smart and read as much as they can. I will do my best to encourage them to read.

> I would like my children to be avid readers, but not to the point of isolation. During my school years, I wasn't a social butterfly and books were nicer than other students. I want them [my children] to be smart and enjoy reading, but not to the point where they shut the outside world out.

> I would like my children to begin reading at a young age. I would like to be reading to them before they learn to read. When they do learn to read I would like them reading at least one chapter per day, with one of those chapters being read at bedtime.

Figure 4. Responses to the question, "Briefly explain what kind of readers would you like your children to be."

Teachers' Comments on their Students' Reading in a Two-year Tribal College

The next logical step in this inquiry was to find out how, if at all, the instructors sense the invisible crisis of reading in a small, two-year tribal college. The online survey I sent out to all full-time instructors (14) yielded 12 (85%) responses from all programs, including science, social science, health and fitness, early childhood education and business. (Unfortunately, no response was entered by the computer studies faculty, who missed the survey). All these programs currently offer certificates, associate degrees or are included in general studies preparing students for transfer. The basic online survey program used for data collections does not allow separating data by segments of responses, but the open ended questions asked all respondents to verbally identify their area of teaching. The first question, "How important are good reading skills in your area of teaching" yielded an almost unanimous response: Ten (90%) instructors believe that good reading skills are very important; one (9%) believes good reading is important (one response was missed or not recorded). On a scale of 5, the average importance rating of reading was 4.91. Similarly, although not so unanimously, teachers agreed or strongly agreed that poor reading skills are one of the main reasons why students struggle with learning in their class, with an average agreement rate of 4 on a 5-point Likert scale.

Then the respondent faculty ranked 12 specific types and skills[7] of reading by importance in their area of teaching. The skills included three more complex skills involved in college-level reading (paraphrasing, interpretation, evaluation) while the rest were related to finding and retaining information from reading. In addition, the survey was intended to gather some data on the responding teachers' perceived importance of fiction and non-fiction books in their students' reading experiences. The results confirm the assumption discussed earlier about the more practical, vocational orientation of teaching in two-year colleges. The most important function of reading, according to the surveyed tribal college teachers, is to read and follow instructions precisely. The finding is corroborated by anecdotal evidence: Teachers frequently complain that students do not read instructions well, or do not read instructions at all on assignment sheets, or they read textbooks, but do not retain content well. However, as research in many different forms is becoming indispensable in any area of study, and as it increasingly involves searching the Internet, the importance of evaluating texts for reliability—a complex analytical skill—is also becoming increasingly important. The rank list of importance of types and skills of reading, based on the average rating by 12 full-time teachers, is shown in Table 4.

A more specific list of text types or genres were also rank listed (see Table 5). It is worth noting that paraphrasing and selecting passages for quoting were considered relatively less important in spite of accumulating anecdotal evidence (and

---

7 The terms "skills" or "types" were not precisely defined for the purpose of using an accessible language. Similarly, when teachers were asked to rank text types or genres, no precise applied linguistic definition of genres was implied. I tried to use terms that are commonly known by all faculty and selected categories by their practical familiarity. I tested these items through conversations with faculty.

actual increase in the number of instances) of plagiarized papers. Although techniques of paraphrasing, quoting and source attribution, strictly speaking, are considered to be the responsibility of English/writing teachers, the task is too complex and time consuming, especially if it is not supported by all faculty giving guidance to students on acceptable ways of incorporating read information in students' writing in each specific content area. However, as such important professional matters are rarely discussed among faculty beyond personal exchanges, this survey demonstrates the relative disadvantage of two-year colleges in terms of lack of professional consensus. In other words, writing across the curriculum is endorsed, but not really implemented, and the faculty is not unified in valuing (or even articulating) some of the more complex reading skills. Typically, responsibility for poor reading or writing skills is placed squarely on the shoulders of the Communication (or English) Department. This attitude often masks lack of understanding that complex literacy skills need a consistent and supportive environment to grow. In addition, tribal college instructors often lack advanced college degrees themselves, and—sometimes even admittedly—lack knowledge of how to support their students' reading and writing skills.

Table 4. Average Importance Rating of Specific Reading Skills by Faculty in a TCU

Twelve Reading Skills from Most Important to Least Important (n=12)	Average rating (1=most important)
1. Reading instructions precisely and following them	3.14
2. Reading to get the general or main ideas fast	4.6
3. Evaluating texts for reliability of information	4.8
4. Reading for finding new information	4.88
5. Reading for retaining content	4.89
6. Interpreting reading for multiple possible meanings	5.12
7. Reading to find specific details fast	5.33
8. Reading and paraphrasing content	7.0
9. Reading and memorizing content	7.73
10. Reading books of non-fiction	8.09
11. Reading and marking passages to quote	8.22
12. Reading books of fiction	10.33

It certainly appears to be the case that reading books, and reading fiction, are no longer seen as closely related to learning to be good readers in college, and the fluid spectrum of efferent and aesthetic reading is becoming broken up and separated. The once typical college experience of reading great books is being slowly eroded, without being replaced by any kind of books. Although the average ratings of types and skills of reading that faculty consider important are not wide spread, no one ranked great fiction or, for that matter, informative <u>books</u> as most important. As a matter of fact, no instructor assigns books to read other than the textbook, with the exception of one history teacher, who requires Voltaire's *Candide* in his world history class.[8]

Table 5. TCU Teachers' Rank List of Most Important Genres for Students to Read in College

Genre	Average rating (1=most important); n=12
Short, informative texts (non-fiction)	2.50
Quality news magazines	3.64
Long, informative books (non-fiction)	3.67
Peer reviewed articles (scholarly, professional)	4.20
Anything they like and enjoy (young adult books, fiction)	4.22
Local newspapers	4.70
Great books of classical literature	4.78

Research papers, however, are still required in some of the higher-level content classes, but those research papers are increasingly based on information from short, informative pieces available on the Internet, and quality news magazines are the most reliable sources that teachers can realistically expect students to read and incorporate. In addition to the general reading crisis, two-year colleges tend to have a larger percentage of students who enter college with pre-college level reading and writing skills, making the research paper an increasingly impossible mission, not just because of the writing, but now because of the low level of reading skills. Instructors of science and social studies sometimes require source readings from peer reviewed periodicals; however, it is unlikely that many students are prepared both in terms of background knowledge and the refined reading skills that reading such texts effectively would require.

Viewed from the vantage point of a small, two-year tribal college, college-level reading needs to be (re)defined. As the anonymous author almost two hundred years ago recognized, education came "with a book in hand" and with an

---

8   Retrieving the age old "literary canon" debate is beyond the scope of this paper. It is worth noting, however, that after the critical revision/rejection of the canon, there seems to be a confusion in the high school community about what to read or how to teach good reading. Many of the popular young adult books, in spite of their important role in motivating young readers to read, arguably do not prepare students sufficiently for the complexity of textbooks and other non-fiction materials commonly read in college (Cunningham and Stanovich, 2001; "What kids are reading," 2014).

expectation that it will bring a new, fearful power of learning. The power of education has become part of oppressive colonization and has been abused in many ways, the discussion of which is not pertinent to the topic of this chapter. It would not be surprising if these tribal college students were hostile toward books and reading because "education by the book" has been typically used to eradicate their cultural heritage, but the data presented in this chapter do not show evidence for hostility. Although a few students believe that they do not learn well from books, amazingly, their ancestors were generous and wisely learned to value the book in spite of enduring suffering from the imposing hand holding that book. Most students are surrounded by parents and elders who read ferociously, and who are the most loyal patrons of the community library located on campus. It is safe to conclude that nothing in the survey indicates that, at least in one TCU, students negatively associate reading with colonization.

(Re)Definition of College-Level Reading: Bringing the Book in from the Cold?

The data selectively collected for this chapter from a small, two-year tribal college were meant to illustrate how the general neglect and misunderstanding of reading in college can affect a particularly vulnerable student population disadvantaged by geographical isolation, low socio-economic status, and a cultural heritage of ambivalence about formal education. There is a need for (re)defining college-level reading to acknowledge the diversity of college experiences and the growing gap between high school reading and college expectation as well as the gap between two-year and four-year colleges. However, as many two-year college students consider transfer to earn a bachelor's degree and go even further, all of us who teach in two-year colleges should find ways to decrease or at least bridge these gaps by reconsidering the role of reading in our teaching.

One way of addressing the problems is to give in or give up. As an instructor of mathematics said, "I don't think we can continue to assume that they [our students] are readers and capable of comprehending what they read. I hate to say it, but we need to change our teaching strategies to include less reading" (see Appendix A: Teachers' voices). This response, so it seems, has been quite typical in our college classrooms, as Anson's anecdotal introduction to his chapter in this volume also shows. Textbook publishers also read the writing on the wall and design texts for students who don't read. One textbook of college writing, for example, which just came out with its 6th edition, shows a mixed response to the declining reading skills of students. The author began including readings in the 5th edition, but made the chapters and the explanations of grammar points shorter, with fewer examples. The added readings are one-and-a half-page essays, written by "student writers," mixed with brief, blog-like texts, or short excerpts from professional staff writers, followed by multiple-choice comprehension and vocabulary tests. The text itself shows signs of simplification. For example, the word "comprehension" is replaced with "understanding the reading." These kinds of revisions may not be a general trend in all textbooks and they may have been inspired by other factors than the students' changed reading habits, but seven (58%) instructors in the teacher survey agreed strongly or more or less that textbooks in their field have been simplified over the past few editions; five (41%) responding faculty disagreed or strongly disagreed.

Another way of addressing the decline of reading is to "force" students to read (otherwise they won't, as one teacher assumes), or as a social studies instructor phrased it, "it behooves the colleges to require some readings of the classics," and the same instructor was brave enough to suggest books, including some controversial titles. The unpopularity of such measures along with the ineffectiveness of isolated incidents can be mitigated by a joint effort of faculty, for example, by taking turns in choosing one book every semester that every student in a college would read, and every instructor would agree on designing assignments related to the "book of the semester" in a creative way, seeking connections with the book in their disciplinary area. One good example of such efforts is the Common Read programs presented in this volume by Maloy et al. Forcing students to read, however, can easily become counterproductive unless it goes together with meaningful learning activities. Again, it is helpful to bear Louise Rosenblatt's ideas in mind that it is not so much what students read that matters, but how they read it. Unless the reading is followed by some analysis, evaluation and reflection, it may not create the much needed transformative learning experience (see Gogan in this volume). Therefore, it is necessary to supplement the required reading assignment with a more systematic approach outlined in this volume in Anson's chapter. This approach not only connects reading to writing, but it also sets up four criteria for making such efforts meaningful: the reading assignment has to be motivating, cognitively complex, creative in its design and resonant with collaborative learning (Anson, in this volume).

There are more productive ways of addressing the emerging crisis of reading than by apathetic submission or by force. Carillo (2015) Anson, Davies and others in this volume provide not only compelling reasons for paying attention to and a general framework for approaching reading, but also examples of activities that all teachers, not only those who teach first-year composition, can apply. The suggested assignments go beyond the routine comprehension questions and require students to summarize and respond to chapters, shorter, but important passages, or related articles in creative ways, for a particular audience or purpose. Four instructors (33%) in my survey admitted that they don't expect students to learn from the book, and they use gestures, images, Power Point presentations or other ways to communicate the textbook content to students. (Average agreement on a scale of 5 was 2.65). But what if these instructors assigned these tasks to students who would be responsible for creating the visual-verbal conversions of texts or textbook chapters for the class? These assignments would "force" the students to read the chapter carefully and to understand its content well enough to be able to explain it to others. Collaboration with librarians on taking students to the library and showing them how to find sources there; source evaluation exercises, modeled annotation (teacher shows what to underline, how to write marginal notes, then students can do the same with subsequent readings) and handouts with directed questions can help students acquire higher-level reading processes and develop good reading habits.

In 2008, Gerald Graff in a seminal article bemoaning the deplorable condition of college writing classes suggested that college writing faculty should end their misery, isolation and abuse by pairing up with other faculty and teach writing in collaboration to bring writing "in from the cold." The core of his proposal was that faculty has to "reach a consensus on what they are looking for in student writing" instead of pointing fingers and placing blame on writing instructors for poor writing in college. Perhaps now it is time to bring the book and reading "in from the cold." Faculty has to collaborate even more on reading because there is no equivalent of first year composition class teaching "first year reading" to be blamed for students' inadequate reading habits. (Good examples of such collaboration are presented by Maloy et al. in this volume). As Scholes (2002) pointed out, unlike bad writing, bad reading is not visible, but if we could see how poorly our students read, we would be equally shocked. Now the next step is to accept what many who did research on reading found out; namely, that we have to teach and model the cognitively complex reading processes we expect from our students to perform and also to transfer to various academic and career related reading situations because it won't automatically happen (Anson and Davies in this volume; Carillo, 2013).

College-level reading has to be (re)defined, book by book, text by text, with faculty reaching a reasonable degree of consensus on what to read, how to evaluate a text for credibility, how to find, analyze and interpret information, and how to apply a broad spectrum of efferent and aesthetic reading essential not only for college-level academic work, but for making sense of an increasingly complex world around us.

Notes

1. The author would like to thank Mickey Parish, President, and Steve Yanni, Director of Development and Research, at Bay Mills Community College for their approval of and support for this project.

2. Since the data interpreted from 2010 were part of a grant funded research (American Indian College Fund) that was cleared by our institutional research board

and the sample of the follow up was considered both too small and low risk, I was recommended not to go through the usual IRS procedure. Nevertheless, all student and teacher participants in my surveys were informed about the purpose of the survey and the use of their information; they were given the option not to participate and were thanked for their contribution.

References

Carillo, E. C. (2015). *Securing a place for reading in composition: The importance of teaching for transfer*. Logan: Utah State University Press.

Cunningham, A. E. & Stanovich, K. E. (2001, Summer). What reading does for the mind. *Journal of Direct Instruction 1*(2), 137–149.

Ede, L. S. & Lunsford, A. A. (1991). *Singular texts and plural authors: Perspectives on collaborative writing*. Carbondale: Southern Illinois University Press.

Gogan, B. (2013, December 11). Reading at the threshold. *Across the Disciplines, 10*(4). Retrieved from http://wac.colstate.edu/atd/reading/jamieson.cfm.

Graff, G. (2008, Summer). Bringing writing in from the cold. [Reprinted from *MLA Newsletter*]. Retrieved from https://www.mla.org/blog?topic=123.

Holbrook, T. H. (1986, May). Reading needs at the 2-year college level. *Journal of Reading, 29*(8), 770–772.

Horning, A. (2011, October 6). Where to put the manicules: A theory of expert reading. *Across the Disciplines, 8*(2). Retrieved from http://wac.colstate.edu/atd/articles/horning2011/index.cfm.

Horning, A. (2007, January–December). Reading across the curriculum as the key to student success. *Across the Disciplines, 4*. Retrieved from https://wac.colostate.edu/atd/articles/horning2007.cfm.

Hyatt, M. (2015, May 4). 5 ways reading makes you a better leader: The science behind reading and influence. Retrieved from https://www.nyu.edu/classes/stephens/Death%20of%20Reading%20page.htm.

Jolliffe, D. J. & Harl, A. (2008). Texts of our institutional lives: Studying the reading transition from high school to college: What are our students reading and why? *College English, 70*(6), 599–617.

Keller, D. (2013). *Chasing literacy: Reading and writing in an age of acceleration*. Logan: Utah State University Press.

Melis, I. (2013). Mission not so impossible: Standardized testing in a tribal college. *Mellon Tribal College Journal, 1*, 106–148.

National Center on Education and the Economy. (2013, May). What does it really mean to be college and work ready? The mathematics and English literacy required of first year community college students. Executive summary. Retrieved from http://www.ncee.org/wp-content/uploads/2013/05/NCEE_ExecutiveSummary_May2013.pdf.

Reschly, A. L. (2010). Reading and school completion: Critical connections and Matthew effects. *Reading & Writing Quarterly, 26*(1), 67–90. http://dx.doi.org/ 10.1080/1057 3560903397023.

Rosenblatt, L. (2005). *Making meaning with texts: Selected essays.* Portsmouth, NH: Heinemann.

Scholes, R. (2002). The transition to college reading. *Pedagogy 2*(2), 165–172. Retrieved from https://faculty.unlv.edu/nagelhout/ENG714f10/ScholesTransitiontoCollege.pdf.

Stephens, M. (1991, September 22). The death of reading. Will a nation that stops reading eventually stop thinking? *Los Angeles Times Magazine.* Retrieved from https://www.nyu.edu/classes/stephens/Death%20of%20Reading%20page.htm.

Tinberg, H. & Nadeau, J. P. (2010). *The community college writer: Exceeding expectations.* Carbondale: Southern Illinois University Press.

Voorhees, R. A. (2003, August). *Characteristics of tribal college and university faculty.* Littleton, CO: Voorhees Group LLC. Retrieved from http://www.collegefund.org/user files/file/TCUFacultyPaper11.pdf.

Weissmann, J. (2014, January 21). The decline of the American book lover. *The Atlantic.* [Online]. Retrieved from http://www.theatlantic.com/business/archive/2014/01/the -decline-of-the-american-book-lover/283222/.

What kids are reading. (2014). *Renaissance Learning.* Retrieved from http://doc.renlearn .com/KMNet/R004101202GH426A.pdf.

Appendix A: Teachers' Voices

Excerpts from content area instructors of a two-year tribal college responding to questions on what they expect from their students reading for their classes, and what they consider as strengths and weaknesses in today's students' reading skills:

> Science instructor: Students are able to find information on the web, but they lack the skill to know what exactly they found and process it. Processing and retaining what they have is weak. Reading will remain vital in education. Students do not read as in depth or as challenging material as in the past. Hopefully, there will be more access to peer-reviewed articles, so students will need to be able to read these texts.

> Social studies instructors: I think reading classic Western lit-erature is vital although I do not think students for the most part read any of it. I think it behooves colleges to require some reading of classics like the Persian letters, Candide, The vicar of Wakefield, or even more touchy books like Justine, Catcher in the rye, and even the Scarlet letter.

***

> Students will continue to rely on the visual electronic medium and not read anything of great import unless forced to by teachers.

***

Unless it is one Social Media or the Internet, I do not think students read anything voluntarily. Sociology students are used to reading in quick bites. They have trouble reading a long research document for analysis. If the research is summarized, especially into a story-like manner, students are captivated by the story and will generally read and understand the summary.

<u>Mathematics</u>: My students need to be able to read the textbook and grasp some of the content. I don't believe many of my students read much of anything. I don't think we can continue to assume that they are readers and capable of comprehending what they read. I hate to say it, but we need to change our teaching strategies to include less reading.

<u>Early Childhood Education</u>: I see today's students as users of technology to solve problems. Students are more engaged in the process of learning if they are given the opportunity to think about information, not just "fill in bubbles." For example, I assess student learning with at least 50% essay response. The essay questions are questions students should be asking themselves as they read the chapters. I want students to develop a metacognitive approach to learning: read, read, reflect, apply. I ask students questions about the reading, followed by how will you apply this to the work you will be doing.

<u>English</u>: I teach English. Today even students who say they are avid readers read books that I am not familiar with. This creates an enormous gulf between me and my students. When I was a student, some books were shared by most people around me. Sometimes we viciously disagreed about the value and meaning of those books, but we were able to have a conversation nonetheless. This is gravely missing today, and it is a struggle to teach anything that involves a text because texts are full of allusions and can be very hard to work through with students without dozens of oral footnotes from the teacher. Technology does not bother me that much: I read on Kindle, too. Another thing that is different today is that my students do not even realize how much easier it is for them to reach those great books that they do not care to read anymore.

***

Students do not read. Students have no command of the English language because they have no vocabulary. No vocabulary or articulation is the result of never learning to read.

***

I am sorry, but I do not think today's students bring a lot of strengths to college reading tasks. I have seen them misinterpret even Facebook posts. Here is a list of possible reasons for declining reading ability: An insistence on multi-tasking; refusal to turn off/shut out distractions; a deep seated belief that all tasks should be completed within the shortest possible time frame; disinterest in reflection and introspection, stemming from having grown up in a society that occupies itself with massive amounts of external stimuli, leaving no time for quiet examination of ideas. The generation defines itself by online connections rather than values and beliefs. Reading is necessary to form individual values and beliefs. It also tends to be a self-absorbed generation with little interest in the matters beyond their own narrowly defined world. They have little sense of control over their world. A high school curriculum that emphasizes literature over reading for information. A school system that has low expectations for reading to begin with. A rural culture that values social interaction over the introspective activity of reading.

Health and fitness instructor: I see students not reading and learning because it is easier to look up the question online and get an answer, even though they do not understand the answer themselves. All of my classes require extensive reading. There are many formulas, charts, graphs and tons of valuable information including current studies and findings. Students have a hard time with looking at what is a credible material. They tend to look online, and whatever it is that they find must be accurate. But deciding what is actually credible information is hard for them. In the health and fitness industry, there is a lot of false information out there that people read and believe.

Appendix B: Full Text of the Poem "Sacred Ground"[9]

Sacred Ground
O Father Of Education,
You Come
With A Book In Your Hand.
A Monstrous Task;
Be Careful,
Your Expectations Are Great.
The Native People Are
Children Of The Earth;
Walk Slow and Softly
Into These Holy Lands,
For The Red Children
Are Its Sacred Places.
Nurtured With Grace;
A Way Of Life,
Kept These Human Beings
In Spiritual Harmony.
The Family Of The Universe:
The Fathering Sun.
Mother Earth,
The Morning Star.
And Her Relatives.
O Father Of Education,
Please Be Careful,
For You Have Entered
Sacred Ground.

---

9   Although I made several attempts, I could not get any information of the author and original context of this poem. I found copies of it hanging in teachers' offices or on various (English) department notice boards, including one in my own school. With some guesswork, we dated it to the second half of the 1800s, and the inquiry is still on. I found the sentiment in this poem that places reading in a colonial context very important and deserving more inquiry. Overall, my experience is that (modern) education is embraced and supported in the tribal community I work in, but the poem reminded me that books may not always have been welcome around here.

Multiliteracies and Meaning-Making: Writing to Read Across the Curriculum

Mary Lou Odom

KENNESAW STATE UNIVERSITY

Faculty dissatisfaction with the ways students read and write in college is widespread, yet faculty development initiatives typically focus almost exclusively on writing. This chapter treats reading, like writing, as a complex, transformational process of meaning-making and thus looks to writing-based initiatives such as writing across the curriculum to inform approaches for improving college reading. Just as faculty involved with WAC re-examine why and how they ask students to write, faculty concerned with reading should consider the complexities created when students accustomed to an increasingly multiliterate textual environment enter college and are asked to read unfamiliar genres and formats in unfamiliar ways. Based on data from the first six years of a study of WAC faculty at a large, comprehensive state university, the chapter suggests three foundational principles essential for supporting student reading in this context. First, faculty must recognize ways in which they impact student reading behavior—beyond assigning texts or writing related to texts. Second, faculty must articulate to students their goals for student reading. Third, faculty must be willing to provide guidance for students reading complex, discipline-specific texts that may look quite different from much of the reading that has occupied their textual lives until this point.

In many ways, higher education perpetuates a curious dichotomy between reading and writing. Young children are taught both skills together, learning to form letters as they also learn to identify them. As students progress in school, however, the discourse surrounding literacy education changes: barring signs or diagnoses of serious reading difficulties, students can expect little reading instruction once they have mastered the skills taught in elementary school. Even the Common Core State Standards (National Governors Association Center for Best Practices, 2010), claiming to promote "wide, deep, and thoughtful engagement with high-quality literary and informational texts that builds knowledge, enlarges experience, and broadens worldviews," devote explicit attention to teaching reading only through fifth grade. Beyond that, the Standards focus largely on the actual texts themselves, laying a foundation in schools for what Thomas Newkirk (2013) has referred to as "a sterile view of reading" (p. 2).

But academic literacy, though shaped by both the production and consumption of texts, is far from sterile and far from an isolated process easily confined to one stage of learning or school. As Chris Anson has noted earlier in this volume, however, reading tends to be seen as an "independent" precursor to the work, including writing, that students do—even when that work directly pertains to or relies upon their reading. One reason for this frustrating contradiction was suggested by Robert Scholes (2002) in an opinion essay for *Pedagogy*:

> We normally acknowledge, however grudgingly, that writing must be taught and continue to be taught from high school to college and perhaps beyond. We accept it, I believe, because we can see writing, and we know that much of the writing we see is not good enough. But we do not see reading. We see some writing about reading, to be sure, but we do not see reading. (p. 166)

Seeing both writing and reading—and determining how to use what we know pedagogically about the former to advance our approach to the latter—is the goal of this chapter.

This goal is a complicated and at times uncomfortable one because it requires recognizing that, despite the fact that writing can indeed be a tool to promote learning and reading (Langer & Applebee, 1987; Smith, 1988; Graham & Hebert, 2010), it does not do so automatically. In fact, a successful pedagogy that uses writing to enhance reading requires considerable effort on the part of educators to recognize the reality, as literacy scholar Deborah Brandt (1994) explained, that "What motivates and brings meaning to acts of reading or writing may not always be texts" (p. 460). Determining what does bring meaning to our students' textual experiences is a crucial first step in developing pedagogies that make successful reading, writing, and learning connections for students.

Reading in a Time of Textual Change

Success in higher education today rests, as it always has, largely on expectations of literacy. One key component of those expectations holds that irrespective of discipline students will learn, to borrow from M.H. Abrams, by "doing things with texts." Few and far between are those college classes that do not incorporate and depend on reading, yet as we know from Jolliffe and Harl (2008) attention to "careful reading" has "become a smaller blip on the higher educational radar screen" (p. 600). Such inattention is especially problematic in light of the intricate processes and complex materials that increasingly characterize college reading practices today.

Ironically, unlike the silence that typically accompanies consideration of these intricate reading processes, the nature of what constitutes "text" has become a subject of vigorous debate. This contrast represents a missed opportunity to attend to concerns about reading, for as Charles Kinzer (2010) has noted, "The definition of literacy is tied more closely than ever to the specific medium in which literacy practices occur" (p. 53). Given the seismic shifts in the variety, availability, and nature of texts seen in recent decades, this inextricable link between reading and texts should demand some recalibration of faculty expectations for student reading. Indeed, today's students enter college with reading behaviors appropriate for texts that are less linear and permanent, more dynamic and multimodal, and that require greater agency on students' parts than much of what they likely encounter in their classes. By focusing its attention on the mediums but not the processes of reading, however, higher education has continued to operate with an alarmingly incomplete understanding of these literacy practices.

At least since the New London Group's 1996 manifesto on "A Pedagogy of Multiliteracies," there has been a degree of recognition that non-school-based literacy practices offer potential avenues for engaging and empowering students as readers. Julie Coiro (2003) characterized online reading as a process requiring students not only to develop new reading strategies but also to expand their approaches to traditional "text elements, reader elements, activities, and sociocultural contexts" (p. 463). Kinzer (2003, 2010) and others have recorded numerous ways in which making meaning from digital and multimodal texts involves students in the simultaneous processes of decoding alphabetic and visual material, assessing and prioritizing competing information, and determining if and how additional knowledge needs to be obtained.

In their article revisiting the New London Group publication, Bill Cope and Mary Kalantzis (2009) considered the implications of these new and complex meaning-making processes and explained why it is imperative for teachers to comprehend how their students experience text: "Old logics of literacy and teaching are profoundly challenged by this new media environment. They are bound to fall short . . . disappointing young people whose expectations of engagement [with text] are greater" (p. 173). We may grimace at the English major reading Moby Dick on her smartphone, but we also must be open to the idea that such substantive changes in the nature of texts may have provided her with some of the very behaviors we desire—and yet identify as absent—in how she and her peers read in college.

Many faculty already acknowledge this evolving literacy landscape in the writing they assign in their classes: consider the composing students do on class discussion boards, wikis, or blogs and the projects they complete in multimodal or digital formats. Thus, as college writing has changed, so too can college reading. To that end, this chapter operates on a definition of college reading as, at its best, a complex, transformational process of meaning-making influenced in often subtle or even invisible ways by the social, disciplinary, and technological forces that shape today's texts and today's students' lives. By looking at successful efforts to understand and teach student writing with these influences in mind, we can gain insight into college reading both as it is and as it could be.

Reading in a Writing Across the Curriculum Program

As we seek to understand and improve student reading, examining the ways faculty perceive—or more accurately what they *mean* when they refer to—"student reading" is critical. Faculty expectations for reading in college are highly nuanced, demanding critical literacy skills often inaccessible for students who, as Horning (2007) has described them, have little "experience working with extended texts and the world of ideas from which they arise." Much as the Common Core's relegation of reading to the category of "Foundational Skills" may limit its overt instruction beyond elementary school, faculty who overlook college reading's complexity may unwittingly restrict the knowledge and skills about reading they might profitably share with their students.

When students lack both experience and instruction in the kinds of reading necessary for their success in school, they unsurprisingly fall back on strategies used for the reading they do know how to do—the kind of reading and interacting with non-school texts that is not, on its own, typically adequate for college. As a result, many students become less likely to read for school at all, and their reading behaviors that so frustrate educators become a self-perpetuating cycle that is all the more difficult to break when it, like reading, operates virtually unseen.

The mismatch between faculty expectations for and student performance on reading-related tasks has been well documented throughout this collection and elsewhere, but two key points warrant special emphasis here: first, faculty dissatisfaction with student reading is profound; and two, such dissatisfaction is widespread throughout all majors and subject areas. This extreme, cross-disciplinary outcry over student reading ability echoes concerns often voiced about student writing. But whereas few pedagogical movements have emerged to address reading at the college level, writing across the curriculum (WAC), as Susan McLeod and Eric Miraglia (2001) explained, has exerted considerable influence on how college faculty teach:

> WAC, more than any other recent educational reform movement, has aimed at transforming pedagogy at the college level, at moving away from the lecture mode of teaching (the "delivery of information" model) to a model of active student engagement with the materials and with the genres of the discipline through writing. (p. 5)

The early WAC movement provides promising context for considering how to engage faculty in improving student reading. In addressing "How Well Does Writing Across the Curriculum Work?" Toby Fulwiler (1984) explained that "to improve student writing we had to influence the entire academic community in which writing takes place, to make the faculty sensitive to the role of writing in learning as well as to the relationship of writing to other communication skills—reading, speaking, and listening" (p. 113). This encompassing view of WAC not only confirms how well suited it is to address college reading, but it also reminds us again of the multi-faceted and interconnected nature of literacy, including reading, throughout higher education.

McLeod and Miraglia have suggested that one source of WAC's success and longevity is this attention to "writing as an essential component of critical thinking and problem solving, key elements in a liberal education" (p. 3). Because much of what faculty want from good student reading mirrors their goals for good student writing—engagement, critical thinking, depth of understanding—writing across the curriculum provides a valuable lens through which to examine the ways faculty can influence how their students read. Additionally, WAC programs can serve as sites in which faculty perceptions of and approaches to student reading can be probed more deeply.

This article draws on data from the first six years of an ongoing study of WAC faculty at a large, comprehensive state university. The university's institutional review board determined that this study qualified for exempt status under DHHS (OHRP) Title 45 CFR Part 46.101(b)(4). WAC faculty come from the university's largest college, the College of Humanities and Social Sciences, which, as of this writing, is the only college to support a WAC program. After self-selecting to participate in a daylong workshop on WAC with a nationally recognized WAC scholar, up to ten faculty members are supported in the following semester as they redesign and teach a course to include the implementation of WAC principles. At the conclusion of this semester, they submit reflective reports on their experiences along with survey data from students in their WAC-focused courses. Each semester's group of faculty tailors survey questions based on their particular approaches and interests, but six core questions are asked each semester. Of these six, one directly addresses reading.

Initially, reading had not been a focus of either the WAC program or this study, both of which sought primarily to assess WAC's efficacy for enhancing student learning and engagement with course material and for impacting teaching as it pertained to those goals. However, faculty concern about student reading became such a consistent refrain in both monthly WAC faculty meetings and in their reflective narratives that reexamining faculty and student data for insight into student reading within the context of the program was essential.

Analysis of student data compiled throughout the study indicates that students overwhelmingly found writing facilitated their reading of course material. Of the 869 students surveyed, 85.6% agreed or strongly agreed that the writing assigned by their professor "helped me understand the reading assignments." Only 6% of all students surveyed expressed any level of disagreement with this statement. However, feedback from faculty on WAC's ability to impact student reading was far less decisive, and narrative analysis and coding of the faculty's reflective narratives ultimately revealed stark differences between the WAC strategies of those faculty who perceived improvement in student reading and those who did not.

Typical of many faculty throughout higher education, participants in this WAC program expressed a variety of concerns about student reading. Uniformly frustrated at students who simply did not read assigned material, WAC faculty also articulated specific complaints about the reading their students did attempt. A psychology professor lamented her students' lack of "in-depth" reading; a political scientist reported students "struggle" to carry out any "critical assessment" pertaining to course readings or research, and a history professor noted that students often give complex historical documents little more than "a cursory glance." Difficulties with student reading extended beyond homework readings or professional texts as well. One anthropologist noted that many students struggled with peer review because they lacked "the ability to read a paper critically." No discipline was immune to problems with student reading: several English faculty described their upper-level students as unable to engage in "critical reflection" and simply "unprepared to discuss the literature" they had read.

What Doesn't Work

Despite the considerable success most WAC faculty reported in rethinking how and what they asked students to write, some remained deeply disappointed in their students' reading. The reflective narratives of these faculty suggest that their difficulty in effecting positive change in this area can be traced to two key assumptions about the relationship between writing and reading. Both of these assumptions, furthermore, seem deeply rooted in an uncomplicated and ultimately problematic view of reading itself. First, these faculty members assumed that requiring students to write about their reading would ensure that they read more and that they read more actively and carefully. Second, these individuals assumed that this writing would automatically show that students were engaged with text in critical and meaningful ways. Unfortunately, as these faculty members discovered, the requirement to write on its own does not necessarily provide sufficient motivation or instruction for students to read in the ways faculty may desire.

A faculty member teaching an upper-level psychology class endeavored to use online discussion postings to encourage students to engage more critically with textbook material that she would eventually put on their exams. The professor had selected these particular topics from material that had proven the most difficult for students in previous semesters, and, while she used the word "prompts" throughout the semester, the discussion board material she posted asked students for responses to very specific questions (for example, "How do brain imaging studies provide evidence for distribution of activity?"). In her end-of-semester narrative, the professor reported that while "students' discussion posts were generally thorough, they did not necessarily address in detail the evidence underlying our existing knowledge of selected discussion topics."

Student survey comments in this course indicated little interest in the readings and presented a picture of student engagement with course texts in line with the findings of Jolliffe and Harl: "Students were reading, but they were not reading studiously, either in terms of the texts they were engaging with or the manner in which they read them" (p. 611). This professor had imagined her discussion format to be a task like those Art Young (2006) has challenged teachers to devise—tasks for which "students need to be actively involved in thinking and solving problems, in developing knowledge and applications" (p. 47). Yet her students simply saw places to deposit information they could find easily by scanning their textbooks—a far cry from the kind of transformative work with text we hope college reading can be.

Of those WAC strategies that proved unsuccessful, the most common by far involved the use of writing to compel students to read. The following excerpt from the narrative of a political science professor is representative of a number of faculty who used this approach. Her account demonstrates how faculty assumptions about student reading can lead to missteps in how they incorporate reading into their courses:

> Students completed many in-class writing activities. On occasion, students would be asked to write about the reading for the day; such writings served as a sort of "reading quiz" and were intended to encourage students to come to class prepared. I found that these assignments were the least successful [among her WAC efforts]. Students usually did poorly on these assignments, particularly if they covered the reading from the textbook, and I found myself discouraged from using them.

Even well-intentioned teachers like this one can create a disconnect between what they want students to do with texts and what they ask students to do with texts. The professor wanted students to read thoroughly, and she believed that thoroughness would appear in their writing in ways not easily discerned on a quiz. However, without further guidance from the professor as to what that kind of reading looked like (particularly it seems when reading from their textbooks), students responded with reading and writing behaviors just like those they were accustomed to using for quizzes. Much like the students of the psychology professor who retitled reading questions as "prompts," these students responded to tasks based on their nature and not their name.

Why the quiz/coercion approach so reliably failed speaks to the nature of what both faculty and their students expect of reading done in college. Although some research into how quizzes might encourage student reading compliance has shown a positive correlation (Sappington, Kinsey & Munsayac, 2002; Berry, Hill & Stevens, 2011), Linda Nilson (2010) has argued persuasively that when students lack a "perceived need" or a "perceived payoff" their motivation to read is significantly reduced (p. 212–213). Indeed, nowhere in her extensive discussions of teaching strategies to improve student reading has Nilson cited research that test or quiz-like exercises prove useful for this goal.

But perhaps the most compelling evidence that improving student reading depends on understanding something of students' perceptions of reading comes from the students themselves. Such was the case for one WAC faculty member in public administration who began each meeting of her graduate course by having students freewrite in response to questions posed regarding their homework reading. Although this individual began the semester believing her course's heavy reading load made it ideally suited for the use of WAC strategies, she was continually disappointed that the freewriting she received indicated little engagement with course texts: "Only a handful of students provided insightful and reflective thoughts . . . strategies on how to get students to read remain a challenge for me."

Eventually, this faculty member sought feedback from the class on her use of these new writing assignments, and she was both shocked and enlightened to see how differently she and her students perceived the reading-based writing she had asked them to do:

> I realized, based on the comments received, that students
> thought that the writing assignment was a quiz, and that made
> them nervous. I realized that I had not made it clear at the be-
> ginning of the semester of the purpose of the writing assignment;
> I had mentioned to the students that the assignment would not
> be graded, but somehow the students took it as a weekly quiz.

The professor noted that in the future she would articulate earlier and more clearly for students how she perceived assigned reading and writing to function in the course. She explained that in assigning freewriting to enhance student reading of course texts, she would immediately point out to students "The purpose of the writing . . . how it will help students engage with the material and how it will strengthen students' understanding of the material."

This teacher's resolve to make her reading goals clear for her students is one strategy Horning (2007) has also espoused. In discussing goals inherent in the complex types of reading students need to do in college and beyond, she noted, "It is also difficult for students to read well enough to achieve these goals if they are not stated explicitly, taught directly, and required in students' work" (Defining Reading section, para. 3). Helping students see writing as a tool designed to help them understand and make meaning from what they read is an idea many students would no doubt find revelatory—particularly when their previous experiences with writing about reading seemed designed primarily to test reading compliance. Furthermore, the notion that students should engage in an active process of meaning-making for all texts—not just those that they interact with in digital or visual realms—also needs to be made clear if students are to read less passively and with greater transformative purpose.

Tellingly, faculty who reported little or no productive change in student reading behaviors (or work dependent on student reading) were those individuals who did little to reconsider the role and purpose of the reading they assigned in their classes. They may have changed writing assignments, and they may have become more creative with delivery or prompts of reading-based writing, but they remained frustrated at student interaction with text because they did little to alter the nature of student interaction with text, particularly those texts that might have been less familiar and thus more difficult for students. Productive change in attitudes and approaches toward reading does not come easily, but change is possible, as a number of other WAC faculty and their strategies show.

What Works

Attend a writing across the curriculum workshop or meeting and you are likely to hear considerable discussion about designing effective writing assignments. An assignment's purpose, goals, and guidelines, even its length and tone or style, as well as the teacher's expectations are all issues faculty who participate in WAC programs learn to consider. Doing so helps to create writing assignments that students can complete successfully and that, in the words of Young (2006) "are embedded in the unique goals of each course and are integral to the building of knowledge in that course" (p. 5). Yet while invested faculty often write and rewrite essay assignments and assessment criteria, and while they often spend considerable class time reviewing these assignments with students, few college teachers could so readily recount a time they labored over instructions for assigning reading.

But for WAC faculty who made substantive changes in how they asked students to approach and engage with their reading, real improvement in student comprehension and engagement with text resulted. Furthermore, students who read in these more transformative ways were far more successful in using what they read to their advantage throughout the course. Understanding the success behind strategies that produced this sort of improvement begins with examining how these faculty members stated their goals.

Faculty who were willing to rethink not only writing but also reading in their courses tended to have goals for student reading that went beyond the simple evaluation of whether or not students had read what had been assigned for homework. For example, in contrast to one English professor who assigned blogs "in place of quizzes, as a way of seeing who is keeping up with the reading," another WAC faculty member from the same department set out to use blogging with very different goals in mind.

This professor implemented blogs into her general education literature course to address her concerns about how—not just if—her students had read in the past. In particular, she wanted her blog assignment to increase student preparation for and comfort with in-class discussions of the literature they read for homework. With these goals in mind, she set up an assignment that allowed students to interact with the course blog much as they would with a blog in a non-academic setting:

> I wanted students to feel they could reflect on any part(s) of
> the reading that appealed to them most. In order to ensure
> this, I did not ask students to respond to a question or series of
> questions. Students were expected to reflect on the first read-
> ing of each text in a casual nature. The writing would be sim-
> ilar to writing that might be found in a journal. I did specify
> that students were not to summarize the reading but to work
> through their reactions to the text . . . I [also] had students post
> an introduction entry. In this entry, they were asked to not only
> introduce themselves to the class but also to talk about what
> they hoped to learn from the course and what works of literature
> they've enjoyed in the past.

What is notable about this professor's approach to student reading is her lack of focus on reading completion. Rather, she emphasized engagement with text—even the texts students had read and enjoyed at other points in their lives.

A point value was assigned for each blog entry, but the value of this assignment went well beyond that for both students and teacher. At the conclusion of the course, the professor reflected positively on the role that the blogs had played in enhancing a number of the course's learning outcomes: "The blogs facilitated better class discussions. Students were more prepared since they had already posted their initial reactions to the blog and were able to better articulate what they enjoyed or didn't enjoy about the reading. . . . The blogs also made for a class that appeared to be more intimate."

As Anson has also discussed in this collection, creative, lower-stakes writing activities such as this one can make reading more meaningful for students in any discipline. Indeed, students in the class acknowledged how much this approach supported their reading, with one student describing the blog entries as "wonderful avenues for expression and creativity on the material."

In many ways, this assignment is a model for how to blend the informal writing-to-learn strategies of WAC with existing knowledge about current reading practices. While reading literary texts may not have been part of these students' everyday literacy experiences, the use of a blog allowed them to draw on their more typical reading and writing behaviors such as writing or replying to public blog posts or stating an opinion in the online comments section of an article. Similarly, by sharing their personal reactions to readings in the blogs, students established a connection with the traditional and in many cases centuries-old texts they were reading. Much as expressivists have argued that students become more engaged with writing when they begin with a topic or idea that is familiar and personal, so too can students who connect on a personal level with a text engage more deeply in their reading. Notably, such connections did not mean students learned to privilege personal feeling at the expense of critical thought: the faculty member noted that the quality of the students' critical essays was higher than in any previous semester.

The fact that students are able to transfer initial personal engagement with text to more complex acts such as analysis or synthesis is key for faculty who want or need to assign more academic kinds of writing. A professor in the university's conflict management graduate program chose to use John Bean's well-known RAFT (Role-Audience-Format-Task) heuristic to revise a longstanding, highly structured assignment called "Memo to Self." While in the past, the professor had provided a list of elements from the course readings that students were to address in their memos, this new assignment asked students to compose a more clearly situated, rhetorical piece of writing to "revisit and critique a negotiation in which you were a primary party." Additionally, students were to provide "recommendations to yourself, specifically meant to improve your handling of any similar negotiation."

This professor explained that his goal in having the class apply their reading of course concepts to a real-life scenario was to "Push students to recognize and record those lessons on paper, and thus (hopefully) internalize them more deeply." It is after all this type of purposeful exercise Young (2006) encouraged when he made the following appeal: "One ongoing task, which I hope you will share with me, is to develop writing-to-communicate assignments and classroom practices that encourage sincere and authentic communication" (p. 49). The results of this authentic communication for the conflict management professor were truly positive. Not only did the writing he received demonstrate "students' application of abstract principles to concrete experiences," but he also was gratified by student responses on his end-of-semester evaluations: "The memo to self helped me learn how to apply the readings to real life situations."

In reality, this assignment was doubly authentic. First, the guiding task of the assignment—a Memo to Self—immediately encouraged the sort of connections between text and self that students experience in their reading outside of school. Second, when students returned to their course readings, it was not simply to gather a requisite number of sources to fulfill the assignment. Rather, this task required them to pay careful, focused attention as they read to be sure the material they included aligned with the goals of their memos.

Connecting the work of their courses to the "real world" is a thread that runs visibly through many of the most successful reading and writing across the curriculum intersections attempted by the WAC faculty in this program. A sociology professor who was "looking for a way to make social problems come alive" for her class decided to engage students in identifying readings appropriate for inclusion in the course. Using what she had learned from a WAC workshop about crafting assignments and making tasks seem genuine to students, she established clear guidelines for students to find, read, and analyze recent articles about contemporary social problems.

Not only was the professor thrilled with the quality of the texts students selected, but 96% of her students stated they found the assignment beneficial. For this teacher and others like her, blurring the lines between writing to learn and reading to learn by connecting to the world outside the classroom proved a successful approach even for reluctant or inexperienced college readers. Furthermore, by allowing students to go "outside" the course to find texts, this teacher implicitly recognized the value inherent in the reading her students did beyond school.

Like most teachers, the WAC faculty in this study found their experiences with student reading varied widely among different classes and even among different tasks and texts in the same class. What we can learn from these variations is how to apply what we now know about student reading through a range of approaches that can promote student learning. That is not to say that students do not need to learn material found in their textbooks, nor is it an argument that students do not need to learn how to read those textbooks in order to access that material. But using strategies that recognize the many other kinds of texts and ways of reading that exist in students' lives can clearly be successful.

In a surprising turn of events, the political science professor so discouraged at the failure of her in-class writing "reading quizzes" decided to embark on another kind of in-class writing activity—but this time with great success. In marked contrast to her first WAC strategy, she asked students to respond to current event articles in the *The Economist* using any of the concepts from their course readings. Her description of that experience and her students' resulting reading and writing differed markedly from her reflection in the previous section:

> Students seemed much more likely to have completed the
> required current events readings and seemed to enjoy using
> these events to help explore the course concepts in greater detail.
> Students tended to do very well on these assignments, sometimes
> applying concepts in ways that I had not even considered. I
> think that these assignments were particularly successful because
> they were able to utilize something that students were more
> interested in (current events) and thus students were a bit more
> excited about doing them. From my perspective, they were quite

> successful in that they really forced students to think about the
> course concepts and theories in an analytical way and helped
> them build the skills to use these concepts in their future inter-
> national affairs courses and in their lives.

Rather than coercion, it is meaningful reading of this sort that will be key to solving the problems student face when reading in college.

Jolliffe and Harl (2008) have suggested faculty pursue more ways to establish these sorts of linkages for students, but the success of their charge that "faculty members need to teach students explicitly how to draw the kinds of connections that lead to engaged reading" requires an understanding of evolving literacy practices deep enough to establish these valuable "text-to-world and text-to-text connections" (p. 613). Just as many of the students and teachers in this study were able to do, the political science professor and her students took an important step in that direction. In having students connect course readings to actual events beyond the classroom, students also could begin to see that the reading they are asked to do in college is not wholly separate from their outside worlds.

Rethinking Reading in College

Student reading is a complexity at any level. Characterized by a transparency that renders it too easily and too often overlooked, explicit reading instruction tapers off precipitously after elementary school as students, teachers, and testing begin to focus on the texts being read rather than the strategies used to read them. It is no surprise, therefore, that faculty dissatisfaction with student reading in college is vocal and widespread. When looking for ways to address this challenge, WAC, already proven to be a transformative force for teachers, is a natural place to turn.

Just as writing across the curriculum encourages faculty to consider the ways they ask students to write, efforts at improving student reading must begin with a conscious awareness that we ask and expect students to read in particular and highly contextual ways that may not always be familiar to them. Pam Hollander, Maureen Shamgochian, Douglas Dawson, and Margaret Pray Bouchard have noted in this collection that as teachers we eventually must ask ourselves "What are we communicating to our students directly or indirectly about reading?" By no means do the experiences of the WAC faculty in this study represent the complete range of answers to this question. Likewise, their experiences do not encompass every strategy that might productively change the way we assign, teach, or assess reading in higher education. What we can draw from these examples, however, are key principles that will support and encourage student reading far more than faculty across disciplines tend to do now.

First and foremost, faculty must see that they have a role—beyond simply assigning texts or writing related to those texts—to play in student reading behavior. Second, in this role, faculty must be able not only to articulate their goals for student reading but also to make those goals clear to students. Third, faculty must be willing to provide guidance for students reading complex, discipline-specific texts that may look quite different from much of the reading that has occupied their textual lives up until this point.

Student consumption of many outside-of-school texts has much in common with the transformative, meaning-making work we hope for in college reading and learning. However, the fact that less traditional reading behaviors can prove advantageous for developing competent college readers is helpful only if students ultimately can transfer those skills to their college literacy tasks. Students who have not developed reading strategies appropriate for extracting and processing meaning from college texts will struggle to complete both reading and writing tasks.

The faculty and student experiences with reading in this study echo the growing body of research demonstrating that open, explicit work on how to read for and in college needs to be undertaken. Just as McLeod and Miraglia (2001) urged that "It is an error to see writing to learn and writing to communicate as somehow in conflict with each other," it is an error to see reading and writing as entirely separate and thus not able to benefit from similar pedagogical approaches. Using strategies gained in their endeavors in this writing across the curriculum program, many faculty found ways to begin to make meaningful connections with reading possible for their students.

Russell (1990) has suggested that WAC encourages us to consider who plays what role in determining what and how we teach, and he has argued that "WAC ultimately asks: In what ways will graduates of our university use language and how shall we teach them to use it in those ways?" (p. 70). In essence, Russell's question urges us to pursue a broader view of literacy throughout higher education, a goal already inherent in much WAC work. Steve Parks and Eli Goldblatt (2000) have extended this pursuit and called for a much more explicitly comprehensive approach and spirit within the WAC movement:

> The argument is not that WAC needs to abandon its traditional
> support for writing in the disciplines, but that we should imag
> ine our project as one that combines discipline-based instruction
> with a range of other literacy experiences that will help students
> and faculty see writing and reading in a wider social and intellec
> tual context than the college curriculum. (pp. 585–586)

As is evidenced by the WAC faculty narratives examined here, reading is rarely far from the minds of teachers who want to encourage student learning. Making reading a more overt element of our pedagogies and better articulated in our expectations to students can only serve to reduce teacher anxiety and frustration and improve students' performances with regard to reading.

College students today do read. And they read frequently and often with great enthusiasm. However, as Jolliffe and Harl found, rather than reading assigned school texts, students read for reasons such as "values clarification, personal enrichment, and career preparation" (p. 600). These reasons are laudable, and they are not absent in the texts we ask and need college students to comprehend. Too often, however, our students come to college in possession of inaccurate notions of what it means to read for school while at the same time clinging to inadequate reading strategies that do not enable them to correct those misconceptions and recognize that the elements they look for in texts can exist in less familiar venues and formats such as their course readings.

The ramifications of a system of higher education that does not resolve this disconnect and that thus does not produce individuals in possession of critical and evolving reading skills are sobering. Scholes (2002) argued that such reading, by its very nature, is challenging to achieve but indisputably essential: "The basis of an education for the citizens of a democracy lies in that apparently simple but actually difficult act of reading so as to grasp and evaluate the thoughts and feelings of that mysterious other person: the writer" (p. 171). Helping our students become better readers—in college and in the world that awaits them well beyond—will require the rethinking of existing approaches to literacy and pedagogy by educators in all disciplines.

References

Abrams, M. H. (1991). *Doing things with texts: Essays in criticism and critical theory*. New York: W. W. Norton.

Bean, J. (2011). *Engaging ideas: The professor's guide to integrating writing, critical thinking, and active learning in the classroom* (2nd ed.). San Francisco: Jossey-Bass.

Berry, T., Cook, L., Hill, N. & Stevens, K. (2011). An exploratory analysis of textbook usage and study habits: Misperceptions and barriers to success. *College Teaching, 59*(1), 31–39.

Brandt, D. (1994). Remembering writing, remembering reading. *College Composition and Communication, 45*(4), 459–479.

Coiro, J. (2003). Exploring literacy on the internet: Reading comprehension on the internet: Expanding our understanding of reading comprehension to encompass new literacies. *The Reading Teacher, 56*(5), 458–464.

Cope, B. & Kalantzis, M. (2009). "Multiliteracies": New literacies, new learning. *Pedagogies: An International Journal, 4*, 164–195.

Fulwiler, T. (1984). How well does writing across the curriculum work? *College English, 46*(2) 113–125.

Graham, S. & Hebert, M. A. (2010). *Writing to read: Evidence for how writing can improve reading. A Carnegie Corporation Time to Act Report*. Washington, DC: Alliance for Excellent Education.

Horning, A. S. (2007). Reading across the curriculum as the key to student success. *Across the Disciplines, 4.* Retrieved from https://wac.colostate.edu/atd/articles/horning2007.cfm.

Jolliffe, D. A. & Harl, A. (2008). Studying the reading transition from high school to college: What are our students reading and why? *College English, 70*(6), 599–617.

Kinzer, C. K. (2003). The importance of recognizing the expanding boundaries of literacy. *Reading Online, 6*(10). Retrieved from http://www.readingonline.org/electronic/elec Jndex.asp?HREF=/electronic/kinzer/ index.html.

Kinzer, C. K. (2010). Focus on policy: Considering literacy and policy in the context of digital environments. *Language Arts, 88*(1), 51–61.

Langer, J. and Applebee, A. (1987). *How writing shapes thinking: A study of teaching and learning.* Urbana: National Council of Teachers of English.

McLeod, S. H. & Miraglia, E. (2001). Writing across the curriculum in a time of change. In McLeod, S. H., Miraglia, E., Soven, M. & Thaiss, C. (Eds.). *WAC for the new millennium: Strategies for continuing writing-across-the-curriculum programs* (pp. 1–26). Urbana, IL: National Council of Teachers of English. Available at https://wac.colostate .edu/books/millennium/.

National Governors Association Center for Best Practices, Council of Chief State School Officers. (2010). *Common Core State Standards (English Language Arts Standards).* Washington, DC: National Governors Association Center for Best Practices, Council of Chief State School Officers.

Newkirk, T. (2013). Speaking back to the common core. In postscript to *Holding on to good ideas in a time of bad ones: Six literacy practices worth fighting for* (pp. 1–7). Portsmouth, NH: Heinemann. Retrieved from http://heinemann.com/shared/online resources%5CE02123%5C Newkirk_Speaking_Back_to_the_Common_Core.pdf.

New London Group. (1996). A pedagogy of multiliteracies: Designing social futures. Harvard *Educational Review, 66*(1), 60–92.

Nilson, L. B. (2010). *Teaching at its best: A research-based resource for college instructors* (3rd ed.). San Francisco: Jossey-Bass.

Parks, S. & Goldblatt, E. (2000). Writing beyond the curriculum: Fostering new collaborations in literacy. *College English, 62*(5), 584–606.

Russell, D. R. (1990). Writing across the curriculum in historical perspective: Toward a social interpretation. *College English, 52*(1), 52–73.

Sappington, J., Kinsey, K. & Munsayac, K. (2002). Two studies of reading compliance among college students. *Teaching of Psychology, 29*(4), 272–274.

Scholes, R. J. (2002). The transition to college reading. *Pedagogy, 2*(2), 165–172.

Smith, C. (1988). Does it help to write about your reading? *Journal of Reading, 31,* 276–277.

Young, A. (2006). Teaching writing across the curriculum (4th ed.). Upper Saddle River, NJ: Pearson.

Integrating Reading, Writing, and Research for First-Year College Students: Piloting Linked Courses in the Education Major

Tanya I. Sturtz, Darrell C. Hucks, and Katherine E. Tirabassi
KEENE STATE COLLEGE

This chapter discusses Keene State College's *Reading, Thinking, and Writing Initiative*, a pilot program that offers a cohort of first-year Education majors the opportunity to take two linked courses across the academic year. The first semester Education course focuses on reading and research strategies, college expectations and pre-professional dispositions, and accessing campus resources. The second semester course focuses on integrating reading, writing, and research strategies in the required first-year composition course, and this same cohort of Education majors work on researching and writing individual semester-long research projects. Both courses are designed to encourage students to connect their learning across courses, to improve their critical reading, thinking, and writing skills, and to form systems of support with classmates and professors to help them transition into college. The Education professors who team-teach these courses and the first-year writing coordinator detail the history, implementation, and future of this initiative, share resources that they have developed to help students in this program to transition from high school to college-level work, and discuss what students who have been part of this initiative have said about their learning through focus groups.

Creating Keene State College's *Reading, Thinking, and Writing Initiative*

Keene State College (KSC) is a public, liberal arts college in the small New Hampshire city of Keene, with a population of approximately 5,000 students. The majority of this population is undergraduates; 41 percent are first-generation college students, and ten percent receive services from the Office of Disability Services. In 2007, KSC launched a new general education program called the Integrative Studies Program (ISP). Integrative Thinking and Writing (ITW) 101, the new first-year composition course required of all incoming students, became one of two foundational courses in the ISP, the other foundational course focusing on quantitative literacy. ITW 101 replaced a more traditional English 101 Essay Writing course, the original course including essay assignments in various genres, including personal narratives, critical analysis, and a researched essay; ITW 101, conceived of as a themed course proposed and developed by each instructor, asks students to work on just one sustained and extensive researched essay across the semester. As they engage in reading and discussion at the beginning of an ITW semester, students develop creative and complex questions to research, and write multiple drafts of a longer inquiry-based essay. Students learn together the value of ongoing and constructive feedback through in-class workshops, peer reviews, and writing conferences with faculty. The course is capped at 20 students, to keep the size small for a writing course, and 55–60 sections are offered each year, split evenly across two semesters.

Another key difference between English 101 and ITW 101, was that English 101 was taught exclusively by full-time and adjunct faculty in the English Department, while ITW can be taught by faculty across disciplines and departments. This intentional design fosters a campus-wide commitment to the teaching of writing, at least for faculty teaching first-year students. Faculty who are interested in teaching ITW develop a course theme proposal in which they discuss both the content and key questions of the course, and also how they would guide students through the process of developing a semester-long research and writing project.

In the 2012–13 academic year, Tanya and Darrell, two Education faculty members, proposed a yearlong pilot program, linking a new experimental Education course on critical reading with a new ITW course on educational reform. In this chapter, we will discuss the implementation of what we called *Reading, Thinking, and Writing Initiative*, integrating the teaching of critical thinking, reading, research and writing for a cohort of first-year Education majors. Part of the rationale for this program was that, while the college offered a challenging and rich inquiry-based writing course, Tanya and Darrell had noted that their incoming education students lacked the reading and research skills that they needed to be successful, not only in ITW, but also in their other college courses, including those in their intended major. In addition to providing explicit teaching of reading, research, and writing strategies, this two-semester initiative invites first-year education majors to enter into conversations about current issues in educational reform by reading, researching, and writing about educational debates, and by discussing those debates with other classmates, their professors, the campus community beyond the classroom, and local educators and community leaders. Students in the program become familiar with some of the language and genres used by scholars in the field, and they begin to use this language in their courses and to develop strategies to help them read and write at the college level.

To implement this initiative, now in its fourth year, incoming Education students receive an invitation to participate in the program. The first 25–35 volunteers are enrolled in a required foundational course in the education program and the Fall Reading and Writing in Education course. The reading course focuses on integrating reading, research, and writing strategies, understanding college expectations, exploring pre-professional dispositions, and accessing resources on campus. During the second semester, this same cohort of students takes the required ITW 101 course, with the same instructors guiding them through the processes of formulating research questions, researching, outlining, and writing, revising, and editing drafts of longer inquiry-based essays. Both courses are designed to provide opportunities for students to improve and integrate their critical reading, thinking, and writing skills, to connect their learning across courses within and beyond their major, and to form systems of support with a cohort of classmates and professors to help them transition into college.

College Induction, Retention, and Literacy Challenges

The transition, retention, and success of incoming first-year students continue to be topics of serious discussion and concern in higher education and certainly at our institution (Odom, 2014; Reeves, 2010; Tinto, 1998). As the editors of this book discuss in their Introduction, the literacy skills, particularly with regard to reading, essential for successful transition from secondary education to higher education is an area of study that has recently gained serious scholarly attention (Horning, 2007; Kirby, 2007; Rachal, Daigle & Rachal, 2007; Young & Potter, 2013; Carillo, 2015). College students are often challenged by the volume and complexity of reading that is expected of them across different areas of study (National Survey of Student Engagement, 2011). They may lack good experience or instruction with how to engage in reading more complex texts or unfamiliar genres (Odom, 2014). Typically, children learn and master reading in the primary and early secondary grades; however, any gaps in reading skill development may not have prepared them for reading at the college level, resulting in students who "don't, won't, [or] can't" do the reading for their classes (Horning, 2007). In using the term "college-level" in connection with reading, we have developed the following definition, and based on our work with students in the linked course initiative: college-level readers construct meaning by monitoring, through writing and discussion, their understanding of the texts they are reading, enhancing understanding by making connections to prior knowledge and previously learned material, acquiring and actively using what they have learned, and developing insights that they can draw on in discussing and writing about these texts. To develop these college-level reading skills, students need to learn and master strategies like comprehension monitoring, summarizing, use of graphic and semantic organizers to engage them in critical reading and in their learning (Kamil, 2003; National Institute of Child Health and Human Development & National Institute for Literacy, 2007; Nokes & Dole, 2004). When educational institutions or programs such as the *Reading,*

Thinking, and Writing Initiative, target the explicit teaching of such skills, students will play a substantially more active role in their own academic development and achievement (Elton, 2010; Taraban, Kerr & Rynearson, 2004). Over time, successful college-level readers come to see the importance of reading in academic inquiry, research, and writing, and that these processes should be integrated.

Although primary and secondary schools often address these literacy skills separately, the reciprocal relationship between reading and writing was demonstrated through composition research during the 1980s and 1990s (Bartholomae & Petrosky, 1986; Flower, Stein, Ackerman, Kantz, McCormick & Peck, 1990; Lindemann & Tate, 1993). Patricia Harkin (2005) notes that returning to and building on this work (as scholars have done recently) can help us to understand more about *how* readers make meaning, so that we can better understand how to integrate the teaching of reading and writing (p. 422). One book that Harkin mentions, and that seems especially relevant to the concerns raised by faculty at our institution regarding students' issues with integrating their reading and writing, is Linda Flower et al.'s *Reading-to-Write: Exploring a Cognitive and Social Process* (1990). Harkin describes this book as "a thoughtful and comprehensive account of interconnections between reading and writing processes" (p. 417).

Flower et al.'s study and findings raise key issues about the integration of reading and writing that are relevant in current conversations, especially for the initiative we're discussing in this chapter. Flower defines *reading-to-write* as "the goal-directed activity of reading in order to write" and that "Each process is altered by the other" (pp. 5–6); this concept offers insight into how students read differently for different purposes. Based on their study documenting a group of first-year students as they negotiated the complexities of reading and writing in college, Flower et al. argue that in *reading-to-write* "The reading process is guided by the need to produce a text of one's own. The reader as writer is expected to manipulate information and transform it to his or her own purposes. And the writing process is complicated by the need to shape one's own goals in response to the ideas or even the purposes of another writer" (p. 6). Flower et al. demonstrate that, from the interpretation of the assignment itself to the final product, students are constantly working to frame and reframe the nature of the writing project itself, and how their reading impacts their thinking and writing.

The ITW 101 course at KSC requires students to do a great deal of reading-to-write as they work on their sustained writing projects, though reading is not usually discussed or defined in the ways that Flower et al. discuss. Faculty teaching the course regularly talk together about what strategies could help students to read more critically, more in-depth, and more carefully. Reading has always been a priority in ITW 101, at least in terms of the first-year program's student learning outcomes, which include the following three reading outcomes:

- Use reading for inquiry, learning, thinking, and communicating
- Analyze and evaluate the rhetorical features of peer and published texts (audience, thesis or main argument, quality of evidence, structure)
- Understand the importance of reading in academic inquiry and research

However, given that ITW is a one-semester first-year composition course, faculty teaching in the program have found it challenging to balance teaching reading, critical thinking, writing and information literacy outcomes. Discussions about helping students to learn to read with a purpose, to develop, focus, and refine their ideas and overall arguments through the reading that they do have emerged more recently. As faculty raise concerns about students' increasing difficulties with weaving research into their writing, we've turned to current research on reading pedagogy to help guide our thinking and curricular revisions.

As a year-long experience, the KSC Reading, Thinking and Writing Initiative represents our initial efforts to provide students with more time to learn how to integrate their reading, research and writing more fully within a specific disciplinary context. To help students reflect on their growing understanding of the integrated nature of these processes, we ask them to consider how their approaches to reading different types of texts have played a part in their prior (and current) writing and researching experiences. We also ask students, at various points across the year, to discuss and write about how their reading, which is primarily focused on educational reform, has impacted their developing understanding of the field itself and their thinking about their developing research projects. This reflective work, achieved through class discussions and reading logs, among other strategies, builds on the metacognitive work used in earlier reading research of the 1980s and 1990s, and more recent discussions about the value of reflecting on and analyzing texts using a variety of reading approaches, such as Ellen C. Carillo's concept of "mindful reading." Carillo argues that mindful reading helps students "become knowledgeable, deliberate, and reflective about how they read and the demands that contexts place on their reading" (pp. 10–11). Noting David Russell's point that in order for students to understand disciplinary contexts and conventions, they need to participate in that discipline, Carillo states that first-year writing instructors can help students to try, to "experiment with and reflect on which reading practices work more productively in various contexts" (pp. 15–16). Because KSC's Reading, Thinking and Writing Initiative focuses on the field of education and first-year education majors, and is taught by Education professors, the genre conventions and reading approaches that would be most effective or appropriate in this context are a constant point of discussion in class.

Another key reflective element of the Reading, Thinking and Writing Initiative includes a series of focus groups with students who participated in the year-long program, during that first year and, as a way to track students' reflections on the impact of the program in their academic career, in each subsequent year until graduation. To ethically collect this data, as well as data from students' literacy autobiographies and other writing samples, we have submitted annual IRB proposals and received exempt status. Despite the exemption, we provided a verbal overview of our project to students and collected consent forms from each cohort. In addition to what students reported in focus groups, we reviewed samples of students' written work and their overall performances in their college courses to consider whether their reading and writing skills were improving over time, in various courses including those in their majors. Through this research, some of which we will share in this chapter, we are working to better understand the ways in which reading and writing are linked and to contribute to current trends in educational and composition research regarding reading at the college level (McGonnell, Parrila & Deacon, 2007; Young & Potter, 2013; Carillo, 2015).

Understanding Prior Knowledge in Teaching Today's College Students

Education and composition research suggests that while reading and writing are connected and should be integrated, these skills are typically addressed separately in primary and secondary schools, and reading is often under-addressed at the post-secondary level (Fitzgerald & Shanahan, 2000; Scholes, 2002; Kirby, 2007; Rachal, Daigle & Rachal, 2007; Hong-Nam & Swanson, 2011). To learn about our students' prior experiences learning to read and write in schools, we drew on a familiar genre in FYC courses, the literacy autobiography. We wanted to hear how students described their developing literacy, and whether their descriptions would support the notion that explicit instruction on reading receded as instruction about writing became more emphasized. Also, creating a profile of the students from this generation had to be considered before we could fully address how to teach reading to our undergraduate students. The prior schooling experiences of today's college students have changed with the implementation of the *No Child Left Behind Act* (NCLB, 2001). NCLB reform and subsequent reform efforts such as the Common Core State Standards Initiative to our public school system, with its emphasis on standards and testing, greatly affected the reading and writing experiences of the current generation of students entering college.

In her chapter in this collection, Mary Lou Odom notes that students' prior reading experiences involve "texts that are less linear and permanent, more dynamic and multimodal, and that require greater agency on students' parts" than most college reading requires; Odom argues that we need to learn more about how students are reading when they come to college, so that we know how to help them negotiate college-level reading expectations more successfully. In the literacy narrative, we ask students to reflect on their elementary, middle, and high school experiences with reading and writing. Below is an overview of the themes that emerged from these autobiographies.

Autobiography

Students reported having fond memories of their reading and writing experiences in the primary grades. Several reported being more engaged in school and in the joy of learning how to read. For example, one student stated, "When I first started to read, it was so new and fascinating that I wanted to read all the time." Many felt that their teachers liked and cared for them, noting that these teachers encouraged them to be creative with their work and made learning fun across subject areas. Students' memories of reading in elementary school ranged from keeping reading logs listing the books they'd read to more "hands on" read-aloud and reading comprehension activities in class. Students also reported that their families were very involved in supporting their early reading efforts. One student shared, "My mom made it a requirement to read every day, at least 20 minutes until 5th grade. Even in the summers, she made me pick a bunch of books and I would get a reward for reading all of them by the end of the summer." While some students talked about struggling with reading and writing early on, overall, reading and writing in elementary school was enjoyable. But, as students progressed through the grades, struggling with reading and writing became more prevalent.

For most students, the transition to middle school required more independent reading and writing. In terms of the curriculum, students' stories highlighted the separation of reading and writing; most students noted that, by the end of middle school, explicit instruction on writing took precedence over reading instruction. Because there was less conversation about literacy processes in the classroom, some students reported that middle school is when they began to receive additional support for their reading. Those receiving additional support in reading felt that needing this support marked them as being deficient in their literacy development, an association that they felt became part of their identity as learners. One student shared, "My IEP (Individualized Education Plan) haunted me throughout middle school." Others who had negative experiences with reading and writing in middle school noted that it's likely they would have benefitted from additional support, because they were unaware until much later that they were actually a bit behind in both areas.

Many students reported having positive relationships with their middle school teachers, saying that those teachers were influential and inspiring with regard to their reading and writing development; these teachers served as sponsors of students' literacy, offering the more positive elements of Deborah Brandt's (1998) definition of sponsors as those who " enable, support, teach, and model" literacy

(p. 166). Several students shared stories about one or two specific teachers who made writing an enjoyable experience by using creative activities and approaches in class. One student stated, "My favorite teacher made learning fun, so it didn't matter what or how much we read or wrote about. I've always liked reading for fun, but when it came to school books, I procrastinated a lot because I just didn't want to read them and take notes on a book I didn't want to read in the first place." By middle school, expectations about reading changed, focusing more on the number of books that students read rather than their engagement with these texts. Students talked about a marked shift in reading instruction, moving from learning *how to read* more complex texts and new genres or discussing whether students were understanding what they were reading to an assumption that comprehension, analysis, and synthesis were naturally occurring. This shift persisted and deepened as students moved to high school.

Many students reported that they had difficulties transitioning to high school due to increased academic challenges. Some attributed the challenges to personal issues that occurred outside of the school context or teachers who didn't seem to be invested in teaching them the increased literacy skills they needed. Many students reported being overwhelmed with the number of books they were expected to read and as a result, some avoided reading altogether. One student stated, "Once I got to high school, it got a whole lot worse; the books became harder and harder as I got older and there were more books every year." Another student shared, "In high school is when it all went downhill; my papers were always 'C' quality. I used a lot of run-on sentences, never knew where to put commas, colons, and semicolons. I didn't know how to incorporate "big words" into my papers; I would use 'nice,' 'good' instead of 'extravagant' or 'awesome.' Most of the sentences were incomplete and the paper didn't flow." Like in middle school, several students reported receiving additional support or tutoring to improve their reading and writing skills. For most, reading and writing instruction in high school shifted to vocabulary building and writing research papers without a great deal of attention on how to break down and accomplish these tasks.

Engaging Students in College-Level Reading and Thinking

The goals of the first-year linked course initiative are to build on and develop students' reading, thinking, research, and writing skills through guided instruction, class activities/assignments, strategies and resources, and on-going feedback. As Mary Odom points out in her chapter in this volume, "students who have not developed reading strategies appropriate for extracting and processing meaning from college texts will struggle to complete both reading *and* writing tasks." In the area of reading, the goal of comprehension is to construct meaning. Students construct meaning by monitoring their understanding of the materials they are reading, enhancing understanding by making connections to prior knowledge and previously learned material, acquiring and actively using what they have learned, and developing insight. In addition, students need to learn the content through reading as well as the process of how to learn and understand the material (Harvey & Goudvis, 2007). Because students need multiple opportunities to engage in these learning experiences to increase their academic success, the strategies we've developed through this initiative provide students with tools they need to become active readers, to understand and write about complex content and theoretical concepts, and to increase participation in classroom discussions.

To help students become what John Bean (2011) calls "deep readers" who "focus on meaning" and "interact with texts, devoting psychological energy to the task" and who understand the integration of reading and writing, we created a textbook reading guide (Appendix A) that leads students through pre-reading, reading, and post-reading strategies (p. 162). Students use the whole guide in the beginning, with the understanding that as they internalize the process through repeated use of the guide, they can modify it later to meet their individual course note-taking needs. The textbook reading guide starts with asking students to review headings and subheadings before predicting the focus of the chapter. The guide includes sections for students to take notes, and to write down questions that arise and terms or concepts to know while they are reading. After finishing the reading, students write a two-to-three sentence summary, and questions to ask a classmate or the professors.

Overall, the textbook reading guide applies a lower stakes "writing to read" approach that Chris Anson defines as "a reciprocal model of reading and writing that sees them as intertwined" (this volume). The guide asks students to return to the text multiple times, building on concepts of previewing, questioning, clarifying, and summarizing that aid students through the reading process (Vaughn, Bos & Schumm, 2011). According to the 2011 National Survey on Student Engagement (NSSE, 2011), only 60% of first-year students reported taking careful notes while reading. This reading guide provides a format for students to take notes and ask questions of each text. We include a summary as part of the guide to help students build their mastery of the material, focus on the important content of the text, and restate the main points in their own words (National Institute of Child Health and Human Development & National Institute for Literacy, 2007). Bean notes that asking students to write summaries allows them to locate "the hierarchical structure of an article" and to help them focus on the writer's key points (p. 178). The textbook reading guide serves as a tool to engage students in the reading process by providing a graphic organizer that creates a visual representation of the text's content and identifies relationships among the ideas, concepts, and information in the text (Kamil, 2003; National Institute of Child Health and Human Development & National Institute for Literacy, 2007).

After teaching the students how to use the reading guide with textbooks, we focus on teaching students how to read scholarly articles. This class activity draws on students' extracurricular reading experiences, beginning with asking them to bring in magazines they like to read, and discussing differences between the ways that they read for pleasure versus the ways that they read for classes. We ask students to select an article from their magazine to read silently during class. Afterwards, they share summaries of the articles and what they observed about each article's organizational structure. Next, to introduce a more complex text that is by educators for an audience of educators, we hand out teacher practitioner journals. Students choose an article of interest and read it in class, again silently. The students again share summaries of the articles and compare and contrast the organizational structure. Finally, we hand out educational research journals to the students and again, they select an article of interest and complete the tasks as described above, followed by a discussion comparing and contrasting all three articles. To acknowledge the students' concerns about comprehending the research articles, we spend time breaking down the organizational structure of the article together, and discussing a variety of reading approaches and strategies that students can try to read the article. After this activity, our students note that they feel less overwhelmed about reading scholarly articles for class.

Many educators will have used a version of a reading guide such as the one described above to help their students develop a cache of reading strategies that they might choose from, depending on the context and type of reading task. Another essential element of the reading process that is not often discussed, but that we like to emphasize with our students, is how they position their bodies when they read. As students read the magazine, teacher practitioner, and scholarly articles in the above in-class activities, we also ask them to pay attention to how they sit while reading each article. During our class discussions, students share their realization that shifting their body position, specifically how and where they sit, can affect how they engage with, understand, or even complete the texts they are reading. This discussion often reveals to students that their habits can help or hinder their academic success. In reflecting on her changed practice, one student, for instance, shared she was now less anxious at the prospect of reading a scholarly article; she noted that, in a first read-through of an article, she chooses to sit comfortably in her favorite reading chair, and in her second read-through, she sits at her desk, ready to take notes. Through this process, she enhanced her overall reading experience, her understanding of the material, and how she felt when she began to read. In focus groups, several students cited this in-class activity in convincing them that body position and other environmental factors such as physical study environment are essential parts of the reading process to consider.

For most college students, reading aloud is something that they stopped doing in elementary school. But, because we are working with future educators of children, one of the things that they will be doing daily is reading aloud. Reading aloud is also an important strategy for comprehension. To reacquaint students with the value of reading aloud, we have students select a children's book to bring to class and read to their classmates. While each student reads aloud, we provide feedback on the student's pace, tone, projection, clarity, ability to connect with the audience, and to consider the rhetorical situation of the book (its intended audience, purpose, context, etc.). We extend this opportunity to more challenging college-level texts, asking students to read scholarly articles aloud in class, but the goal is the same, to help students consider reading aloud as a strategy to aid in (or identify lack of) comprehension.

Another class activity that engages students in understanding and exploring college-level reading is the book club that we start during class. We select a book for the class book club, setting the expectation that as college students and future teachers, they have a responsibility to be (or to become) avid, critical readers. Each week, students read a chapter from the book and submit a reflection on what they read that includes their thoughts, opinions, and connections to life experiences. During in-class book club discussions, we teach the students how to take the lead in sharing their thoughts, opinions, and reflections on these chapters with each other. We ask them to tell the class what page they are referencing and to give examples that support their points. When students finish talking, they say the name of a classmate who wants to share next, building on each other's comments. The students learn that their voice and opinions have power when they can articulate their understanding of the material with supporting evidence from the reading or their own life experiences; this class experience creates an environment in which reading once again becomes an enjoyable process that leads to dialogue and to learning. Our goal in the book club experience is to help students to understand why reading should be a part of their lives, not just something they have to do.

Because, as we've noted earlier, summarizing is a proven effective comprehension strategy (Harvey & Goudvis, 2007) that students often struggle to master, one final assignment that we'll describe here is the research notes assignment (Appendix B). This assignment, which builds on students' newly established familiarity with reading guides, asks them to write two-sentence summaries for each source they're reading for their research projects. The overall goal of this guide is to help students work on analyzing their sources and begin synthesizing their developing ideas about the argument they want to make. Practically-speaking, the guide asks students to write the reference citation at the top (in APA format for Education), a summary of the article, book, or website, paraphrased notes or quotes, and finally, keywords, topics, or citations they want to research next. The students use the research notes guide for every source in their research paper. These notes help students to organize and synthesize their research and to begin drafting their essays. By the end of the first semester, students have ten research notes completed on their educational topic of interest. At the beginning of second semester, we have the students reread their research notes and weave the information together in a written overview of what they have gathered thus far. This overview assignment asks students to reflect on what they have read in their own words, analyze where the gaps are in their research, and plan their next steps in the research process. In the following section, we will share what students have said in focus groups about what they've learned from using this guide and the other strategies we've discussed.

Focus Group Data

For four years of the *Reading, Thinking, and Writing Initiative*, Tanya and Darrell have conducted two focus group meetings with each student cohort to gather data on their transition to college and on the strategies and resources they have learned in the program that they've found beneficial. Based on the data from these focus groups, the program continues to improve, as we've been able to identify which in-class activities, strategies and assignments students have found most useful and why. As Wardle (2007) has argued, focus group data can help researchers understand what students emphasize about their learning and how they describe transferring literacy skills across contexts and to identify areas for further study. Considering college-level reading in particular, we have analyzed the focus group transcripts for themes emerging from the students' voices. We summarized four years' worth of data into three major categories: transition to college, the relationship between college reading, thinking, and writing, and the impact of strategies and resources taught in the program.

Transition to College

The main themes that emerged when students shared their struggles with transitioning to college were unrealistic college expectations, inefficient time management, and the social demands and distractions of college. Students reported having difficulties adjusting to the less structured college schedule, noting that they were more used to the scheduled lifestyle of high school, with full days spent in classes, and afternoons and evenings spent in after-school activities or on nightly homework. They shared how having classes once or twice a week affected their time management and their ability to remember what they had to do and by when. With so many readings and assignments to complete prior to class time, and without personal connections with professors like those they had developed with their high school teachers, many students reported being unsure about how to manage the volume of the workload and unsure about who to ask for help.

Many students talked about anxiety over courses with grades based on just a mid-term and a final. These stressors were compounded by the fact that they could no longer study in their rooms, since socializing, music, television, and their roommates easily distracted them from schoolwork. Students noted that learning how to be self-motivated to balance their academic and social lives was, in itself, a significant challenge in their transition to college. Due to these distractions, students reported having to search for new places to study across campus, including the library, residence hall study areas, and even the laundry room. As they adjusted to new academic demands, students also talked about having to learn how to communicate with roommates, to make new friends, and to get enough sleep, factors that often affected and complicated their daily lives, and, in some cases, their academic success.

Time management was a universal theme mentioned in the focus groups. Students came from highly structured high school environments to a college setting where classes do not fill each day. When they did not have class at eight in the morning, students stayed up late, socializing. They reported having to learn how to set schedules that prioritized being prepared for classes and completing assignments, so they did not fall behind in their coursework. One student said,

> There are a lot of those classes where you will go into class and the teacher will just reiterate everything you read. So the week before, when you are saying should I read for that class that I am just going to relearn everything in or should I do this other assignment, sometimes you have to choose that the other assignment takes precedence because you know, by that point, I really do not have to read that chapter because it will not apply to my next class.

Students who were successful in completing their reading talked about learning to chunk their assignments, making checklists to break down the assignments into smaller tasks.

Integrating College Reading, Thinking and Writing

In the focus groups, students reflected on how their approaches toward reading impacted their ability to understand and complete their assignments. Some students shared that they could still succeed in high school by just skimming books, but that in college, if they did not complete and understand the reading, they were largely unprepared for class discussions and quizzes. In addition, they realized that reading for class helped them to understand the course content, especially given that the content itself was more complex and the reading more extensive.

To learn how to read critically, students said that they needed to figure out how to organize their thoughts, their reading styles, and take useful notes on the important points in an assigned reading. One student shared how, at first, she did not know what notes to take.

> I feel like I never used to be able to pick out the important
> points. When we would have to do notes from a textbook, I
> would write too much. I would not really know what was im-
> portant. The first semester [of the linked program], we focused
> on how much you do not need. You need to know the main
> points and how to take notes. That was really helpful. Now I can
> pick out the important points and not overload.

Other students found that their reading skills, especially identifying key questions, points or arguments, grew stronger after they learned what to look for in the reading.

To help them practice what to look for in the reading, students cited the text-book reading and research notetaking guides as two being most useful. By learning how textbooks and articles were organized, for instance, students said that it was easier to locate the important points in readings. These resources, students told us, served as a starting point in helping them to rethink and expand their reading pro-cess to include pre-reading strategies like skimming in order to grasp what an article was about and then, in a more careful read-through, deciding how to organize the information that they had read in a useful way. The reading and research notetaking guides helped students to develop a framework for identifying and summarizing key points in a text and expanding their overall reading process. One student talked specifically about how the research notetaking guide had become an integral part of her reading process:

> If I had research notes available to me, I would definitely use
> those to organize the article. If I didn't, I would probably take
> notes, the first parts in the notes part, and then I would probably
> do a summary of it. I would follow the same structure, even if I
> did not have those [guides]. (So, you internalized it) Yeah.

Students shared that learning to identify important points in a reading, writing summaries, as well as learning to write more thoughtful marginal notes, helped them to retain information, and draw connections between concepts so that they could begin to synthesize what they were reading, skills that they used frequently as they worked on their semester-long research projects in ITW and in their courses across the curriculum.

Strategies and Resources

Finally, in the focus group meetings, students talked about strategies and resources that they learned in the linked course series, and the extent to which they were using these strategies in other courses. As we noted earlier, most students in the focus groups cited the reading and research notes guides as being especially important to their literacy development in their first year of college, encouraging them to complete their reading, and to work to comprehend and write about what they'd read; as a result of learning how to use the guides, students talked about becoming more engaged in their reading and research overall. One student shared:

> Research notes, I really like them just like the outline for research notes, I never really used before. It makes a really big difference as you are reading textbooks for other classes especially if it is something that you are not interested in because it forces you to become interested in it and make it clear for yourself, even if you do not want to. For me personally, I can read an entire page and not even comprehend a single word of it. It just all goes over my head. I don't know why. So for those, it definitely helps me because it makes you put it in your own words and write a summary.

In talking about the integration between reading and writing, other students reported that writing research notes helped them get their thoughts down and organize their ideas while reading. One student talked about the research notetaking guide helping him to synthesize ideas, "I liked the way it was structured, because you also had to organize your thoughts and put it in your own words and paraphrase." Several students talked about being surprised how much they could draw on these notes as they began to draft their researched essays. The framework of the research notes showed students how integrated the processes of reading, writing, and research are; they noted that summarizing and synthesizing their research notes helped them to take stock of what information was missing, to develop a plan for further research, and to begin writing their essays.

Connected to their reading experiences while in college, students found that learning how to differentiate between various kinds of articles and how to use a variety of new reading strategies was beneficial in understanding more complex, scholarly readings in multiple courses. One student shared that learning how to read a textbook and take useful notes in the first-semester course helped her to use these strategies in her sociology course. Wardle (2007), quotes David Guile and Michael Young's point that transfer is "a process of transition between activity systems," such as two courses in different disciplines. In order to transfer learning from one context (or activity system) to another, Guile and Young note that "Learners need to be supported to participate in an activity system that encourages collaboration, discussion, and some form of 'risk taking'" (p. 68). We have worked to create this collaborative environment for students in the *Reading, Thinking, and Writing Initiative*, and to talk with students about how they are (or could be) using what they've learned about reading and writing processes in their other courses.

Finally, students talked about how the strategies they learned in the first semester helped them to become better writers in the second semester ITW course and other courses. For example, one student rediscovered the usefulness of outlining in guiding her writing process:

> I just thought the outline was very helpful. In high school, people told me to use outlines and I never did. . . . You guys brought the outline back and I thought it was very useful. It made me want to use it. I have a paper due in sociology and I made an outline and it definitely helped.

Several students talked about the importance of learning to read aloud as a strategy that helped them not only to better comprehend their reading but also to improve their writing. In addition to excerpts from course readings, we ask students to read their essay drafts aloud as part of the revision process, and to share their research with the class in a formal presentation. Students noted that this focus on reading aloud and presenting their work gave them confidence to speak up in other classes. This confidence has extended beyond the classroom, as students from each year's linked course experience have presented their research on educational reform at the campus' annual Academic Excellence Conference, and shared their research findings in formal and informal meetings with local educators and community leaders. As first-year education majors, these students realized that their voices matter, and that, in order to engage in conversations about current issues in education, it was important to learn more about the language, issues, values, and genres of their intended field of study. As we've learned from our ongoing work with these students, they have developed a sense of civic responsibility and many students in this initiative have chosen, during their first year in college, to work in broader educational contexts far earlier than their fellow Education majors, giving back to their communities through after-school and head start programs, youth camps, fundraising, and tutoring, among other activities.

The Future and Implications of the *Reading, Thinking, and Writing Initiative*

After the first year of implementation, news of the Reading, Thinking and Writing Initiative in the Education Department spread across the campus. Tanya and Darrell offered a faculty workshop in May 2013, to share what they had learned about the benefits for both teachers and students involved in a department-based first-year experience in conjunction with the Thinking and Writing program. Katherine, as ITW Coordinator, worked with faculty from departments across campus to create full-year experiences for students interested their majors; an introductory film analysis course for majors linked with an ITW course on Writing About Film has been a popular addition to the linked course initiative. The Building Excellence in Science and Technology (BEST) Program, a new academically themed living learning community (LLC), also linked a ITW course with a interdisciplinary first-year course the following semester. The aim of this yearlong initiative is for students to apply insights they gain through their ITW research to develop community-based projects focusing on science and technology. Opportunities to extend our research to a broader spectrum of students across the curriculum may provide further evidence of the benefits of a linked course first-year model at KSC and elsewhere.

In the past few years at Keene State College, there has been discussion about creating a first-year seminar program; however, due to budgetary and staffing constraints and administrative turnover, a firm proposal for a first-year seminar has never developed. The Reading, Thinking and Writing Initiative has provided an alternative model to the first-year seminar and generated renewed interest among faculty across the curriculum in teaching the ITW 101 course. As higher education institutions across the nation face similar reading and writing challenges with their incoming student populations, and budgetary and staffing constraints precluding the addition of new first-year courses, the idea of a year-long first-year experience drawing on existing courses and resources may be a more viable and desirable option.

The research findings for KSC's Initiative, thus far, indicate that the majority of students have benefitted from the work being done via the first-year linked courses, particularly in terms of their academic success and retention. As retention scholar Vincent Tinto (1998) has shown, integrated first-year academic programs such as linked or clustered learning courses, or, specific to his research, learning communities, can help students to persist in college, giving them a greater sense of belonging to the institution, and encouraging a sense of shared knowledge, learning and responsibility among the cohort of first-year students participating in such programs (p. 7). In advocating for a more integrative approach to first-year instruction, Tinto argues that first-year students also need a stronger connection to full-time faculty as mentors and advisors; as we've seen from our experience, a full-year linked course initiative can facilitate those essential connections. Often, those advocating for retention and student success argue that the goal is to keep all students at the institution, but we would caution that equating student success with retention shouldn't be the main priority.

Part of our responsibility as advisors and mentors during this yearlong experience with first-year students is to help them determine, earlier than their junior year (when such decisions usually occur), whether they are particularly suited to become teachers. By treating our students as pre-service teachers from the beginning and talking with them about their interests and career goals, some students realize that they need to choose a different path—changing their majors or sometimes, choosing to change schools or take time away from college to explore other options. The relationship faculty can build with students through the linked course initiative allows for this type of informal advising. Despite the fact that not all students in linked courses remain in the major, students tell us that this experience has helped to clarify their path while in college, and that their connections with their first-year cohort and with faculty in the program and the strategies they've gained and used in other courses have made the experience worth doing. The first-year experience has also allowed students who did not bloom the first semester to have another semester to grow, to develop literacy strategies and to talk with their instructors and cohort about what connections they were making in their other college courses.

Chris Anson (2016) has noted that our understanding of "the phenomenon of transfer," or how transfer works, is still developing, and that there are a number of factors yet to be studied that impact transfer from context to context (p. 519). The structures of full-year linked courses, learning communities, and clustered learning programs connecting two or more courses that typically involve the same faculty and students, offer researchers interested in transfer further opportunities to study how a whole cohort of first-year students apply, transform, integrate and reconstruct their learning about reading and writing processes across contexts, including those that the students have in common within the linked course program (Nowacek 2011; Wardle 2007). Studying FYC courses designed specifically for first-year students in a particular major, taught by faculty in that field, also could offer some insights into whether such a focus has the potential to help students transfer what they've learned about integrating reading and writing processes as they move to new, similar disciplinary contexts, such as other courses in that major, and then, as they generalize or "recontextualize" (Nowacek, 2011) their learning in courses beyond the major.

From our observations working with four cohorts in the Reading, Thinking and Writing Initiative, we have seen students who want to become teachers take on the identity of teacher-learner sooner than students part of the full-year experience. Though we have not yet looked at *how* transfer is occurring across courses, we have heard students talk about how they've drawn on skills and strategies they've learned as they move through the education program, through their second required major, and through the Integrative Studies (general education) program. Sophomores who were part of the linked first-year program have shared in focus groups that in their sophomore-level major courses, they felt more confident in the knowledge they'd already gained about the field during the first year, and found that they had an advantage because they could identify and build upon the language, genres, debates, and research that they had begun to study during their first year. In a future study, we plan to consider how students have transferred and integrated their reading and writing skills as well as their developing knowledge of the field in subsequent Education courses. A wider study of discipline-specific first-year courses or full-year initiatives at institutions of various kinds may have implications for further study in many areas of interest, including retention theory, student success models, teaching for transfer, and, of particular interest to us, teaching reading and writing in and across the disciplines.

References

Anson, C. (2016, June). The Pop Warner chronicles: A case study in contextual adaptation and transfer of writing ability. *College Composition and Communication, 67*(4), 518–549.

Bartholomae, D. & Petrosky, A. (1986). *Facts, artifacts and counterfacts: Theory and method for a reading and writing course.* Upper Montclair: Boynton/Cook.

Bean, J. C. (2011). *Engaging ideas: The professor's guide to integrating writing, critical thinking, and active learning in the classroom.* San Francisco: Jossey-Bass.

Brandt, D. (1998, May). Sponsors of literacy. *College Composition and Communication, 49*(2), 165–85.

Carillo, E. C. (2016, January). Creating mindful readings in first-year composition courses: A strategy to facilitate transfer. *Pedagogy 16*(1), 9–22.

Carillo, E. C. (2015). *Securing a place for reading in composition: The importance of teaching for transfer.* Logan: Utah State University Press.

Elton, L. (2010). Academic writing and tacit knowledge. *Teaching in Higher Education, 15*(2), 151–160.

Fitzgerald, J. & Shanahan, T. (2000). Reading and writing relations and their development. *Educational Psychologist, 35*(1), 39–50.

Flower, L., Stein, V., Ackerman, J., Kantz, M. J., McCormick, K. & Peck, W. (1990). *Reading-to-Write: Exploring a cognitive and social process.* New York: Oxford University Press.

Harkin, P. (2005). The reception of reader-response theory. *College Composition and Communication 56*(3), 410–425.

Harvey, S. & Goudvis, A. (2007). *Strategies that work: Teaching comprehension for understanding and engagement* (2nd ed.). Portland, ME: Stenhouse Publishers.

Helmers, M. (Ed.). (2002). *Intertexts: Reading pedagogy in college writing classrooms.* Mahwah, NJ: Laurence Erlbaum Associates, Inc.

Hong-Nam, K. & Swanson, M. (2011). K-8 preservice teachers' attitudes, knowledge & confidence in application of content literary strategies. *National Teacher Education Journal, 4*(4), 23–33.

Horning, A. S. (2007). Reading across the curriculum as the key to student success. *Across the Disciplines, 4.* Retrieved from https://wac.colostate.edu/atd/articles/horning2007.cfm.

Kamil, M. (2003). *Adolescents and literacy: Reading for the 21st century.* Washington, DC: Alliance for the Excellent Education.

Kirby, J. R. (2007). Higher education students with reading and writing difficulties. *Exceptionality Education Canada, 17*(2), 129–134.

Lindemann, E. & Tate, G. (1993). Two views on the use of literature in composition. *College English 55*(3): 311–21.

McGonnell, M., Parrila, R. & Deacon, H. (2007). The recruitment and description of university students who self-report difficulty acquiring early reading skills. *Exceptionality Education Canada. Special issue on Adult Dyslexia, 17*(2), 155–174.

National Institute of Child Health and Human Development (U.S.) & National Institute for Literacy (U.S.). (2007). What content-area teachers should know about adolescent literacy. Washington, DC: National Institute for Literacy.

National Survey of Student Engagement (NSSE). (2011). *Fostering student engagement campuswide—annual results 2011.* Bloomington: Indiana University Center for Postsecondary Research.

Nokes, J. D. & Dole, J. A. (2004). Helping adolescent readers through explicit strategy instruction, in Jetton, T. L. & Dole, J. A. (Eds.) *Adolescent literacy research and practice* (pp. 162–182). New York: Guilford.

Nowacek, R. S. (2011). *Agents of Integration: Understanding transfer as a rhetorical act.* Carbondale: Southern Illinois University Press.

Odom, M. L. (2013, December). Not just for writing anymore; What WAC can teach us about reading to learn. *Across the Disciplines, 10*(4). Retrieved from https://wac.colo state.edu/atd/reading/odom.cfm.

Rachal, C. K., Daigle, S. & Rachal, W. S. (2007). Learning problems reported by college students: Are they using learning strategies? *Journal of Instructional Psychology, 34*(4), 191–199.

Reeves, D. B. (2010). The write way. *The American School Board Journal, 197*(11), 46–47.

Salvatori, M. R. & Donahue, P. (2012, November). *What is College English?* Stories about reading: Appearance, disappearance, morphing and revival. *College English, 75*(2), 199–217.

Scholes, R. J. (2002). The transition to college reading. *Pedagogy, 2*(2), 165–172.

Taraban, R., Kerr, M. & Rynearson, K. (2004). Analytic and pragmatic factors in college students' metacognitive reading strategies. *Reading Psychology, 25*, 67–81.

Tinto, V. (1999). Taking retention seriously: Rethinking the first year of college. *NACADA Journal, 19*(2), 5–9.

Vaughn, S. R., Bos, C. S. & Schumm, J. S. (2011). *Teaching students who are exceptional, diverse, and at risk in the general education classroom* (5th ed.). Boston: Pearson.

Wardle, E. (2007). Understanding 'transfer' from FYC: Preliminary results of a longitudinal study. *WPA: Writing Program Administration, 31*(1–2): 65–85.

Young, J. A. & Potter, C. R. (2013, December 11). The problem of academic discourse: Assessing the role of academic literacies in reading across the K–16 curriculum. *Across the Disciplines, 10*(4). Retrieved from https://wac.colostate.edu/atd/reading/young _potter.cfm.

Appendix A. Textbook Reading Guide

Created by Tanya Sturtz and Darrell Hucks (2012)

Preview

- What are the title and subtitles?
- What do you think you will be learning in this chapter?

Main Points & Questions

- What questions do you have about the reading?
- What terms do you need to learn or remember?
- What main points do you want to remember?

Summary

- Write a brief summary about the chapter.
- Any questions you still have that you should ask a classmate or your professor?

Appendix B. Research Notes

Created by Tanya Sturtz and Darrell Hucks (2012)

Citation (In APA style)

Summary

Notes

Reference to Research

Afterword

Patrick Sullivan
MANCHESTER COMMUNITY COLLEGE

Howard Tinberg
BRISTOL COMMUNITY COLLEGE

We are deeply honored to be participating in this innovative collaboration—what amounts to a scholarly, multi-volume summit meeting on the state of reading instruction in America. These two volumes contain front-line news reports from across the nation written by teachers seeking innovative ways to make reading instruction more effective, more vital, and more transformative for students. It is rare in our discipline to see two books—companion volumes—developed collaboratively on the same subject, and this obviously speaks to a renewed interest in theorizing reading as foundational for any kind of understanding of academic learning and meaning-making. Both of these volumes theorize reading and writing as collaborative, generative, powerful forms of thinking and reflection—and when teachers do their work well, reading and writing become forms of deep thinking, exploration, and meaning-making. Increasingly in our discipline, reading ability is acknowledged as essential to the development of strong writers. Our book is entitled *Deep Reading: Teaching Reading in the Writing Classroom* (2017), and it was developed collaboratively with Alice, Deborah, and Cynthia. The full table of contents is provided below.

Although it may appear at first glance that these two volumes focus primarily on college-level concerns and practices, in a variety of significant ways they also focus considerable attention on the still largely unexplored intellectual and pedagogical spaces, gaps, and interstices between high school and college. There is a great deal of "news," wisdom, and current research contained in these two volumes that English teachers at all levels of instruction can benefit from, especially grades 6–13. As we know, college readiness and issues related to articulation have been central concerns for our discipline for many years now. These two volumes address this issue directly by theorizing a new approach to reading, writing, and creative and critical thinking for the 21st century, one that deliberately counters the reductive, instrumentalist approach to reading embodied in standardized testing regimes like the Common Core. Furthermore, these two volumes theorize *the teaching of reading* as a pedagogical activity essential to teaching practices across all disciplines and all grade levels. The primary goal of these two volumes, following reading scholar and Global Teacher Prize recipient Nancie Atwell (2007), is very ambitious, indeed: To help nurture skilled, passionate, habitual, critical, creative, and joyful readers across all grade levels and especially across institutional boundaries in America's high schools and colleges.

We began our work on this project with a great sense of urgency. Data suggest that America is currently experiencing what might be described as a reading crisis. Many students in America appear to be reluctant, unhappy, and unskilled readers. Kelly Gallagher (2009) has famously suggested that reading as it is now taught in school systems across the nation has produced a condition that he calls "readicide"—"the systematic killing of the love of reading, often exacerbated by the inane, mind-numbing practices found in schools" (p. 2). Much of this is the result of the central place that standardized testing now occupies in primary and secondary school systems, the reductive way that standardized tests theorize the act of reading, and the increasing unwillingness among legislators and powerful philanthropists to use disciplinary knowledge to inform teaching practices and goals. Our two books actively seek to address these problems.

Ominously, as Elizabeth Wardle (2012) has suggested, current reading instruction in school systems—driven by standardized testing—appears to promote superficial kinds of cognitive engagement. We find Wardle's distinction between "problem-exploring dispositions" and "answer-getting dispositions" particularly important in this regard. Problem-exploring dispositions, Wardle suggests, "incline a person toward curiosity, reflection, consideration of multiple possibilities, a willingness to engage in a recursive process of trial and error, and toward a recognition that more than one solution can 'work'" (Problem-Exploring vs. Answer-Getting Dispositions section, para. 1). Answer-getting dispositions "seek right answers quickly and are averse to open consideration of multiple possibilities" (Problem-Exploring vs. Answer-Getting Dispositions section, para. 1). These dispositions are created primarily through the approach to reading we privilege in our classrooms. Wardle concludes that

> the steady movement toward standardized testing and tight
> control of educational activities by legislators is producing and
> reproducing answer-getting dispositions in educational systems
> and individuals and that this movement is more than a dislike
> for the messiness of deep learning; rather, it can be understood
> as an attempt to limit the kind of thinking that students and
> citizens have the tools to do. (The State of Current Educational
> Dispositions section, para. 5)

The work we have undertaken in these two volumes can thus be theorized as activist in nature, seeking to nurture skills and dispositions that will help further democratic ideals and the development of a reflective, thoughtful, independent citizenry. Like Wardle, we regard this work as a high stakes enterprise. As it turns out, and each in their own way, the contributors in these two volumes all actively promote reading practices in the classroom that nurture creative and critical thinking, flexibility, curiosity, open-mindedness, metacognition, and problem-exploring dispositions.

In many important ways, our work on these two volumes devoted to reading is a continuation of our series of books focused on college-level writing: What Is "College-Level" Writing? (2006) and What Is "College-Level" Writing? Volume 2: Assignments, Readings, and Student Writing Samples (2010). As we note in the introduction to our book, we would like to suggest—after many years of reflection and research on the complex question that frames these two books: "What is 'college-level' writing?"—that reading must be theorized as foundationally linked to any understanding of writing. A great deal is at stake, therefore, as we seek to deepen our understanding of the vital role that reading plays in teaching and learning in the writing classroom.

We cheer the serious and thoughtful approach taken in this volume toward reading at the college-level, a subject that too often has been ignored by higher education scholars. The assumption by many college faculty today is that teaching reading is the responsibility of K–12 teachers. As advances in neuroscience have shed light on the development of the human brain over an individual's life course—and the impact of reading on that development—more and more college faculty have recently begun to pay attention to reading in the college classroom. If, as Maryanne Wolfe (2007) and other researchers attest, reading changes a brain, then it is the responsibility of all educators, K through 16 and beyond, to actively nurture that transformative process. In that spirit, we deeply appreciate Brian Gogan's focus in this volume on reading as more than a mechanical, skills-based exercise, but one that is instead deeply transformative, both of the reader and of the reader's understanding of the world. We are reminded of Paulo Freire and Donaldo Macedo's (1987) revelatory aphorism: reading the word equates to reading the world—effecting self-improvement while assisting in political and social change (p. 29).

In addition to the insightful approach to reading as a transformative subject, this collection does us all a great service by reminding us of a crucial fact: that reading instruction needs to take into account the institutional and disciplinary differences when readings are assigned and taught. Community college faculty, for example, will appreciate Jennifer Maloy, Beth Counihan, Joan Dupre, Susan Madera, and Ian Beckford's contribution, which focuses on reading and reading pedagogy at a diverse, open-admission, urban community college. Ildikó Melis's essay about teaching reading at a two-year tribal college—serving a geographically isolated, low-income, rural student population—offers another important perspective related to institutional and disciplinary diversity that has been largely ignored in our scholarship. As Melis notes, "In the less privileged institutions of higher education, the students' reading experiences tend to be more limited."

Moreover, we are grateful that the editors of this collection take as perhaps their most fundamental understanding of reading pedagogy the fact that responsibility for reading instruction must be actively engaged across the curriculum by teachers from all disciplines. Teaching reading at the college level simply can no longer be theorized ever again as simply the responsibility of one department (English) or one course (first-year composition). This important work must be theorized and practiced much more broadly and inclusively across disciplines. Creating a college curriculum suffused with rich, vibrant reading assignments—augmented with instruction focused on how to read these different kinds of texts—must be the concern of all faculty, both in college and in high school. The essays included in this volume make the case for this kind of approach to reading across the curriculum—and reading instruction across the curriculum—with great eloquence and power. Mary Lou Odom's essay, for example, reports on a research project that revealed three foundational principles essential for supporting a reading-instruction-across-the-disciplines approach to teaching reading:

> First, faculty must recognize ways in which they impact student
> reading behavior—beyond assigning texts or writing related
> to texts. Second, faculty must articulate to students their goals
> for student reading. Third, faculty must be willing to provide
> guidance for students reading complex, discipline-specific texts
> that may look quite different from much of the reading that has
> occupied their textual lives until this point.

Laura J. Davies's essay in this volume offers a fascinating case study approach for how this pedagogical practice might be accomplished in one specific discipline, the science classroom. Readers may be surprised to see how deliberately and carefully Davies instructs students to read different kinds of texts frequently encountered in the science classroom: 1. the popular science trade book and magazine article; 2. the science textbook; and 3. the empirical research article published in a peer-reviewed journal. As Davies notes, "Scholars who study the rhetoric of science have long argued that scientific writing and scientific research are neither "objective" nor "detached" (Kuhn, 1962; Gross, 1990; Bazerman, 1988). Rather, scientific knowledge is produced through persuasion and shifting social structures and relationships." This is precisely the kind of patient, careful, discipline-specific reading instruction we'd like to see practiced across disciplines.

Creating a climate of support for reading across the curriculum poses significant challenges and requires concerted effort, as Pam Hollander, Maureen Shamgochian, Douglas Dawson, Margaret Pray Bouchard attest in their essay. Allies abound for this effort, including composition colleagues such as Chris Anson, whose essay here examines the fundamental relationship between writing and reading.

We celebrate this collaboration, and we are deeply thankful for the honor of being able to work closely with Alice, Deborah, and Cynthia on this project. As Maryanne Wolf (2007) has noted, reading "changes who we are" and "what we imagine we can be" (p. 8). Our books are both dedicated to precisely this transformative process—and providing it systematically to students across all grade levels and across all institutional boundaries.

References

Atwell, N. (2007). *The reading zone: How to help kids become skilled, passionate, habitual, critical readers*. New York: Scholastic.

Freire, P. & Macedo, D. (1987). *Literacy: Reading the word and the world*. Westport, CT: Bergin and Garvey.

Gallagher, K. (2009). Readicide: *How schools are killing reading and what you can do about it*. Portland, ME: Stenhouse.

Sullivan, P., Tinberg, H. & Blau, S. (Eds). (2010). *What is "college-level" writing? Volume 2: Assignments, readings, and student writing samples*. Urbana, IL: NCTE.

Sullivan, P., Tinberg, H. & Blau, S. (Eds). (2017). *Deep reading: Teaching reading in the writing classroom*. Urbana, IL: NCTE.

Wardle, E. (2012). Creative repurposing for expansive learning: Considering "problem-exploring" and "answer-getting" dispositions in individuals and fields." *Composition Forum, 26*. Retrieved from http://compositionforum.com/issue/26/creative-repur posing.php.

Wolf, M. (2007). *Proust and the squid: The story and science of the reading brain*. New York: HarperCollins.

Table of Contents for *Deep Reading: Teaching Reading in the Writing Classroom*

Contributors

William M. Abbott is Associate Professor of History at Fairfield University, Connecticut. He holds a D.Phil. in modern British history from Oxford University and a B.A. from the University of California at Berkeley. His primary field of historical expertise is 17th-century England with a specialty in church-state relations; more recently he has conducted research on animal protection movements in Victorian Britain. His pedagogical research focuses on interdisciplinary teaching methods and also on grade inflation at American universities.

Chris M. Anson is Distinguished University Professor and Director of the Campus Writing and Speaking Program at North Carolina State University, where he teaches graduate and undergraduate courses in language, composition, and literacy and works with faculty across the disciplines to enhance writing and speaking instruction. He has published 15 books and over 120 articles and book chapters relating to writing and has spoken widely across the U.S. and in 28 other countries. He is Past Chair of the Conference on College Composition and Communication and Past President of the Council of Writing Program Administrators. His full c.v. is at www.ansonica.net

Ian Beckford, Director of Policy Analysis for General Education and Student Learning Outcomes, has over 20 years of experience in assessment and evaluation research both in the private sector and higher education. Since joining Queensborough Community College in 2011, Dr. Beckford has assisted faculty in developing instruments to measure student learning outcomes, offered workshops to faculty and staff on assessment and evaluation issues and conducted implementation and impact evaluations of various initiatives. Dr. Beckford has a B.A. in Psychology from Hamilton College and an Ed.D. in Policy, Planning and Evaluation from the University of Pittsburgh.

Margaret Pray Bouchard is a retired Professor of Education at Worcester State University, where she taught Literacy Education courses and coordinated the Graduate Reading Program. Before that she was an elementary school teacher and a reading specialist at several public schools in Massachusetts. Dr. Bouchard has helped many public school teachers through professional development workshops and has presented research drawn from her teaching nationally and internationally.

Beth Counihan is in her fifteenth year as a member of the English department at Queensborough Community College of the City University of New York. She earned her B.A. in English at Fordham University, her M.A. in English at Lehman College-CUNY and her Ph.D. in English at The CUNY Graduate Center. Her teaching and research interests include oral history and high impact practices such as service learning and the Common Read and her work has been published in *The Journal of Basic Writing and English Education*.

Laura J. Davies is Assistant Professor of English and the Director of Campus Writing Programs at SUNY Cortland, where she teaches in the professional writing & rhetoric and English education programs. Her scholarship focuses on the history and practice of writing program administration, teacher preparation and development, education policy, and the intersection of secondary and college-level writing instruction. Davies' work has appeared in *WPA: Writing Program Administration* and *Composition Studies*. She received her Ph.D. in Composition and Cultural Rhetoric from Syracuse University in 2012. In her free time, she loves to watch her kids play Little League games.

Douglas Dawson received his bachelor's degree in Biology from Princeton University and his doctorate in Neurobiology from the University of California at Irvine. For many years he worked at the New England Science Center (now the EcoTarium), presenting inquiry science workshops and week-long summer institutes on Earth and Space Science, Ecology, Physical Science, and Life Science for K–8 teachers. At Worcester State University, Dr. Dawson teaches science methods for prospective teachers at the early childhood and elementary levels, with an emphasis on hands on, inquiry-based experiences that promote student investigation and exploration, and challenge student misconceptions.

Joan Dupre earned her Ph.D. in English at The CUNY Graduate Center and teaches literature, pop culture, and memoir writing at Queensborough Community College/City University of New York. Her research interests include the intersection of politics and music, and the representation of mental illness on television. She finds that her teaching is greatly enriched by high-impact practices such as the Common Read and Global Diversity Learning.

Leora Freedman is Associate Professor in the teaching stream and the coordinator of the English Language Learning Program in the Faculty of Arts and Science, University of Toronto. She works intensively with academic departments to embed instruction in scholarly reading, academic writing, and professional speaking into courses across the curriculum. She also teaches non-credit courses which support multilingual students' academic acculturation and development in reading, writing, speaking, and listening. Her article "Using Close Reading as a Course Theme in a Multilingual Disciplinary Classroom" appeared in the October 2015 issue of *Reading in a Foreign Language*.

Brian Gogan is Associate Professor at Western Michigan University, where he teaches courses in the rhetoric and writing studies program. Among the courses he regularly teaches is an undergraduate course titled "Transfer and Written Communication," which views both reading and writing as transformational. His work has appeared in journals such as *College Composition and Communication* and *Across the Disciplines*, as well in collections including *Microhistories of Composition* and *Who Speaks for Writing: Stewardship for Writing Studies in the 21st Century*.

Deborah-Lee Gollnitz is Coordinator for Assessment and Program Evaluation in a K–12 public school district in the Midwest. After spending over 10 years in the high school English classroom and several years as a leader in curriculum-technology integration, she pursued the study of feedback and the role it plays in student writing development. She comes to the instruction of English Language Arts through a love of writing and focuses on the importance of reading with full comprehension in the development of strong written language skills. Her current work includes oversight of the district's K–12 ELA, World Language, and Reading departments.

Cynthia R. Haller, Professor of English and Faculty Fellow at York College/City University of New York, teaches writing and rhetoric and has served in a number of administrative positions, including Writing Program Director, Writing Center Director, WAC Coordinator, First-Year Composition Coordinator, Deputy Chair of English, and Interim English Department Chair. Her published articles have appeared in the journals *WPA: Writing Program Administration, Written Communication,* and *Technical Communication Quarterly,* and she has contributed chapters to *Reconnecting Reading and Writing, Environmental Rhetoric and Ecologies of Place,* and *Information Literacy: Research and Collaboration Across Disciplines.*

Pam Hollander, Ed.D., is Assistant Professor of Education at Worcester State University, where she teaches literacy education and developmental reading courses. She is the author of several refereed journal articles and book chapters, with most of her work focused on the literacy education of college students, including using popular culture in the college classroom. Her article "Elevate My Mind: Women's Identities in Hip Hop Love Songs" was anthologized in the Bedford/St. Martin first-year composition textbook *Reading Popular Culture* (2016).

Alice S. Horning is Professor of Writing and Rhetoric at Oakland University, where she holds a joint appointment in Linguistics. Her research over her entire career has focused on the intersection of reading and writing. Her work has appeared in the major professional journals and in books published by Parlor Press and Hampton Press. Her most recent books include *Reading, Writing, and Digitizing: Understanding Literacy in the Electronic Age* published in 2012 by Cambridge Scholars Publishing and *Reconnecting Reading and Writing* co-edited with Beth Kraemer, published in 2013 by the WAC Clearinghouse and Parlor Press.

Darrell Cleveland Hucks is Associate Professor of Elementary Education at Keene State College. He received his Ph.D. in Teaching & Learning from New York University. His research interests include the schooling experiences of Black and Latino males, collective achievement, teacher education, culturally responsive pedagogy, college student development and retention, civic engagement, and literacy and technology integration. He is the author of *New Visions of Collective Achievement: The Cross-Generational Schooling Experiences of African American Males.* He is one of the editors of *Literacy Enrichment and Technology Integration in Pre-Service Teacher Education.* He was a New York City public school teacher.

Debrah Huffman is Associate Professor of English at Indiana University Purdue University Fort Wayne. She teaches first-year courses regularly as well as graduate courses for master's students specializing in writing. As director of writing she oversees the writing program and fosters the professional development of its part-time instructors. With research in the scholarship and teaching of college reading, her most recent work has been the creation and development of an introductory college reading course at her university. Her active interests also include writing and reading across the curriculum, writing program administration, and the scholarship of teaching and learning.

Susan Madera holds a Bachelor's degree in English from Queens College, CUNY and an Associate's degree from Queensborough Community College, CUNY. In 2006, she joined the Office of Academic Affairs at QCC as the Learning Communities Coordinator for the MDRC grant, Demonstration of Learning Communities. In 2009, she became Administrative Coordinator of High-Impact Practices, where she promoted the relevance of these distinctive pedagogies as a key component of QCC's Freshman Academies, the College's model for students success. In Fall 2011, she directed QCC's first Common Read as a Common Intellectual Experience, an initiative that continues to flourish under her direction. In 2013, she became a member of the College's Center for Excellence in Teaching & Learning, where she serves as the Academic Program Manager of High-Impact Practices.

Jennifer Maloy is Assistant Professor of English at Queensborough Community College/City University of New York, where she teaches English-as-a-Second Language courses, basic writing, and freshman composition. Her research areas include identity formation of multilingual students and designing service-learning projects for ESL and basic writing students. She has published articles in Teaching English in the Two-Year College and the Basic Writing eJournal.

Ildikó Melis earned her first degree in English and Hungarian Studies in Budapest, Hungary, an MA in English as a Second Language and a Ph.D. in Rhetoric and Composition from the University of Arizona. She is a full-time writing instructor, department chair, and publication editor at Bay Mills (Tribal) Community College on Michigan's Upper Peninsula, and the 2010–2011 recipient of the American Indian College Fund—Mellon Research Fellowship. Her work is published in Goodburn, A., LeCourt, D. & Leverenz, C. (2013). Rewriting success in rhetoric and composition careers, and in the *Tribal College Faculty Research Journal* where she is also an editorial board member.

Kathryn A. Nantz is currently chair of the Department of Economics and Roger M. Lynch Chair of Economics at Fairfield University. Her research interests are in the areas of education—particularly the role of the GED in preparing adult learners for work—and economics education. Kathy has been involved in a variety of grant-funded projects, nationally and internationally, that have involved faculty development and the scholarship of teaching and learning. She teaches courses in applied microeconomics, and won a teaching award in the College of Arts and Sciences in 2009 for her work in the classroom.

Mary Lou Odom is Professor of English and Director of the Writing Center and Writing Across the Curriculum at Kennesaw State University. Her research seeks to interrogate assumptions common in writing center/writing program administration and in the teaching of writing. Most recently, her work has appeared in *WLN: A Journal of Writing Center Scholarship* and *Across the Disciplines*.

Charlie Potter is Director of Accreditation and Assessment at Spokane Community College. She previously worked in education policy for the State of Washington. Prior to her experience in public policy, she taught English at several higher education institutions for over a decade. Additionally, she has worked as an academic librarian.

Maureen Shamgochian is currently Professor Emeritus of Biology at Worcester State University in Massachusetts. Dr. Shamgochian received her doctorate in Molecular and Cellular Physiology from the Graduate School of Biomedical Sciences at the University of Massachusetts Medical School. She has over 25 years of experience in higher education, having held positions as Professor and Chair of Biology and Associate and Interim Vice President for Academic Affairs prior to her recent retirement. She is interested in science education and has done research on the physiological regulation of gene expression in the brain.

Tanya I. Sturtz, Ed.D., is Associate Professor in the Education Department at Keene State College. Dr. Sturtz earned a doctorate degree in Special Education from the University of Virginia and has been teaching at Keene State College in both the undergraduate education programs and the graduate program in Special Education. Her research interests are in the reading, thinking, research, and writing experiences of first-year students during linked-courses their first-year in college and in the literacy beliefs and knowledge development of pre-service teachers in teacher education programs.

Patrick Sullivan teaches English at Manchester Community College, in Manchester, Connecticut. He is the editor, with Howard Tinberg, of *Deep Reading: Teaching Reading in the Writing Classroom* (NCTE, 2017). He is also the author of *A New Writing Classroom: Listening, Motivation, and Habits of Mind* (Utah State University Press, 2014) and *Economic Inequality, Neoliberalism, and the American Community College* (Palgrave Macmillan, 2017). Patrick has also edited, with Christie Toth, *Teaching Composition at the Two-Year College: Background Readings* (Bedford/St. Martin's, 2016). Patrick is currently serving as a member of the editorial board of *College Composition and Communication*.

Howard Tinberg is Professor of English at Bristol Community College, Massachusetts, former editor of the journal TETYC ,and former chair of CCCC. He is the author of *Border Talk: Writing and Knowing in the Two-Year College* and *Writing* *with Consequence: What Writing Does in the Disciplines.* He is co-editor of *What is "College-Level" Writing?* and of *What is "College-Level" Writing? Vol 2.* He has published articles in a variety of academic journals. In 2004, he was recognized as U.S. Community Colleges Professor of the Year by the Carnegie Foundation and the American Council on Education.

Katherine Tirabassi (Ph.D., University of New Hampshire) is Associate Professor of English and Center for Writing Director at Keene State College, where she coordinated the first-year writing program from 2010–2014. She teaches composition theory, creative nonfiction, professional writing, and coordinates writing and publishing internships. She has published articles on archival research, composition pedagogy, and writing center theory/practice. Her dissertation, "Revisiting the 'Current-Traditional Era': Innovations in Writing Instruction at the University of New Hampshire, 1940–1949" received the 2008 College Composition and Communication Conference James Berlin Memorial Outstanding Dissertation Award, and she is developing this project into a book.

Martha Townsend is Professor Emerita of English at the University of Missouri and former director of its internationally renowned Campus Writing Program. Townsend's publications have played a central role in the conceptualization and development of writing-across-the-curriculum programs in the United States and abroad. She is a former literacy consultant to the Ford Foundation.

Justin Young is Associate Professor in the English department at Eastern Washington University, where he directs the English Composition Program and Writers' Center. His research focuses on the transition to college and reading and writing instruction across the P–16 continuum. He is particularly interested in how writing instruction and writing center support can better prepare students across the K-16 continuum to communicate effectively in both print and in digital environments and to succeed in college.